From Millet to Léger

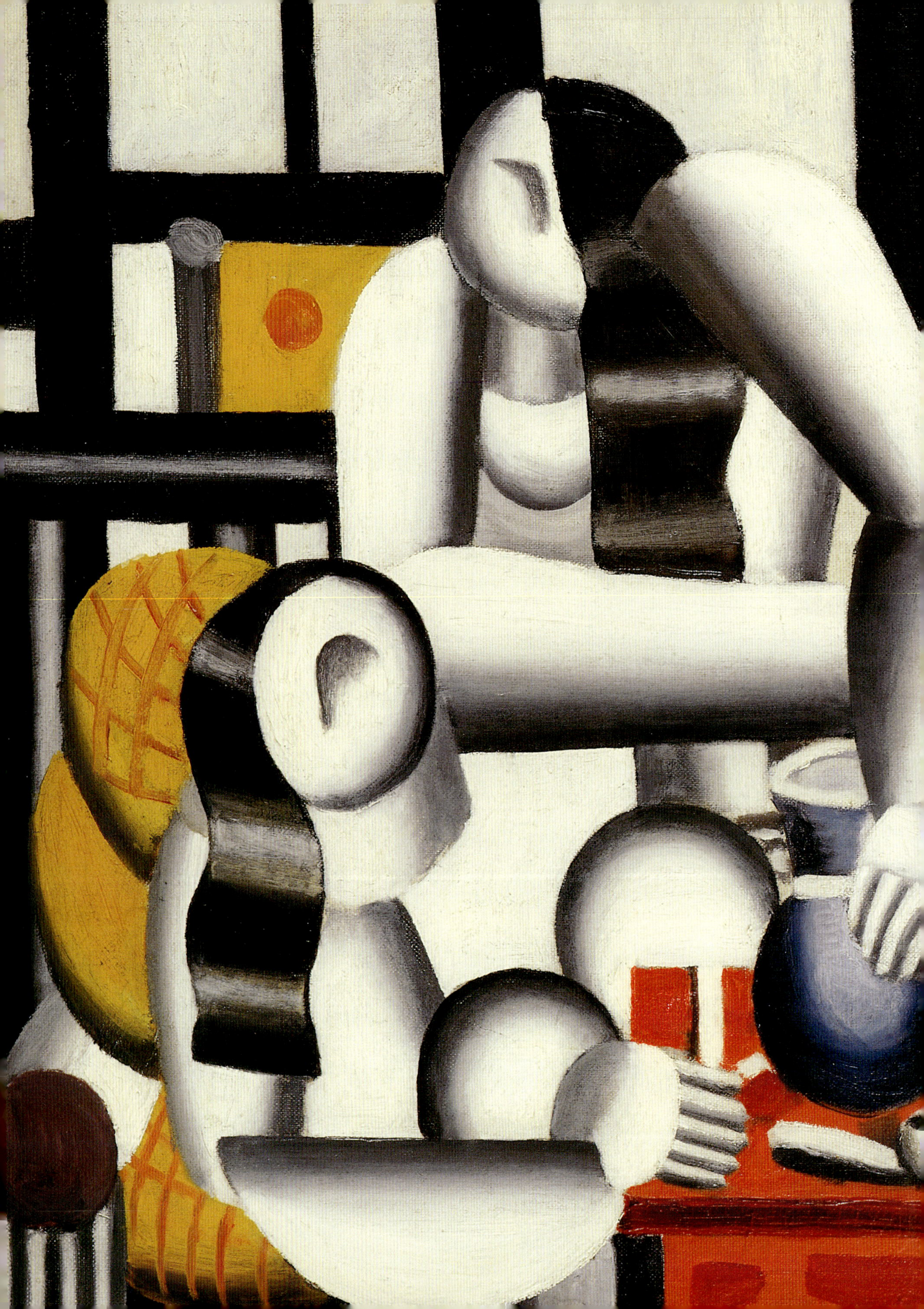

From Millet to Léger

Essays in Social Art History

Robert L. Herbert

Yale University Press
New Haven & London

To Alan and Martha, and to friendship

Designed by Elizabeth McWilliams

Printed in China

Library of Congress Cataloging-in-Publication Data

Herbert, Robert L., 1929–
From Millet to Léger : essays in social art history / Robert L. Herbert.
p. cm.
Includes bibliographical references and index.
ISBN 0-300-09706-9
1. Art and society – France. 2. Art, French – 19th century.
3. Art, French – 20th century. I. Title.
N72.S6 H43 2002
759.4'09'034 – dc21
2002001895

A catalogue record for this book is available from The British Library

Frontispiece: detail of fig. 46.

Contents

Preface

To say how I explain social art history is to explore my own biography – yet I've always disliked the confessional in historians, much as I love it in artists. I want to believe that my writings speak for themselves and are convincing on their merits; my personal views need not concern the reader although I know they are implicit in what I publish. To assert one's opinion is not a sufficient form of reasoning. This belief results from my being turned off in the early 1950s by the dogmatism of Stalinism. I adopted a Marxist view of class structure and of property-based greed that enfranchises capitalism, but Milovan Djilas's *The New Class* (1957) confirmed my belief that the dictatorship of a vanguard party was the central evil of Stalinist communism.

By that time I had read Meyer Schapiro's writings on modern art and talked him into two tutorial meetings about my dissertation on Seurat. (I had first met him at a meeting in New York of the Young People's Socialist League which he had addressed.) He right away made clear his distrust of generalizations; his conversations were far franker and less generous to his colleagues than his writings. He confirmed my suspicions of all generalizing theories, political and non-political, including those that purported to explain whole cycles of art history.

With Schapiro as my hero and socialism as my political home, I balked at much of the art history I was studying. It is true that from my teachers – and equally from studio artists whom I met – I learned a lot about looking at pictures, about how to assess color, drawing, brushwork, and composition. I learned that the means of representation differ from the objects represented and have their own histories. This let me see that socialist realism, by giving nearly exclusive attention to subject matter, denied both the visible traces of an individual artist and also the importance of technique and pictorial structure. However, the histories of style and form that satisfied most of my teachers struck me as mere chronology. I came from a working-class family and not only rebelled against the authorities I was confronted with – they were analogs of my factory and railroad bosses – but also I thought the stuff of ordinary daily life should enter into art history. I realized that nineteenth-century artists were just as involved with the art market, contemporary art reviews, street theater, and everything else that makes up culture, as the artists I saw working around me.

At the same time, warned off by blinkered socialist realism, I did not think that the art historian should begin with major social crises and then seek the art that reveals them. For France from the 1850s to 1880s, economic historians could deal with the rapid expansion of the railroads, seaport traffic, and international trade, but I was looking at paintings of rural villages, refurbished city streets, cafés and café-concerts, urban parks and gardens, suburban pleasure boats and seacoast leisure. I wanted to restore the flesh of real painters and their culture to the bones of style and form. I did not find it in the hero-worship of such writers as John Rewald: while I acknowledge a big debt to Rewald, his publications, like those of most of his contemporaries, spoke for an artistic elite instead of offering critical insights into their subjects' work.

When I think over my career as writer, I realize that everything began with my dissertation on Seurat. During George Hamilton's graduate seminar at Yale I became fascinated by the apparent disparity between Seurat's "scientific" paintings and his moody nocturnal drawings. In college I had loved the history of science, so studying Seurat in graduate school led me irresistibly into the history of color theory. I found Seurat's images of peasants hoeing, market porters, street cleaners, elegant strollers, nurses with children, drawbridges, and café singers to be full of life, a whole social spectrum. I wondered why they were written about solely as abstract forms. Commentary on Seurat struck me as overly influenced by abstract art or, rather, by twentieth-century artists and critics who found irrelevant the social content of his drawings. I love abstract art, but I don't feel obliged to defend it by claiming that the work of earlier artists was merely imitative and lacked symbolic and social meanings.

It was the study of Seurat's drawings – they still take my breath away – that taught me, in turn, to look at Millet's drawings. These didn't at all conform to the view I had inherited of that artist's "sentimental" art. Instead of seeing an artist who sacrificed form to Christian moralizing, I saw a powerful draftsman, the heir of Rembrandt and Goya. I took a perverse pleasure in being a young historian looking anew at an artist generally neglected when not despised as hopelessly old-fashioned. It was also through studying Seurat (in this case, the paintings) that I came to admire Léger, whom I saw as Seurat's descendant. Those are the three great love affairs I've had with painting and drawing: Seurat, Millet, and Léger. Although I can see how each of them involved me with issues of social art history, I began studying them with what I still feel: an immense joy when I look at their work.

In Millet, my pleasure comes from his engrossing use of black conté crayon to construct forms memorable for their extraordinary distillations of gesture and shape. Their force comes from sculptural silhouettes that stick in the mind as the very meaning of hoeing or sowing. Form preceded social meaning, not the reverse. Structure created meaning, but the meaning resulted from a dialog with what the artist had seen and felt. For Léger, I was happy to find out that most of his pictures have forms and colors painted over or added (*pentimenti*), changes of mind that show how much he was a craftsman responding to the process of painting, and not a geometrician coolly applying a pattern. He seldom used a straight-edge and his contours have a handmade attraction that sets up a dialog with the large geometry of his shapes. It was in creating what he called "form-objects" that he constructed social meanings. In the small scale of reproduction his pictures look like perfect geometries, leading me to realize how vital it is to seek out the originals and to let them be the starting-points of a process in which I try to get rid of my former assumptions about both style and subject matter.

I realize that my empirical writings make me appear as the typical male who presents himself as the omniscient master of historical narrative. Like lots of leftists of my generation, I believed that it was the historian's job to question outmoded ideas of art history and also to fight for racial and economic equality against the profit motive as the arbiter of corporate and private actions. Class and race were far more important than gender. However, over the decade of the 1970s, I introduced gender issues in my courses, and eventually I left Yale University for several years of teaching young women at Mount Holyoke College. I won't pretend that this shifting interest grew out of solitary self-inquiry. It was due instead to my wife, the historian Eugenia W. Herbert, and to the constant give-and-take with mostly younger peers and students bright enough to challenge their teacher.

I have always recognized the subjectivity of my writing and in recent years I have acknowledged the open-ended nature of history which is characterized as much by questions as by seemingly objective answers. I continue to believe that no matter how unwittingly prejudicial is my mustering of historical and visual evidence, I can still construct a persuasive view of past history. I know that I cannot reach total objectivity, but the struggle to do so is a prop that keeps my passions from spilling over into mere prejudice. Objectivity is neither passive nor disengaged. The tensions that arise from my writing make me aware of just how moral and passionate is the search for what paintings and drawings meant in the artists' time. I study works of art made by individuals, and yet these works participate in a culture (including the viewer's) that by definition is a collective. Joining the two is the purpose of my work, much as reconciling individuals with social structures is the aim of good politics.

My method is the transparent one of juxtaposing documented events and settings, customs, locations, and institutions to the forms and subjects of specific pictures and then make broad deductions. I say "juxtapose" because artists hardly ever make direct connections between their art and its ramifications in social history. It is the absence of such explicit statements that encourages opponents of social art history to classify my writing as mere "context" or "background." Of course Millet didn't say that his peasants were related to the industrial revolution, and Léger didn't write that his "Animated Landscapes" make nature subservient to the city, but both deductions are obvious when paintings and contemporaneous history are placed side by side.

Rather than steer readers overtly by putting my views between them and the pictures, I lay out the historical record so that it can be examined and the same conclusions as mine be reached. Of course this conforms to the methods of the nineteenth-century naturalists to whom I've always been drawn, and reveals my personal relationship to my subjects. Unlike the Romantics who favored affective melodrama, the naturalists (Flaubert, Degas, and so on) seemed to be mere reporters of what they saw while subtly planting in the viewers' and readers' minds the salient elements that comprised their interpretations. And most of them avoided theorizing in favor of the pursuit of the "natural," a constantly redefined conception that nonetheless had the least common denominator of empirical vision and practice. No better evidence of my own involvement in the history I write than my delight when I found Millet's long, handwritten excerpts from the writings of the sixteenth-century sage Bernard Palissy. Millet's copies emphasize Palissy's constant opposition of abstract theorizing to practice based on nature, including this pithy excerpt that could have served as epigraph to my preface:

> *Theorique.* Et où est-ce que tu as trouvé cela par escrit, ou bien di-moy en quelle escole as-tu esté, où tu puisse avoir entendu ce que tu dis?
>
> *Pratique.* Je n'ay point eu d'autre livre que le ciel & la terre, lequel est connu de tous, & est donné à tous de connoistre & lire ce beau livre.[1]

Social art history is not neutral: the historian is conscious of putting it together. Neither is it predetermined nor reductionist. It is not "background," either, but the analysis of how art reaches the public through dealers, exhibitions, journalism, biographies, and historical writings. Each of these is a complex social construction that helps determine how one looks at art. In more particular focus, social art history is the study of materials, techniques, and subjects – all three of these! – that arise from both handcraft and industry, from writings about art, from prior practices of art, from artists' knowledge of human figures and animals, of buildings, cities, villages, and landscapes, of museums and exhibition spaces, of sister arts, of social and political events. Artists do not have to be aware of the ingredients of these interactions, many of which enter gradually into their craft until they become instinctual.

The historian's job is to pry into those components, to work backward from the artists' forms and subjects toward the unstated founding agencies of their art. It is necessary to surround works of art with every bit of history and circumstance that might involve them, and then select those that are relevant. These include the investigation of what an artist omits. While drawing premodern peasants, Millet excluded all the new agricultural tools and practices that actually had invaded Barbizon, so as to give images of unmediated hand labor. Monet systematically expunged traces of tourism in Etretat (no hotels, no casinos, no bathers, no restaurants), although its fame and viewers' comprehension of his pictures relied on the seaport's renown as a tourist spot. Léger never made collages because his pride as artisan required that he make all the pieces of his art.

It is their distance from everyday reality that makes me regret my younger contemporaries' addiction to what, in shorthand, we call "theory." It is a way of retaining the elitist position of old-fashioned fine arts. Too many of its practitioners write for other initiates. They use a specialized jargon with the result that their internalized discourse excludes even a generally well-informed reader. Furthermore, such writers are often guilty of an extreme form of subjectivism because they have little faith in making contact with history. They feel sure only of what they see in front of them, consequently their vision is skewed by the myopia of present-day culture. To me the height of subjectivity is to discard historical evidence while claiming to have direct knowledge of a given visual or literary text. Reduced to semiotic structure or to the psychology of vision, the art work loses its resonance with its author's culture. Richard Powers, an artist, put it well in a novel in 1985 when he defined the "trigger point" of modernist culture as the moment

> when the progress of a system becomes so accelerated, its tools become so adept at self-replicating and self-modifying, that it thrusts an awareness of itself onto itself and reaches the terminal velocity of self-reflection. [. . .] Art that was once a product of psychological mechanisms is now *about* those mechanisms and – the ultimate trigger point – about being about them.[2]

I know that I cannot escape romantic individualism and Freud, and that I automatically posit an artistic self when I look at paintings. However, I try to resist psychological readings which are too often used by writers as a substitute for historical reasoning. Ironically these writers use available histories to get at the psyche of dead artists who cannot be put on the psychoanalyst's couch. They substitute their own belief in connections between a biographical self and the art that flows from it. Most such writing is a form of circular reasoning in which one deduces from the work of art a psychological state which "explains" it. I have similar objections to claiming to know an artist's intentions. I stick with the effects on the viewer of what artists do, regardless of what they may have intended (as if we could know what that was!).

Although most of my publications have been centered upon individual artists and are rooted in specific works of art, I have occasionally addressed myself to broad issues of social art. The present volume results from friendly suggestions that I bring together such essays because they are scattered in periodicals, books of essays, and exhibition catalogs, and are somewhat apart from my best-known writings on Impressionism and Seurat.

I have included ten essays. The first three deal with the second half of the nineteenth century, the last three involve the first thirty years of the twentieth century. They are mostly concerned with the ways in which art can be seen to engage in the widest currents of Western cultural history of the modern era. I am often out on a limb on these – only a few of the essays include examples of close looking into specific paintings or prints – but I take my chances because I am confident that they deal seriously with important issues.

R. L. H. South Hadley, October 2001

Acknowledgments

For close readings of my preface I am very grateful to Eugenia W. Herbert and Alan Armstrong. My warm thanks go also to Ruth Thackeray, who copy edited my manuscript with sharp-eyed vigilance. I am also indebted to Elizabeth McWilliams for the care and flair with which she designed this book. While debating what essays to include, I benefited from the advice of Anne Higonnet, Anne McCauley, Richard Shiff, and Nancy Troy, especially from the fact that they had different thoughts from one another. Several colleagues helped me with information and permissions, including Brigitte Hedel-Samson, Dorothy Kosinski, Carolyn Lanchner, Jean-Cédric Michel, and Michelle Yun. For permission to reproduce a previously unpublished letter of Léger's, I am thankful to Laura Rosenstock and her colleagues at the Museum of Modern Art, New York.

Author's Note

Texts have not been revised from my present-day vantage point, except to take account of obvious anachronisms, unclear phrasing, and undue overlappings of one text with another. Titles of works of art have been anglicized but the French is used whenever strong tradition favors it. Translations from the French are my own, unless otherwise credited, and are very literal, at the expense of grace and rhythm, in order to convey the exact meanings of the original texts; the French is given only when its original flavor needs to be provided. Paintings are assumed to be oil on canvas unless otherwise stated, and dimensions are rounded to the nearest ⅛ inch and nearest 0.1 cm.

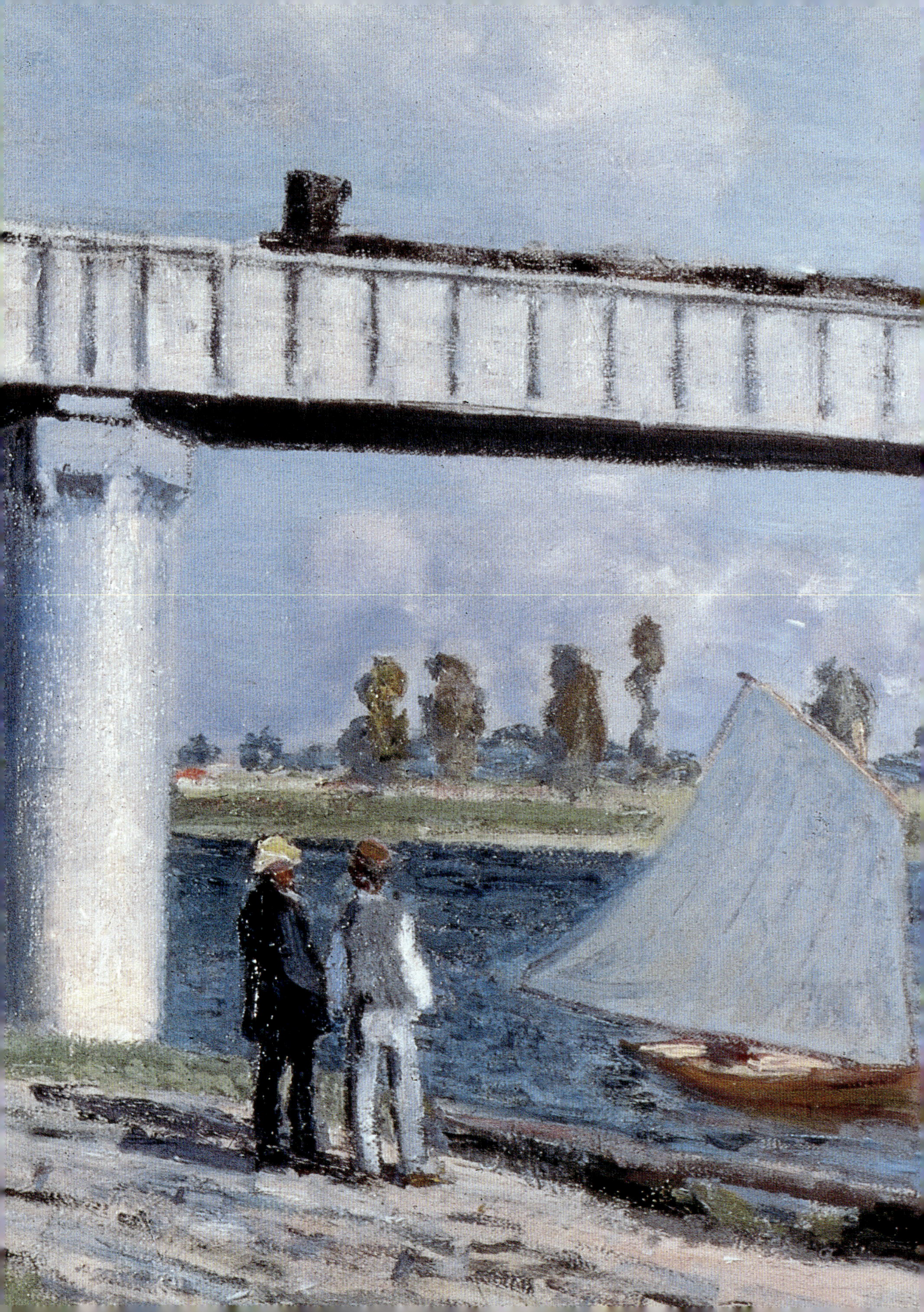

Chapter 1

Industry in the Changing Landscape from Daubigny to Monet

In communicating with his colleagues outside his own specialty the art historian is often guilty of mystification. By stressing the several components of pictorial structure (line, color, shape, arrangement) he protects his profession by identifying it with a set of arcane mysteries that are hidden from the uninitiated. Historians not principally concerned with the visual arts are tempted to conclude that art really consists of these mysteries and either they exclude art from the evidence they use in their own work, or else, despairing of their role as outsiders, they merely use art as an embellishment. It is true that most art historians believe that they deal with history. They demonstrate that artist Y has borrowed a portion of his composition from the earlier artist X, and usually they deduce from this a causal relationship. However, this is often a false teleology. Simply by stating that one pattern has preceded another, the art historian feels that he has been engaged in "history," when all he has done is to name a chronological sequence. Real historical analysis, which would tell us how Y's painting fits into its culture, is set aside in favor of the conviction that forms of art have their own teleology, independent of the cultures that gave them birth.

Two related assumptions support the false teleology that dominates art history, and both come from the hegemony of abstract art, apparent successor to the nineteenth century's art-for-art's sake.[1] One is the belief that art springs only from the subjectivity of the artist and therefore that the historian is free to ignore socio-cultural history. The other, already mentioned, is that the forms of art, to the extent that they are not purely subjective and idiosyncratic, are related principally to one another, as distinct from the society in which they have found existence.

These assumptions are often strengthened when the art historian sees others use art merely to illustrate historical events. Such use, confined to the subject matter of art rather than to its complicated inner workings, convinces the art historian that she or he is right to separate art from social history. This is all the more true when the user is that kind of historian who begins with a critical event, say a revolution, and then goes out to find art that "illustrates" it. Such art

1 *(facing page)* detail of fig. 7.

• From *French Cities in the Nineteenth Century*, ed. John M. Merriman (New York, 1981): 139–64

frequently is not that which itself is revolutionary, not that which is the real bearer of a new pictorial language, but art which only represents socio-political events. An example would be the historian of late nineteenth-century France who shows us pictures of factories, strikes, and political leaders rather than the landscapes of Monet or the café scenes of Manet and Degas.

The historian who uses art for its subject matter alone is just as remote from the history of art as the specialist who talks only of color and composition. The historian who wishes to deal meaningfully with art must explain why its subject cannot be understood properly unless its structure is analyzed. Pictorial structure interprets subject. Each is proper evidence for the cultural historian, but his work is incomplete unless he demonstrates their interdependence.

The first examples of paintings that I give offer a good introduction to the general theme of this essay. Corot's painting (pl. 2) and Sisley's (pl. 3) show the same road southwest of Paris. Camille Corot (1796–1875) was a long generation older than Alfred Sisley (1839–99), and his view of the road, a fresh and new vision for his day, speaks for the values of the mid-century. Although artfully contrived, it appears natural. Two rural persons are moving slowly along the road at a pre-industrial pace. The dirt road has slightly irregular edges, grass and foliage on both sides are abundant, and the view towards the outskirts of Paris is a deep one that contributes to a sense of expansiveness, in this serene meeting of countryside with city.

Sisley could have chosen a similar view, but instead takes us further down the same road, nearer to Paris. The increased traffic along such routes has led to the use of urban modes of road building. Along the edge of the road a cobblestone drain has been placed, and a curb erected. Relatively young trees, spaced with military precision and regularly trimmed, mark one side of the road in contrast to the more countrified aspect of Corot's roadside. In moving from one picture to the other, we have gone from country to suburb or, rather, from a relatively unmodernized suburb to an urbanized one. We have entered the world of modern France, and we sense the presence here in Louveciennes of Baron Haussmann's and Louis Napoleon's imperial order. From Paris have been exported the canalized edges of the road and the implacable regularity of the trees, visible signs of the growing grasp of Paris upon the nearby suburbs, and of the suburbs upon the countryside.

To this partial analysis both the historian and the art historian might object that the images Sisley painted were really there, and therefore that I have identified only subject matter. The first reply to such an objection is an obvious one. Sisley chose that view, and merely by doing so, he draws attention to the modernization of Louveciennes in preference to a more untouched rural road which he could easily have found in that vicinity. That his choice of view is an intentional one is indicated by the fact that the estate whose wall shows to the right is that of the famous Mme. Du Barry. A conventional representation of this site by an earlier artist would have disclosed more of the château in order to evoke

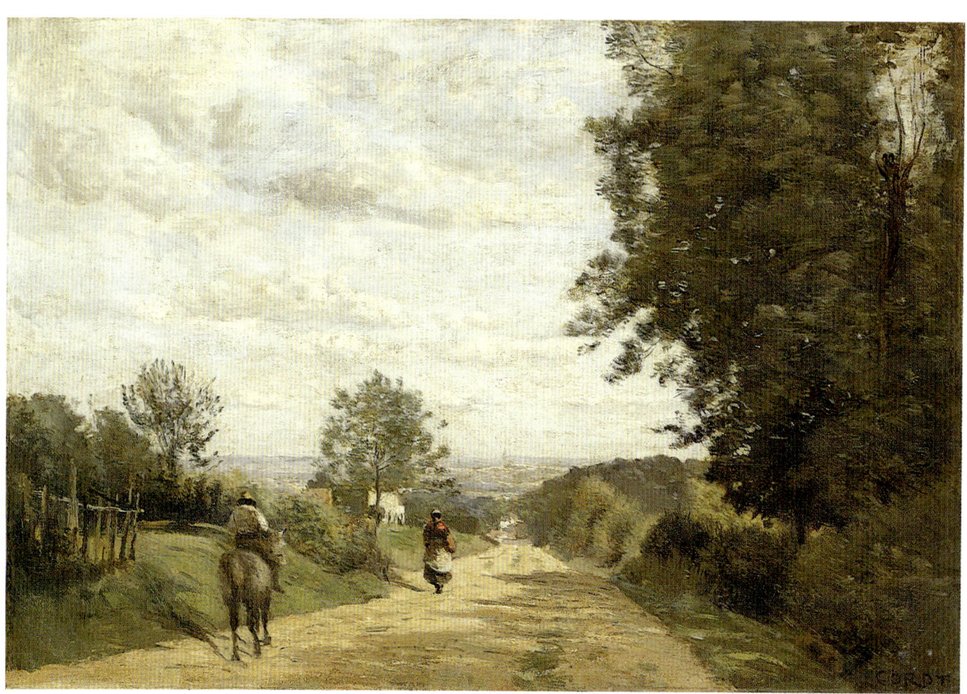

2 Camille Corot, The *Sèvres Road*, *c.* 1865. $13\frac{3}{8} \times 19\frac{1}{4}$ in. (34 × 49 cm.). Musée d'Orsay, Paris, R.F. 1352.

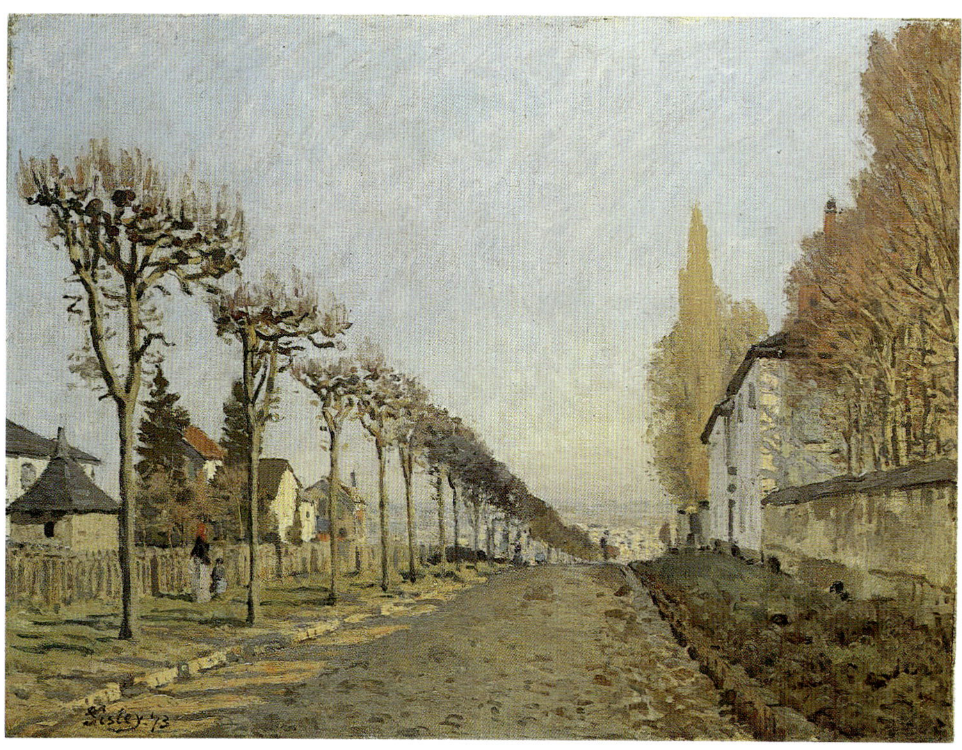

3 Alfred Sisley, *Louveciennes, Chemin de la Machine*, 1873. $21\frac{1}{2} \times 28\frac{3}{4}$ in. (54.5 × 73 cm.). Musée d'Orsay, Paris, R.F. 1079.

history more overtly. Sisley was an adherent of naturalism which in turn was the style of progressive bourgeois culture. Naturalism meant a facing towards the present, a turning of the back upon history, a rooting out of values, both pictorial and social, that attached to monarchy and theocracy. Into this banal view Sisley has introduced Mme. Du Barry's estate in a matter-of-fact way that assimilates it by giving it a new modesty, a plainness that puts history in its place.

The second reply to the objection that I am dealing only with subject matter is to point to the intimate connection of Sisley's pictorial structure to his subject. Considered simply as a piece of abstract organization, Sisley's painting, compared with Corot's, is a taut network of geometric forms. The road makes a truncated triangle whose abrupt termination emphasizes its rather flat shape. The ground to the right is a five-sided polyhedron, and to the left the regularity of the trees is reinforced by the block-like patches of sunlight along the road. Compared with the Corot, Sisley's sharp perspective and the sudden plunge over the brow of the hill have an almost automotive speed. He seems to have absorbed the spirit of the imposition of order and regularity over nature which is more than a metaphor for the Second Empire's alteration of the environs of Paris: it is its very embodiment. The forms of his art are in inextricable harmony with his subject, not because he consciously made them so, but because experience and instinct led him to a point of view and a pictorial organization that suited his endeavor.

Most artists of Corot's generation had sought out relatively unaltered roadways and villages, despite the encroachments of the growing urban-industrial revolution, and they favored a correspondingly softer, more irregular set of forms. It is no accident that the Barbizon artist Théodore Rousseau, painter of the villages on the fringe of Fontainebleau forest as well as of the forest's exuberant growth, consistently fought the government's piercing the forest with new macadamized highways.[2] His love of the intertwined branches of forest and the thatched cottages of villages was also the love of a matching set of lines, colors, and shapes. They would prevent him from seeing Sisley's site as anything other than ugly.

Such comparisons of Impressionist and pre-Impressionist paintings are therefore instructive because they show us how to deal with the formal language of paintings as well as with their subjects. In providing the context for the study of forms, they deal with the two generations which witnessed the rapid suburbanization of the environs of Paris. Reactions of artists to these changes were not always predictable – far from it. I now go on to explore other comparisons of the two generations, with Monet as the exemplar of Impressionism, and for the preceding generation, an artist he knew well, Charles Daubigny (1817–78). The choice is not arbitrary, for Monet learned a great deal from Daubigny and he painted along the same riverbanks and the Norman coastline the older artist favored.

Daubigny, known today principally as a painter, was also a prolific printmaker and illustrator.[3] In both media he stands as one of the principal artists devoted to the suburbs and the countryside near Paris. As is true of many artists, his oils and prints display two different ranges of subject matter, and the contrast between them is illuminating. In making prints, whether or not illustrations to specific texts, Daubigny represented a relatively large number of topical subjects. Prints often embodied present concerns and, since they were serially reproduced and cheap, they shared in an active circulation of artistic and social ideas. When he worked in oils, however, Daubigny's instinct was to choose more "permanent" subjects suitable to the more disinterested mood that he and most others associated with painting. This contrast of the typical and the reflective was also the contrast of city activity and country solitude. Printmaking was more commonly a social enterprise than painting, which was a rather private activity often associated with release from the city. Daubigny's friend Frédéric Henriet praised his paintings in 1857 because "they provide us abundantly with some of the illusions of repose, liberty, and solitude which are near to happiness."[4]

Daubigny's prints and illustrations include a number that deal with the industrialization of the countryside. Among them are those he provided for the 1851 edition of the *Fables* of Pierre Lachambeaudie.[5] Although commissioned works, the illustrations probably reflect Daubigny's sympathies with the author's Saint-Simonism. Daubigny was an ardent republican, and apparently friendly to the utopian ideals of the Fourierists and Saint-Simonists which appealed to so many artists who matured in the 1840s. Lachambeaudie's constant message is the need to accept industrialization and to overturn the royalists and landowners who oppose progress. Once radical, by 1851 this view was the spearpoint of entrepreneurial capitalism in France, and erstwhile Saint-Simonists began to enter the government of Louis Napoleon in increasing numbers.[6]

In *Steam* (pl.4), Daubigny shows an old man and his son looking out over a broad landscape (Daubigny seems to have based it upon Le Havre). Two trains pass over a viaduct, and in the distance, maritime commerce is indicated in the plumes of smoke from two steam vessels. In his fable, Lachambeaudie has the father, fearful of the train, ask his son what it is that he sees, the child of Providence or of the Devil. The son replies that steam conquers natural obstacles by harnessing nature's own force for its purposes. By bridging chasms and rivers, and defeating time, it will bring products to remote places and join peoples heretofore separated. Myths of old will become reality:

> Au nouvel Amphion, qu'à ta voix enchantée
> Naissent des monuments utiles, glorieux;
> Poëte, à la douleur que ton luth fasse trêve;
> La vérité bientôt remplacera le rêve,
> Et la réalité sera le merveilleux.

> [To the new Amphion, at the sound of your enchanted voice
> Monuments are brought forth, both useful and glorious;
> Poet, may your lute call truce to pain;

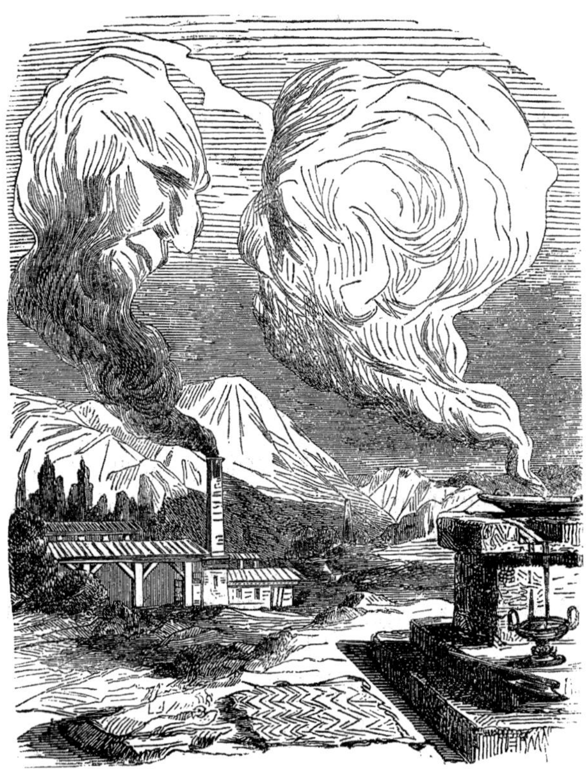

4 Charles Daubigny, *Steam*, engraving for Pierre Lachambeaudie's *Fables* (Paris, 1851).

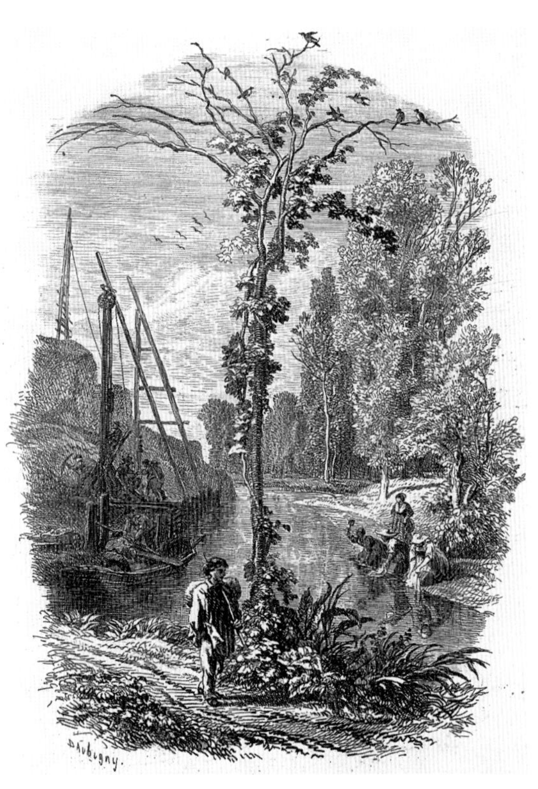

5 Charles Daubigny, *Two Riverbanks*, engraving for Pierre Lachambeaudie's *Fables* (Paris, 1851).

Truth will soon supplant the dream,
And reality will be marveled at.]

Lachambeaudie recognizes that industry transforms the countryside, and he is sensitive to the loss that nature (and the poet) must bear. In the *Two Riverbanks* (pl. 5), Daubigny interprets the poet's most autobiographical and most bittersweet fable. Lachambeaudie writes that in his childhood in the country, both banks of the river were equally verdant. At age sixteen, when he was leaving home to seek his fortune, one riverbank was taken over by industry and new construction replaced the trees. Now old, the poet hopes that progress will not have removed the last plants of his ideal domain. The course of life has two banks. In youth, both are flowered, but later, need takes over one half of our illusions. The fable ends:

Heureux, quand la vieillesse arrive,
Si quelques fleurs encore restent sur l'autre Rive!

[There is happiness, when old age arrives,
If a few flowers remain still on the other Shore!]

Daubigny interprets the fable quite directly. Construction has taken over one bank while opposite, four washerwomen symbolize the traditional use of the

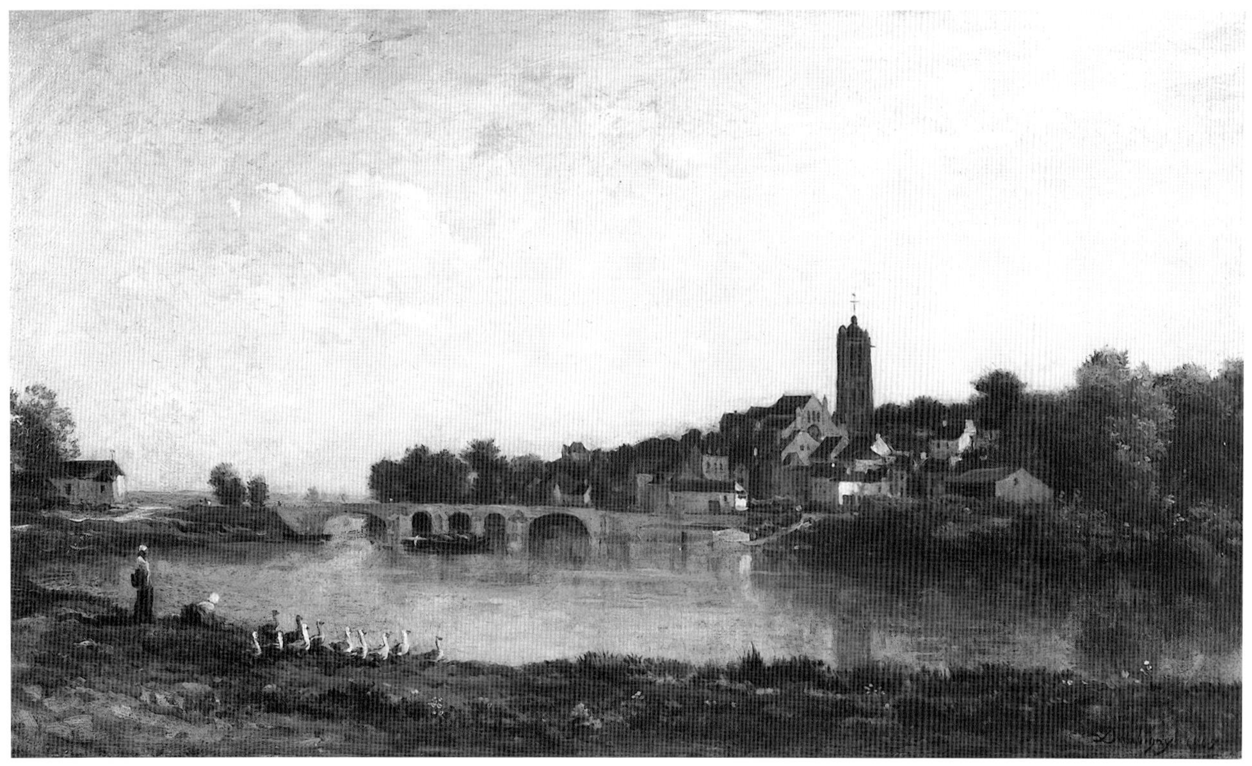

6 Charles Daubigny, *Bridge between Persan and Beaumont-sur-Oise*, 1867. $15\frac{1}{2} \times 26\frac{1}{2}$ in. (39.4×67.3 cm.). Sterling and Francine Clark Art Institute, Williamstown.

river, whose banks they leave untouched. The tree overhead divides the two worlds with its dead limbs to the left, a vine and live limbs to the right. The boy poet on the near bank leaves both worlds behind, but in Daubigny's spirit, if not in Lachambeaudie's, he puts his back to industry and walks toward the world of nature and illusion.

For the two sides of the *Two Riverbanks* are the two realms of Daubigny's artistic activity. His prints frequently show the transformation of the countryside, but his oils represent instead the unsullied villages, meadows, and riverbanks of France. Typical of his paintings is the *Bridge between Persan and Beaumont-sur-Oise* (pl. 6). Avoiding the rail line along the bank to the left, and the small industrial center of Persan, he painted the old road bridge and the village of Beaumont, precisely because they were unaltered. The women and the geese in the foreground are witnesses to the unchanging life he sought out, and the absence of any steam traffic on the river permits the water to reflect the illusions of timelessness. Daubigny hardly ever painted the steamboats along the Seine and the Oise, although we know that they were so common as to inspire the hatred of riverside innkeepers, ferrymen, and towpath workers, rapidly being done out of their livelihood. In several etchings in his autobiographical album of 1861, Daubigny represents both steamboat and train. *Departure* shows the train which often took him back and forth to Paris, and the steam tugs which plied the rivers. The world of oil painting was a different, and an ideal, realm. For Daubigny, as well as for Théodore Rousseau, Corot, and Millet, nature and the traditional village formed an ideal world in which they actually lived, one that was carefully nurtured in their paintings, protected from the incursion of insistent modernity.

Daubigny's paintings are the chief witnesses to this retention of a pastoral ideal, but occasionally his letters are especially revealing. In September 1854, returning to Avallon to seek out a favored site, he found it so changed by progress that he fled it immediately. To his friend Geoffroy Dechaume he wrote:

> Decidedly, old chap, I am unfortunate. Everything I wanted to paint has been torn down: trees cut, no more water in the river, houses knocked down! Therefore as a last resort I am clearing out and will see if the Eternal Father has not rearranged the mountains of the Dauphiné. I hope not.[7]

A few days later, settled in the countryside not far from Lyon, he opposed the calm of nature to the international preoccupation over the Crimea. His anti-war republicanism shows in his references to Barbès, to the "ratapoils" (Daumier's invented right-wing figure) and to Pierre Dupont, Lachambeaudie's friend and fellow *poète populaire*:

> So poor Barbès is really out of prison? Have you read what he has said about the war? Here they are more or less ratapoils, and the words war and victory are not spared. When one observes the great calmness of nature, the vain quarrels of European governments, as Pierre Dupont says, appear the vainer, and one asks oneself what it serves to kill people who are not tired of being alive.[8]

The contrast that Daubigny felt between the repose of nature and the cares of contemporary life continues the age-old yearning for release and tranquility that is a constant theme in Western art and literature from Pliny to van Gogh.[9] It is nonetheless essential, when dealing with the cultural history of France in the third quarter of the century, to point to the awareness of both worlds, city and country, because neither was independent of the other. The rapid industrialization of France lay behind the rise of landscape, which is nothing other than its counter-image. The fact that Impressionism eventually replaced Renaissance art as the dominant world style is proof enough of the need to look into its origins.

Monet, the greatest of Impressionist landscape painters, reveals the dichotomy of city and country in many aspects of his rich and varied work. His subjects range more widely than those of Daubigny, and they include many paintings of Paris as well as of a number of villages along the Seine and the Norman coast. Especially revealing and especially wonderful are his paintings at Argenteuil, where he lived from 1872 to 1878. Argenteuil was a suburban village that bore the evidence of a wholesale transformation under the impact of the urban-industrial revolution.[10] It is an especially good site for study because it was neither city nor country. Monet's paintings there give witness to the complicated pattern of change in a region that was indeed "nature" and that lent itself to "landscape," but one that was neither Paris itself nor the relatively untouched villages favored by Daubigny.

In his *Railroad Bridge, Argenteuil* (pl. 7), Monet reveals his unstated ambition to be the painter of modern landscape. The contrast with Daubigny's bridge at Beaumont (pl. 6) is striking in several regards. Because formal structure interprets subject, we might begin by noting the abruptness, bordering on harshness, with which Monet presents the bridge. Daubigny's bridge is woven into his composition by its environing foliage and by the shapes of nearby buildings which echo its arches. We see both ends of the bridge, where one comes from and where one goes, and we sense the firm anchor it has on both banks. Not so Monet. His bridge hurtles in from the left edge, unmediated by foliage, and it cuts sharply across the canvas.[11] This harsh presentation suits the bridge, for it carries trains, not foot passengers, and this particular rail line was relatively new, cutting across the eastern side of Argenteuil to a new station on the edge of the older section of the village. The bridge is of new design, for the comforting arches still used in metal bridges of the 1850s have given way to a compound structure that is put together in units, then hoisted atop the piers.

In the foreground of Monet's picture, instead of Daubigny's restful grass, flowers, and reeds, there is a homely pathway showing signs of the recent construction. Along its edge is a low barrier that retains the new embankment. It is of utilitarian design that makes no concession to traditional railings (to a modern eye it looks like a highway divider). It helps speed the eye along the near shore (we linger in the Daubigny), and makes all the more striking the rightward leap of the bridge. The spanning of the river is made the more dramatic by the way it dwarfs the figures below. That we are below the huge bridge is evident from the way Monet constructed the events on the ground plane. From the two men our eye passes to the near sailboat, then on to the other sailboat in an oblique line that reinforces, but does not parallel, the diagonal of bridge and piers. The alternating light and dark of the piers is repeated in the two sailboats and in the men's clothing, aiding the march of our eye off to the right, and providing a rhythmic contrast and support for the straight thrust of the bridge above.

The two men are at a key spot in the whole network of crossing diagonals. They stand along the axis of the shore, an angle which their own shadows accentuate. The tops of their heads just touch the line of the opposite shore, another instance of Monet's artful organization. That shore is another of the slanting lines of this composition. The two men look out along the receding diagonal formed by the boats. Like the engineers or onlookers pictured in nineteenth-century books devoted to the marvels of modern construction, they are witnesses to the Promethean triumphs of new industry. As if there were invisible strings in their hands, they stand within Monet's network of geometric forces, his organizing lines whose unflinching straightness is the very embodiment of modernity. This

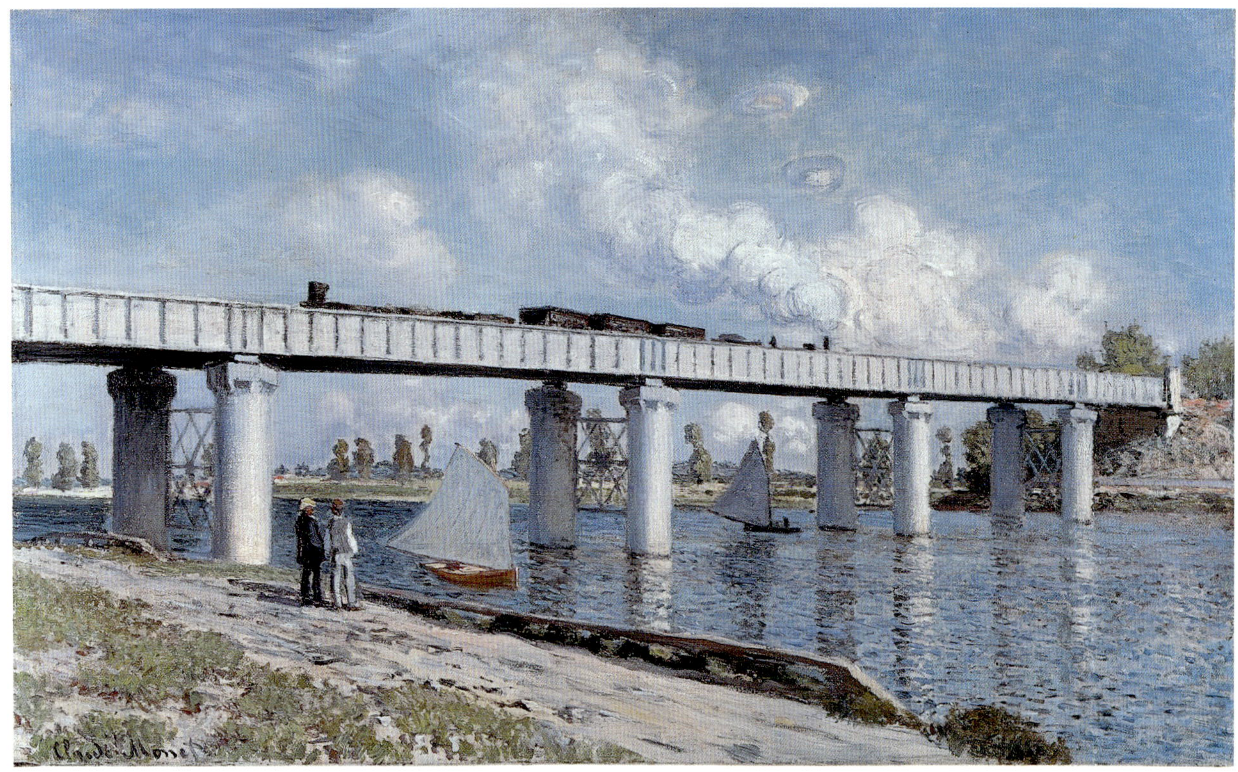

7 Claude Monet, *Railroad Bridge, Argenteuil*, 1873. 22⅞ × 38¼ in. (58.2 × 97.2 cm.). Private collection.

is because they record man's ability to surmount nature, to span her waterways and chasms, to defy her with the unyielding patterns that man imposes upon her for his own purposes. Their modernity, both in Monet's painting and in actuality, resides in their very unnaturalness.

The starkness of the bridge is somewhat relieved by the merging of the train's windblown smoke with the clouds above. They form a canopy of blues and whites that symbolizes the peaceful blending of manmade and natural vapors. The wind that blows the smoke also propels the sailboats below and they, too, soften the impact of the bridge, thanks to their association with natural pleasures. The near boat beats upwind as the other runs in front of the strong breeze. Although they move in opposite directions, their paths cross under the span, caught there along Monet's organizing diagonal.

Another picture of pleasure boating at Argenteuil (pl. 8) shows the same bridge, this time from upstream. Its composition is not at all the same, and the differences are revealing. To the art historian, these differences are of vital importance even though, superficially, the subject is the same in both pictures. In this second painting, done about a year after the first, Monet has moved upstream along the same bank of the Seine, going under the bridge to arrive on the other side. This places the viewer perhaps 200 yards from the vantage point of the other painting. To our right is the talus of foliage-covered earth which supports the railroad

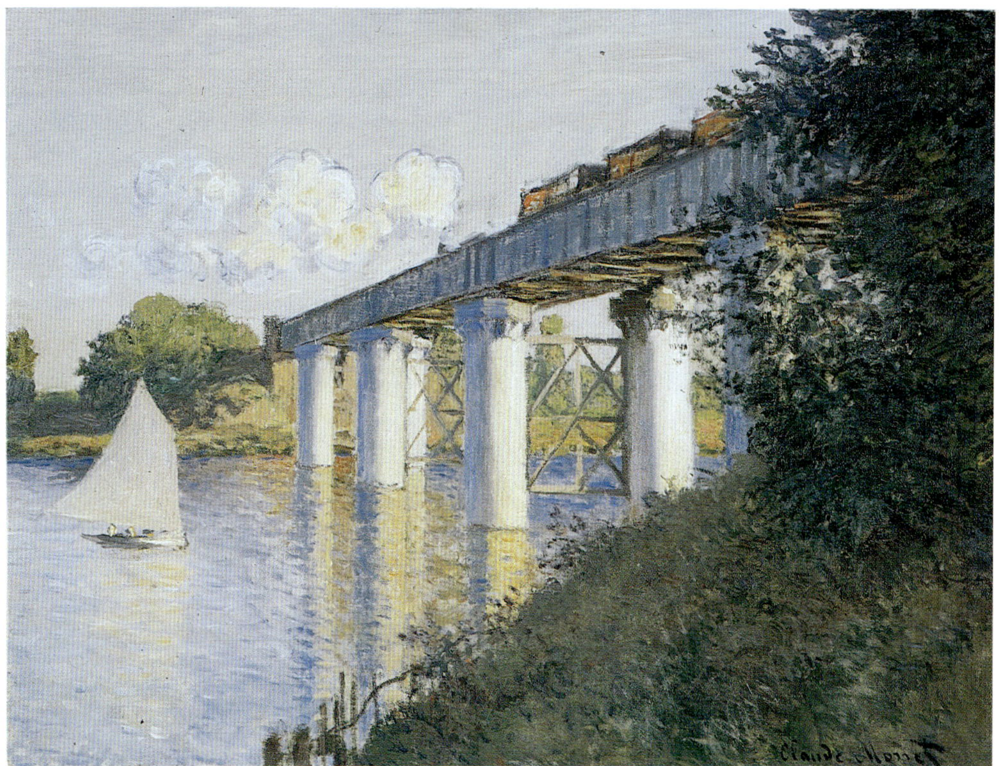

8 Claude Monet, *Railroad Bridge at Argenteuil*, 1874. 21¾ × 29 in. (55.4 × 73.5 cm.). Philadelphia Museum of Art, John G. Johnson Collection.

tracks above. This artificial mound and its growth form a pictorial cushion for the bridge, giving it a different feeling from the abrupt geometry of the other canvas. In fact, the more we compare the two, the more we realize how unalike they are. It is true that in the fiction of the later picture, the bridge darts dramatically back into space to give us a sense of the movement of the train, but it is also true that the foliage at the right softens the juncture with the picture's edge. Our imaginary position is on this verdant bank, no longer on the scruffy embankment of the earlier painting, and so our associations are with the colorful natural growth here and on the shore opposite. This integrates the bridge with its setting at Argenteuil, as distinct from the stark separation it exhibited in the earlier painting (pl. 7).

Nature, in other words, is arranged by the artist so as to enframe his dynamic bridge and train. The strong afternoon sun which comes from our right is seconded by the wind which pushes the train's smoke to the left. The sailboat is tacking against the wind, which must be fairly strong because it pushes the train's smoke sideways. By stressing that sun, wind, and sailboat are all going along the axis of the river, at right angles to the bridge, Monet reinforces the symbolic confrontation of the boat, symbol of leisure, with the train. Together the boat and the railroad stand for the new Argenteuil: the modern suburb which has given up its agricultural role to the pressures of urban leisure and industry. Both boat and railroad represent the new forces that were radically altering Argenteuil, forces that disrupted traditional life in this village, creating wholesale changes in the use of the river and its shore, in landownership and land use, in the types and numbers of local residents and in the work that they did.

A special word needs to be said about boating at Argenteuil, for the risk is that we do not recognize Monet's sailboats for what they really were: principal agents in the transformation of Argenteuil from country village to suburb.[12] Before 1840 Argenteuil's economy depended upon several kinds of agricultural produce and scattered local industry, including the plaster called "plaster of Paris." A few people made their living taking care of towpath horses, maintaining riverside inns and the local ferry. All this changed with astonishing rapidity in response to the expanding population of Paris and its need for leisure. The Seine widens at Argenteuil and this makes it one of the best spots near Paris for sailing. Boating clubs were established there,[13] and thanks to the railroad, the village was only fifteen minutes (six miles) from the Gare St. Lazare. Boat rental agencies took over some of the shoreline, and renting villas to vacationers loomed ever larger in the local economy.

Monet's willingness to address himself to these alterations of riverside life did not, however, mean a wholesale adoption of the industry which was rapidly expanding at Argenteuil. It is true that artists of the preceding generation, such as Corot and Daubigny, could not bring themselves to paint pleasure boats nor new railroad bridges, which embodied changes they could not tolerate. By comparison with them, Monet seems more of a spokesman for the changes affecting the once-rural villages along the Seine. Nonetheless, there is abundant evidence that at Argenteuil he screened out much of the rapidly growing local industry, showing factories only at a considerable distance, with few exceptions, or else avoiding them entirely. In the second of his bridge pictures discussed here, the whole truth about the site will reveal why his reconciliation of nature and railroad is a surprisingly complicated issue.

Were we able to stand where Monet places us in the Philadelphia picture (pl. 8), we would realize how artful his choice of view was. Immediately behind us and to our left were several large factories, and along the shore just to our left were industrial warehouses and loading docks.[14] The industrial uses of the river, which Monet uniformly avoids at Argenteuil, and the factories, which show in only a few pictures, are hardly hinted at in his painting of the bridge. Instead he literally put that all behind him, and shows us the sailboat, and the train as it leaves Argenteuil for Paris. The excitement of the train, as it hurtled over his head, and the opposed movement of the sailboat, were the images that distilled his sense of modern Argenteuil and its relationship to Paris. In this distillation they stood for the reconciliation of city and country, of industry and leisure, of railroad and river, of metal bridge and green foliage, of industrial steam and natural wind. Steam and wind are forces which move things, and motion is the very essence of change.

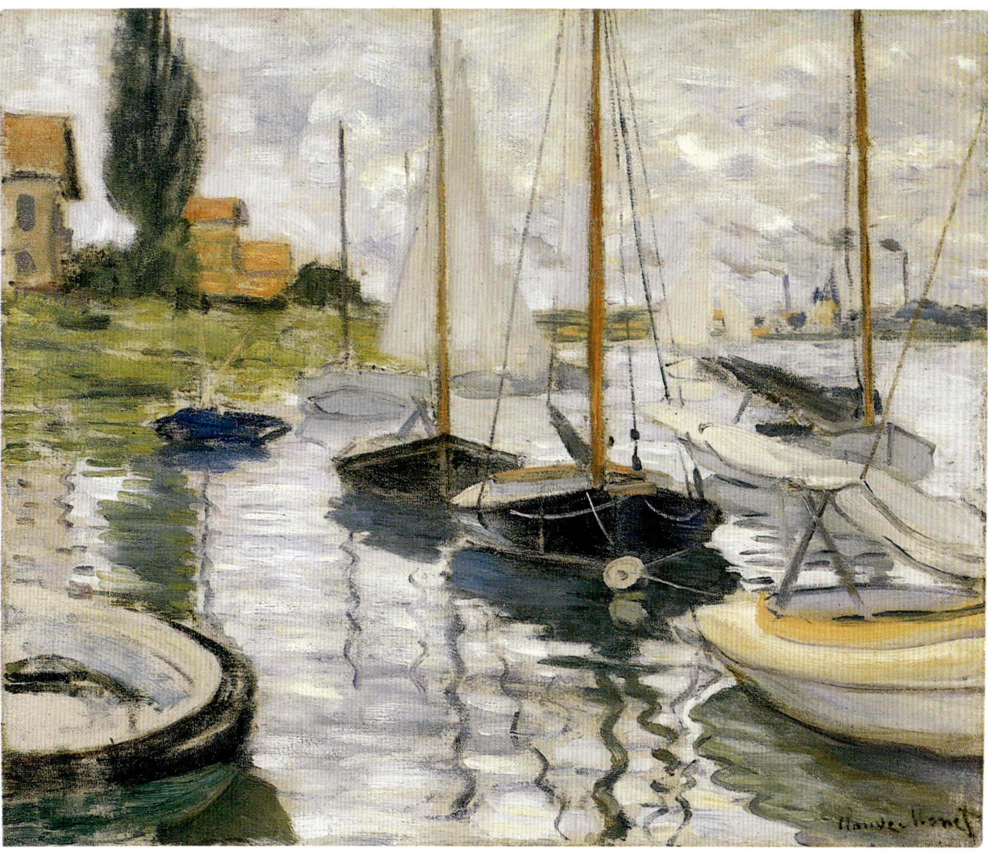

9 Claude Monet, *Sailboats on the Seine at Argenteuil*, 1874. 21¼ × 25⅝ in. (54 × 65 cm.). The Fine Arts Museums of San Francisco, Gift of Bruno and Sadie Adriani, 1962.23.

The factories and docks that surrounded Monet as he painted this picture were embodiments of industry and therefore of change, but they were not easily reconciled with the river and with natural light and movement. Monet's break with Barbizon art was not a complete one, in other words. The natural light and wind, and the riverbank foliage that Daubigny and Corot had so loved, are still present in Monet's painting, even if accompanied by suburban boat and train. Strong effects of outdoor nature were Monet's link with the preceding generation, and permitted him to blend old and new. It is symptomatic that in the only painting at Argenteuil which shows factories in relatively large scale,[15] Monet put them in mid-distance rather than in the foreground, and represented them under the softening effects of snow.

In most cases, when Monet showed factories at Argenteuil, they were far off in the distance of his pictures, as in *Sailboats on the Seine at Argenteuil* (pl. 9).[16] In this view we are across the river from Argenteuil, looking over a group of moored sailboats toward the easternmost extension of the village, marked by two smoking factory chimneys. Monet probably painted this picture from his studio boat, a device he had borrowed from Daubigny. It permitted him a variety of views that would otherwise be difficult, as well as the convenience of a modestly equipped floating studio. In this painting we feel the intimacy that resulted from being on the water, so close to other boats that the nearest ones are cut off by the edge of the frame. The undulating reflections, like so many eels, seem to work their way right under our feet. In mid-distance two sailboats are getting under way, their favorable wind made clear by the smoke from the distant chimneys. Once again industry and leisure are juxtaposed, and once again industry is peacefully absorbed, this time by integrating it with the river view. We see part of industrial Argenteuil across a broad reach of luminous water, as though it were some suburban Venice, purified by its exposure to brilliant light and air.

Other subjects that Monet painted at Argenteuil also reveal his conception of suburban life, even those which seem innocent of any contemporary references. *Gladioli* (pl. 10), for example, is one of a large number of paintings that show his wife in their richly flowered garden. Properly understood, it becomes a "modern" picture that shows how Argenteuil reflected the impact of Paris. In fact, this painting reeks of the city dweller.

Thanks to the work of Rodolphe Walter, and Daniel Wildenstein's collaborators,[17] we know a good deal about Monet's life at Argenteuil. From 1872 to 1874 he rented a house from a notable local landowner, Mme. Aubry-Vitet. He transformed its garden into a flowery wonder and often painted his wife and child, in proper middle-class dress, surrounded by blossoming plants. From the first rented garden he could see a new house being built next door, on a portion of Mme. Aubry-Vitet's land that had recently been sold and subjected to *lotissement*. Its owner and builder was one Alexandre Flament, an enterprising local carpenter and furniture maker. In 1874 Monet moved his family into Flament's pavilion, becoming its first tenant. Once again he turned his passion for gardening to good account and filled his rented yard with all manner of flowering plants. *Gladioli* shows his wife Camille in this second garden, one of a great many in which she appears, sometimes with their son or a friend.

In the preceding generation, most notably in paintings and drawings by Millet at Barbizon, a village garden was presented as such: it had Brussels sprouts or cabbages, and chickens pecked among them. The most common flower was that of the fruit tree, whose produce is edible. Millet had rented his village house, as Monet did later, but through his paintings he associated himself and his family with traditional villagers. Monet, by contrast, identifies himself with the transplanted city dweller who gets rid of the cabbages and chickens, and instead plants the flowers which transform the rented yard into a miniature estate. Despite his enormous debts – or perhaps because of them – Monet was living high off the hog (to use an anachronistic, small-town phrase), and he shows his wife as though she were the mistress of a château. The situation is a distillation of the suburbanization of Argenteuil. The local carpenter's land grows more valuable

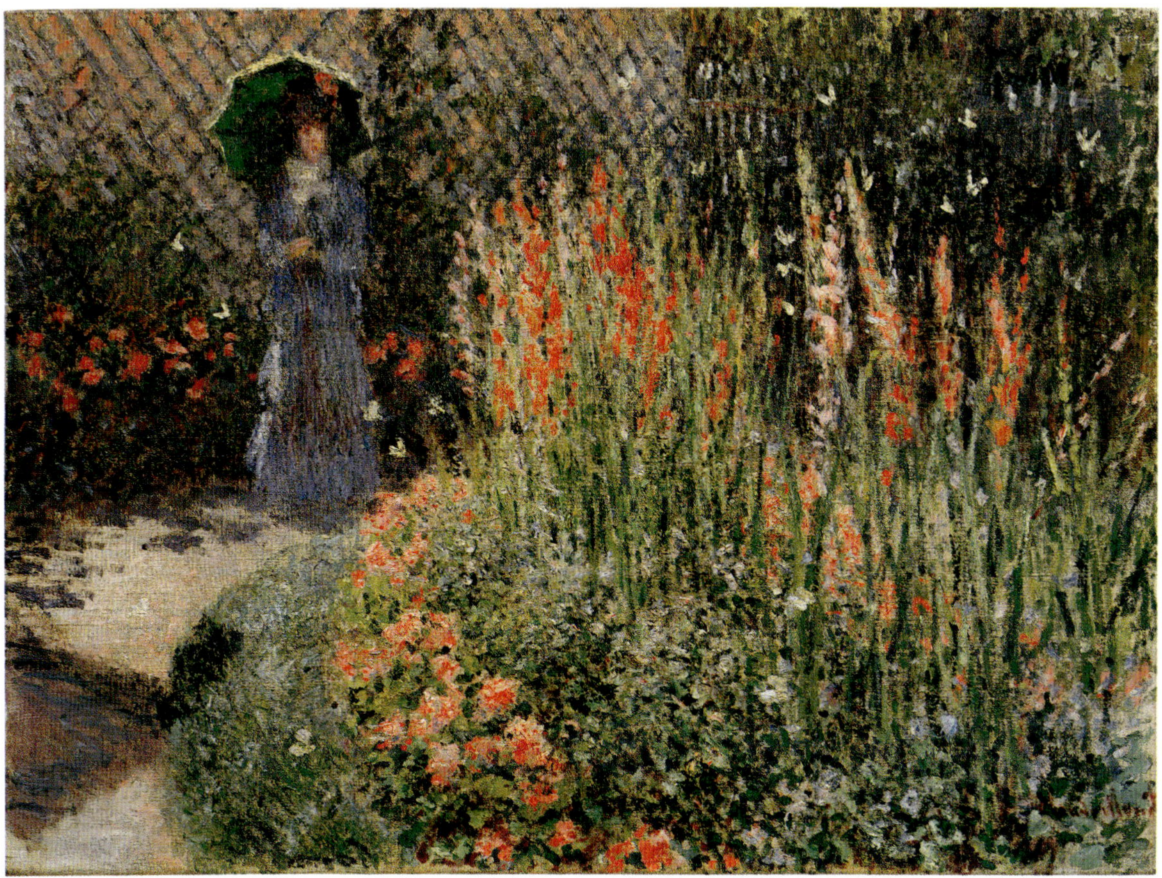

10 Claude Monet, *Gladioli*, 1876. $23\frac{5}{8} \times 32$ in. (60×81.5 cm.). Detroit Institute of Arts.

as Argenteuil expands, so he builds upon it a villa whose rental income is greater than he could obtain from the land itself. The city artist to whom he rents comes to Argenteuil to find suitable subjects to paint, not far from Paris where his market is located: dealers, exhibition galleries, and clients.

The contrast between Millet's vegetable garden and Monet's flowers is that between a premodern village and a suburb. Millet's ideal was the rural community untainted by the modernization of urban life, which he had deliberately fled. Monet's ideal was that of the middle-class city dweller who thinks of the village as a place to build his domain, a garden of color and beauty which will be a compensation for the need to work – and from which vegetables, those symbols of need and of work, will be excluded.

Some contemporiaries lamented the conversion of such villages as Argenteuil to suburban extensions of Paris. Adolphe Joanne, the relatively sober author of guidebooks to the environs of Paris, could not hold back his opinion of the new suburban villas:

> These habitations, more pretentious than picturesque, affect all forms and styles of architecture. Here is a garden of a few square meters, possessing a jet of water in a tiny basin, some statues, a gazebo, and a greenhouse; it is called an English garden. There, the façades of houses are erected, some on the model of the Alhambra, others on that of Herculaneum or Pompeii.[18]

Fortunately Monet's taste was not that which Joanne deplored, but the flowers that he cultivated nonetheless stood for the bourgeois who surrounded himself with a garden of his own devising that contrasted with the traditional use of the land. Even an enclosed village garden of former days, managed by a typical resident, would have had vegetables and a few chickens. The great geographer Elisée Reclus, in an essay of 1866, lamented the loss of these traditional village gardens with their farmyard aspect: "For strollers walking down the muddy lanes of this make-believe countryside, nature is only represented by well-trimmed bushes and masses of flowers seen through the bars of fences."[19]

We need not, in consequence, attack Monet for debasing village traditions. I have wanted instead to make evident the particular truth of his real and his painted gardens. They represent the creation of an ideal environment, away from the city, released from immediate urban pressures, an environment shaped to his own liking as the recipient of natural light and air which, then, his artificial pigments could reconstruct.

Monet's rented villa was on the eastern side of Argenteuil, a district that had been undergoing drastic alteration since the Franco-Prussian War. The railroad used to end across the river, on the Paris side, but now it was brought across the new bridge – the one Monet painted (pls. 7 and 8) – into the edge of the village, where a new station was erected. Monet's villa was diagonally across the street from the station.[20] He often had to leave his flowered garden and take the train to Paris, in search of the money he constantly needed. His frequent use of the Gare St. Lazare led him, in 1877, to paint his famous group of twelve pictures of the great train shed and its outlying tracks. To complete this review of industrial images in Impressionist painting, we should look at one of these paintings of the Gare St. Lazare, and we should juxtapose it with the contemporary painting of his garden at Argenteuil. The truth of Impressionism is found in the juxtaposition, not in either picture alone. Like Daubigny's and Lachambeaudie's *Two Riverbanks* (pl. 5), there are still two sides to Monet's pathway in 1877, one flowered and the other industrialized.

In order to paint the Gare St. Lazare, Monet rented rooms nearby and frequently stayed there, although his wife and child remained in Argenteuil. His choice of subject was a daring one in 1877. Some courageous critics had called for paintings of modern buildings, but generally they were considered suitable only for commemorative pictures. A few artists however, including Manet and Caillebotte, had made paintings of the tracks and bridges near the Gare St. Lazare.[21] Like these two artists, who were among his friends and supporters, Monet was committed to a form of naturalism which sought the characteristic

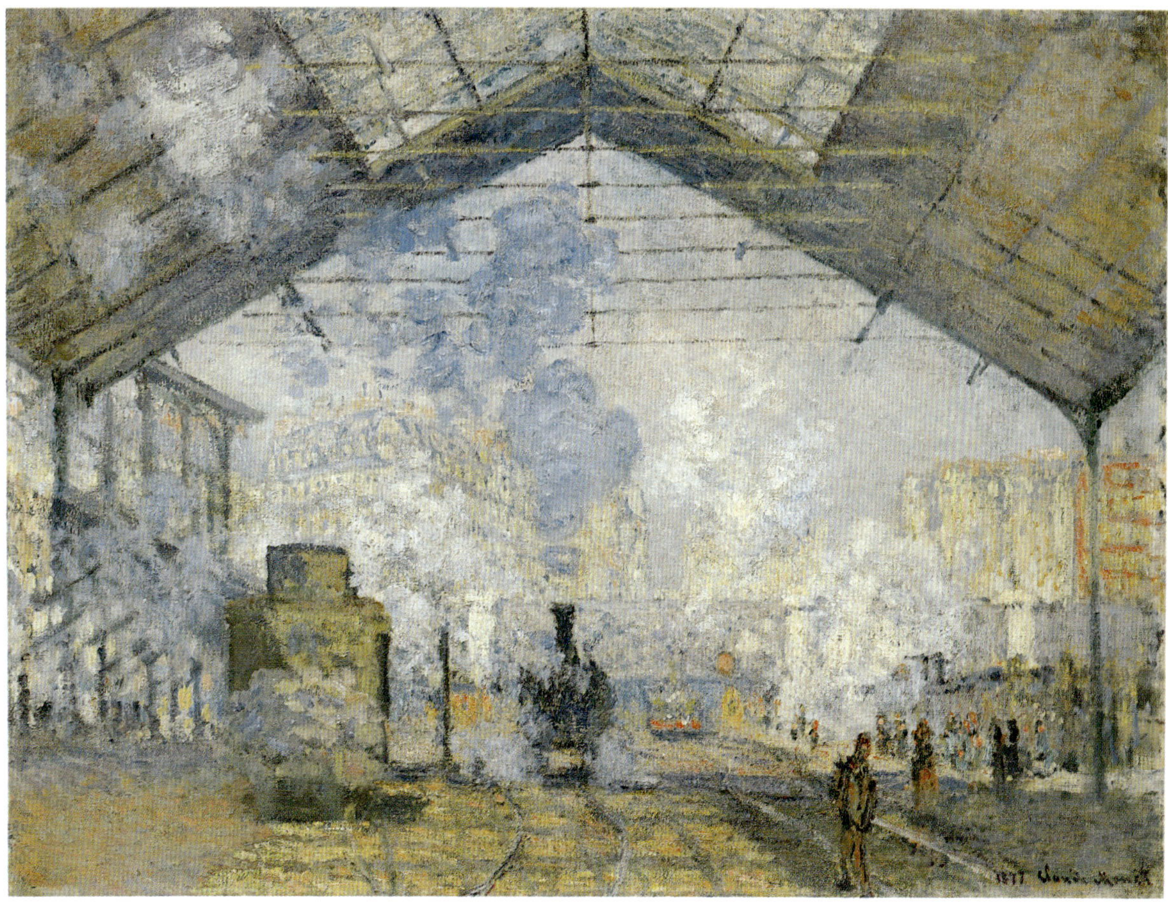

11 Claude Monet, *Gare St. Lazare*, 1877. 29¾ × 41 in. (75.5 × 104 cm.). Musée d'Orsay, Paris.

truths of a scene or activity. For that reason he did not portray the façade of the station nor the great waiting hall which contemporary chroniclers made so much of. Instead he took the viewer out in the shed (pl. 11), and even there, it is not just the train but the structure and the whole activity of the station which is his subject. The locomotive is relatively small and, because it is seen frontally, it lacks the mass and power often associated with it. The puffs of steam on the ground at either side hide its wheels and further diminish its threatening power, making it float in an atmosphere of light, steam, and smoke. We can see by the placing above of its clouds of blue smoke that it has just entered the shed. Nearer to us on the left is a stationary caboose, also seen from one end so that movement is denied. To the right are a trainman in the foreground and passengers further back on the quai. It is a classically balanced picture, given a great control by its overall symmetry. Not only is the overhead vault centrally placed, but also its vertical supports are the same distance from the left and right edges.

Monet has drawn our attention to these spindly iron columns on either edge. In doing that he has caught the spirit of Eugène Flachat, the engineer who had made of this shed one of the most daring of contemporary structures. Clever use of iron supports and overhead braces let Flachat construct a very wide span, which he pierced with huge skylights. Monet lets the sunlight flood down from the skylights onto the tracks in the foreground, and he gives as much prominence to the geometric shadows of the overhead network as to the tracks. In fact, we come to understand this picture as a celebration of the moist outdoor sunlight that occupies the whole center of the composition, the sunlight that penetrates the station. The smoke and steam that join outside with inside also join industrial vapors with nature's atmosphere.

The whole picture is therefore a homage to modern engineering, and more particularly to Flachat's having overcome solid mass in favor of light and air. Is this not the very ambition of this gifted landscapist in his own art? When we think of the Impressionists, do we not think first of their denial of traditional sculptural mass and darkness in favor of light and air? And can we not recall that Louis Napoleon and Baron Haussmann had brought light and air into Paris by widening streets and creating new parks and squares? To carry these analogies one step further, we need only remember that one of the demands of progressive social forces in France, as in England, was for ridding cities of dark, fetid courtyards and streets, of dark, windowless factories and slums, in favor of clean air.

In the preceding generation, Lachambeaudie's enthusiasm for modern engineering was precisely because it could bring about more vital and healthier conditions of travel and work. Flachat himself had been a prominent Saint-Simonian – he was one of Père Enfantin's original group of disciples – and his rebuilding of the Gare St. Lazare was the fruition of what had once been a utopian ideal. By Monet's day, progressive capitalists had adopted many of the Saint-Simonists' ideas. The railroad trains and bridges that Corot, Millet, and Daubigny were unable to countenance could now be assimilated into the poetics of painting. In the most profound sense, the light and air of Monet's railroad station were interwoven with social issues.

If the history of Monet's painting ended with the Gare St. Lazare, the historian would have an easy job of it. His art had ranged sufficiently over city, suburb, and country to encompass train station, railroad bridge, factories seen at a distance, seaports, pleasure boating, private gardens, village streets, meadows, and riverbanks. Industry had its place in this broad adoption of the contemporary landscape, and there was little reason to assume that it would not continue to figure in his pictures.

Yet after the series of paintings of the Gare St. Lazare in 1877, Monet never again painted any subject that could be construed as an industrial one. No more railroad bridges, no more factories appeared in his paintings. Furthermore, he never again painted the buildings and streets of Paris, with the exception of a few pictures of parks and gardens, and even these disappear entirely after 1878. In that year he moved to Vétheuil, on the Seine beyond Mantes, and remained there after his wife's death the following year. By then he was living with Alice Hoschedé; their combined children numbered six. He began painting often on the Channel coast, and at the end of 1881 established residence at Poissy (which he detested, and refused to paint save for two or three pictures). Then in 1883 Monet settled his expanded family in Giverny, on the Seine halfway to Rouen, and there he spent the rest of his life. Giverny was beyond the reach of immediate Parisian influence and had nothing of the suburb about it. Besides Giverny, Monet's subjects were the cliffs and small ports of Normandy (with evidence of tourism expunged), the rocky coast of Brittany, the Mediterranean coast, the meadows, villages, and riverbanks of Normandy, the cathedral of Rouen, and his own estate and water gardens. These gardens were the fulfilment of the dreams first sketched out in his rented gardens at Argenteuil.

Art historians will offer Monet's own subjectivity as the explanation for the abrupt termination of his interest in both city and suburb and in the transport that linked them. His wife's lingering death in 1879, followed by his combining families with Alice Hoschedé (whose bankrupt husband gradually took his distance), were emotional events of the first order. Forsaking Paris and its suburbs can be seen as a search for the tranquility of unspoiled village and rural subjects, that release from city cares which Daubigny and Millet had sought in the preceding generation.

And yet the historian of culture concerned with its social meaning cannot rest content with explanations rooted in the subjectivity of one artist. Of course it would be foolish to ignore such evidence. The richness of psychological inquiry is especially apparent when dealing with the poetics of art. Such inquiry, however, should supplement and not usurp the role of social history.

In the work of Monet's younger contemporary, Vincent van Gogh, there are instructive parallels. Van Gogh's social mission and his art were interwoven in the early 1880s, when he drew and painted the peasants and townspeople of the Borinage. During his two years in Paris he learned the new palette of the Impressionists and painted a number of subjects similar to theirs. The tensions of living in the French capital were too great for him, and when he went to the south of France in 1888 it was in search of an ideal world in which cultivated fields and valleys were in sight of the small towns he preferred. The community of artists he hoped to establish in Arles would have re-established a society whose loss he regretted, a society devoted to the pre-industrial truths of town work and field labor, and to their celebration in art. His Japan, he called it, out of conviction that Japanese artists lived in co-operative communities; he also thought of it as a revival of seventeenth-century Holland, knit together by common beliefs.

Van Gogh's utopian dream could not survive its abortive test in the presence of that egocentric bully Gauguin, and eventually Vincent was driven north to

Auvers, where he could seek the help of Dr. Paul Gachet, artist, collector, friend of the Impressionists, and specialist in mental disturbance. In Auvers van Gogh tried to achieve balance, painting those magnificent last pictures of thatched cottages, wheat fields, and gently rolling countryside. He committed suicide out of awareness of the distance there was between reality and illusion.

When we are reminded of van Gogh's poignant odyssey, we are so drawn to its familiar, purely personal events that we are apt to forget how much it speaks for modern man. For in a larger sense, van Gogh and Monet are alike. Industry and the suburbs enter prominently into their art, but tensions inherent in creating an ideal world in painting drove them away from images of railroad bridges and large cities. In flowering trees and haystacks, wheatfields and villages, they chose images that would cleanse modern people of the effects of industrialization.

If the art of either painter had been entirely isolated from that of his fellows, we might be entitled to interpret it as purely subjective and purely idiosyncratic. This is not true, however, for Monet and van Gogh shared a number of aspirations, and the effect of their art on subsequent generations is owing to their having touched a chord that vibrates deep within modern man. Moreover, in the paintings of Cézanne and Pissarro, of Winslow Homer and of Giovanni Segantini, early modern art came to us peopled by peasants, fishermen, and villagers.

It was still possible in the late nineteenth century to hold up such images to the face of industrialization as a world towards which to aspire. Despite the vitality of the rural communes of the 1960s, and despite the attractions of living the winter in Vermont or Colorado by a wood stove, we no longer believe that we can return to a pre-industrial condition. It is unlikely that Monet believed he could, either. In the last decades of his life, dominated by his paintings of water gardens, he had to be aware of the degree to which his art was an illusion. In order to get from his house to the water gardens he had built (detouring a local stream for the purpose), he had to cross over the branch railway that bisected his estate. Although he never showed this rail line in his paintings of waterlilies, we must take it into account if we are to comprehend the inner meaning of his art.

Le cours de notre vie a toujours deux Rivages;
Tous deux, dans notre enfance, et fleuris et joyeux,
Sont pleins de doux pensers, de chants insoucieux.
Plus tard, sur une Rive étendant leurs ravages,
L'intéret, les besoins et les prévisions
Emportent la moitié de nos illusions.
  Heureux, quand la vieillesse arrive,
Si quelques fleurs encore restent sur l'autre Rive![22]

[The course of our life has always two Shores;
Both, in our childhood, are enflowered and joyous,

Full of gentle thoughts, of uncaring songs.
Later, over one Shore, ravages are spread by
Interest and need, and anticipated wants
Take away half of our illusions.
  There is happiness, when old age arrives,
If a few flowers remain still on the other Shore!]

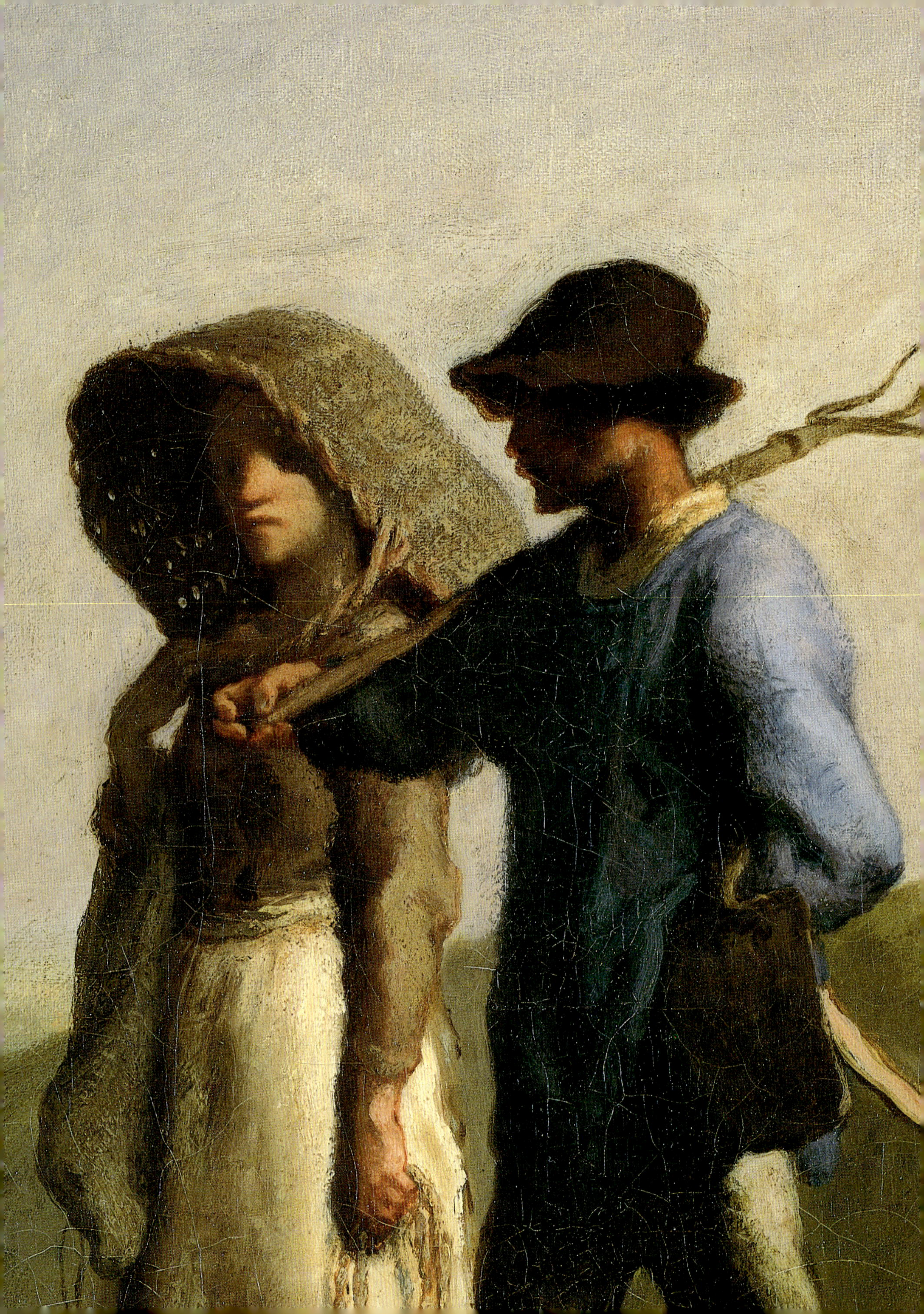

Chapter 2

City vs. Country: The Rural Image in French Painting from Millet to Gauguin

Images of the modern city, its factories, its machines, and its workers, would not provide a sufficient basis for a study of the way art is related to the urban-industrial revolution. On the contrary, such images are relatively rare, and it is frequently latent or indirect imagery which provides the essential clues. For example, the art of the early twentieth century showed a stubborn retention of traditional images despite the wilful expression of a new dynamism. The Futurist Boccioni, regardless of his revolutionary statements about machinery, retained the nude human form and the horse in many of his major works. Duchamp-Villon's principal sculpture evokes a horse, and Brancusi often chose birds and fish, pre-industrial images whose natural state suggested speed and streamlined form. Kandinsky embodied his apocalyptic visions in floods, tottering city walls, and horsemen.

In nineteenth-century painting, direct references to the urban-industrial revolution are not common. The Impressionists, it is true, occasionally painted railway stations, busy riverports, and the new parks and boulevards which Napoleon III and Baron Haussmann had added to Paris. Nevertheless it is fair to say that themes of urban entertainment, suburban relaxation and rural nature dominate French art of the nineteenth century, to the near exclusion of machine and worker, those basic constituents of the cataclysmic changes taking place.[1]

This does not mean that the artists were unaware of the ways in which the city and individual lives were being altered. Renoir, painter of suburban dalliance, wrote diatribes against machinism. A major artist of the preceding generation had written in 1853:

> Will steam stop before churches and cemeteries? And will the Frenchman, returning to his fatherland after some years, be reduced to asking where it was that his village stood [. . .] ? For villages will be as useless as the rest; villagers are those who cultivate the soil, because they have to stay there where their care is required at every moment; it will be necessary to build cities suited to this workless and disinherited mass of people, who will no longer have

12 *(facing page)* detail of pl. 18.

• From *Artforum* 8, 6 (February 1970): 44–55.

> anything to do in the fields; it will be necessary to construct immense barracks where they will lodge pell-mell. [. . .] Instead of transforming the human race into a vile herd, let it keep its real heritage, its attachment, its devotion to the soil! [. . .] Alas! poor peasants, poor villagers! [. . .] With only the slightest hopes, they vie with one another in leaving the work of the fields; they rush to the cities, only to be disappointed; they complete there the perversion of the feelings of dignity which the love of labor gives, and the more your machines feed them, the more they will become degraded.[2]

This passionate statement, which so aptly predicts the rise of urban ghettoes, and which proclaims the conservative virtues of peasant devotion to the soil, is by Eugène Delacroix, the great Romantic master who painted neither the city of which he speaks nor the peasant. He is best known for subjects drawn from Shakespeare, Byron, Goethe, and North African life. The lesson is a simple one: we need not find a direct association between an artist's known social feelings and the subjects he chooses.

My general thesis therefore, perhaps surprisingly at first glance, is that the peasant was among the most important subjects for the embodiment of artists' attitudes toward the urban-industrial revolution. To give emphasis to materials I know best, and to provide continuity as I deal with relationships often based on intangible and circumstantial evidence, I focus on Jean-François Millet (1814–75). He has been known as the "peasant painter" since the 1850s and any interpretation of peasant art would have to be measured against his work, in any event.

First we should recall the phenomenal growth of Paris in the nineteenth century, and its effects on the countryside. City cannot be divorced from country, and once studied together, the relationship becomes clear between urban and rural upheavals on the one hand, and the painting of peasant subjects on the other. Perhaps the best way to indicate the changes in Paris in the middle of that century is to record the fact that in the Department of the Seine, encompassing Paris and its suburbs, the population between 1790 and 1831 rose by only 10,000, or about 1½ per cent. This was over a period of forty years. But between 1831 and 1851, only twenty years, the population doubled, that is, it grew by 100%.[3] To accommodate this burgeoning society, Napoleon III and Baron Haussmann undertook the massive transformation of Paris which gave the city much of its present aspect. From 1852 to 1857 there were about 24,000 new buildings erected in the capital and its suburbs, let alone the hundreds of miles of new streets.[4] (It should be noted that the stonebreaker, prominent in the work of Courbet, Millet, and many others, although ostensibly a rural image, is thereby an echo of the building campaigns in the city; Fontainebleau forest, favorite site of the Barbizon school, contained some of the quarries for Paris.)

Where did the mushrooming population of Paris come from? Principally from the countryside. France's birth rate then, as now, was very low, and between 1846 and 1856 there was a net rise of only 640,000 for all of France. To give some measure of the dominance of Paris, its population rise in the second half of that ten-year period was 305,000, roughly equal to the national total. What really happened was what the French were already calling the "depopulation of the countryside." Most of the eighty-six departments lost people at the expense of the large cities and industrial regions. The northeast departments lost 200,000 between 1851 and 1856, except for Le Nord, the industrial region, which gained 56,000. In the Ile de France, the departments which touched Paris on all sides lost 55,000, many of them counted among the capital's phenomenal increase.

The only word for this vast shifting of rural peoples is migration. So great were the numbers leaving for the city, and so great was the utter disruption of traditional harvesting and culture, that by 1860 a total of nearly one-sixth of people who lived on the land left their villages each year, some of them as migratory agricultural workers who would later return, but many never to come back.

How did artists react to these dramatic changes? It so happens that statements directly on the subject, like the one by Delacroix already cited, are relatively rare, and we must rely on circumstantial evidence, essentially the juxtaposition of peasant subjects and the changes in city and country. To move from juxtaposition to interrelationship, a higher form of analysis, is easier when we learn that there was in general, at least among sensitive observers, an awareness of the connection between the new city and the plight of the countryside.

Evidence of an awareness of rural depopulation appears as early as 1846, in the book published that year by Eugène Bonnemère, *Les Paysans au XIXe siècle*. It was the winning entry among forty-nine in a competition sponsored that year by the Academy of Nantes on "The causes of emigration from the countryside to the cities and the means of stopping it." From this time onward, there was an increasing amount of attention paid to rural emigration. In 1848 the National Assembly ordered an investigation of the emigration and ways to prevent it. There was, as we see, an assumption that it was bad and must be halted, and although the need of the city for labor was apparent, many reformers were willing to call a halt to city growth, if necessary, to stem the disruption of country life. After the Revolution of 1848 or, rather, after the consolidation of Louis Napoleon's power in 1852, the number of sociological studies of rural emigration grew very suddenly, and by the end of the decade they were commonplace. Between 1855 and 1862, about fifteen major books appeared, and a number of learned competitions were sponsored by various provincial and national academies. The national census became much more sophisticated, and it was not hard to find evidence of the great upheaval taking place. The government was well aware of the phenomenon and embarked on a number of investigations and remedial programs which we should compare with the pre-1848 period. For example, in 1846 there had been a national subsidy for the royal theaters amounting to 1,144,000 francs, but subsidies for agriculture for the entire nation came to only 900,000 francs.[5] That had all changed by the mid-1850s, when agriculture and rural workers became one of the central issues of the day. It is against this background of the sudden rise to prominence of the depopulation of the countryside that we must place the exactly parallel rise of peasant art in mid-nineteenth-century France.

As 1848 approached, there was an increasing significance given to genre and popular subjects which could be associated with that new hero, the common man. Mention began to be made of the Le Nain brothers, nearly forgotten painters of the seventeenth century: in 1847 Thoré compared Millet with them;[6] in 1848 the new and rather revolutionary staff of the Louvre reattributed pictures by the Le Nain brothers that had been given to other artists, and gave them prominence in new installations; in 1850 Courbet's friend Champfleury published his first article on the Le Nains, and the revival continued until his brochure of 1862, which drew together the life and works of these major ancestors of peasant painting.

Another example of the mid-century's concern with peasant subjects is the appearance of rural themes in contemporary poetry, song, and novels. Admitting that there had always been rustic themes in literature, we nonetheless find that on the eve of the 1848 Revolution, the German writers Hebel, Gotthelf, and Auerbach appear in their first translations; their French counterparts, Courbet's friend Max Buchon (who translated many of the German works), Gustave Mathieu, and Pierre Dupont, all come to public attention at the same time.[7] Unlike former writers, these men treat rural life with considerable realism, and with relatively little of the embellishments of Romanticism. Besides, the relationship to current political and social upheaval was apparent since Buchon, Mathieu, and Dupont were all political radicals. Dupont, the writer of populist songs and poems, claimed a social role for his writing in the preface he wrote in 1851 for his collected works: "My rustic songs have found their echoes and have opened the way to social or political refrains;" and later on the same page he flatly states that his writing foretold the revolution.[8]

For painters of peasant themes we will have very few such statements. Gustave Courbet is the notable exception. He openly proclaimed his political radicalism, and many of his most important paintings, such as *The Stonebreakers* (lost) and the *Burial at Ornans* (Musée d'Orsay, Paris), both of 1849, were controversial precisely because they claimed for rural subjects an equality of pictorial rank with themes from religion, mythology, and history. However, the pervasiveness of peasant motifs can be demonstrated to be not the political expression of one or of a few artists, but a social and artistic phenomenon of remarkable extent related to the Revolution of 1848 and its aftermath. All these allied events began in the late 1840s, reaching peaks in the 1850s: the growth and renovation of Paris; an awareness of the depopulation of the countryside; the upsurge of peasant themes in literature and popular music; the revival of the Le Nain brothers; the rise to great prominence of landscape as a major category of painting, and the simultaneous mushrooming of animal and genre painting; the concomitant development of vast city parks (landscapes for city dwellers); the great boom in riverine and seacoast resorts (seascapes for city dwellers on vacation); the sudden notoriety of Courbet and Millet. The critic Castagnary, one of the chief spokesmen for the new naturalism, summarized it most succinctly:

> Religious painting, and historical or heroic painting, have gradually been weakened, in proportion to the weakening of theocracy and monarchy, the social organisms to which they refer; their elimination, nearly complete today, is bringing about the absolute domination of genre painting, landscape, and portraiture, which stem from individualism: in art as in society, man becomes more and more man.[9]

The new man, ostensibly stripped of religious, mythological, and historical references – actually still present, but transformed – appeared in some of the most notable early works by Millet and Courbet. Millet's *Winnower* (National Gallery, London), a vigorous standing male shaking his basket, became the embodiment of the spirit of 1848 when it appeared in that year's Salon, its red kerchief unconsciously echoing the great Revolution of a half-century earlier. Courbet who, like Millet, had exhibited hardly any peasant subjects before 1848, took the figure of the *Winnower* in the following year for his famous *Stonebreakers*, turning him to a three-quarter view and substituting stones for grain. The second figure in Courbet's painting has the marked monumentality of Poussin (and recalls a figure in the Louvre's *Et in Arcadia Ego*), for it is evident that in the laborer and the peasant, both artists found reincarnations of the heroic figures of Renaissance and Baroque art. Millet, a more conservative man and artist than Courbet, devoted himself to peasant life more unreservedly. He moved to Barbizon in 1849 and passed his life there, seldom departing from rural subjects; Courbet became a Parisian by adoption and challenged many of the great subjects of the past, including portraiture, the nude, and urban genre.

In his first few years at Barbizon Millet gave to his paintings a passion and an energy we should associate with the mood of 1848 and the mid-century celebration of work.[10] His *Woodsawyers* (Victoria & Albert Museum, London) and *Faggot Gatherers* (pl. 13), both of 1850–51, show peasants sawing wood and binding faggots with Michelangelesque gestures. Shoulders rise up in great curves which are continued by the sweep of active arms, forming continuous pictorial movements which cover naturalistic detail, the better to induce a feeling of integral thrusts of power. Other figures have limbs drawn tautly toward the body, squeezing, pressing, and gathering in centripetal energy, as though steel springs were being wound by the artist. How different these figures are, both individually and as naturalistic groups, from the famous *Arrival of the Harvesters* (pl. 14) by Léopold Robert, shown at the Salon of 1831. Robert's Italian peasants are, by comparison, of a past era when they were looked upon as actors on a stage, not as real men really living the lives of peasants. They strut and posture and in the great variety of their types and their poses, they are intended to reca-

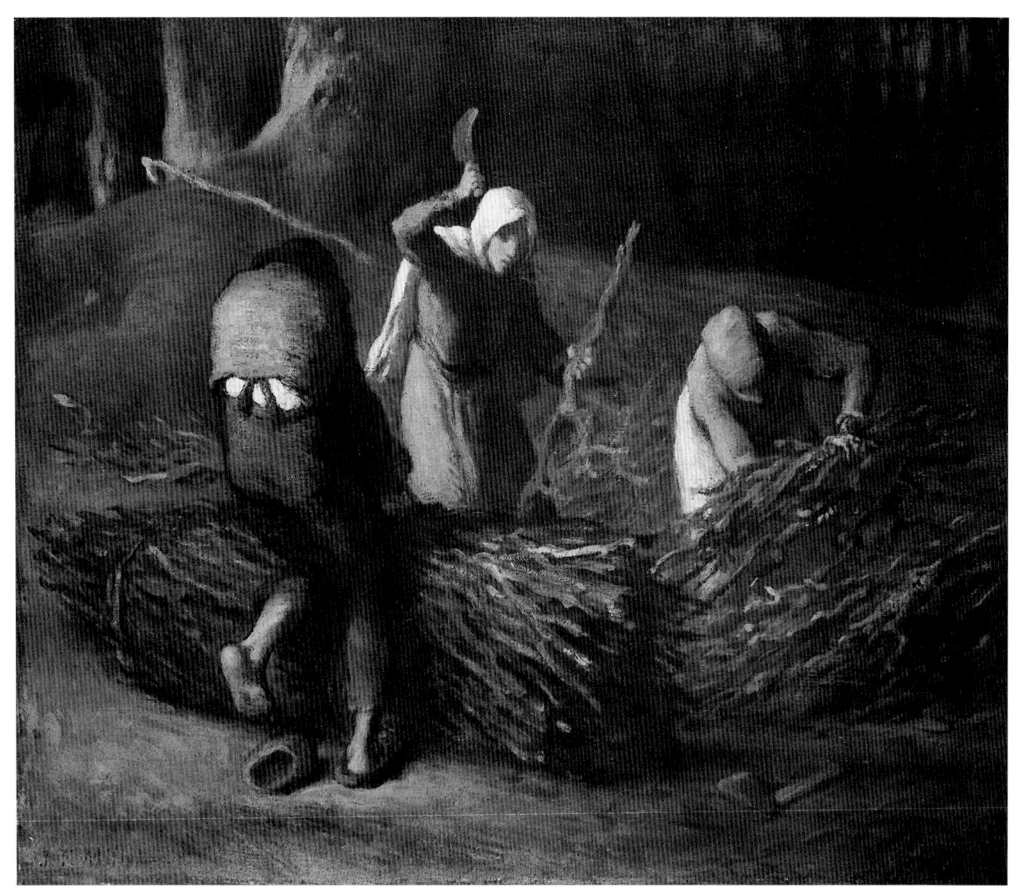

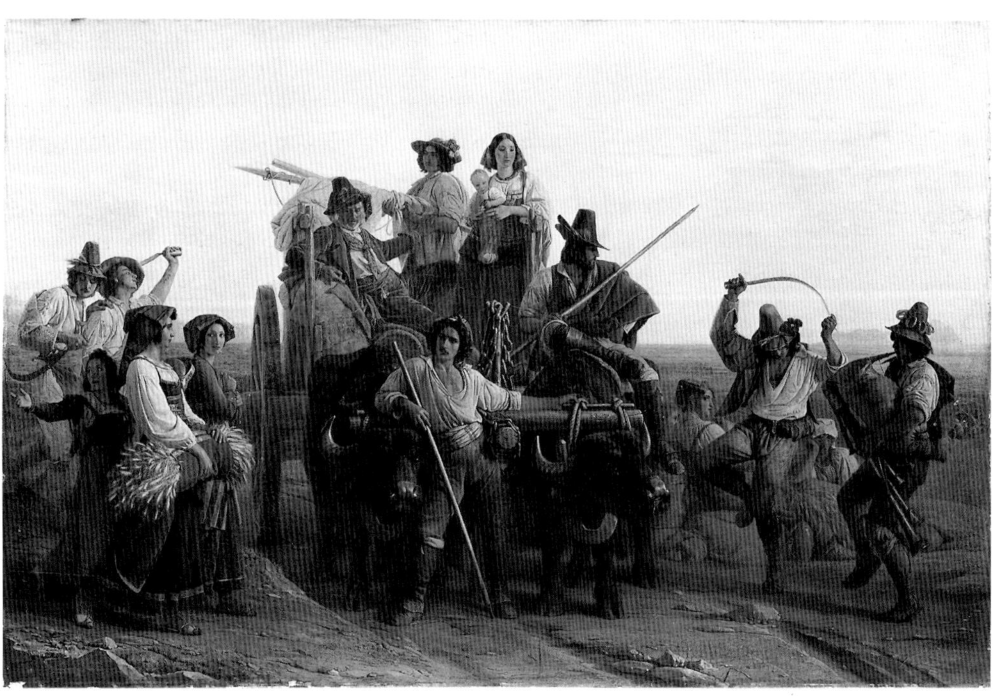

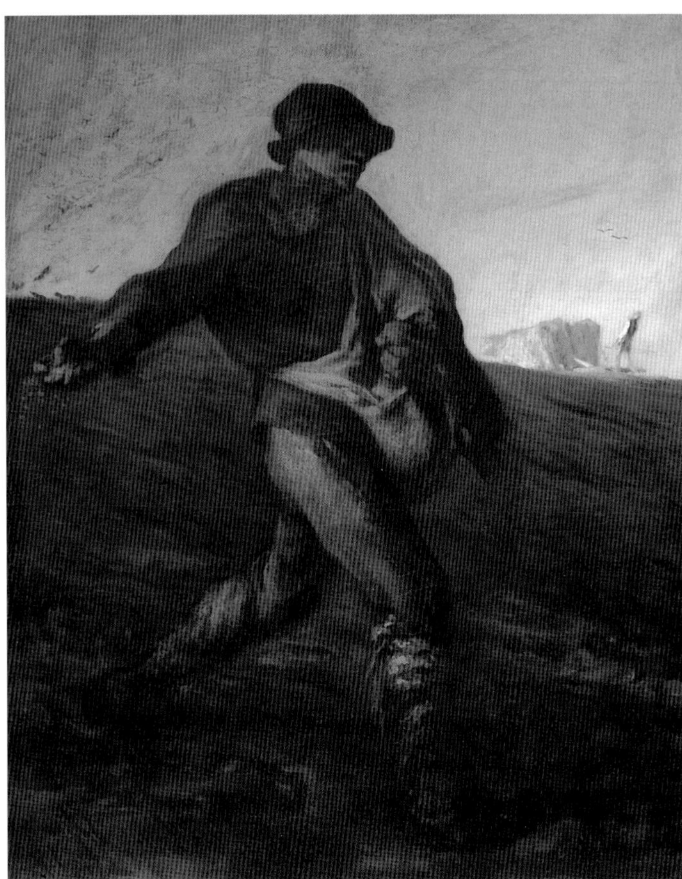

15 *(left)* J.F. Millet, *The Sower*, 1850. 40 × 32½ in. (101.6 × 82.6 cm.). Museum of Fine Arts, Boston, Gift of Quincy Adams Shaw.

13 *(facing page, top)* J.F. Millet, *Faggot Gatherers*, 1850–51. 15 × 18 in. (38 × 45.7 cm.). Norton Museum of Art, West Palm Beach, Gift of Mr. and Mrs. Wiley R. Reynolds, Sr., 59.13.

14 *(facing page, bottom)* Léopold Robert, *Arrival of the Harvesters*, 1830. 55¾ × 79¼ in. (141.5 × 212 cm.). Musée du Louvre, Paris.

pitulate much of peasant life all in one picture, rather than to show a particular and everyday action. Furthermore, Robert takes the observer outside France to Italy, whereas Millet strips away the literary and anecdotal trappings and forces the observer to a direct confrontation with living French peasants in the midst of their labors.

The Sower (pl. 15), exhibited in the winter of 1850–51, is Millet's most famous early work, and right away it was accepted as the celebration of the new man.[11] One observer compared it directly with Robert's *Harvesters* and concluded that:

> These two painters, in different degrees and under different climates, have understood and rendered the ideal of the poetry of the countryside from the modern point of view. The one [Robert] sought it in the melancholy and grandeur of old Roman types; the other in the suffering of the race of the Gauls, in the miseries of the rustic proletariat.[12]

This last phrase was typical of the public view of Millet. He was greeted as a reformer who painted the peasant in order to bring about an improvement in his lot. The peasantry had become a radical force in the period 1848–52, and memories of earlier peasant revolts and an awareness of the social ills following upon the vast shifting of rural peoples made Millet a figure of immediate concern. Liberals saw in him the very essence of contemporaneity:

> Come, poor laborer, sow your seed, throw out to the soil your fistfuls of grain! The soil is fertile and will bear fruit, but next year, as this, you will be poor and you will work by the sweat of your brow, because men have so well arranged things that work is a malediction, the work which will be the only real pleasure of intelligent beings in a regenerated society. His [the Sower's] gesture has a Michelangelesque energy and his tone a strange power [. . .]; he is a Florentine construction. [. . .] He is the modern Demos.[13]

Conservatives also regarded Millet's peasant as a contemporary figure but one calculated to stir rebellion. When *The Gleaners* (Musée d'Orsay, Paris) was shown in 1857, Paul de St. Victor was somehow prompted to think of the Reign of Terror and called the three women, although they are inertly performing a peaceful act, the "three fates of pauperism."[14] This was an extreme reaction, but one finds on all sides similar points of view expressed. A simple picture of a beautiful young shepherdess seated by a hedge stimulated one critic to regret the "stupidity and [. . .] indifference in her facial expression" and to refer to her as "this poor idiot."[15] And others wondered why Millet did not dress his peasants in beautiful clothes, instead of "rags of poverty" or the clothes of "a village beggar!"[16]

It is undoubtedly correct to assume that Millet's *Death and the Woodcutter* (pl. 16) was rejected by the Salon jury of 1859, despite its evocation of La Fontaine, because it seemed to solicit the sympathy of the public for the plight of the peasant. Conservatives must have felt justified in their view when they saw Alexandre Dumas take up the cudgel for Millet. Incensed at the exclusion of the picture, he published a pamphlet which stated that the woodcutter as Millet showed him "is not the peasant of 1660, but the proletarian of 1859,"[17] thus associating the artist with contemporary radical views.

When we pause to examine such paintings as *Death and the Woodcutter* and *The Gleaners* in the light of Millet's own views, a very different attitude emerges, paradoxically, an opposite one. For the artist the woodcutter represented not a cry for change, but the age-old struggle of man for existence, a struggle which would continue forever unchanged. Millet was a fatalist who saw no possibility of reform, but instead found in the peasant of his day the proof that life had continued unaltered since time immemorial. He wrote to his friend Sensier in 1851:

> You are sitting under a tree, enjoying all the comfort and quiet which it is possible to find in this life, when suddenly you see a poor creature, loaded with a heavy bundle of faggots coming up the narrow path opposite. The unexpected and always striking way in which this figure appears before your eyes reminds you instantly of the sad fate of humanity – weariness. The impression is similar to that which La Fontaine expresses in his fable of the Woodcutter!

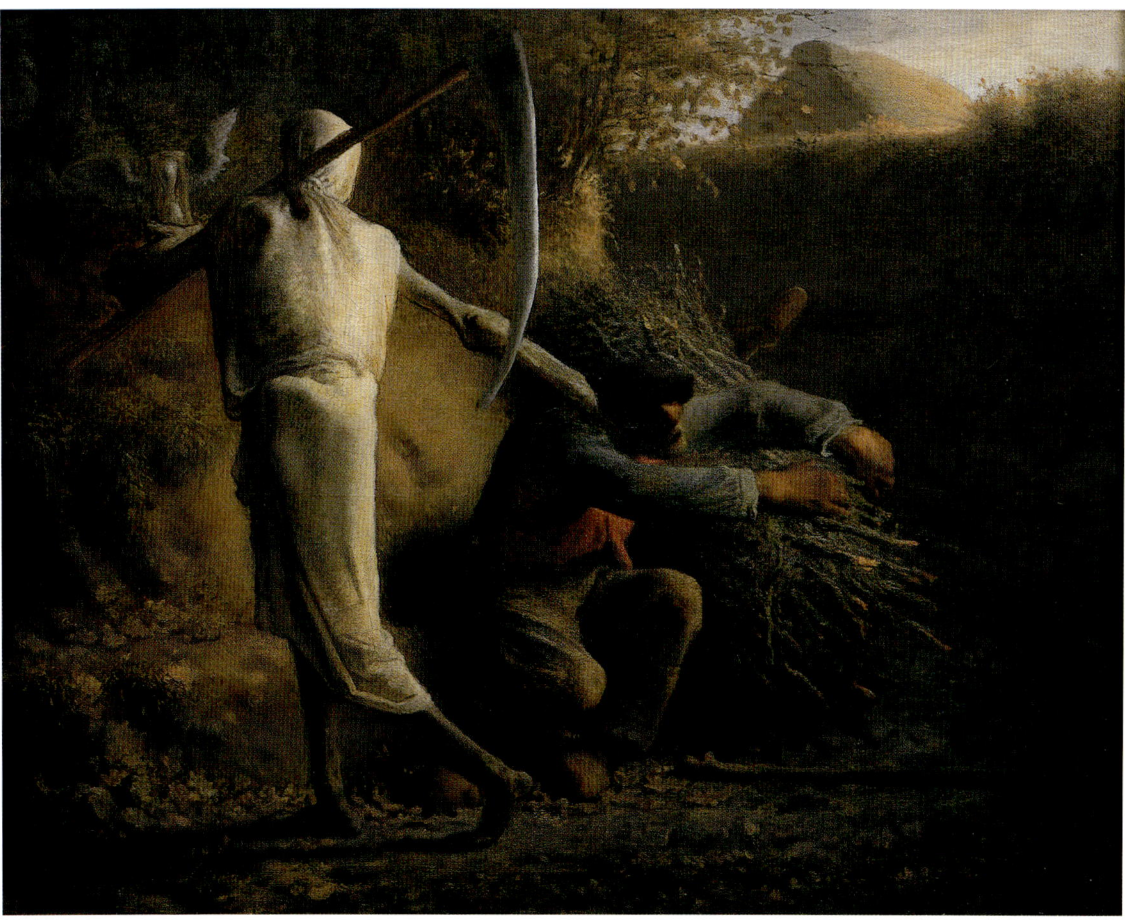

16 J.F. Millet, *Death and the Woodcutter*, 1859. $30\frac{1}{2} \times 38\frac{3}{4}$ in. (77.5 × 98.5 cm.). Ny Carlsberg Glyptothek, Copenhagen.

> Quel plaisir a-t-il eu depuis qu'il est au monde?
> En est-il un plus pauvre en la machine ronde?[18]

We might also recall that in La Fontaine's fable, the woodcutter proclaims his misery and longs for final release from life's cares. When Death appears before him, however, his instinctive grasp upon life – no matter how miserable his existence – reasserts itself and he asks Death to help him shoulder his burden, so that he may after all continue to trudge through life.

The same fatalism had been expressed in *The Gleaners* two years before. In contrast to the bustling harvesters in the background of the painting, the three women are condemned to gather one by one the stray gleanings left behind. The weariness and the implacable fatality of their task are embodied in the repeated rhythms of bodies and arms, great curves forced down toward the earth. Castagnary was one of the few who understood Millet's fatalistic outlook. He wrote of *The Gleaners*:

> This canvas, which recalls frightening miseries, is not at all, like some paintings by Courbet, a political harangue or a social thesis: it is a very beautiful and very simple work of art, free of all declaiming. The motif is poignant, it is true, but treated as it is in the highest style, with breadth, sobriety and frankness, it raises itself above partisan passions; far away from lies and exaggeration, it reproduces one of these pages of true and grand nature found by Homer and Virgil.[19]

More declamatory than *The Gleaners* is the *Man with a Hoe* (pl. 17), exhibited at the Salon of 1863. Here one cannot escape the impact of the brutalized image, for every aspect of his form carries to an extreme point the artist's sense of helplessness and despair at man's fate. Millet's instinctive pessimism, his fatalism, and his humanitarian feelings are cast over the figure like so many leaden shrouds, burdening him with the weight of ages and denying him any spark of rebelliousness. It is no accident that in the thorns and thistles one sees in *Man with a Hoe*, especially in the left foreground, there is expressed both the traditional and the personal association of barrenness, toil, pain, and the Passion of Christ.

Millet's wish to show the eternity of man's burdensome life was grafted on to a period of profound social upheaval, and therefore his pessimism and his fatalism became vehicles for others' social protest, if not his own. *Man with a Hoe* was accepted in 1863 as the outcry of common man against society. It was a transposition which we can now see was inevitable. Millet made a somber outcry against fate, but his contemporaries claimed that fate was nothing other than an instrument of social oppression. In this equation, Millet's fatalism, the intermediate quality (but to *him* the ultimate one), was finally suppressed so that *Man with a Hoe* and other peasant figures became *ipso facto* images of social protest.

How could it have been otherwise, with all the attention being paid to the depopulation of the countryside, with all the urgency given to social reform? The burdened peasant was already the hero of social literature, and Millet could not escape this context. For example, in 1856 Bonnemère wrote the following, which could stand as a caption for *Man with a Hoe* of seven year later:

> You can multiply schools, you can make education free, but you will have accomplished nothing, nothing at all, as long as you have not changed the conditions of existence of this man who, brutalized and bent over his furrow every hour of every day of his whole life, arrives at the end of his career as ignorant and about as miserable as at the beginning.[20]

One might think that Millet could not have escaped the association of his pictures with such social commentary, regardless of the particular mood his work projected. It is tempting to believe that any image of a peasant would bear the same message. This is not so, however. Charles Jacque, Constant Troyon, Jules

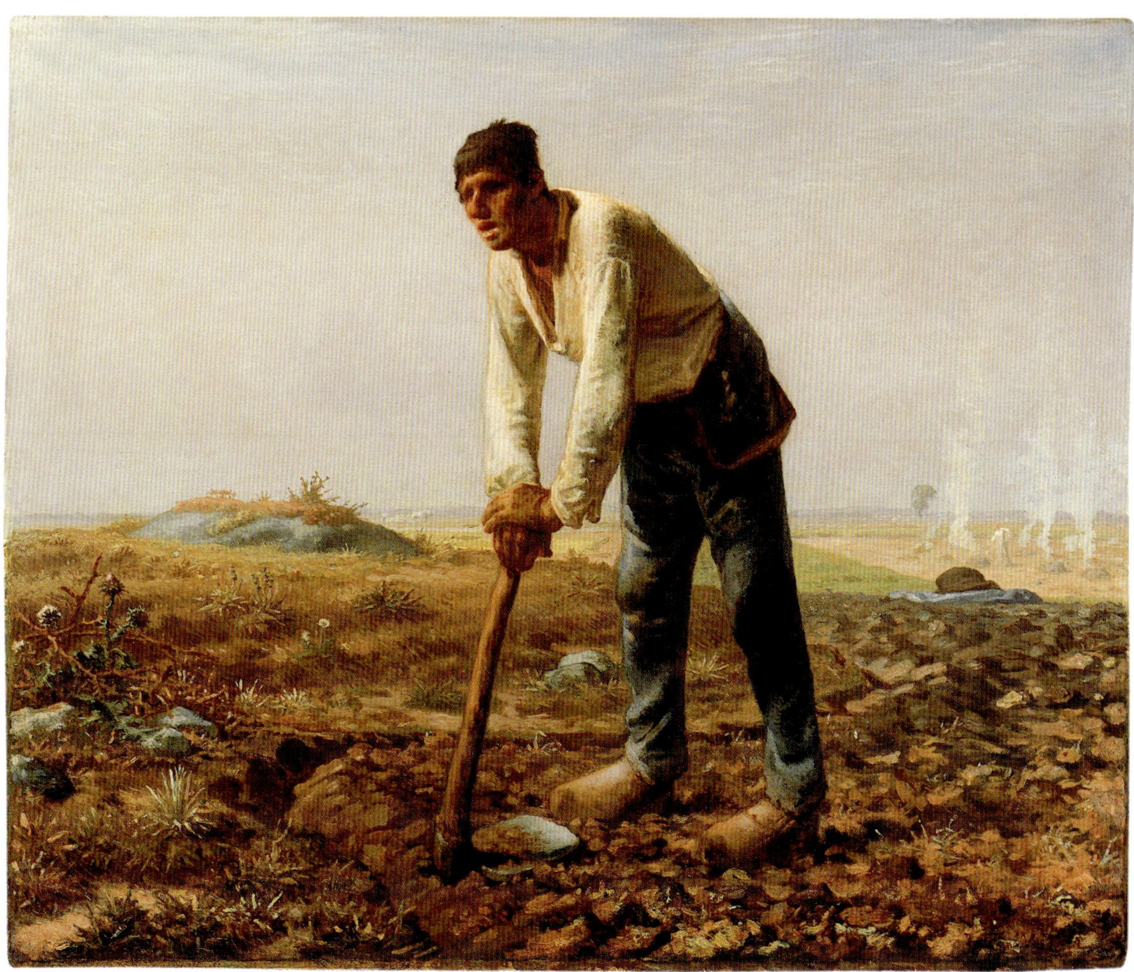

17 J.F. Millet, *Man with a Hoe*, 1863. 32 × 39½ in. (80 × 99 cm.). J. Paul Getty Museum, Los Angeles.

Breton, and many others, despite their peasant subjects, were widely admired and honored by conservatives. The reason is found in the realm of qualities hard to articulate, but instantly understood with the actual pictures at hand. Troyon and Jacque represented the peasant in relatively small scale, peacefully engaged in the happy tasks of rural life. Breton did show the peasant in large scale, but with an idealized, pretty face and with a mood of gentle devotion to nature's bounty (a mood that is really the artist's, not the peasants'). Unlike theirs, Millet's figures, at least those so far mentioned, make a neutral reaction impossible. Instead of confirming the middle-class view that life on the farm is a happy round of healthy tasks, Millet brought the laboring peasant directly into the observer's presence, with a sense of the grueling, wearing tasks he performs. He usually showed the peasant in a struggle with obdurate nature, which only reluctantly yields to dogged effort, a dialectic in which nature stands for fate, and therefore one which embodied Millet's sense of the meaning of life: man versus fate. This dialectic, as already noted, became transformed in the minds of contemporaries to that of man versus the social order.

The history of Millet's radical presence in the public eye is essentially limited to the thirteen years between *The Sower* of 1850 and *Man with a Hoe* of 1863. The latter was about the last of his paintings to cause a public stir. His *New-Born Calf* (Art Institute of Chicago), shown at the Salon of 1864, still caused some unreconstructed conservatives to gnash their teeth (at what they regarded an overly ceremonial presentation), but thereafter he exhibited less often, and in any case turned increasingly to landscape. A discussion of Millet's peasant naturalism should not end here, however. The historian must be concerned with qualities of art that help explain social phenomena, qualities which are not merely those of obvious subject matter. Millet's importance to history is not that he provided us with a pictorial commentary on rural life, but that he created a memorable art. His work was a powerful force because it drew together past art and present aspiration, melted in the crucible of a rare talent. We shall find that far from being a simple transcription of what lay around him, Millet's rural naturalism was a compound of literary predilection, nostalgia for the past, an instinctive humanitarianism, and a profound pessimism. It was a compound also of religious and mythological themes transposed into secular actuality.

In the first decade of his life as a professional artist, from 1837 to the Revolution of 1848, Millet, although the son of Norman farmers, was not at all a painter of peasants. He devoted himself at first to portraits and to the female nude. About fifty to sixty oil portraits survive from these early years, and they are so beautiful – although little known – that they would have sufficed to guarantee Millet a reputation. The same is true of his paintings and drawings of nudes, especially those of the period 1845–48. They make him one of the principal masters of the female figure in the nineteenth century. When he first broached rural themes around 1845, it was in the rather voguish taste of Diaz de la Peña and the *petits romantiques* who carried on the eighteenth-century tradition. By 1847 he had developed a stronger, more sculptural and heroic style, and his subjects came closer to the mood then building towards 1848: homeless mothers with children; despairing fisherwomen waiting on stormy rocks for absent husbands.

Coinciding with the Revolution of 1848, and owing much to its liberating spirit, came Millet's fully fledged naturalism. With funds provided by a commission given him by the republican government (another link to the events of 1848), Millet left Paris in late 1849 for Barbizon, where he remained for the rest of his life in an atavistic return to the land. Like the heroes of so many *Bildungsromanen* in the nineteenth century, he had grown up on the land, and had then become a city dweller, in his personal life mirroring the transformation of Europe from an agricultural to an urban-industrial society. With the culture and outlook of a professional artist (sixteen years in Cherbourg, Le Havre, and Paris), he found in Barbizon the actual environment toward which his subjects had been slowly groping.

Not that he began to copy, even now, the rural scenes about him. Fleeing the city meant not so much a direct plunge into contemporary peasant life as a rediscovery of the past, his own past life as a boy in Normandy, that personal past which would become equivalent to the pre-industrial past for European sensibilities. The proof of the high place that nostalgia for his youth had in these first years at Barbizon is readily found. Many of his pictures and drawings are not of Barbizon, but of distant Normandy. *The Sower* of 1850 throws his seed out against the steep hillsides of his native Cherbourg region, and not onto the flat land of the Brie where he actually painted the picture. It was only in the mid-1850s after several years at Barbizon that Millet habitually represented his figures against the horizontal plains of the region.

It is appropriate to insist on the degree to which rural subjects and the actual rural environment signaled for Millet an escape from the city. When he later recalled his arrival in Paris in 1837, he used terms that recur in his letters all his life, images evocative of noise, confusion, unrest, and fear:

> And then Paris, black, muddy, smoky Paris, where I arrived one evening, made the most painful and discouraging impression upon me. It was on a snowy Saturday evening in January that I arrived there; the light of the street lamps was almost extinguished by the fog. The immense crowd of horses and carriages crossing and pushing each other, the narrow streets, the air and smell of Paris seemed to choke my head and heart, and almost suffocated me. I was seized with an uncontrollable fit of sobbing.[21]

In clear relief from such impressions, his surroundings at Barbizon brought him an exhilarated peace of mind. "If you could but see how beautiful the forest is! I run there whenever I can, at the end of the day when my work is done, and each time I come back crushed. The calm and grandeur are tremendous, so much so, that at times I find myself really frightened."[22]

The sense of his rediscovery of a primeval past, untainted by the city, is found in any number of paintings. *Going to Work* of 1850–51 (pl. 18) has some of the feeling of Masaccio's famous *Expulsion from Paradise* (Brancacci Chapel, Santa Maria del Carmine, Florence). It is pre-industrial and even pre-urban man, "primitive" man in short, going out to the fields to earn his salvation. "It is an old truth," wrote Castagnary, "that eclogues and idylls have nearly always been the reflection of social agitation. Jostled by the tumult of events, poets and dreamers seek refuge in the peace of the countryside, in the contemplation of calm and serene nature."[23]

To Millet the "peace of the countryside" was associated with the favored reading of his youth, the Bible and Virgil; he constantly quoted from both in his conversations and letters. *Going to Work* is perhaps an unconscious evocation of biblical times, but the monumental *Grafting a Tree* (Neue Pinakothek, Munich) of 1855 seems a deliberate realization of Virgil's well-known "Insere Daphnis, piros; carpent tua pome nepotes" ("Graft thy pear tree, Daphnis; posterity shall pluck thy fruit"). In a Barbizon setting, a young peasant grafts a tree while his wife (her form derived from Roman sculpture) stands nearby, holding their child, the result of the human graft. What appears to be an acceptably naturalistic scene is a programmatic pictorial statement, drawing attention to the continuation in the present of the Virgilian past.

To the extent that the style of "naturalism" would seem to require a presentation of present-day reality, Millet's devotion to age-old unchanged life strikes us now as paradoxical. Yet the very heart of the present argument is that the rural past became the perfect expression of contemporary urban sensibilities. We are sure, in any event, that Millet's and Courbet's peasants were accepted in their day as fully avant-garde, and we are also sure that naturalist critics did not require or even prefer the new urban-industrial imagery as expressions of modernity. Castagnary, in so many ways Millet's counterpart among the critics, saw that rural subjects embodied present aspirations, with the virtue of being aloof from the most obvious contemporary polemics and therefore endowed with greater permanence. The past enters here into a curious dialog with the present, and country with the city. This is why it is not surprising to learn that Castagnary can proclaim the modernity of age-old rural life and simultaneously denounce ostensibly modern subjects. In his Salon of 1857 he attacks the radical painter Jeanron, friend of Louis Blanc and illustrator of his writings, for destroying his concept of landscape by inserting an electric telegraph:

> The *Placing of the Electric Telegraph in the Rocks of Cap Gris-Nez* (Pas-de-Calais) [by Jeanron] is a firm and vigorous landscape, which deserves only one reproach, but a capital one: why this electric telegraph? What does it signify, I don't mean in this painting, but in any painting? What is there in common between this brass wire, this utilitarian industrial product, and landscape, which is the seeking and expression of beauty in nature? Obviously it is nonsense.[24]

Millet himself edited out all references to modern instruments. He had a particular predilection for the most old-fashioned peasant tools: the hoe-like *bèche*, the wheeled wooden plow and the handheld distaff. The one modern farm in Barbizon, within sight of his house, appears prominently in only one major painting, *The Gleaners*, where it forms the background. It is significant that this farm, modern for its large size and use of teams of laborers, is the foil for the timeless labor of the gleaners in the foreground: past versus present again. Millet strove hard to retain in his pictures the very forms of agricultural life which were being rendered useless by the industrial revolution. One of his most common subjects is the spinner, of which he made many oils and innumerable drawings and

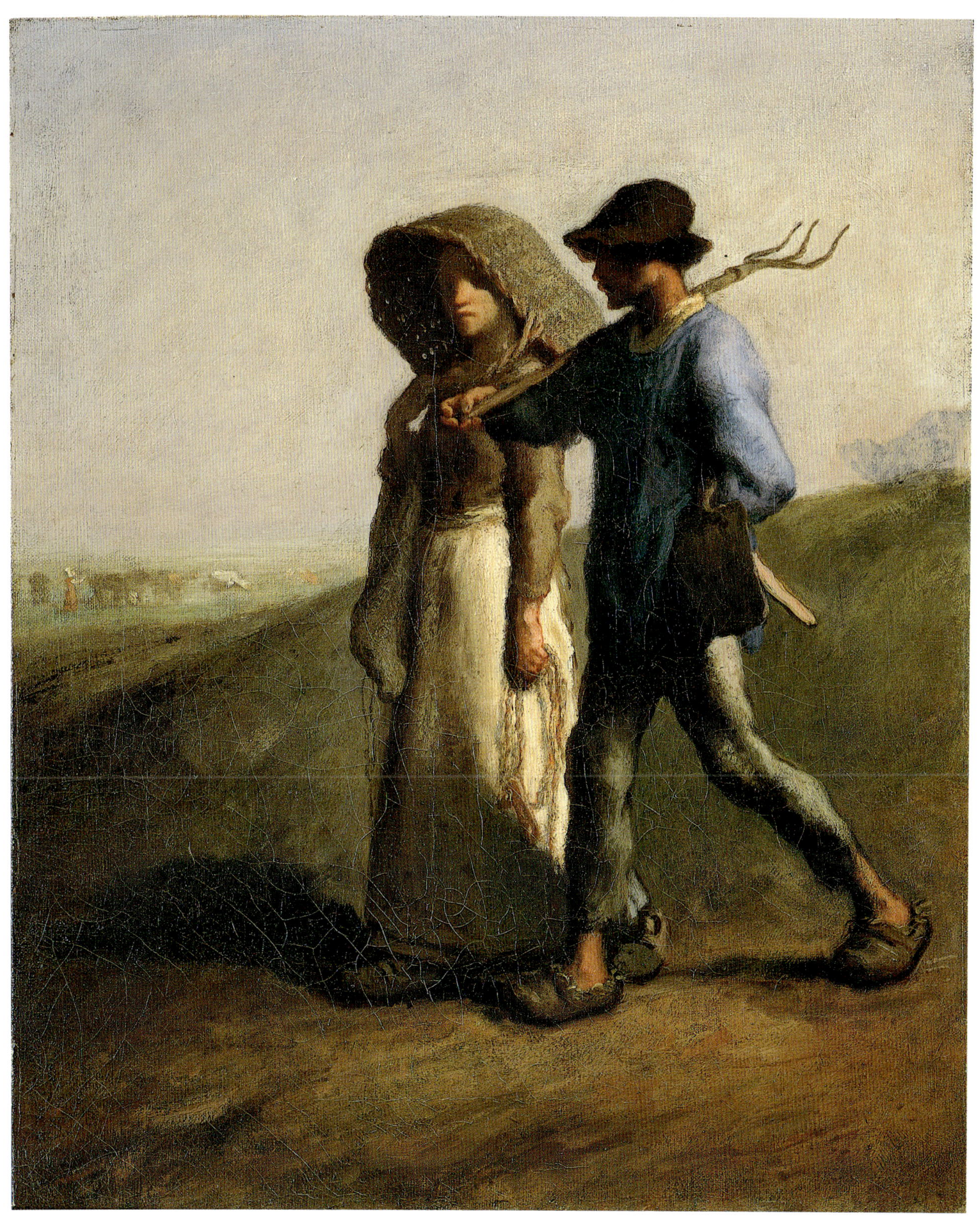

18 J.F. Millet, *Going to Work*, 1851. 22 × 18 in. (53.3 × 45.7 cm.). Cincinnati Art Museum, bequest of Mary M. Emery.

pastels. The spinner was one of the chief victims of the industrial revolution, and the development of modern textile methods, one of its central agents. Bonnemère wrote in 1856:

> It is rigorously true to say that the most skillful spinner does not earn 10 centimes a day: she earns nothing. The city has taken from the country this precious resource: it is toward the city that the peasant turns his face, in order to follow with his regrets this richness which has forever flown, in order to contemplate these powerful machines which have broken under the first turn of their wheels the distaffs of all the peasants.[25]

To preserve such old-fashioned institutions as the spinner, in face of the industrial revolution, was therefore Millet's self-appointed task. Such subjects could nevertheless incorporate contemporary attitudes for several reasons. First, as always in art, it was a question of feelings, and these did not require textile machinery for their expression. Next, although increasingly anachronistic, spinning and the other rural occupations were active, and embraced the mood and the morality of labor, so important to the middle class in the nineteenth century. Third, the peasant was that contemporary figure, the common man, in whose name so much social progress was sought. Fourth, the peasant gave Millet and other artists the opportunity of translating religious and mythological themes, somewhat in disgrace among progressive circles, into acceptably secular terms. This last requires further comment.

It was the fashion later, after Millet's death, to comment on the depth of his religious feeling, and he was presented to posterity as a kind of lay saint. However, in the generation of 1848, conventional religious subjects were largely discarded by major artists in France. Millet, Courbet, Corot, Rousseau, and Daubigny painted very few religious pictures and, by the 1860s, Manet's two pictures of Christ are among the rare religious subjects in the markedly secular generation then forming. After 1848, Millet painted only one religious picture of great fame, *The Angelus* (Musée d'Orsay, Paris); only one other, the *Parents of Tobit Awaiting his Return* of 1860 (Nelson-Atkins Gallery, Kansas City), can be called a major composition.

Mythological subjects also fell into relative disgrace among advanced artists after 1848, largely because of an ostensible inappropriateness to contemporary reality, and also because of their association with discredited academic circles. In the mid-century generation, Corot alone continued to give overt classical themes any importance; Millet's only significant venture here was a cycle of decorations he painted in 1864 for the Hôtel Thomas in Paris.

It was nonetheless difficult for the post-1848 generation to renounce overnight the centuries-old saturation in religious and mythological subjects. Between the Romantics and the Impressionists, they stood as a generation of transition who secularized old themes. In this process, Millet had a major role. *Grafting a Tree* has been mentioned already as a covert homage to Virgil, and *Going to Work* as a contemporary expulsion from the Garden of Eden. As it happens, the majority of Millet's paintings can be viewed as transpositions of religious and mythological themes. *Ruth and Boaz*, begun in Paris on the eve of the Revolution of 1848, was subsequently completed as *The Harvesters* (Museum of Fine Arts, Boston) and so exhibited in 1853, a typical example of what should be called the "secular shift." Couples shown going to work in the fields, the wife and child astride a donkey led by the husband, are restatements of the flight into Egypt. Young girls learning to spin or sew recall the common medieval theme of the Virgin's education; a peasant pointing the way to lost travellers echoes the pilgrims of Emmaus; a mother seated with her swaddled child held between her knees is a peasant Madonna and Child. More generally, the labors of field and farm Millet so often represented are the very ones which from medieval times had represented the months of the year, the four seasons, and the hours of the day, and his shepherds come from the *Eclogues* and *Georgics*, no longer labeled "Daphnis" as in the 1840s, but just as clearly Virgilian.

In transposing and secularizing classical and biblical themes for his age, Millet also transformed the art of the past. When looking at his paintings, one is perhaps inclined to accept them as naturalistic images and not think of their collateral function, which was to filter past art in the light of contemporary sensibilities and pass it on to following generations, properly enriched. For van Gogh, Pissarro, and many artists later in the century, Millet's art was a vital source in itself, but it was also a lens which focused on certain aspects of earlier art. As E.H. Gombrich has so admirably shown,[26] there is no such thing as merely "copying" natural form, and when he forged his naturalistic style, Millet went back to those arts which nourished both his subjects and his style. Without this absorption of earlier arts, peasant genre would not have had such wide currency in the nineteenth century, for it would not have had this deeply sensed cultural substructure, it would not have contained these associations – both conscious and unconscious – which surround a form and give it meaning.

Millet incorporated in his paintings and drawings the vital currents that emanated from the great repositories of peasant subjects. It has already been noted that he drank deeply from the literary reservoirs of peasant life: Virgil, the Bible, La Fontaine. He also admired what was considered in his day "gothic" art, from anonymous wooden sculptures, which he collected, to Quattrocento Italian painting and sixteenth-century art in the North, which he also collected in the form of engravings and a few oils. A number of his drawings and paintings of single figures who are carding wool, carrying faggots, mending baskets, and the like, have the very gestures and compacted forms of medieval sculpture. His several compositions of a young family going to work in the fields seem to be rather directly derived from the composition of the flight into Egypt found perhaps first in Dürer's engraving, but at about the same time in the school of Patinir (Raleigh, North Carolina) and the Venetian school (Carpaccio or Bellini, National Gallery of Art, Washington). Even more to the point is Dutch art, which so thoroughly penetrated Millet's style in the 1850s that one should speak of a "Dutch period." Countless oils, drawings, and pastels of humble interiors that show women sewing, sweeping, spinning, or feeding children bring to mind Dutch genre of the seventeenth century (Maes, de Hooch, Netscher) and their French heirs of the eighteenth (Chardin, Lépicié).

The artist who looms largest in Millet's work from the 1850s onward is Bruegel the Elder, the sixteenth-century master of village and rural genre. Millet owned several oils attributed to him, but the evidence in his pictures and drawings hardly needs this confirmation. His large pastel of *The Reaper* (Museum of Fine Arts, Boston) is a direct descendant of the same figure in Bruegel's engraving *Summer*, and the powerful and handsome *Meridian* (Philadelphia Museum of Art), another pastel of the mid-1860s, stems from the reclining figures in the Flemish master's *Land of Cockaigne*. Gnarled and sinewy old men, especially those in *Death and the Woodcutter* (pl. 16) and the *Parents of Tobit*, echo the protagonists of the *Blind Leading the Blind*, while the litter bearers of the *New-Born Calf* recall the soup bearers of the famous *Peasant Wedding*.

To the extent that Millet and his contemporaries found in the peasant a contact with the stable past, that is, a feeling of permanence and continuity in the face of the great upheavals taking place, then the representation of peasants in past art was particularly appealing.[27] In other words, style rejoins social history, and we must accept as one cultural phenomenon the rise of peasant subjects in contemporary literature and painting, the heightened interest in peasant art of the past, the alliance of both in the realm of style, and the underlying relationship with the living peasants of France, the objects of passionate social concern as victims of the massive displacements of the urban-industrial revolution.

In the quarter-century following Millet's death in 1875, peasant subjects enjoyed a widespread popularity never before equaled. Nostalgia for the pre-industrial past, which Millet had sensed with dignity and heroism, became adulterated and sentimentalized. His own work, by now forming part of the past, was subjected to a curious process which drained away its initial meaning and superimposed over it Victorian associations of prettiness, rusticity, and picture-book morality. Collectors vied with one another in acquiring works by Millet, Josef Israëls, or Rosa Bonheur, at prices equal to those for eminent Old Masters. It became commonplace for railroad magnates and industrial leaders to surround themselves with paintings of peasants and rural scenery. The leading exemplar is James Staats-Forbes, who filled his apartments in the upper reaches of Euston Station in London with several dozen works by Millet, Israëls, and Corot. If such collections were not sufficient proof of the role peasant subjects played as expressions of industrial sensibilities, we would not be at a loss for other forms of corroborating evidence. The period 1875–1914 was the heyday of books and articles on peasant art, particularly on Barbizon art. It is hard to estimate the relative place occupied by such writings compared with other subjects, but it was clearly one of the most prominent. Of all titles ever published on rural genre and its masters, down to the present day, more than half come from that period. In the same years, the Arts and Crafts movement had its rise. Its anti-machine, anti-urban ethic was suitably clothed in peasant imagery, and numerous schools and colonies devoted to the handicrafts were established in the countryside (often, if memory serves correctly, subsidized by the wives of wealthy industrialists). At the same time, second- and third-generation Barbizon art became immensely popular throughout Europe and the Americas and every country developed its own native school devoted to rural genre. Most young artists studying in the last decades of the century passed through an apprenticeship to peasant subjects, which become the lingua franca of art schools, and in some countries – one thinks of Segantini and Northern Italy – the most progressive movements were devoted to such subjects.

Among major painters active in France in the last quarter of the century, several gave peasant themes an important place, including Pissarro, van Gogh, and Gauguin. However, the nature and the meaning of such themes were no longer the same, and considerable caution must be used in their study. The sense of permanence and continuity with the past, which Millet and Corot had felt, was hard for the next generation to sustain in face of the growing evidence of wholesale changes in modern society. It had been possible for the earlier artists to suspend their knowledge of the urban-industrial colossus which was dislocating the countryside, and to indulge in the fiction that portions of unsullied rural nature represented a meaningful form of life that might somehow endure. (Their awareness of the fiction involved shows in the veil of nostalgia which Corot cast over his works, and the despairing seriousness Millet gave his.) In the 1860s and 1870s the same pressures which had led to this seeking of permanence and stabiliy were heightened until artists were pushed beyond the underlying fiction into a devotion to impermanence, mobility, and the hedonistic moment of the present. They often turned to the rapidly expanding suburbs, that intermediate zone between city and country whose relatively open spaces and ready access permitted an enormous growth of swimming, boating, and picnicking, those essential escapes for city dwellers which were so beautifully celebrated by Renoir. In Impressionism, the social realism of the mid-century was replaced by suburban realism.

This did not mean that the artists were immune to the dialog between city and country. In the evolution of Monet's landscape, the progressive abandoning of urban and suburban environments meant the release of his feelings in front of untrammeled nature, the inner necessity to isolate himself from the city in order to cultivate an increasingly private dialectic with nature and vision. Renoir made his feelings more explicit than Monet did. He wrote veritable diatribes against the machine and industrial society, prompted by his having been a victim of technological unemployment (when he was only seventeen, he had lost his position as a master porcelain painter because new industrial techniques had supplanted handicraft methods).[28] Renoir did not invest these feelings in pictures of contemporary peasant life, however, but in images of an ideal world of nymphs, flowering fields, and undulating hillsides that overlap with only a small part of Millet's oeuvre: those moments of Virgilian charm and beauty in his less ambitious pictures.

Alone among the Impressionists, Pissarro gave the peasant a central role. Older than the others, and of a more conservative temperament as an artist, he carried to the end of the century more of the characteristics of Barbizon art. His landscapes are predominantly of rural villages and fields (most of his paintings of Paris and Rouen date from the end of his life), and his pictures of the human figure are with few exceptions devoted to peasants and villagers. Unlike the other Impressionists in another regard, Pissarro was a political radical and adherent of Pierre Kropotkin, the chief theoretician of the Anarchist-Communist movement.[29] He contributed money and drawings to the cause, and was on intimate terms with party leaders. The Anarchist-Communist credo of the end of the century strikes us now as rather idealistic and anachronistic, even within its own generation, and Pissarro's peasant subjects require some comment in this light.

When Pissarro gave his composition of a plowman at work as a color supplement to the anarchist journal *Modern Times* in 1902 (pl. 19), he provided an ideal pictorial symbol for anarchist beliefs and for his art. We see not just a plowman, but one using the old-fashioned wheel plow for, like Millet, Pissarro preferred the unchanging ways of the countryside. The incarnation of "modern times" in an archaic plowman did not strike him as an anachronism, because it incorporated his ideas of health, honest labor, and dignity which he set against the pollution and degraded labor of the city. In Kropotkin's theories, industrial techniques were welcome to the extent they would permit rural-based communes to use labor-saving devices, and retain a proximity to the land. (We often find in Pissarro's landscapes, especially in the 1870s, small factories serenely smoking along verdant riverbanks, the very image of the kind of modernity to which he was drawn.) Society, Kropotkin held, was to be decentralized and village-oriented, because in large cities the workers could only become prisoners of oppressive economic and institutional patterns which could not be reformed. This was very different from orthodox Communism, which saw in these patterns the necessary last step before the assumption of working-class power.

The essential Romanticism of Pissarro's view, and its actual disparity with an increasingly urbanized society, shows in the nature of his peasants. Despite his proximity to Millet, from whom he frequently borrowed, he does not endow his figures with a fully believable capacity for the work they are engaged in. A curious kind of wooden lassitude characterizes them, as though they were primarily artists' models, performing their actions under instructions. During the twentieth century we became deprived of a naturalistic vision, and therefore might not be immediately struck by this anomaly, but when Pissarro is viewed alongside Millet and others of the earlier period, it is one of the striking differences. There is nothing of the pejorative in this, of course, because quality in art

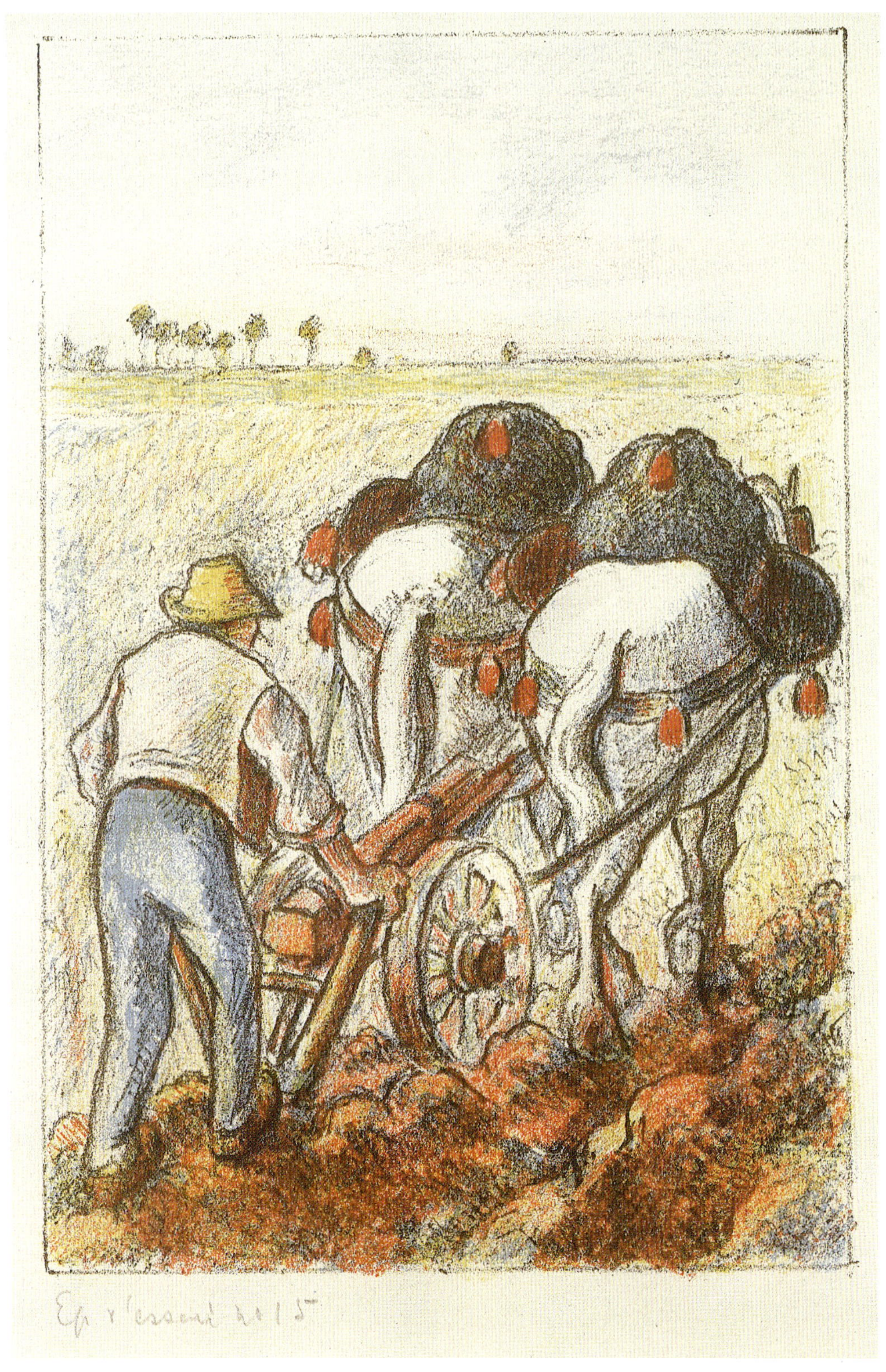

19 Camille Pissarro, *The Plow*, 1902. Color lithogragh. Sterling and Francine Clark Art Institute, Williamstown, Massachusetts.

does not require believability of action, but attention must be drawn to it as a phenomenon typical of the late nineteenth century. Even Pissarro, living close to the land and convinced of the merits of his subjects, was unable to accept peasant life as coequal with reality.

Van Gogh is another major artist on whom Millet had a profound impact. He was more than twenty years younger than Pissarro but had a rather similar orientation because of his early and lifelong devotion to artists and writers of the mid-century: Daumier, Millet, Delacroix, Monticelli, and Michelet among them. His political and social views coincided with Pissarro's on many grounds, and the peasant entered prominently into his work for many of the same reasons. The greater intensity which marks his painting should not be attributed solely to his personal makeup, but also to his Protestant origins.[30] Unlike Pissarro, who had an essentially secular formation tinged by Jewish culture, van Gogh was raised in that kind of Northern Protestant environment which consists of pairs of opposites in great tension: social work versus theological abstraction, individual works versus disciplined communal action, private agony versus inhibition and repression. We might call Pissarro's orientation secular-political, and van Gogh's religious-social, both traditions embracing a profound humanitarianism and a preoccupation with the peasant as victim of social change and as exemplar of the biblical laborer.

Van Gogh's early drawings and paintings of peasant life grew directly out of the then contemporary style in Holland, where the mid-century impulsion toward rural subjects had flowed into the tradition of genre painting that had continued strongly from the seventeenth century. Both the peasant and the worker coexist in his paintings of the early 1880s, as they did in the Borinage district where he tried to adapt himself to a social-religious mission. Since the factory worker was so often a displaced villager, the two were not so separated in those areas where the industrial revolution erupted in the middle of cultivated fields.[31] In a large urban center like Paris, it might have required some effort to see the relation between city and country, but not here.

When van Gogh went to Paris in 1886, it seemed natural that he devote himself to scenes of the city, especially of the sites and the society of the artists among whom he moved. Peasant subjects were left behind and did we not know better, we might have thought that his evolution would parallel that of Georges Seurat (1859–91) or any number of artists coming to maturity in the same decade. Seurat, another disciple of Millet for a time, had concentrated on peasants and country landscapes in the early 1880s in his remarkable oil paintings (in his drawings, the city and its humble citizens like vendors and ragpickers were conspicuous so that he, like van Gogh, incorporated both city and country in his work). However, upon increased contact with Impressionism, Seurat turned to the suburbs for his subjects, and after 1883 there are hardly any peasant motifs in his work. The balance of his short life was spent on paintings and drawings of city parks and entertainments, alternating with summer pictures of Channel seaports. In retrospect, therefore, Seurat's peasant compositions seem to share in the obligatory apprenticeship of most young painters to the current studio practice, a youthful phase that is passed by when expanded contact with the modern city introduces rival stimuli and hence a new concept of what is "modern."

Stimulated by the Impressionists while in Paris, van Gogh also abandoned peasant subjects, but only for a time. His return to the countryside in 1888 – for Arles was a small city that gave him easy access to adjacent fields and orchards – responded to a deep need to renew that interlocked set of realities which constituted one final reality for him: peasant and village surroundings, their images transformed in art, his concern for the role the artist would have in a society he saw buffeted and sundered by cataclysmic changes. In his writings as in his paintings, he reminds us of the literal materialization of his ideas in the clay-like pigments he used, that raw matter he handled with a peasant clumsiness and which he opposed to the refined city-bred techniques of other artists "à la Baudelaire." That is, the "clay" with which he molded his images of peasants and villagers and which he accused contemporary Paris artists of not appreciating became for him a parallel to the clay from which God "this great artist" had molded the human form. It was also a parallel to the direct technique of earlier artists he so admired: Hals, Rembrandt, Delacroix, Millet, Daumier, and Monticelli, and in general to the immediacy and tangibility of expression which Pissarro had meant when he claimed for himself and Cézanne the qualities of the "savage" and the "primitive." For van Gogh, this synthesis could only be realized in an environment which recalled his youth, his religious mission, and the unspoiled pre-industrial past.

It is no wonder that in his last years van Gogh turned again toward Millet and copied many of his works, for Arles, St.-Rémy, and ultimately Auvers are all his Barbizon. But forty years had passed since Millet had quit Paris for the forest village, four decades in which was developed so much of the industrial belt around Paris that van Gogh had painted, so much of the industrialization of the Lowlands that he had painted earlier and had left behind. The fiction which Millet had been able to maintain, with the rumble of the city barely heard in the distance, was no longer possible for van Gogh. Millet had already written:

> Art is not a picnic. It is a combat, a set of gears which grinds one up [. . .] . I am not a philosopher, I do not want to suppress pain, nor find a formula which would render me stoical and indifferent. Pain is perhaps that which makes an artist express himself most forcibly.[32]

How much stronger was the pain in van Gogh, when the wheels of industrial change were all the nearer, all the more present to his feelings as he tried to reconcile the elements of his despair by placing his canvas in front of rural society and nature.

For Paul Gauguin, the dialectic of city and country, of modern life and the untouched past, was worked out on a broader terrain. His Barbizon, at first, was Brittany. More remote than Barbizon, which by the 1880s was a world-famous site, Pont-Aven had welcomed artists since the 1860s. Brittany had long been of special interest because of its retention of some Celtic characteristics, its distinctive architecture and costumes, the whole more archaizing and "medieval" than Millet's village had been in mid-century. Very much the cynic and the artful contriver, Gauguin seemed to look upon the Breton peasant and his farm as a series of pictorial motifs, but we are not fooled.[33] He had a deep need for these images of the "primitive" and the "savage," words he often used in this context. Brittany, before the South Seas, meant Gauguin's search for identity, for the lost paradise of pre-industrial man.

Feeling little of the direct self-identity with the peasant that Pissarro had, Gauguin went much further toward treating his subject as mere motif, so that from Millet to Pissarro to Gauguin there is a progressive decline in believable action, a slackening of an acceptable fiction of reality. The rural villager and the farm worker remain counter-images of the urban-industrial world, but now with an awareness, even an exploitation, of the fundamental unreality involved. In his zincograph of the *Joys of Brittany* (1889) Gauguin gave his farm women the heads of Egyptians and removed their pitchforks from their hands, suppressing the tools but leaving the gestures. His figures enter upon a kind of ceremonial incantation which predicts much of his art in Oceania.

When Gauguin left Europe for Tahiti, it was in order to find the opposite of modern urban society. We can state the equation that Oceania was to Gauguin as Barbizon was to Millet. The intervening years had required a heightening of the sublimated dialog of city versus country, but the mechanism was essentially the same. A South Seas couple striding along, like the figures of Millet's *Going to Work*, are Adam and Eve condemned to earn their salvation; an Oceanic mother and child, like Millet's peasant group, are the Madonna and Child; nude women bathing in wooded streams, figures chopping wood, watering horses, or gathering fruit are in the work of both painters descended from the eclogues and idylls of classical literature.

Both Millet and Gauguin proclaimed the superiority of their rustic Eves over sophisticated ladies of Paris, both had an instinctive preference for wooden shoes, clumsy homemade tools, rough stone and wood. These qualities, properly called "primitive" in the sense of first, or preceding, are those which industrial man has felt the need to seek, in release from the mechanistic, the smooth, the well-regulated, the machine-made. They are admired instinctively, for their own sake, and also because they call to mind non-industrial societies and their freedom from mechanization. Gauguin carried this canon outside Europe, all the while preserving a Western viewpoint, and his art was the most important precedent for the next step in Western sensibilities. This was the adoption of African sculpture (and eventually of African music, the music *par excellence* of industrial man in the twentieth century) which began among advanced artists in Paris around 1903, the year of both Gauguin's and Pissarro's deaths. What had happened since the middle of the nineteenth century was an increasing polarization of the colloquy between city and country. Millet left Paris for nearby Barbizon; van Gogh left his homeland and eventually the whole industrial North for Arles; Gauguin left Europe entirely. Finally, sculpture from black Africa, partly because it was misunderstood and thought to be the result of spontaneous outbursts of emotion, entered modern art as the ultimate counter-image of industrial man.

African sculpture is the heir to the profoundest aspirations of Western artists which had been manifested in the second half of the nineteenth century in images of rural peasantry. There is another heritage as well, probably secondary in absolute significance of expression but, in effect, more obvious. This is the retention of images of the peasant in painting throughout the world, Western and non-Western, usually as the visual concomitant of the beginnings of rapid industrialization, or the anticipation of it. Since Marx's day, it has become apparent that advanced industrial societies are not the ones that lend themselves to drastic revolution; it is instead peasant societies (Russia, China, Egypt, Cuba, and so on) which, thirsty for industrialization, hope to leap over intermediate stages to fully fledged mechanized cultures. Almost invariably, such revolutions or their anticipations are characterized by a marked devotion to images of the peasantry. This is partly because their labor provides the plus-value which permits rapid industrialization and, as in Western Europe and the United States in the nineteenth century, the dignity of labor becomes central to the governing ethic. Thus in the USSR the existing tradition of peasant realism was expanded and officially sponsored from the early 1920s onward and later, in Mao's China and Nasser's Egypt, an utterly Western concept of the human figure replaced native imagery, leading to the strange appearance of peasants and workers steeped in European style striding across posters which proclaim the virtues of indigenous ideals.

In Western countries or those already under the economic tutelage of industrial nations, anticipations of revolutionary change and periods of pronounced social reform have also been characterized by the prominence of pictures of rural and village life. In Mexico, the twentieth century's greatest art of social concern, headed by Rivera, Orozco, and Siqueiros, gave the peasant a leading role. The advanced artistic movements of many Latin American countries incorporated a concern for the villagers who had partly escaped the Westernization process and who therefore went back to Millet's Barbizon peasants as elements of artistic sensibility. Too often it is assumed that such subjects are but expressions of leftist sympathy (witness Renato Guttuso in postwar Italy), but this is not so. The American Scene movement in the 1930s, including Grant Wood, Thomas Hart Benton, John Steuart Curry, and the critic Thomas Craven, was essentially a very conservative impulsion. (Wood's famous *American Gothic* is, incidentally, an American version of Millet's *Peasant Family*, now in the National Museum of Wales, Cardiff.)

* * *

In a generation shaken by the peasant masses of China, Southeast Asia, and Africa, it has seemed appropriate to investigate the peasant as an image of the urban-industrial revolution. The force of this tradition must be traced to the second half of the nineteenth century in France, when the artist, one of whose roles it is to sense the critical aspirations of his fellow men before they can articulate them, found in his construction of rural subjects the vessel into which so many of his longings could be poured. It represented release and freedom from the regularity of mechanized life, from the impurity of city slums, from the degradation of factory labor. It permitted the expression by proxy of feelings hard to articulate directly, feelings of an extraordinary range, from nostalgia for that past being assaulted and torn asunder by industrialization, to admiration for the nobility of women and men whose gestures force a pattern upon nature. The peasant called forth a host of associations with past literature and art, permitting the transposition into secular terms of religious and mythological themes that gained new force in the process.

The power of the peasant image to modern man is shown in the fact that van Gogh is the most widely known painter on earth. To that extent his art is a contemporary phenomenon, entering into the construction of the popular image of the world, which is an agonized one.

Chapter 3

Peasants and "Primitivism"

> It is ever true that rude and humble labors awaken our sympathy more readily than magnificent labors, because we have a kindly feeling towards the humble effort, whereas accomplished power does not seem to need our sympathy. A poor little rustic bridge makes us share the satisfaction of the villagers who erected it; a great railway viaduct is only what is called a triumph of science.
>
> Philip Gilbert Hamerton,
> *Imagination in Landscape Painting*, 1895

"Nostalgia isn't what it used to be!" This slogan, found on the walls of American colleges in the 1970s, declared the end of romantic yearnings for an idyllic past. Those yearnings can still be found, however; they never disappeared. Along residential streets within three miles of Mount Holyoke College are several rustic wells, one sylvan bridge, a mailbox mounted on the handle of an old plow, another on a disk harrow, and several on wagon wheels, to say nothing of the ubiquitous geese, sheep, and deer which form immobile lawn parades. Nostalgia for a rural past enters profoundly into middle-class culture as compensation for fragmented and anxious times, and this has been so since the early days of the urban-industrial revolution. Never mind its fairytale unreality: it has been a powerful cultural and political agent throughout Europe and the Americas. Travel writers born and bred in cities have often referred without irony to their "return" to nature. Today in France politicians must proclaim sympathy for peasants, still considered the backbone of the nation although numbering fewer than 2 million out of a population of 58 million.

The exhibition *Peasants and "Primitivism"* documents the extraordinary prominence of peasants in French prints from the 1840s to the turn of the century.[1] It traces some of the reasons why yearning for a rural world was a prominent counterweight to the drastic alterations of society under the impact of the industrial revolution. Oil paintings by J.F. Millet, Camille Pissarro, and Vincent van Gogh are the best known embodiments of "peasant art," but etchings, lithographs, and engravings had a vastly greater audience. I do not speak just of prints by famous artists but also of those in art reviews and the illustrated press, as well as popular broadsides. Examples of all of these are in

• From *Peasants and "Primitivism:" French Prints from Millet to Gauguin* (exh. cat., Mount Holyoke College Art Museum; Museum of Art, Rhode Island School of Design; University of Chicago, Smart Museum of Art, 1995–96): 11–19.

the exhibition, including prints by such artists as Auguste Lepère, whose activity defied the usual separation of "fine art" from the mass media.

Simply to display images of peasants and villagers would have little merit because the meaning of a print depends as much upon its structure as upon its subject. For that reason the catalog entries pay attention to the forms and techniques of prints. When artists represented rural people, they often used techniques that were primitive in comparison with the dominant styles. This twinning of primitive subject and primitive technique was so widely assumed that by the middle of the nineteenth century the famous makers of popular broadsides, the Pellerin firm of Epinal, cultivated a pseudo-primitive style actually produced with the aid of modern industrial technology. And as we shall see, there were several primitivisms, for the term encompasses a whole range of arts whose only common thread is their anti-illusionism. Alphonse Legros's prints of the 1890s have an archaizing look far removed from the Art Nouveau of Lepère's woodcuts of the same decade. Pissarro's peasants are modeled in the round and have a stable platform of perspective; Emile Bernard's and Gauguin's are but slightly modeled and embedded in flat decorative patterns.

The chief reason for exhibiting nineteenth-century prints of peasants is to examine the interrelationships of subject, technique, and style. But there is a second reason. The concept of primitivism is now attached to the dialog of modernism with non-European peoples, a consequence of the conquests of colonial powers. Most studies of primitivism are limited to this dialog, omitting or paying scant attention to nineteenth-century peasants, those Others (called "farmers" and "farmhands" in England and the United States) found within national borders. When we see how peasants and villagers were pictured, we will learn that many of the assumptions about non-European primitivism were already in the minds of Parisians whenever they pondered the world of the peasant. And Paris is indeed the locus of the culture we will examine: it was the principal market for the prints, and the home or training-ground of most of the artists.

City and Country

The stable rural life which Parisians yearned for was more myth than reality. In fact, farming, peasant society, and villages were all undergoing major changes, slowly and spottily at the beginning of the nineteenth century, more rapidly and widespread at the end. Traditional uses and ownership of the land changed under the impact of new transport and new agricultural techniques which meant greater involvement with city capital and commerce. Increasingly peasants left the land to join the corps of workers engaged in urban industry, commerce, and domestic service. Already by the 1840s this internal migration reached such proportions that it was referred to as the "depopulation of the countryside."[2] In Paris alone tens of thousands of peasants became workers for Louis Napoleon's ruthless remodeling and extension of the city in the 1850s and 1860s. Nonetheless, despite the abundant proofs of the interpenetration of city and country, many Parisians, including those risen from the peasantry, continued to make sharp distinctions between the two realms.

The work of journalists, art critics, travel writers, and authors of rustic novels shows how much those distinctions were based on long-standing beliefs about rural life that the bourgeoisie clung to. They needed these myths to cope with, or excuse, their actual devotion to "progress," to throw a cloak over its consequences, especially the spread of industrial squalor and the growth of an urban underclass. Of course townspeople elsewhere in Europe and America clung to comforting ideals of rusticity in reaction to the century's rapid industrialization. In Paris, however, the myths had special resonance because the violent overthrow of monarchy in the Revolution of 1848 confirmed with unusual suddenness the arrival of the "common man." Peasants came to new political and cultural prominence in the wake of that upheaval, and for the rest of the century they were the domestic primitives of France's somewhat belated industrial expansion.

Myths of primitivism, many of them still with us, have always derived their meanings from opposition to the city. They did not originate in the Romantic era (indeed, they were already prominent by the eighteenth century), nor were they limited to rural life in France since they referred also to "savages" and children. Rather, it was in the 1830s and 1840s that they joined together to form the colored lens through which French artists viewed peasants. Some elements of this primitivism can be summarized under the following headings:

Simplicity. The Bible and the secular texts (Virgil, Pliny) that underlay French education portrayed bucolic worlds free of the corruption of cities, for cities had long been treated as the sites of temptation, complexity, and change, where country folk risked the loss of their innocence. The simplicity of rural societies, although it had roots in earlier centuries, was one of the prominent illusions of nineteenth-century Romanticism, a major recompense for the unwelcome alterations of modern life. Images that conjured up this simplicity include shepherdesses and shepherds, haymakers, wool carders, faggot gatherers, and humble but prosperous families. All of these were personified in the Bible where Christ is the shepherd and the faithful, his flock.

Virtuous work. Viewed from a distance, the direct relationship of peasant to animal or land seemed to have none of the complexities of modern city life: no money visible, no employer, no organized labor, no slum, no unemployment. The work ethic so valuable to industrialization, but so troublesome in images of factory labor, could be celebrated in pictures of isolated rural and artisanal workers. In addition, Christian morality praised the humbleness that rural labor ideally embodied, in contrast to the rebelliousness that marked the urban underclass according to the bourgeoisie, frightened by the uprisings of Parisian workers and artisans in 1848 and 1870–71.

Innocence, childhood, arcadia. Simplicity and virtue were attributes of the mythical countryside, thought to be untarnished by the negative aspects of modern industrial and urban transformations. While looking at images of shepherdesses or men herding cattle, city dwellers could think of their parents' childhoods or their own. Grain and cattle were more welcome images than iron girders or rails, systematically excluded from the category of "art." Rustic myths were associated with poetic expression since the reigning conception exalted art above ordinary life. Pictures of the idealized countryside allowed imagined journeys into the past, more innocent than the troubled present. For the anarchist Pissarro, these were also journeys to the utopian future.

Consequently, threats to the myths were often fiercely objected to, particularly in the 1850s after some peasants had opposed Louis Napoleon's seizure of power, actions that stimulated memories of earlier peasant revolts. Moreover, art was supposed to offer a noble ideal, and as long as contemporary peasants were threatening, they could hardly personify bourgeois aspirations. Courbet's huge painting *Burial at Ornans* offended Parisians in 1851 for its monumental "ugliness," and Millet's poor women in *The Gleaners* (both Musée d'Orsay, Paris) were attacked as the "three fates of pauperism" who denied the progress that the Second Empire was supposedly bringing to the countryside.[3] In opposing the new realism, bourgeois critics confessed the fragility of their myths, for lurking behind arcadia was their conception of the bestial and unthinking peasant. Typically these were men (Millet's *Man with a Hoe* is the best-known exemplar); for most nineteenth-century artists the countryside of peaceful pastoral myth was largely inhabited by women. The work of Jules Breton, contemporary of Millet and Courbet, was far more acceptable than theirs because his fruitful fields were staffed by women whose studio beauty confirmed the myths.

By the time the Second Empire ended in the short-lived Franco-Prussian War of 1870–71, bourgeois attitudes toward the peasant had changed. Louis Napoleon had eventually received massive support from rural voters in his plebiscites, and peasants seemed truly conservative in contrast to the *communards*, the insurrectionists who took over Paris during the war. By the 1870s Millet had become quite acceptable, and when academic naturalism triumphed among the middle class in the last third of the century, prints and paintings of an unidealized peasantry proliferated. No longer threatening, and often subjects of solicitous reform, peasants could be shown in homely plainness. Representations of unvarnished daily aspect were taken as a kind of ethnographic examination of a people far removed from urban culture, and now safely categorized and disarmed by apparently scientific rendering. Before the end of the century, however, the example of the Impressionists had pushed modernist art away from that kind of naturalism, a development that is chronicled in the prints and paintings of such artists as Gauguin, Lepère, Camille and Lucien Pissarro, Rivière, and van Gogh.

Alienation and Primitivism

For artists like Millet, Adolphe Hervier, Legros, and Gauguin, peasants did not embody bourgeois ideals. Marginalized by bourgeois society whose authoritative agencies rewarded artistic conformism, these artists treated peasants not as pretty maidens but as neglected Others who signified their own alienation. Industrial capitalism had fragmented the relationships and institutions of premodern societies, including those of artistic patronage. Artists now had to sell their wares like other producers, but the new marketing institutions (dealers, illustrated art reviews, non-government exhibitions) brought comfort only to a few. Expelled or self-excluded from the society of official art, many artists took pride in their independence from convention, hence their identification with Bohemians, that is, with gypsies, those permanent marginals.[4] Alienation sometimes meant literal departure from the city, so painters gathered in rural surroundings in Barbizon, Pont-Aven, Worpswede, and other artists' colonies. Their distance from the city was illusory, for just as the word "leisure" has no meaning unless we posit work, so "alienation" cannot stand alone; one must be alienated from something. Artists in Barbizon or Pont-Aven might wear wooden shoes and peasant hats but they were cityfolk, visitors to a native culture. Primitivism and alienation are siblings with common parentage in Romanticism.

Again it will be helpful to discuss primitivism under several headings:

Timeless societies. Rural societies were imagined as stable, well rooted in traditions both secular and religious, offering artists continuity with the desired past and a wholeness denied by the fractured life of modern cities. In Barbizon, Eragny, Arles, and Pont-Aven they used knowledge of earlier images of rural and village life (Bruegel, Rembrandt, Ostade, eventually Millet) to construct an art that was new in relation to dominant styles, but nonetheless well grounded in history. However, they usually suppressed any signs of encroaching modernity, and as a result they denied the actual histories of their Barbizons and Pont-Avens. Millet favored the oldest agricultural and artisanal trades despite the growing modernization of the Barbizon region; Pissarro seldom pictured new agricultural machinery and preferred market gardens to large farms; Gauguin mostly ignored the fishing industry and other signs of Pont-Aven's contemporaneity. Rural societies were held in timeless suspension because otherwise the myths would be shattered.

Instinct and freedom. Artists thought that peasants were free from the restraints of industrial culture based on time clocks, the division of labor, the suppression of individualism, and other signs of the rule of materialism and repressive reason.[5] They were treated as creatures of nature, closer to humankind's original condition before science and reason dampened instinct. Among them, artists could cultivate their own feelings out in a "natural" setting undisturbed by modernity. Romanticism meant above all the separation of the heart from the mind, the triumph of the idea that creativity was dependent upon instinct. Since modern urban culture thwarted spontaneity, how much better to seek a terrain, or at least images of it, that encouraged freedom from the iron grasp of reason.

Primitive: the first, or original. When art-minded Parisians of the nineteenth century referred to "les primitifs," they did not mean peasants or non-Europeans, but medieval and early Renaissance artists: Clouet, Fouquet, van Eyck, Fra Angelico. These were deemed painters who stood at the beginning of the modern tradition, therefore primitive in the sense of first, or original. With the triumph of a biological conception of history came the search for the first peoples or ideas in a chain of development. Accordingly, ancient European and Near Eastern arts too were labeled primitive: Assyrian, Egyptian, early Greek, Etruscan. The imperfections of their forms and techniques were adduced to exalt the superior ones that followed in Western European societies. (This distinction of inferior and superior underlay the racist conceptions that supported colonial conquests.) For artists who opposed the authorities of official art, that reasoning was reversed: imperfections were signs of originality therefore artistically and morally superior. Artistic energies could be recovered by "returning" to earlier conditions, that is, by stripping away the overlays of reason and convention that hid creativity. By mid-century there was a widespread anti-classicism most famously proclaimed by John Ruskin, but practiced by Millet, Théodore Rousseau, and other French artists. They deplored the Renaissance because they said it substituted reason, bookish knowledge, and clever illusionism for the instinct, individuality, and imaginative forms and colors of earlier art.

Folkloric arts. One of the principal signs of originality was the mark of handwork. Its irregularities were the proof of individual creativity, in opposition to the smooth perfection of academic style. That perfection was associated with the impersonality of machine production, in turn the product of repressive reason.[6] Printmakers, facing the rapid growth of mechanical means of reproduction which jeopardized their craft, established societies and publications which not only featured their own work, but also early European prints and contemporary folklore. For oppositional artists caught up in the fervor of the Revolution of 1848, the primitiveness of popular imagery was the proof that it emanated from *le peuple*, that it expressed the heartland of France and not the coterie of urban artists sheltered by government and finance. Courbet, George Sand, and the writers Champfleury, Max Buchon, and Pierre Dupont found vitality in popular prints and songs which they associated with the new realism. By the 1870s this viewpoint, no longer radical, led to the founding of the major journals and societies devoted to folklore.[7]

For these views we have an especially appropriate witness, the writer Champfleury, a friend or supporter of Courbet, Millet, Daumier, Hervier, and Legros. A man of the left in the 1840s and 1850s, he held that popular art responded to democratic ideals. He was the biographer of the Le Nain brothers, seventeenth-century painters of peasants, and became a leading historian of caricature and the popular arts. In his history of popular prints Champfleury reproduced primitive woodcuts and nineteenth-century broadsides while documenting such traditional tales as "Old Man Misery" and "The Wandering Jew."[8] He insisted that the awkwardness of popular prints, a natural result of their defiance of conventional rules, makes them closer to the art of genius than the slick products of academic schools. Such prints have great depth because they grew out of peasant culture: "Popular broadsides engraved by the people spoke to the people." Champfleury's praise-words are "naïveté," "innocence," "awkwardness," and "unpretentious and child-like." Although he believed in "men of genius" he argued for school instruction in the popular arts, these "gay and healthy images, unrelated to urban coarseness," and said that if artists could turn their backs on the dominant traditions and look within themselves the result might well be "work that is original, consequently naïve and popular."

Primitive techniques, individualism, and originality. Most of the artists in the *Peasants and "Primitivism"* exhibition were not only attracted to the look and the crafts of rural life, they also cultivated techniques in their own art that defied the well-modeled naturalism equated with metropolitan sophistication and the appearance of machined products. They were not alone in this, for defiance of the machine was also at the heart of the international Arts and Crafts movement of the second half of the nineteenth century. Consistent with their alienated view of modern industry, they disdained the industrial processes that were replacing printing by hand, a disdain that had the passion of self-preservation. Lepère may be the only artist who actually called his technique "a robust peasant,"[9] but from Millet onward artists often emulated earlier graphic arts for perpetuating supposedly crude ways of working wood or metal. The prints in the exhibition show the frank exposure of etched line, the direct cutting of wood, the simplified drawing and flat patterns of lithography, techniques damned as primitive by their detractors, praised by their defenders for the same qualities.

All of these techniques had another virtue for modernist artists: they revealed the artist's hand and therefore artistic uniqueness. Opposition to the classical traditions of art, including polished techniques, was born of distrust of coercive authorities, which is why artistic gestures of individual freedom have become the very core of modernism. Naturalistic art and smooth techniques did not just fade away, they were sabotaged by artists who made them appear to be hopelessly old-fashioned, empty of creativity. They were replaced by "primitive" handling that expressed the creative force of the individual. In Richard Shiff's persuasive formulation, their techniques expressed "finding," not "making" forms in traditional ways. "Making" was associated with the well-known techniques of academic discipline, whereas "finding" involved obvious marks that seemed to be intuitive and personal as though just discovered. The old balance of subject matter and technique was tipped in favor of the latter. As they deserted naturalism, artists found expressive force in what Shiff calls a "technique of originality."[10] Of course this, too, was a learned technique with roots in prior art, but it appeared to be spontaneously found, therefore individual and original.

It is the value that modern culture places on originality that explains how the artistic qualities of primitivism eventually triumphed in the art market, despite having its origins in the opposition to bourgeois conceptions of skill. Millet's paintings that were despised in the 1850s later became celebrated works that made more than one dealer's fortune. A radical stance based upon political opposition and alienation from the norm helps identify originality, and originality is a source of capitalist value.[11] Modernist art relies on this familiar alternation of early rejection and eventual acceptance ("outsider art" is its latest manifestation). Artists like Courbet, Hervier, Millet, and Pissarro did indeed oppose the conservative middle class, but they unwittingly acted for the advanced bourgeoisie. Their attacks upon convention were ways of pushing rigid traditions aside, of reformulating art for their society. Social structures threatened by sclerosis survived and moved on, beneficially altered, without falling apart. Artists who began as rebels were eventually adopted when they established values that offered vicarious freedom from the alienating effects of industrial culture. A leading example is Impressionism, whose apparent spontaneity, naturalism, and hedonism has made it one of the major attractions of industrial societies.

Brittany, a Special Province

Peasants from Brittany are conspicuous in nineteenth-century prints. They are featured in the work of two of the artists presented at the beginning of the exhibition, Olivier Perrin and Hippolyte Lalaisse, and in six of those at its end, Gauguin, Bernard, Armand Seguin, Henri Delavallée, Tony Beltrand, and Henri Rivière. It is Bretons whom we see in a print made at Epinal on the opposite side of France (pl. 23), rather than a native Alsatian, for by the third quarter of the century the generic peasant was from Brittany. Why did the peasant Everyman come from that province rather than from Alsace, Normandy, or the Auvergne? The answer is found in a set of historical circumstances and attitudes that have been brilliantly analyzed by Denise Delouche.[12]

It was in the 1830s that Brittany became widely celebrated as a province with a distinctive character. French artists and writers were then confirming the nationalism inherent in Romanticism by examining the landscapes, legends, and peoples of the provinces, a regionalism that increasingly supplanted the former hegemony of Italy and the Graeco-Roman world. Within this new regionalism Brittany gained distinction from several interconnected circumstances. One was its relative isolation thanks to the forests and marshes which partially blocked off the peninsula and slowed its integration with the rest of northern France. Another was its reputation as particularly religious and traditionalist, above all anti-Parisian, a reputation earned from its steady resistance, military and civil alike, to the forces of the French Revolutions of the 1790s. The adjacent region of the Vendée shared in both circumstances, and the two provinces were often grouped together. However, the Vendée and Upper Brittany were sooner penetrated by national culture, and so Lower Brittany, the outermost portion of the peninsula, came to stand for the whole province. There the Breton language resisted the inroads of French, and the agricultural revolution was delayed until the middle of the century.

Although Lower Brittany (largely limited to the department of Finistère) had begun to change rapidly by 1848,[13] its character was frozen by artists and writers who kept it for the rest of the century in an unchanging world of a strange language, uncivilized peasants, primitive agriculture, and devout religiosity. Their piety was characterized by unusual sculpted calvaries and by periodic "pardons," folkloric festivals when pilgrims paraded in quaint costumes and animals were blessed. This supposed unchanging world was said to be the true old France, the Celtic world uncontaminated by later Latinate peoples and customs. And this was claimed by the Bretons themselves, who founded the Celtic Academy in 1804 at Quimper to celebrate their unique heritage. "Celtomania" was well in place among Parisians by the 1830s, and peasants of Brittany's "ancient race" were well represented in paintings of picturesque rusticity that hung in government exhibitions (the "Salon") of the 1840s. Prints of this supposedly archaic world proliferated in the same decade, including engravings and lithographs appearing in the rapidly growing illustrated press.

Gauguin was therefore a Johnny-come-lately when he arrived at Pont-Aven in 1886. Lalaisse had visited in 1843, and in 1865 the American painter Robert Wylie had settled there to launch a veritable international artists' colony. The plot of Blanche Willis Howard's novel *Guenn*, published in Boston in 1883, revolves around the relationships of Breton girls with the foreign artists whom they serve as models.[14] Howard's young women work in a sardine factory, unlike those subsequently pictured by Gauguin, Bernard, Seguin, Beltrand, and Rivière. These French artists acted like Howard's fictional painters who eliminated signs of modern life (although Howard notes them) and who sometimes referred to Breton women as "coiffes," substituting the headdress for the person. The prominence of huge white coifs in Pont-Aven paintings is but one token of the retention of the masculinized myths of primitivism. They were worn on Sundays and special occasions, not out in the fields as Gauguin and Bernard would have it (Rivière's plainer bonnets are more faithful to field work), and they were rich in local meanings, not signs of strangeness with which the alienated artists endowed them.[15] By creating impressions of unchanging ways, Gauguin, in a manner of speaking, aligned himself with the oldest inhabitants of Pont-Aven, not with his younger models whose French-speaking and cosmopolitan ways would have punctured the myths he had adopted.

Gauguin and the others mentioned above pictured women far more frequently than men. Primitivism, as feminists have shown, is a gendered concept. (This becomes even more obvious in Gauguin's paintings of Tahiti and the Marquesas Islands, where men are hardly ever shown.) Insofar as Gauguin and Bernard were drawn to religion, their predilections were reinforced by what they found in Brittany. There, as elsewhere in France, Catholicism had become a female world, not just by the failure of men to show up at Sunday services, but also by the increase in women's religious societies, an extension of prevalent Marianism in the church.[16] However, it must also be said that men habitually believed women to be ruled by instinct and to be closer to nature, in contrast to men who use reason and its offspring, science, to dominate "her," that is, nature. Women were the basic Other for men, therefore the elemental primitive person. Pissarro's markets, gardens, courtyards, and meadows were women's territories, and so was the Brittany pictured by Gauguin, Bernard, Seguin, and Rivière.

Peasants and Other Primitives

Between about 1890 and World War I, non-European peoples displaced French peasants as the Others who were the chief source of primitivist ideas. Peasants were being more rapidly assimilated into national commerce and culture as a result of decades of homogenizing education, of improved transport and communication, and of the continued decline in the proportion of rural citizens.[17] Their assimilation was all the more apparent because other "primitives" now loomed larger. French colonialism had been growing apace, resulting in sharper rivalries with Great Britain, Belgium, and Germany for supremacy in Africa and the Near and Far East, rivalries that greatly increased the attention paid to non-European peoples and their arts. Instead of visiting a quaint Breton village, one could go to a World's Fair and see native peoples in purportedly authentic "villages." Such "natural" settings, so different from the fairs' exhibits of the latest machinery, had the apparent neutrality of anthropological investigation. It was understood that peoples treated like exhibits in a zoo deserved to be "civilized" by a superior civilization. It was the Javanese village in the Paris World's Fair of 1889 whose dancers were so widely admired and whose imitations of ancient sculpture attracted the attention of Gauguin, a pivotal modernist figure because he shifted from Breton peasants to the natives of Pacific islands.[18]

It is true that Oceanic peoples, Africans, and Native Americans had been treated as primitives since the sixteenth century, not only because of their subjection to superior "science," but also because their non-naturalistic art was believed to express their prelapsarian worlds. Because peasants were now fully enrolled as members of French society, albeit naïve ones, it was colonial natives whose presumed attributes became the most vital auxiliaries in the fight against the repressions and fragmentations of metropolitan culture. In the wake of Gauguin's global primitivism, North African textiles and ceramics inspired Matisse, while African masks and sculpture became the most influential non-European arts for Picasso and hosts of others. The harsh realities of the conquest of non-Europeans could be set aside or excused by assuming that many of the illusory attributes that we have charted for peasant society were also characteristic of colonized natives: simplicity, closeness to nature, timelessness, instinctual creativity, freedom from repressive reason, and the absence of disruptive modernity. The violence of colonial hegemony was, however, confessed in the attraction to magic, ritual, and strangeness which was used by some artists – no matter how grossly misunderstood – as an attack upon conventional art and consequently an ironic comment upon imperial policies.[19] In the twentieth century this dialectic of advanced industrial power and subjugated peoples supplanted that of city and country that we have been examining.

Despite the greater impact of non-European art, primitivism that looked toward peasant culture did not entirely disappear in twentieth-century modernism. It lived on in the vocabulary of critics even when no peasants were present, so that, for example, the sculptures of Maillol and Brancusi were described in terms of "rustic simplicity." In the first decade of the century in Germany, Käthe Kollwitz, Gabriele Münter, and Franz Marc drew upon German folk arts. In Russia at the end of that decade, Natalia Goncharova and Kasimir Malevich constructed their images of peasants in radically flat and strongly colored forms that recalled icons and popular prints which they associated with the Russian peasantry. In the 1920s and 1930s the revolutionary Mexican government cultivated peasant imagery to help weld its disparate peoples into a national culture; Diego Rivera replaced his Parisian Cubism with an influential nativism. In the next decade in the United States, Grant Wood and Thomas Hart Benton denied the disastrous reality of the Great Depression by celebrating rural society in primitivizing easel paintings and murals.

From the perspectives of the turbulent twentieth century, nineteenth-century peasant life featured in the *Peasants and "Primitivism"* exhibition seems quaintly distant. Charles Jacque's pot scrubbers and Rivière's laundresses work in courtyards and fields where hard labor takes second place to the cleansing action of pictorial beauty; Seguin's Breton maidens have the decorative leisure of Renaissance nymphs. Looked at closely, however, these prints come across not only as perpetuated myths of timeless societies, but also as revealing the conflicts of modern culture. Hervier's women and children live in rural slums that look like many of today's Third World settlements; Millet's laboring men and women have the dignity that Soviet poster artists gave to their pairings of factory workers and peasants; Millet, Legros, Lepère, and Pissarro show faggot gatherers and vagabonds who remind us of today's displaced victims of urban-industrial upheavals.

From our perspectives also, we know that the techniques and styles of many nineteenth-century printmakers looked forward to the more outrageous primitivisms of modern artists. Twentieth-century artists assimilated the techniques we have been examining with selected characteristics of the arts remote from centers of European culture: direct cutting into wood or metal, leaving evidence of the hand tools used, instead of the polish of mechanical means; relatively unmodeled and unnaturalistic imagery; a strong penchant for the decorative; striking, unmodulated colors; materials no longer used by industry. All kinds of modern art can be described in such terms, but what the exhibition hopes to show is that they were not merely formal devices, they were rooted in myths about pre-industrial rural cultures. And it is these myths that fueled the anti-illusionism which is the central dialectic of modernist art.

Three entries from *Peasants and "Primitivism": French Prints from Millet to Gauguin* (exh. cat., Mount Holyoke College Art Museum, 1995)

Adrien Lavieille, after J.F. Millet, Reaping, 1853 (pl. 20)

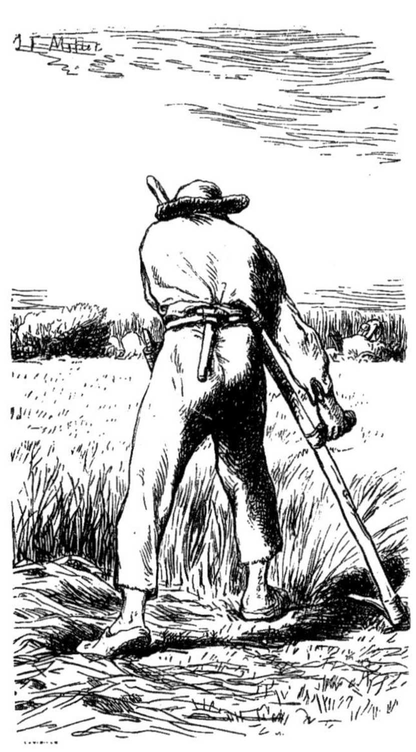

Millet's rustic subjects have echoes of the figures used since medieval times to represent the four seasons and the labors of the months. This print and several others of the series published by *L'Illustration* (later issued separately as "Les Travaux des champs") recall those used for the late summer or fall months (*Raking*, *Trussing*, *Flax-Pulling*, *Flax-Crushing*, *Mowing*, *Threshing*), and the remaining three, winter months (*Shearing*, *Faggoting*, and *Spinning*). In their form – vertical compositions of single figures, evenly divided between male and female work – they also look like a rural version of the long-established series of prints, *Cris de Paris* ("Paris Street Cries"), prints that were particularly numerous in the preceding two decades, devoted to the trades plied in the shops and streets of the capital. Partly because Lavieille's prints made them available, *Les Travaux des champs* are among

20 Adrien Lavieille, after J.F. Millet, *Reaping*, 1853. Wood engraving after drawing on the block by Millet, from *L'Illustration* (February 5, 1853): 93.

Millet's most influential inventions. Van Gogh's oil paintings after them are their most famous heirs but other artists were inspired by them, among them Charles Jacque, Jules Breton, Léon Lhermitte, Jules Dalou, and both Camille and Lucien Pissarro. Millet's fame would have guaranteed some interest in his work but it is the particular strength of these figures that gave them their historical authority. Like his *Sower*, they encapsulate labor in striking silhouettes that remain imprinted on one's memory. Among Millet's surviving drawings there are several for each print.

Lavieille's ten engravings after drawings by Millet were published in *L'Illustration* to accompany an article, "Revue agricole." They were subsequently printed on separate sheets for the album from which these two prints come. In addition, they were copied in drypoint by H.E. Lessore in 1879 and photographically reproduced several times by the end of the century. In effect Millet was better known through such reproductive prints than through original works.

J.F. Millet, *Going to Work*, 1863 (pl. 21)

There is a nearly primeval innocence in these peasants setting out in the morning to dig potatoes, carrying their tools and a jug of water: a nineteenth-century Adam and Eve or a couple from Theocritus. Their path is symbolically flanked by rocks and prickly weeds but farther back Millet's needle traces in ever lighter accents the textures of plowed land, low growth, mounds of straw, and the abandoned plow which signals autumn. Weedy rocks and fruitful soil, hard labor and youth: Millet's idea of humans in nature is a moralizing one whose innate conservatism eventually won him worldwide admiration. These are not doubtful itinerants but a married couple heading out from a peaceful village to dig their own crop. Like some living votive sculpture, the woman peers at us from under that memorable basket. The man could almost have stepped from any number of sixteenth-century engravings where there are similar striding figures. Together the couple has an iconic presence because both man and wife are centered on the page and because their bodies face partly toward us although they walk to our left. Echoes of earlier ages are all the more logical when we learn that in the months immediately preceding his work on this print Millet had plunged into a reading of Robert Burns and Theocritus, and was in the midst of making drawings from the latter. As he noted, "Reading Theocritus proves to me more and more that one is never as Greek as when one renders very naïvely the impressions one has, no matter where they come from, and Burns proves it to me also."[20]

By 1863 the "etching revival" was well under way in Paris, and Millet's etchings were admired by a substantial number of artists and collectors. The idea for *Going to Work* came from his friend Alfred Sensier, who formed a group of ten subscribers each paying 100 francs in exchange for co-ownership of Millet's print. Among the ten was the print fancier Philippe Burty, who demanded that the plate be destroyed so as to create a limited edition of greater value. In an article of 1861 he wrote that Millet's etchings appealed "more directly to sincere friends of nature and of art than to the banal crowd."[21] Millet successfully opposed Burty's demand, for he was quite willing to have his prints in the hands of the "banal crowd," a view that contrasts ironically with that of Pissarro in the next generation, who favored the unique print. On the other hand, he catered to his subscribers' connoisseurship by inserting an artist's joke that most people would not notice. Along the bottom edge, one-third the way across the sheet from the left corner, he etched a minuscule reclining nude resting on one elbow. (She appears all by herself as a trial vignette in one of the fragmentary impressions Millet pulled from the plate before it was finished.) In the plate margin above the lower left corner of the completed etching is the profile of a tiny standing nude. It is less clearly deliberate (it could have been an artist's doodle) but Millet allowed it to remain throughout the printings.

Hand-colored popular broadsides, printed between 1860 and 1880: *Wings of a Rustic Interior* (pl. 22); and *Rural Decorations, No. 23*, 29 × 39 (pl. 23)

These two prints, when glued to stiff paper or cardboard, would have served as backdrop and wings of miniature theaters. They come from a large assortment of such rustic "décors" published by the Pellerin firm. The primitive aspect of the technique suited the images of rural life, creating a make-believe world that appealed to city people. They found in their toy-like charm a rusticity that echoed childhood, not surprising since so many urbanites had originally come from the countryside in the internal emigration that characterized the industrial revolution.

Pellerin, an entrepreneur of Epinal in eastern France, gathered together a number of provincial printmakers late in the eighteenth century. He provided paper, inks, and presses, but despite this form of capitalist factory production he made sure that their prints retained their folkloric, "primitive" qualities. Beginning in the 1840s, Pellerin's successors gradually shifted from woodcuts to lithographs (*imagerie d'Epinal* became a generic term, like "Currier & Ives" in the United States). By 1842 their annual production had reached an astonishing 875,000.[22] Pellerin's success depended on the gap between the actual modernization of urban culture and nostalgia for the premodern past. The firm filled the gap by convincing clients of the genuine "folk" origin of their prints.

Pellerin's two prints embody the dialog of rural ideal and urban market in their very technique which exploited technological advancement in order to suit mass marketing. By the 1860s the firm was using a process patented in 1850 by Firmin Gillot, whose name appears at the bottom of these two prints. Instead of cutting into wood, the artist simply drew in greasy ink on a suitable paper. The drawing was placed face down on a zinc plate to transfer the inked lines, which were then

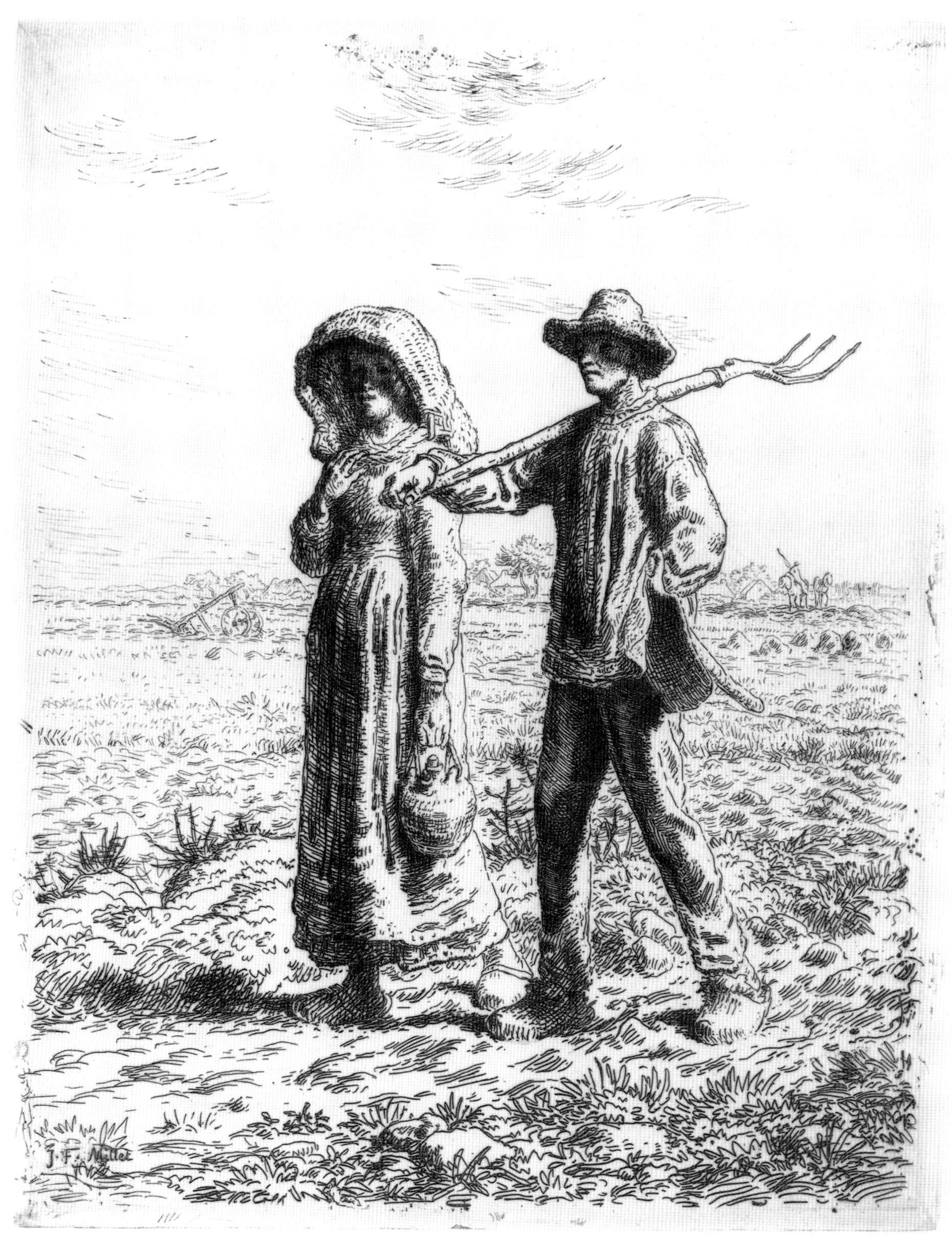

21 J.F. Millet, *Going to Work*, 1863. Etching. Delteil, Melot 19 ii. Collection S. William Pelletier.

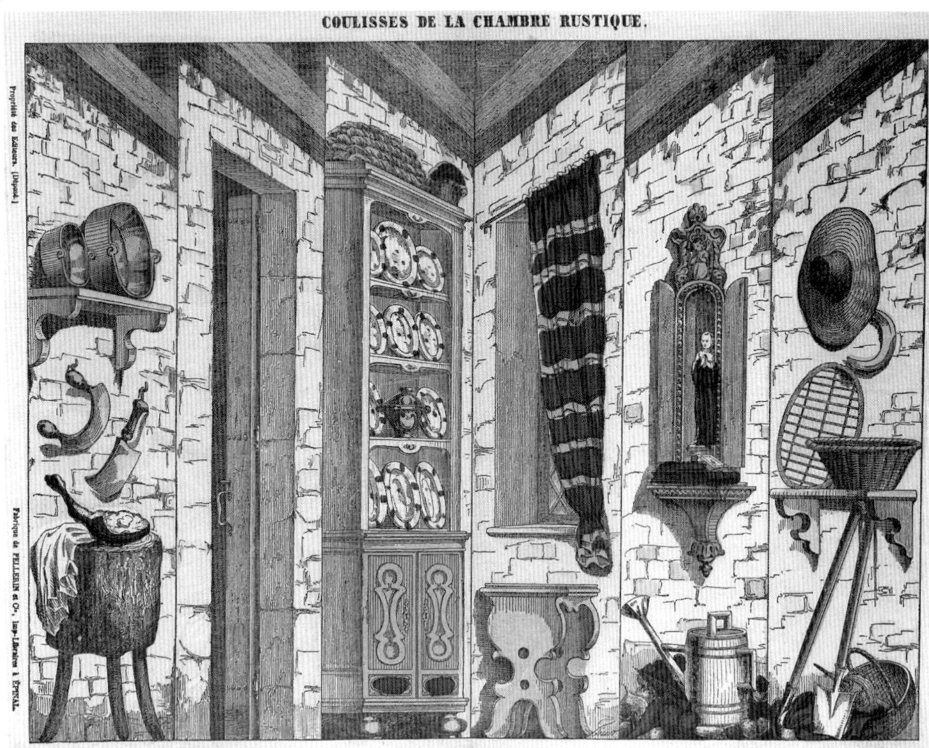

22 “Chaste,” *Wings of a Rustic Interior*, between 1860 and 1880. Gillot-process print imitating woodcut, printed by Pellerin, Epinal. Signed in the plate “CHASTE.” Jean C. Harris Fund. Mount Holyoke College Art Museum, South Hadley, Massachusetts.

23 Anonymous, *Rural Decorations, No. 23*, between 1860 and 1880. Gillot-process print imitating woodcut, printed by Pellerin, Epinal. Jean C. Harris Fund, Mount Holyoke College Art Museum, South Hadley, Massachusetts.

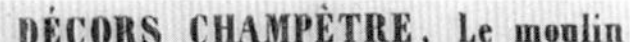

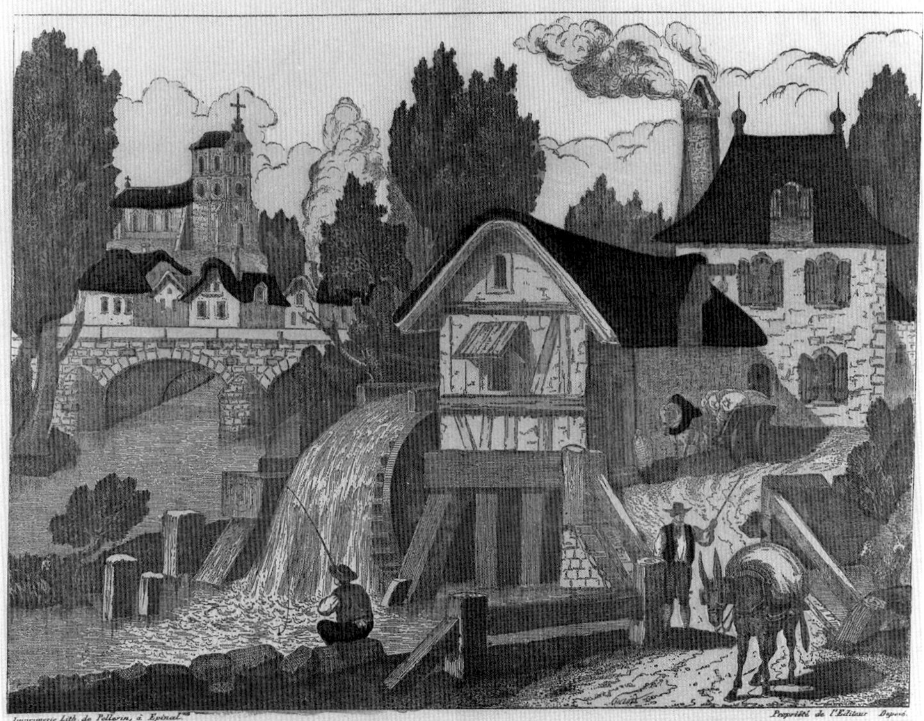

coated with an asphalt or resin that resisted acid. When placed in an acid bath, the untouched metal was bitten away, leaving the drawing in relief. This metal plate could then print in the manner of a relief woodcut, but it was more durable and labor-saving because the acid did the work of hand-cutting. To preserve the illusion of rural primitivism, however, the wily provincials of Epinal disguised their modern process by having artists draw in imitation of the stiff lines of traditional woodcuts. The disguise worked, and still today such prints are often treated as unadulterated pieces of folk art. Their "folk" quality is preserved in the large blotches of bright color, painted with deliberate crudeness through stencils. *Wings of a Rustic Interior* has blood red, tannish-yellow, and (more subtly) two pale tints for the set's walls; *Rural Decorations* has six hues.

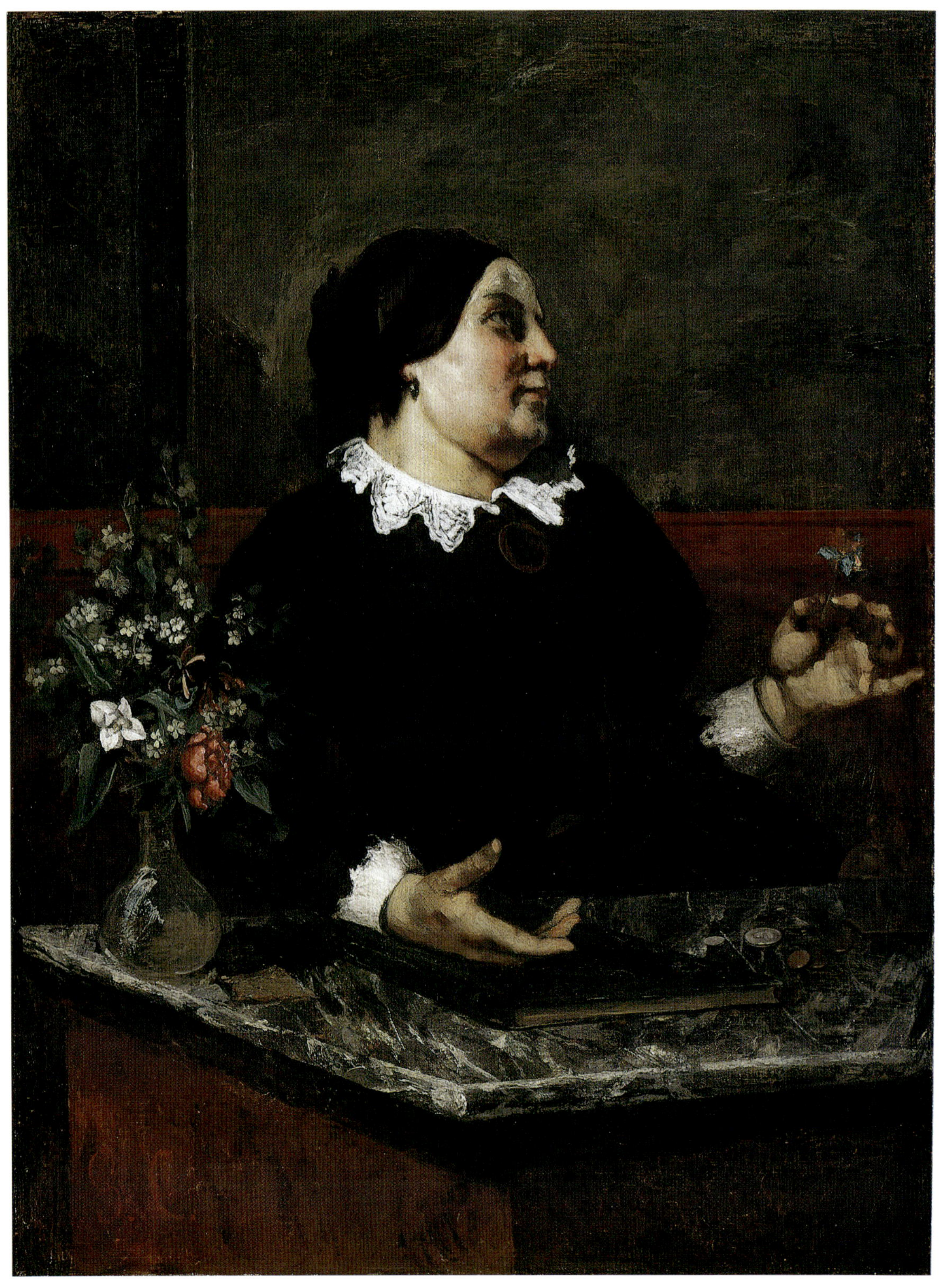

24 Gustave Courbet, *Mère Grégoire*, 1855/67. 50¾ × 38⅜ in. (129 × 97.5 cm.). Art Institute of Chicago, Wilson L. Mead Fund.

Chapter 4

Courbet's *Mère Grégoire* and Béranger

Gustave Courbet's *Mère Grégoire* (pl. 24), one of the glories of the Art Institute of Chicago, was based on the popular poem "Madame Grégoire" by Pierre Jean Béranger. That this escaped notice for so long is principally because Béranger's *chansons* (poems set to popular tunes) are not much read. To explain Courbet's inspiration from the poet is to explain something of Béranger's importance as a popular writer in the middle of the nineteenth century and, even more, something of Courbet's conception of his art. First, it must be established that his painting does indeed derive from the Béranger poem, and then that *Mère Grégoire*, like so many of Courbet's works, raises fascinating social and political issues.[1]

Madame Grégoire

Air: It's Big Thomas

It was during my days
That Madame Grégoire shone.
At the age of twenty I would go
To laugh and drink at her tavern;
She attracted people
With her engaging manner.
More than one brawny guy
Had credit there on his good looks.
Oh, how we'd go
And drink it up at her tavern!

Although she wept over the memory
Of a certain spouse,
None of us
Had known the late Grégoire;
But of replacing him
Who wouldn't have dreamed?
Happy was the table to which
madam

Air: C'est le gros Thomas

C'était de mon temps
Que brillait madame Grégoire.
J'allais à vingt ans
Dans son cabaret rire et boire;
Elle attirait les gens
Par des airs engageants.
Plus d'un brun à large poitrine
Avait là crédit sur sa mine.
Ah! comme on entrait
Boire à son cabaret!

D'un certain époux
Bien qu'elle pleurit la mémoire,
Personne de nous
N'avait connu défunt Grégoire;
Mais à le remplacer
Qui n'eût voulu penser?
Heureux l'écot où la commère

• From *Museum Studies* (Art Institute of Chicago) 13, 1 (1987): 24–35.

Brought her bottle and her glass!
Oh, how we'd go, etc.

I can still see
Her laughing heartily until she cried,
And beneath her gold cross
The fullness of her modest charms.
Ask her lovers:
At the counter, the responsive brunette
Would give them double for their money.
Oh, how we'd go, etc.

The wives of coarse drinkers
Often picked quarrels with her.
How many times did I see
Suitors fighting over her!
While the doorkeeper and the lovers
Were always bickering,
She, a most clever woman,
Would hide the guilty ones in her bed.
Oh, how we'd go, etc.

When it was my turn
To be master of her establishment,
Every day
Was a new feast for my friends.
I'm not the jealous type:
We worked things out for everyone.
Our hostess, pushing her sales,
Surrendered everything including the maid.
Oh, how we'd go, etc.

Everything has changed now:
Having nothing left to tap,
She took leave of
Both pleasure and business.
Alas, how I miss
Her wine cellar and her charms!
For a long time to come each customer
Will cry out in front of her place
Oh, how we'd go
And drink it up at her tavern!

Apportrait sa pinte et son verre!
Ah! comme on entrait, etc.

Je crois voir encor
Son gros rire aller jusqu'aux larmes,
Et sous sa croix d'or
L'ampleur de ses pudiques charmes.
Consultez ses amants:
Au comptoir la sensible brune
Leur rendait deux piéces pour une.
Ah! comme on entrait, etc.

Des buveurs grivois
Les femmes lui cherchaient querelle.
Que j'ai vu de fois
Des galants se battre pour elle!
La garde et les amours
Se chamaillant toujours,
Elle, une femme des plus capables,
Dans son lit cachait les coupables.
Ah! comme on entrait, etc.

Quand ce fut mon tour
D'être en tout le maître chez elle,
C'était chaque jour
Pour mes amis fête nouvelle.
Je ne suis point jaloux:
Nous nous arrangions tous.
L'hôtesse, poussant à la vente,
Nous livrait jusqu'à la servante.
Ah! comme on entrait, etc.

Tout est bien changé:
N'ayant plus rien à mettre en perce,
Elle a pris congé
Et des plaisirs et du commerce.
Que je regrette, hélas!
Sa cave et ses appas!
Longtemps encor chaque pratique
S'écrira devant sa boutique:
Ah! comme on entrait
Boire à son cabaret!

Courbet's painting is a free improvisation based upon the personage of Mme. Grégoire, with particular reference to the third stanza. Although she does not wear a golden cross, Courbet's woman has "a fullness of her modest charms," and "At the counter, the responsive brunette / Would give them double for their money." The sense of this last verse, with its *double entendre*, is at the very heart of Courbet's conception. The woman's right hand rests on her ledger, the palm upward in the traditional gesture of expectation of payment. Coins are on the counter in front of her, and the substantial, marble-topped counter bespeaks the proprietress (or, at least, the cashier) of the establishment. In Mère Grégoire's other hand is a flower, symbol of love, which she presumably offers to an unseen person to her left. This figure is standing, as we can deduce from Mère Grégoire's fixed gaze. Although we do not see him, we know him to be one of the favored customers who is fortunate enough to engage in the dialog of money and love that Béranger's song celebrates.

The vase of flowers on the other side of the composition reinforces the gesture of love; a further reinforcement is found above, in the privacy screen that stands behind the woman's bench. That it is indeed a privacy screen, and not part of a door or mirror, is clear in the original. The frame has brass nailheads or bosses, and the leather surface has a lozenge pattern stamped in gold.[2] Because it hints at a private space behind the counter, the screen takes its place in the compounded dialog of the picture: money and love, public and private, man and woman, coin and flower, ledger and bouquet. Symbols of the dialectic may be carried even further. On the counter to the right is the kind of bell one rings for attention – an emblem of public function. On the left, near the vase, is a flat, grayish-brown object that seems to be either a small coin purse or the kind of pocket notebook in which one would record private debts or assignations. Almost every feature of Courbet's painting, therefore, contributes to the characterization of Béranger's "Madame Grégoire." And it should be noted that, contrary to the commonly held view of Courbet as vulgar and insensitive, he is revealed here as both discreet and subtle. Béranger's verses could easily give rise to any number of ribald interpretations, but Courbet did not take such an easy route. The "fullness" of the cabaret owner's charms is indeed made "modest."

It is instructive to compare Courbet's interpretation with the only one so far found that precedes his: that of J.J. Grandville (pl. 25) for the 1836 edition

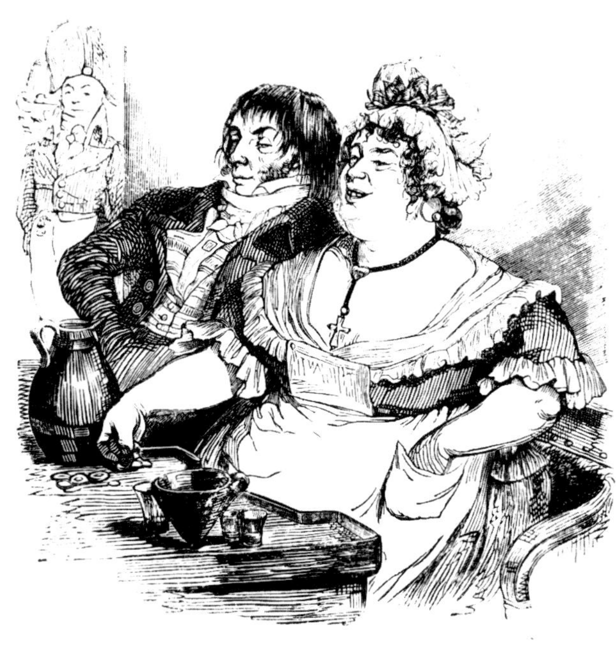

25 J.J. Grandville, *Madame Grégoire*, engraving for *Oeuvres complètes de P.-J. de Béranger* (Paris, 1836).

of Béranger's poems.[3] Grandville's version, unlike Courbet's, shows us a favored client and, farther back, two customers. He represents Mme. Grégoire – with the gold cross, hearty laugh, and modest charms cited in Béranger's third stanza – in the act of doling out coins. By comparison, Courbet's interpretation is very restrained. The restraint is only natural: Courbet's is an oil painting, requiring the autonomy and permanence of its medium, whereas Grandville's is an illustration, deliberately bordering upon caricature, that is attached directly to its text. (Despite the differences, it is likely, in view of his adaptation of Grandville's invention of the unseen client, that Courbet knew the Grandville illustration.)

Courbet's choice of Béranger's "Madame Grégoire" is particularly rich in political and social reverberations. To understand them, we need to look into the origins of Béranger's poem and into his reputation in Courbet's day. Béranger (1780–1857) was a native Parisian whose early reputation was based upon the songs that circulated in Paris in the last years of the Empire (the most famous was "Le Roi d'Yvetot").[4] Most of his poems were written and published between 1815 (when his first album appeared) and 1833, after which he seldom wrote. A self-proclaimed "son of the people," he regarded himself as a spokesman of the ordinary Frenchman, who was the bearer of poetic and national energies. By 1821 Béranger was president of a singing society that congregated at the Moulin Vert (also called the Moulin de Beurre), one of the singing clubs (*goguettes*) that flowered under the Restoration. It was run by a woman called "Mère Saguet" who, according to Béranger's biographers, served as the model for "Madame Grégoire." Others who frequented her cabaret were the young historian Thiers, the artists Raffet and Charlet and, at various times, Hugo, Gautier, Gavarni, and Nerval. Like other singing societies, it was often a rallying point for opponents of current government, who couched their opposition in songs of witty double allusions that were designed to escape censorship.

From the singing societies of the 1820s to the revolutionary cafés and banquet societies of 1848, there was not a great distance, and we shall see that this evolution would logically take us also from Béranger to Courbet. The singing clubs and popular cafés were constant sources of agitation that were kept under surveillance – and often censored – by successive governments from 1820 onward. They bore a popular cachet, and some were truly working-class. The Moulin Vert was apparently typical. When Mère Saguet retired in 1830,[5] her son-in-law, Bolay, allowed the establishment to become more openly political; it eventually became one of the many centers of opposition to the July Monarchy. Also, from 1830 onward, *chansonniers* became more numerous and more prominent, many of them taking their cues from Béranger. The admiration of left-wing literary and artistic circles gave increased prominence to worker-poets and worker-songwriters, and frequent persecutions by the police heightened the social tensions that led to the 1848 Revolution. Because of its ostensible source in the people, the popular song, in the words of Pierre Brochon, became "the means of popular expression, *par excellence*" and, "by its form, its ease of diffusion among the semi-literate, it [was] the most efficacious method of propaganda, a veritable weapon."[6]

With the approach of 1848, the popular song became overtly political, and the *chansonnier* Pierre Dupont, a disciple of Béranger, could subsequently claim that his songs had helped bring about the revolution.[7] Béranger, although he had virtually ceased writing, was by then a national figure and was especially popular among the ordinary citizens of Paris. This was true not only because of his songs, but also because of his standing as a victim of oppression. In 1821 and again in 1828, Béranger had been imprisoned for "outrage to religious and public morals and offense to the king."[8] The second imprisonment constituted a moral victory for the poet; famous people visited him in prison and liberal pamphleteers took up his defense. The incident helped make him the favorite of liberals such as Hugo, Lamartine, and Dumas *père*. In 1848, Béranger was named to the Assembly in a genuinely popular movement, despite his protests that approaching seventy and not concerned with politics, he was not a fit candidate.

Béranger was permitted to resign from the Assembly; he lived until 1857 in retirement, holding himself aloof from politics. New editions of his poems (1847, 1850, 1851, 1853, 1854, 1855) kept him before the public; he was such a national figure that he was widely viewed as a living La Fontaine.[9] His popularity led to homages that took many forms, including an album of songs, *Les Amours de Béranger*, published in 1854 by a number of admirers. His death in 1857 became a national event, in the wake of which there appeared a veritable outpouring of testimonials, songs, and vaudevilles drawn from his poems (five alone were put on stage in the fall of 1857), and even a weekly journal, *Béranger*, which ran from September 1857 to February 1858.[10]

While all of this is true, it is equally important to recall that Béranger's last years were not at all free from polemic. Indeed, the interpretation of Courbet's *Mère Grégoire* is not possible without reference to Béranger's reputation. For one thing, while the poet had a broad popular appeal in the early 1850s, he was also the subject of strong attacks from both left and right. For the left, the republicanism of the elderly man was too moderate; his failure to denounce openly the regime of Louis Napoleon was a fatal flaw. For the right, his republicanism, the popular flavor of his poems, and his anti-clericalism all militated against him. Sainte-Beuve, once an admirer, attacked him in an essay in 1850 for being too vulgar, lacking chasteness, and favoring socialism.[11] Further to the right was Armand de Pontmartin, who attacked Béranger in *Opinion publique*, a legitimist journal, in the fall of 1851: Béranger was guilty of "criminal work" which appealed to "ill-bred libertines." Worse, in his poems, Béranger issued "a call to revolt" and engaged in "perpetual demolition of all the established authorities, the king, the magistrate, the priest."[12] Attacks from the right like this were frequent and reached a high point in 1855, the year Courbet assigned to his *Mère Grégoire*. De Pontmartin's article was reprinted in his book *Nouvelles Causeries littéraires*; his attack was seconded by that of another Catholic conservative,

Louis Veuillot.[13] Although neither critic was enamored of Louis Napoleon, their assaults were sanctioned by his government's actions since 1851. Because the singing clubs and popular cafés, where Béranger's songs were sung, had been among the centers of agitation, they were suppressed in increasing numbers after the *coup d'état*. Research by Susanna Barrows has shown that, from 1851 to 1855, nearly 60,000 Parisian drinking establishments of all categories were shut down (dropping from approximately 350,000 to 291,000);[14] further, we know that suppression and censorship led to the virtual elimination of open political references in popular songs and literature. *Chansonniers* were obliged to use well-disguised analogies, if they were to hint at politics at all.[15]

By 1855, the date given to *Mère Grégoire*, everything about Béranger would have conspired in favor of the painter's choice. Béranger was a notable "son of the people," widely admired by the shopkeepers and artisans of Paris with whom Courbet sympathized. The fact that "right-thinking" critics like de Pontmartin were attacking Béranger would be an additional reason for Courbet's admiration. Many of the attacks on the painter since 1850 had centered on the same qualities that Béranger was accused of having, and the government's suppression of popular cafés and drinking establishments would have fortified the painter's association of himself with the popular poet.

In fact, Courbet's *Mère Grégoire* should probably be seen as a protest – albeit a covert one – against censorship and, by extension, against government authority. Béranger had twice been imprisoned and, since the facts of the life of this popular hero were well known, the very choice of "Madame Grégoire" by a notorious radical could be construed as an attack on censorship. There is abundant evidence that, as the Second Empire grew in power, the government forced writers of plays, songs, and vaudeville to find indirect means of opposing authority.[16] Courbet's *Mère Grégoire* would therefore seem to conform to a widespread pattern.

Why is *Mère Grégoire* so appropriate a selection from Béranger if the painter was thinking of his confrontations with authority? Any evocation of Béranger, after all, could be considered a satisfactory provocation. The answer is that *Mère Grégoire* was probably the kind of document that frequently is found in the history of art, namely, one that elicited an instinctive, subjective response in the artist, and yet one that had social portent. (Dogmatists are wrong in always opposing the subjective and the social.) Béranger's song is a particularly striking instance of the bawdiness in which Courbet indulged himself.[17] Its ribald character, its heroine who is frank and free in her loves, its celebration of drinking and conviviality, its disrespect for conventional morality – all its leading features were admirably suited to the robust artist who held forth in the Brasserie Andler, and who prided himself on his earthiness. Moreover, Courbet was proud of his musical talents and even composed some songs.

The social significance of *Mère Grégoire* stems from these same characteristics, transformed by the pressures of current history. This poem inevitably evoked the singing societies and popular cafés that had been powerful centers of opposition, and whose control had been specifically envisaged in a repressive decree of December 29, 1851.[18] There is even a serious temptation to believe that Courbet was consciously baiting the government in one feature of his painting. The flower that Mère Grégoire holds in her hand has not yet been identified but, unlike any real blossom, it carries the three colors of the French flag: red, white, and blue. If this was a conscious act, Courbet would have been setting the true Frenchness of Béranger against the usurped authority of the government he detested.[19]

If Courbet had exhibited *Mère Grégoire* in 1855, reaction to it might have provided a test of what has so far been stated here. He did not, however, and the truth is that the final judgment of the significance of the homage to Béranger rests on several confusing features of this painting's history. These are the traditional identification of the woman as Mme. Andler, the date of the picture, and its alteration (the canvas consists of two different pieces). Each of these must be dealt with in turn.

The painting, at least since Georges Riat's monograph on Courbet of 1906,[20] has been said to represent Mme. Andler, proprietress of the brasserie that Courbet frequented from 1849 onward. This identification should be discarded. The first documented reference to Mme. Andler dates well after Courbet's death, in the memoirs of his friend Alexandre Schanne, published in 1886.[21] All subsequent references stem from this one, including Riat's in 1906 and Charles Léger's in 1929.[22] Schanne is probably guilty, as are many writers of memoirs, of conjoining several reminiscences of earlier days into an unwitting invention.[23] Because the painting was mentioned by several of Courbet's acquaintances and friends during his lifetime (Silvestre, Thoré, Astruc, Castagnary, Etienne Baudry, etc.), it is logical to assume that one of them, at least, would have mentioned Mme. Andler. When Castagnary and Baudry discovered the painting in a dealer's shop in 1873 (it had been stolen from storage in 1871),[24] and subsequently wrote to Courbet about it, surely they would have made some references to Mme. Andler had she been the subject of the portrait. Moreover, Schanne was inconsistent because he noted that Mme. Andler was hardly a sensualist: a student with a girlfriend had to endure "the fire of thc angry glare of the owner."[25] This character hardly accords with *Mère Grégoire*, unless Courbet was deliberately mocking Mme. Andler.

The possibility that Courbet was insulting Mme. Andler by presenting her as the libertine Mme. Grégoire should at least be mentioned, since it would have been well within the artist's known capacities. However, beginning in 1855, he had a long, bitter dispute with Mme. Andler and her husband over payment of his debts; it was not resolved until 1869. That being so, it is not very likely that Courbet would have taken public revenge by exhibiting Mme. Andler's painting in 1867 at the risk of her denouncing him. Furthermore, were he to have done so, the well-known dispute would have led some observers, at least, to invoke

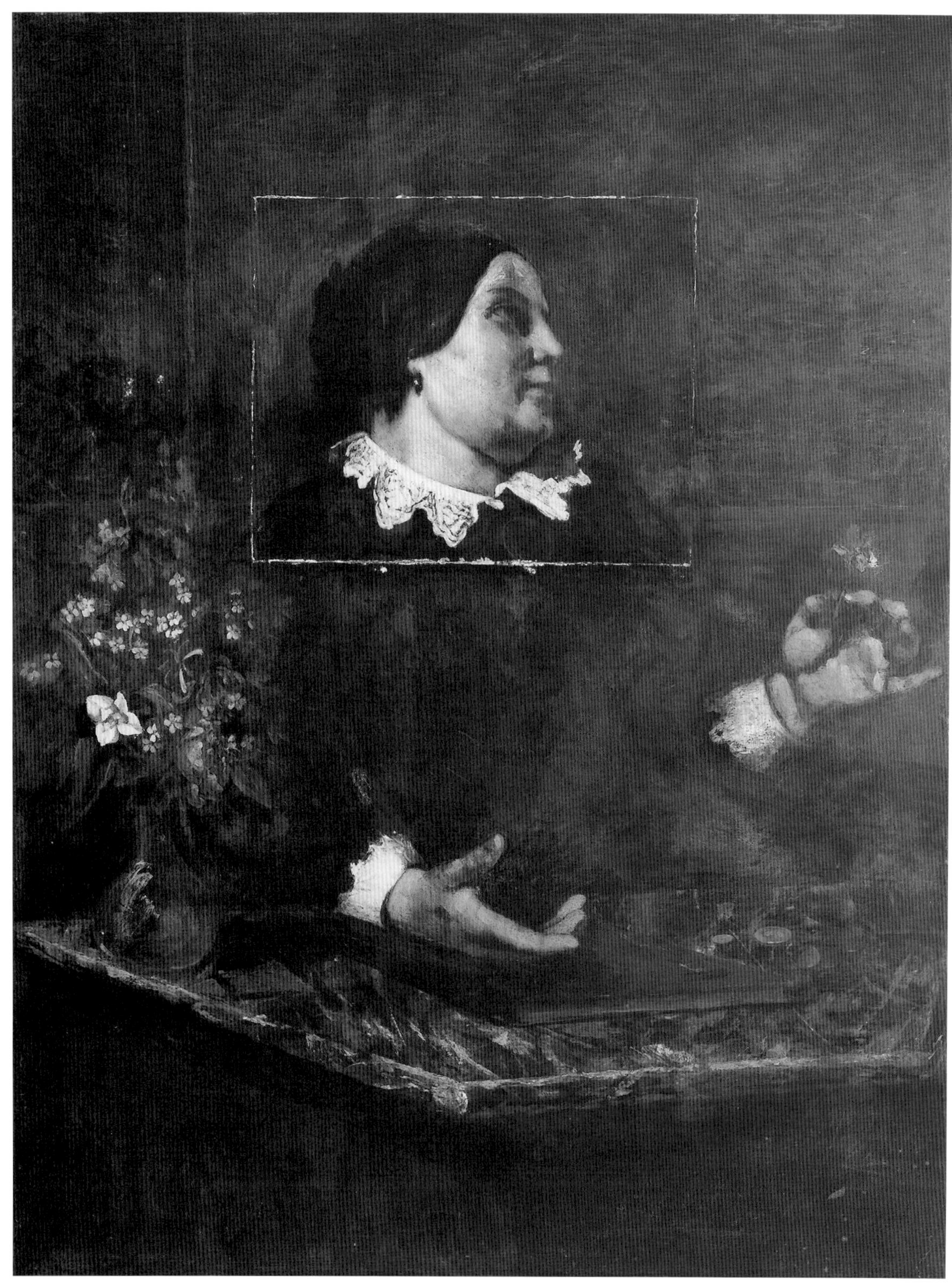

26 *Mère Grégoire* in the process of being restored, 1977.

her name. However, it is logical to assume that the painting, done without Mme. Andler in mind, could subsequently have been associated with her in Courbet's circle. Since Courbet's argument with her centered on money, Mère Grégoire's ledger could have inspired an *ex post facto* association as a way of insulting her. Perhaps this kind of teasing reference lay behind Schanne's erroneous assumption.

It is easier to believe that the lens of Schanne's memory was a bit obscured by time. The fame of Béranger's poem would have led him, and perhaps others, to make a connection between, on the one side, Béranger and the real Mère Saguet, proprietress of the Moulin Vert and model of "Madame Grégoire," and, on the other, Courbet and Mme. Andler. It is even reasonable to think that Courbet would have thought of the parallel between himself, leader of an informal society of drinking friends at the Brasserie Andler, and Béranger, the leader of the singing club at Mère Saguet's cabaret. Nonetheless, although one can readily imagine Mme. Andler to have been the butt of more than one ribald joke, there is no reason to believe that she is the woman we see in Courbet's painting. It is more sensible to conclude that the woman is one of Courbet's models, a deduction endorsed by Hélène Toussaint.[26]

The problem of dating Courbet's painting is intimately linked with the fact that the head of the woman is on a separate piece of canvas, of coarser weave than the rest of the painting (pl. 26).[27] When Castagnary and Baudry found it in 1873, Castagnary wrote Courbet: "O surprise! Madame Grégoire, whose head has been delicately severed, and then reinserted in the canvas. But the signs of the beheading have not yet been covered over."[28] This has sometimes been interpreted to mean that the painting was mutilated after it was stolen in 1871, and therefore that the head might not be that of the original composition. However, Courbet himself gave the explanation in a letter to Castagnary: "It is I who stuck the head of Mère Grégoire onto the large canvas, as usual, out of economy."[29] Castagnary would not have expected that; hence, his surprise in 1873 when the painting, having suffered some damage, exposed its piecing. The dealer, in this hypothesis, was trying to cover over the damage but was not responsible for adding a new section of canvas.

This hypothesis is supported by all the evidence that we now have. The picture was first mentioned by Théophile Silvestre in 1856, in his *Histoire des artistes vivants*. In an often-cited passage, he wrote: "Recently I saw at his place the head of a sleepwalker or card dealer and another woman whom he calls Madame Grégoire, whose hideousness would rout witches and dwarfs that Shakespeare and Velazquez sometimes used as repoussoirs in their vigorous creations."[30] When we add his other reference to the painting, usually overlooked, we see that it is only a head of Mme. Grégoire that he saw. In his list of Courbet's works, he recorded: "– Head of a sleepwalker. – Head of Mme Grégoire. – Portrait of M. Gueymard, of the Opéra (unfinished)."[31] There is no way of knowing whether the head Silvestre saw is the piece of the Chicago canvas or the separate head of

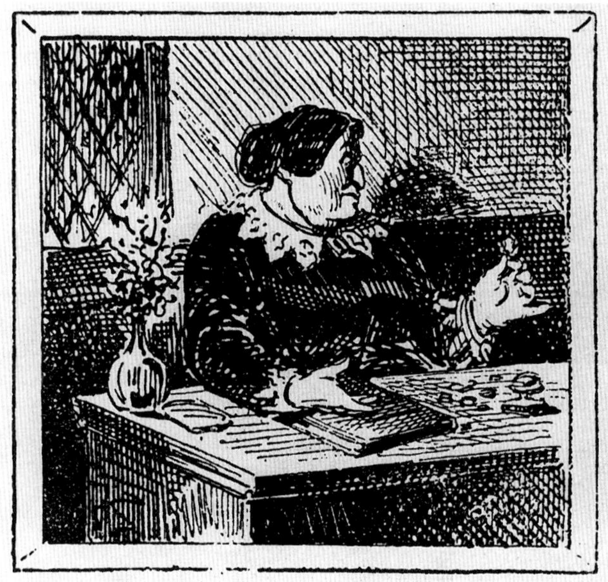

27 Gilbert Randon, *Madame Grégoire*, caricature from *Journal amusant*, 1867, reproduced in Charles Léger, *Courbet selon les caricatures et les images* (Paris, 1920): 69.

the same woman now in the Musée de Morlaix.[32] There is no way of knowing, either, whether Courbet inserted the head into a large, unused canvas, expanding it into the full composition, or whether he removed the head from an already finished composition and inserted the one we now see. In either case, Silvestre's account establishes that the piecing of the final canvas took place after he saw it, that is, after 1855–56 and before 1859, when it was described quite thoroughly by Zacharie Astruc in his article "Les 14 Stations du Salon." Astruc recounted a visit to Courbet's studio, where he saw Mère Grégoire, among other pictures, apparently in the process of being painted: "powerful old gossip dressed in black, collar embroidered at the neck, ruffles."[33]

Courbet included *Mère Grégoire* in his retrospective of 1867 and dated it 1855 in the catalog. The date probably derives from the head that Silvestre saw; that is, Courbet probably dated the composition by reference to its inception rather than to its completion. Although he listed it among his "studies and sketches," the painting was almost certainly completed. In Randon's 1867 caricature of the painting (pl. 27), the woman's head and collar are so close to those in the present picture that it is safe to assume that the inserted piece was already there. This deduction is supported by the careful examination and restoration conducted in Chicago in 1977; the authenticity of both sections of the canvas is not to be doubted. We can be sure only of a date between 1855 and 1867 for *Mère Grégoire*, but palette and brushwork seem to suit the period of the middle 1850s for the whole.

It would be comforting to the analysis of the painting as a homage to Béranger to prove that it was painted about 1855 for, as we have seen, this was the height of the conservative attacks upon the popular poet that might well have led

Courbet to associate himself with him. Of course, Silvestre's witness account of 1856 points to the head entitled "Mme Grégoire," therefore to Courbet's intention of doing a picture after the Béranger, poem. However, the whole period from 1855 to 1867, for all its internal changes, was one of constant polemic concerning Béranger, and Courbet's gesture makes sense at any point in that era. When Béranger died in 1857, there was the outpouring of pro-Béranger publications and plays mentioned above. Louis Napoleon's government, anxious to capitalize on the poet's fame, conducted state ceremonies in his honor, pretending that he had made peace with the Empire. Similarly, it was widely claimed that, before he died, Béranger had declared his allegiance to God. This supposed rallying to both church and state was later disproven but at the time it was generally believed, to the point that some leftists assaulted the poet's memory.

Béranger was also kept in the public eye by the continued popularity of his poems; by the publication of his letters to various correspondents; by the appearance of numerous anthologies of his work, and by the various comic operas, plays, and vaudevilles that were based upon his songs. One of these latter was the comic operetta *Madame Grégoire* by Eugène Scribe (collaborating with Henri Boisseaux and Antoine Louis Clapisson), which began its run at the Théâtre Lyrique in Paris in February 1861.[34] The fact that Béranger's poem was very well known is obvious from the comment of one reviewer of the operetta: "Madame Grégoire, whose reputation for earthiness has, thanks to her cabaret, long been known, has furnished MM. Scribe and Boisseaux the canvas of a joyous intrigue, half carnivalesque, half pompadour, upon which M. Clapisson has embroidered profusely with his habitual spirit his pleasant melodies."[35]

And, in 1867, when Courbet exhibited his painting, Randon, in the text accompanying his caricature, also gave witness to the widespread familiarity with Béranger's original, by which he judged Courbet's derivation: "MADAME GREGOIRE. Is it at all possible that this woman would have had the audacity to pass herself off to M. Courbet as Mère Grégoire, that good and amiable gossip of sparkling eye, ruddy complexion, and laughing mouth, the one we all know? [. . .] Ah! dear and illustrious master! What an error you have made!"[36]

Courbet's "error" had been to reinterpret Béranger, giving the stamp of a real cabaret mistress to a personage many wished to see only as a buxom, laughing, and amiable woman. She is, in Courbet's image, remote from the conventions of beauty, a woman whose ruddy features and self-conscious gesture give her a formidable presence. Courbet has wrenched Béranger's figure out of the pleasant fiction of a song and made her as real as is possible in the illusions of art. And her reality was offensive to Silvestre and to others precisely because of this lack of idealization, this reminder that the models and shopkeepers and ordinary people he preferred were not the middle-class or aristocratic beauties that most contemporaries expected to find in "art."

Courbet's appreciation of Béranger was, in this sense, very well judged, more so than that of his friends Baudelaire, Champfleury, or Proudhon. Baudelaire's sense of the elegant was offended by Béranger, whom he dismissed as vulgar and lacking real talent. Champfleury had more respect for the "national poet," but was hardly enthusiastic.[37] Proudhon did admire Béranger, it is true, and his analysis of the poet was published by Béranger's ardent defender, Arthur Arnould, in 1864, three years before Courbet's painting was shown in public.[38] Proudhon called Béranger "the premier French poet of the nineteenth century," but he said that this was owing to his being the bearer of an old tradition, not to any originality of his own. Proudhon's preference for ideas over sensations made him regret Béranger's "retrograde and licentious love," and he lamented the poet's inability to write epic poems or tragedies.

We cannot really know what Courbet thought of Béranger except what we can deduce from "Madame Grégoire." The qualities that Proudhon least liked – Béranger's sensuality and his love of the women and men of ordinary cabarets – are those that Courbet would have most appreciated. Courbet was a sensual and impulsive man, with a strong dose of anarchism that suited his egocentric temperament. As an artist, he was free to ignore the philosopher's demand for a "higher" form of idea than those in popular songs. As an independent, without attachment to a specific political credo, he was free to identify Béranger's quintessential Frenchness with "the people," from whom Béranger derived his art.

Courbet finished his life in exile, and it is a temptation to liken his appreciation of Béranger to that of many of France's most notable political exiles: Hugo, Blanc, Sue, Leroux, Ledru-Rollin, d'Angers, and Thoré. Their sense of nationhood tested, and perhaps exalted, by banishment, they did not begrudge Béranger his foibles, as did Baudelaire and Proudhon, but honored his achievement as a gift to France. Exiles of other countries, including Marx, Garibaldi, and Heine, also admired Béranger. They and Courbet would probably have endorsed Thoré's words in his letter to Béranger that served as preface to his review of the Salon of 1845:

> You have proved well that there are no small subjects or little forms at all, only small artists; for genius alters the proportions of all things. You have taken the song and elevated it to the ode and the poem. You have taken beggars and made great philosophers of them. You have taken the demented and made them into seers. Writing about bottles and tavern keepers, or just about everything, you have reanimated the French spirit and evoked generous feelings of patriotism and Equality. You are, as Pierre Leroux had said, the son of that great generation of the end of the eighteenth century who made the Revolution. You are common man and philosopher, like Diderot and Voltaire, and like them, you have placed your poetry in the service of Humanity.[39]

Chapter 5

The Decorative and the Natural in Monet's *Cathedrals*

The words "decorative" and "decoration" are not neutral terms like "painting" or "sculpture." They are instead well freighted with the weight that assumptions or prejudices place upon them. In the early 1890s, "décoratif" and "décoration" came to the forefront in the discussions of French art, and were applied to Monet's paintings in series, the *Haystacks* (more correctly, *Stacks of Grain*) exhibited in 1891, the *Poplars* in 1892, the *Cathedrals* in 1895, *Mornings on the Seine*, *Cliffs at Pourville*, views of Norway, and seven more *Cathedrals* in 1898, and the *Nymphéas* (or *Waterlilies*) in 1900. For most conservative reviewers (Camille Mauclair, for example), Monet's series were merely decorative, and lacked the qualities that were required of great painting. For more alert critics, like Georges Lecomte or Gustave Geffroy, the series were great art in part because they were decorative.

To recover something of the complexity of "décoratif" and "décoration" in the 1890s, as applied to Monet's art, we need to be aware of different meanings then, and we also need to recognize the peculiar twist that was given to these terms during the century thereafter. The defense of abstract art grew in part from theories of the decorative but it did so at the cost of denying to the term its real complexity. The twentieth century's need to legitimate abstraction, and its growing distance from nineteenth-century naturalism, led critics and artists alike to stress the pure color patterns of Monet's series, as though nature, that is, subject, had nothing to do with them. In this process, "decorative" was stripped of most of its real weight, and rose to the surface as a virtual equivalent of "abstraction." Monet's series came to be viewed as progenitors of post-1945 serial painting, and instead of regarding each picture of a series for the way it differed from its mates, and for its relation to its subject, critics treated it as one of so many units stamped out by a master decorator.

There are four major components of the "décoratif" in Monet's series:

1. The ensemble, that is, the exhibition of a series as a co-ordinated scheme, whose shared subject and composition gave special meaning to the overall effect the paintings had on the viewer. This permitted them, *grosso modo*, to approximate numerous decorative ensembles in sixteenth- to eighteenth-

• From *Aspects of Monet: A Symposium [1981] on the Artist's Life and Times*, ed. John Rewald and Frances Weitzenhoffer (New York, 1984): 160–79.

century interiors (with the notable difference that they were not commissioned for a fixed emplacement, and were dispersed after being exhibited).

2. Their relative flatness, that is, their stress on surface effects of color and pattern, at the expense of illusions of depth and solidity. In this they seemed to conform to the esthetic of the wall surface, as distinct from traditional easel painting.
3. Their glorification of color, Monet's *enveloppe* of color-light, often in intense hues, which supplanted traditional modeling in light and dark values. To conservatives, the dominance of color was associated with architectural decoration more than with easel painting.
4. Their subjects, which lent themselves to the decorative by eliminating the human figure, and by embodying that kind of natural form (even the weather-worn cathedrals were "natural" architecture) which was conducive to restful contemplation.

The first two of these four components are the ones most congenial to current interests, and they have been well dealt with, particularly by Steven Levine, in his indispensable dissertation of 1974.[1] It is the third and fourth components which need attention, and in this chapter I hope to restore idea content to the concept of the decorative by concentrating upon them, especially upon the fourth. Because Monet seldom wrote directly about art, I am going to rely heavily upon contemporary critics, citing from them more generously than is customary, in order to provide adequate samples of the kinds of evidence I have used.

The first thing to establish is the astonishing redefinition of "le décoratif" which Monet and the other Impressionists helped bring about. As witness, I will call upon Ernest Chesneau, a relatively conservative French critic, and one of John Ruskin's chief admirers in France. In 1881 Chesneau published an introduction to Edouard Guichard's *Dessins de décoration des principaux maîtres*, which states that French decoration had concerned itself too exclusively with form, particularly with servile imitation instead of creative form, with three-dimensional illusion rather than "suitable adaptations" (*la convenance des appropriations*).[2] Artists producing decorative works should not discard nature, but should seek better means of drawing inspiration from her, of opening the public's eye "to the immense, infinite world of admirable forms offered by the exploitation of the vegetable realm in the purely decorative direction" (*dans le sens purement décoratif*). Nature, that is, lies at the heart of decoration, an important parallel to Monet's conception. Reversing the usual order, Chesneau placed color above form in his definition of the decorative:

> As an element of art, color suffices by itself without aid of idea; it can be and it is, in effect, the special aim of a certain application and direction of the art of painting. [. . .] Finally, employed via juxtaposition, with the aid of material of limited extent as in textiles, rugs and wallpapers, or via divided tones, as in painting properly speaking, it constitutes the most active and seductive element

> of decorative art. Color exercises on human faculties an action which varies according to external and to individual circumstances, but a real action which must be reckoned with.[3]

This represents, in French theory, the triumph of ideas going back to Delacroix, then carried forward by the Impressionists, in which color supplants form (that is, light and dark) as the essential element of painting, and of decoration. This was a fundamental revolution, consummated by the 1890s. Some did not like the change. Camille Mauclair, writing of Impressionist landscape in 1895, said that "Their art no longer does anything except charm the eyes. They sense this quite indistinctly, since their great word [. . .] is *the decorative*, that is, an art founded on the delectation of color by itself, applied to distortions of beings, flowers, accessories, according to the fundamental principle of ornamentation."[4] However, all of the critics well disposed towards Impressionism welcomed color as the heart of the new idea of "le décoratif." One of the most interesting texts is that of Georges Lecomte, friend of Seurat and of Pissarro. His article in the *Revue indépendante* of 1892 is a key document in the reconciliation of the senior Impressionists' aims with those of the younger generation. It begins by saying that Impressionist division of color-light

> appears to us, not as a definitive result, not as a pinnacle reached, but rather as a propitious means of embodying more certain bearings: permitting the restitution of the complex elements of natural harmonies, it thus allows the better rendering of their decorative magnificence. And it is precisely this regard for decorative beauty which, it seems to us, beyond any secondary concern, ought to be the distinctive sign of our era in the general history of art.

The article continues by stressing the natural origins of color dominance, while allowing the artist to select from nature, to exercise his artistic judgment: "Above all, are not nature's noble sights, if the eye can remove insignificant and momentary details from them, as much stamped by colors as by lines with the most majestic decorative beauty?"[5] Monet is then introduced as a leader in decorative color:

> Finally, the vigorous talent of M. Claude Monet – who for a long time limited himself, but with what power of evocation! to the rendering of the fugitive intensities of ephemeral natural effects – seems more and more to abstract the durable character of things from complex appearances and, by a more synthetic and premeditated rendering, to accentuate meaning and decorative beauty.[6]

Lecomte's conception of decoration is like that of Monet's close friends Octave Mirbeau, Gustave Geffroy, and Georges Clemenceau: it incorporates a vital sense of nature, for nature and the artificial conventions of art were conceived of as essential components, each requiring the other.

> Naturally the joy of an exquisite ornamentation will only be felt if this search for ornamentation is not too obvious and has not been pursued to the detriment of the character of things. [. . .] In these works, the descriptive aspect of beings and things is never sacrificed to decorative preoccupation nor to amplification of character. Their beauty resides solely in plastic beauty, by virtue of skillful dispositions and harmonies of lines and tones, without deliberate intention, without evading any of the essential plastic qualities in a painted work. And yet the intellectuality of such an art is evident. These evocations of nature pass well beyond reality and purely external ornamentation. From their limpid harmonies thought extricates itself, dream finds its way. They render nature's great mystery. This painting satisfies the soul as much as it enchants the eye.[7]

For Lecomte and others, most particularly for Mirbeau, Clemenceau, Geffroy, and later for Léon Bazalgette and Roger Marx, Monet's special genius was to have formulated a decorative painting that led the viewer to a special realm of "dream," "reverie," and "illusion." And just as the artificial conventions of his art were steeped in nature, so too the *rêve* he provoked was not of an otherworldly, mystical kind, but one permeated by an ardent feeling for nature. Painting, that is, was the result of a collaboration of the subjective and the objective, in which the objective remained of fundamental significance. Mirbeau, writing of Monet in 1889, proclaimed "the truth – unique source of the dream,"[8] and in 1891 he wrote "What enchants, in Claude Monet, is that evidently a realist, he does not limit himself to translating nature. [. . .] The landscapes of Claude Monet are, in a manner of speaking, the illumination of states of consciousness of the planet, and of the supra-sensitive forms of our thoughts." In Monet's art, he concluded, "the dream becomes the reality."[9]

Geffroy also insisted on Monet's bringing poetic reverie, this superior state of a viewer's consciousness, out of deliberate choice of subject:

> For one of the numerous fantasies born of the accidental etiquette "Impressionism" is to believe in the non-choice of subjects by these thoughtful and willful artists. Choice was, on the contrary, always their lively and important concern. But it is thus that legends are made: these painters are customarily portrayed as instruments indifferently aimed at every sight, and the mistake goes along, repeating itself. [. . .]
>
> How can one believe, for example, that Monet has not expressly chosen the admirable décor of verdure which shades the *Branch of the Seine near Giverny*, this double ornamental cut-out of branches profiled on the sky and reflected by the water, this alley of foliage in which glide the delicious phantasmagoria of sky and misty clouds. [. . .] Landscapes familiar and dreamy, dark forms, distant phantoms, mysterious evocations, limpid mirrrors.[10]

For all the writers I have so far cited, Monet's *rêve* was not a religious one, far from it, but one based solidly on nature, in keeping with the goals of

Impressionism. There has been a trend in recent years to link Monet's decorative series too exclusively to the preoccupations of the Nabis and other anti-naturalist artists of the 1890s. This is a serious error, for it denies the markedly secular streak in Monet's art. Lecomte's essay of 1892, from which I have already cited, bears this out. Its second half is an attack upon the Nabis and upon religious art, with his point of view summarized in one sentence: "Now, in painting, the decorative is only acceptable as the prolongation, the logical development, of the true."[11] The attack on Nabis painting (Maurice Denis, Paul Sérusier, et al.) is because:

> It is no longer the simplification of forms, but really the erosion of forms. Well, such syntheses, destructive of the truthful, such interpretations so distant from reality, can no longer seduce plastically, even if they end up in harmonious ensembles. [. . .] What is true for drawing is even more so for color. With the pretext of synthesis and decoration, they cover canvases with flat tones which do not at all restore the luminous limpidities of the atmosphere, which do not at all give the envelope of things, the depth, the aerial perspective. [. . .] One arrives at a confusing image which in no way recalls the harmony, at once precise and suggestive, of the natural décor.[12]

Lecomte went on to complain that in Nabis painting:

> Exterior objects, their proper meaning scorned, are only of concern as material representatives of the ideal archetype, as the finite manifestation of infinite Beauty, of God. They concern themselves with expressing faith by plastic means and, on behalf of religion, they sacrifice the essential plastic qualities.[13]

And he concluded his article with the following words:

> And in truth, out of reaction to the reborn religiosities, our sympathies go out to an Art entirely Modern which, far from being enamored of the past and of fallen beliefs, will find enough pretexts for its manifestations in the study of physical and moral man, envisaged in what his nature has that is general and permanent, in natural splendors with their infinite poetry, mysterious and not mystical, in the greatness of human efforts, and in the justice of new social groupings.[14]

In Lecomte's last phrase we detect the friend of Camille Pissarro, and we need not believe that Monet was much concerned with issues of social justice – certainly not in Pissarro's radical terms. However, the surprising thing is that this laical ideal characterizes the writings of Monet's friends and of those critics who favored his art, and surely reflects the artist's own ideas (at the end of his life he left instructions opposing a Christian burial service). This is even true of the writings about the *Cathedrals* shown in 1895. To explain how paintings of a notable religious monument were regarded as non-religious is the purpose of the rest of this chapter.[15]

When these *Cathedrals* were exhibited, all critics recognized them as secular representations (pl. 28). Conservatives who did not like Monet attacked them for being merely a decorative cycle that failed to do justice to the religious spirit inherent in the building. Camille Mauclair thought that decorative painting was inferior because it did not transport the viewer to higher thought. "The esthetic and the effect of decorative art are not to make one think of a man, but of an order of things arranged by him: it is a descriptive and deforming art, it is an assortment of displays whose function is to be *seen*."[16] As for Monet's *Cathedrals*, Mauclair wrote that "The very idea that the gothic, a cerebral art *par excellence*, serves as theme for this pagan, so superbly sensual, is a bit offensive."[17] A number of modern critics have continued to feel that the decorative content of Monet's series overwhelms the idea content. Kenneth Clark, in his influential text on landscape, called Monet's choice of the cathedral "text-book examples" of decadence.[18]

Of course the most famous defense of the *Cathedrals* is that of Georges Clemenceau. Before turning to him, however, I want to invoke the book *L'Esprit nouveau* by Léon Bazalgette, published in 1898.[19] It contains an entire chapter called "Les Deux Cathédrales, Claude Monet et J.K. Huysmans," in which Bazalgette attacked Huysmans's then recent book, *La Cathédrale*, by comparing it to Monet's series. Huysmans is wrong, he wrote, to believe that traditional faith can survive in an era of triumphant naturalism. Monet is on the right path because:

> Entirely untrammeled by remembrances, by any creed or religious tradition, the painter considered the edifice only as a fragment of nature, according to reality, not according to religion. Occult meanings cannot trouble him for a single moment, nor can Christian symbols. His eye saw, rising up somewhere, on a spot of earth, an imposing architecture which was alternately bathed in light and dark. This caress of light on the melancholy countenance of the sanctuary of yesteryear, this union of the venerable stones and the always living sun, captivated all his being, caught up by the sight. For him it was not a question of liturgy nor of symbolism: no mystery of deciphering, no doubt of interpretation, no theological debate could touch him. Reality was there in front of him, without any ambiguity: he saw it and interpreted it.[20]

Like Lecomte in 1892, Bazalgette traced the triumph of secular naturalism:

> The individual, whom Christian dogma had isolated from nature, felt more and more that between her and himself existed the most indestructible and the deepest attachment. He believed he understood that not only was there no antagonism between his own being and the world's being, but that they were eternally united, consubstantial and interdependent; that there was thenceforth the absolute need for him to plunge, to the depths of his soul, into this fountain of life, into this ocean of nature, from which he drew the best of his abilities.[21]

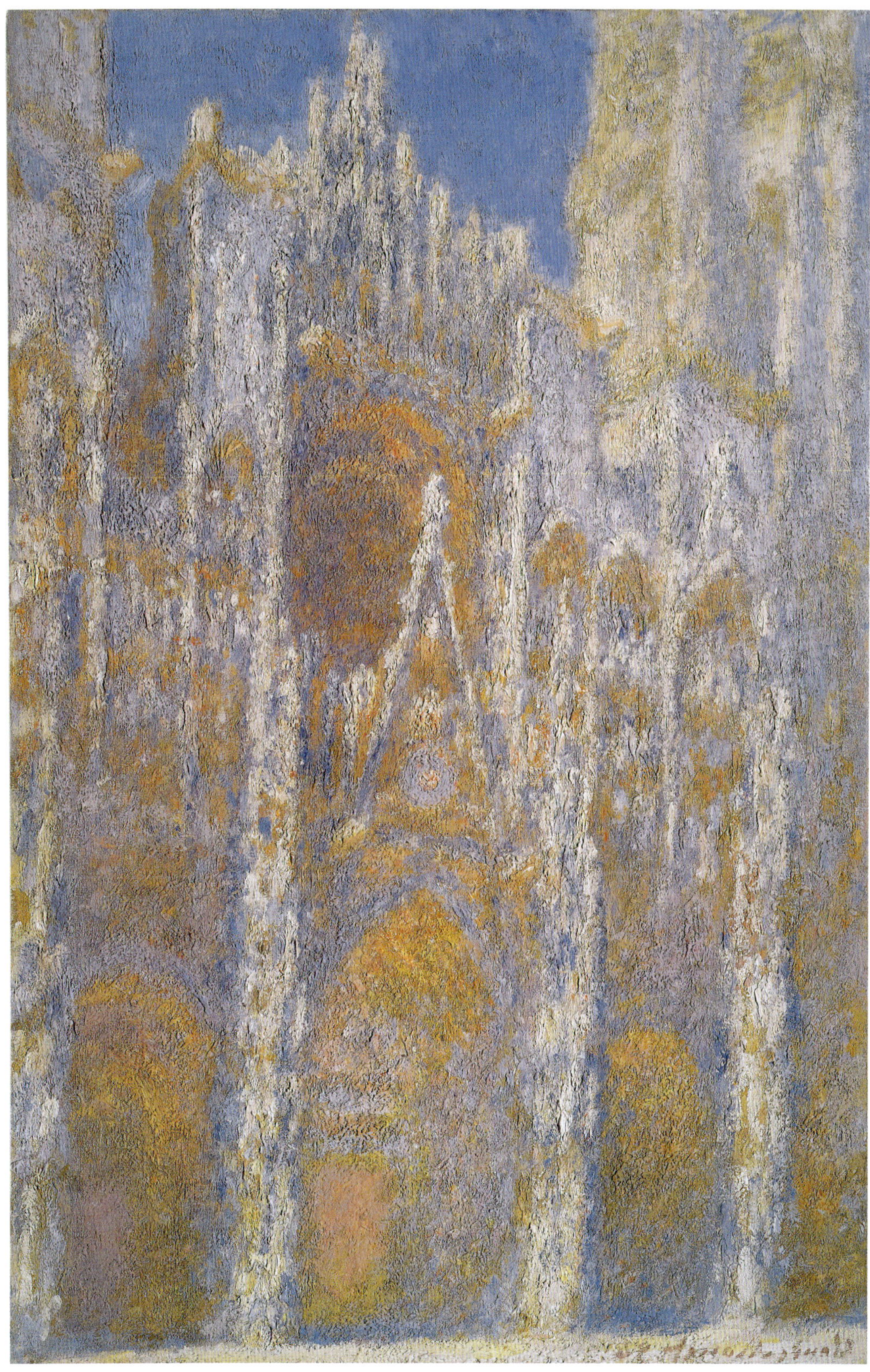

28 Claude Monet, *Rouen Cathedral at Sunset*, 1892–94. 39⅝ × 26 in. (100.6 × 66 cm.). Museum of Fine Arts, Boston, Julian Cheney Edwards Collection.

> Nature, formerly proscribed as a receptacle of impurities, regains its place and its dignity. Nothing exists except through her and every effort hoping to oppose her energies will be in vain. Thought, which no longer accepts any dogma, any revelation, submits the world to its passionate investigation. Truth is born little by little of the free and impartial examination of man, who takes his place in the immense series of beings and of worlds. [. . .] It has been remarked that this conception presents a certain analogy with the doctrine known by the name of pantheism. It leads, it is true, to a new pantheism, infinitely broader than the older conception, wholly impregnated with reality and science. [. . .] The painter of the cathedrals has sprung from there.[22]

After attacking Huysmans again, Bazalgette continued:

> Monet's work appears to us radically different: healthy, frank, vital, realist, alive. With him it is no longer a question of dogma or of resurrection. He squarely faced reality, that of yesterday, of today and of all times: it is with the vision of modern man that he forced it to reveal its secrets. From his canvases life spills out, stripped of every symbol, of every kind of artifice or lie. It is there in front of us, trembling and naked; and how much its reality seems superior to the wan effigies that we have been called upon so many times to admire! If there really is a modern art [. . .], an art linked to today's thought, the painter of the cathedrals, from every point of view, is one of its representatives.[23]

At this point there is a reference to Georges Clemenceau, whose essay of 1895, "Révolution de Cathédrales," profoundly influenced Bazalgette:

> The marvel of Monet's way of sensing things [wrote Clemenceau] is that he sees the stone vibrate and gives it to us vibrating, bathed in luminous waves which collide and break up into flashing sparkles. It is the end of the immutable canvas of death. Now the stone itself lives, one senses it moulting its former life as it turns to its next. No longer is it congealed for the viewer.[24]

"It is the end of the immutable canvas of death." For Clemenceau, as for Bazalgette, the cathedral itself and the priests' use of it represented a bygone era, a faith that no longer was genuine – hence death.[25] Monet, in effect took over the role of the priest, laicizing the cathedral by painting it, restoring it to modern man by re-creating it in the presence of intense natural light.

> And these gray cathedrals, which are of purple or of azure buffeted by gold, and these white cathedrals, of fiery portals streaming with green, red or blue flames, and these rainbow cathedrals, which seem to be seen through a rotating prism, and these blue cathedrals, which are rose, all of a sudden give you a durable sight not of twenty, but of a hundred, a thousand, a million states of the eternal cathedral in the endless cycle of sunlight. It amounts to life itself, as much as sensing it can be granted us, in its most living reality.[26]

By restoring life to the cathedral, Monet transferred the inner essence of the medieval era from the outmoded priesthood to the artist. The artist's creativity is now the locus of true spirituality, that is, of non-material poetic and imaginative thought. Clemenceau repeatedly pointed to Monet's taking over the role of priest as intercessor between man and the universal force of natural creativity. He referred to the paintings as "twenty marvelous revelations," calling them "miracles," and describing their light as "divine mist."[27]

This idea that Monet, and not the priesthood, was the modern interpreter of the cathedral, was widespread in 1895. "A. F.," the correspondent of that very secular journal *Gil Blas*, wrote:

> it is the historic and enflowered cathedral that Monet has wanted to beatify in his recent years of work, because cathedrals have a soul, and one could believe that, after centuries of embodying the mystical aspirations of the multitudes, they have become human, they have become flesh and flower. [. . .] Silence! the smoky monument, where light carves out allegories, seems surrounded by transparent veils; but the sun is seductive and attracts us to the pinnacles, like so many congealed jets of water, and then it is like the assumption of the cathedral.[28]

For this critic, for Clemenceau, Bazalgette, and others, Monet's extraordinary colored light was, in painting, a modern equivalent of the miracle of Gothic architecture. They do not offer more than a vague and general comparison, but they were aware, of course, that the medieval builder, by perforating his walls with openings, had eliminated mass in favor of colored light. Material substance was dematerialized, and series of stained-glass windows were the most remarkable proofs of this. Monet's series of paintings also dematerialized mass and substance, and in a decorative sequence, color-light replaced traditional *chiaroscuro* as the principal structure of art. God's light has become nature's light, and man has seized nature thanks to his own creativity, without the need for God.

That Rouen Cathedral was a deliberate choice on Monet's part is not to be doubted. He could have chosen to paint the law courts or the stock exchange or another kind of governmental or financial institution. We know instinctively that this would be ludicrous for Monet, owing to the different associations with neoclassical architecture. For most of the Impressionists, medieval architecture was associated with naturalism. Government buildings of classical style were associated with authority, that is, with government, with bureaucracy, rationality, rules, and recipes. Gothic architecture was widely believed to be the result of the willing efforts of many artisans and artists, who were given considerable freedom to choose their decorative motifs from nature. This view had gained strength during the Gothic Revival earlier in the century, for which John Ruskin, then William Morris, became the principal spokesmen. It combined several attitudes that the Impressionists found to their liking: the communitarian, or social origins of

Gothic architecture; the presumed freedom of the individual artisan to develop his own motifs as he helped decorate the building; the source in nature of these decorations, and the resultant rich and irregular profusion of forms, rather than the despised regularity of Renaissance and neo-classical architecture. From these ideas had grown the English Arts and Crafts movement which, long before Monet painted Rouen Cathedral, had secularized and humanized medieval art. By the 1890s, Ruskin, Morris, and the Arts and Crafts had made impressive inroads among the avant-garde in France. Ernest Chesneau, already referred to, was one of several major spokesmen in France for Ruskinian ideas, and Bazalgette was an outspoken admirer of the English critic.[29]

Further evidence for the association of naturalism, medieval art, honest craftsmanship, and the decorative, lies in three writings by Renoir. They do not prove the case for Monet, but they do show the prevalence of such ideas in Impressionist circles, and reinforce the interpretation of the *Cathedrals* that rises logically from a study of Monet's critics. The first of Renoir's writings, "L'Art décoratif et contemporain," was published in Georges Rivière's journal *L'Impressionniste* in 1877. The second is his proposal for a "Société des Irrégularistes" sent to Durand-Ruel in 1884, and the third is his preface to Henry Mottez's publication of his father's edition of Cennino Cennini in 1911.[30] In these publications, Renoir attacks modern engineering and machinism, and praises Gothic, early Renaissance, and eighteenth-century decorative arts for the following qualities: they were the result of communities of artists working harmoniously together; the individual artist was allowed considerable freedom in composing his share of the decorative ensemble, and his instincts were encouraged; this instinctual effort was the essence of creativity, itself a natural force that found its models in nature; natural models were varied and irregular, and so was the art that resulted, art which displayed the craft of the hand. The hated enemy was finish, polish, the ruled line of the engineer.

The relevance of these ideas for Monet, Renoir, and Pissarro is easily understood (one need think only of their "rough" brushwork), for of course Renoir is expressing his views rather than speaking objectively for the early eras he admired. Much of what he wrote would have been endorsed by his fellow Impressionists, including his dislike of modern rationalism, which he associated with industry and the despised spirit of commercialism. It was with regret that Renoir noted the demise of traditional faith, which had, he believed, sustained the communitarian spirit and the art he admired. Renoir's lament for the passing of traditional faith, and his reluctant admission of the new secular age, were not in the spirit of Monet, Clemenceau, Geffroy, Lecomte, or Bazalgette, all of them pronounced freethinkers. But his views overlapped significantly with theirs, particularly when he insisted that it is the artist, in the new materialist era, who carries on the essence of the old spirit. In his proposal for a Société des Irrégularistes he wrote:

> Among other conditions of admission, the rules will expressly stipulate for architecture: that all ornament must be made after nature without any motif, flower, leaf, figure, etc., etc. . . . , being exactly repeated; that the slightest form must be executed by hand without the aid of instruments of precision; that as for the plastic arts, goldsmiths, silversmiths, and others . . . will need to exhibit alongside their finished work the drawings or paintings after nature which were used to compose them. [. . .] Photographs of celebrated monuments or decorations which bear evidence of the principle of irregularity will be acquired at the Société's expense and placed at the disposition of the public in a special room.[31]

Renoir, therefore, would have understood why Monet became obsessed with painting Rouen Cathedral, one of these "celebrated monuments or decorations which bear evidence of the principle of irregularity." And Pissarro, rather lukewarm toward Monet's earlier series, was struck with admiration at the sight of the *Cathedrals* in 1895. He wrote to his son Lucien that he was "very excited by this extraordinary mastery" and that "the Cathedrals are much argued over and also much praised by Degas, me, Renoir and others."[32]

That nature was the source of Monet's art, both "real and decorative," is the leitmotif of the writings of his friends Geffroy, Mirbeau, and Clemenceau. His painting was "real" because it was based upon diligent study of nature, "decorative" because it was transformed by artistic creativity, not merely imitated. For Clemenceau, the fundamental argument, one that he never ceased repeating, is that Monet's goal was to translate natural impulses. This was true not just of the *Cathedrals*, of course, but of his other series, including the great *Nymphéas*. "What he proposed doing," wrote Clemenceau, "was to follow nature in every particular; as closely as possible."[33] In discussing the "decorations of the Waterlilies" (*décorations des Nymphéas*, Monet's own phrase), Clemenceau insisted on their intellectual, poetic, and real content. "Decoration" was not, as later critics would have it, a withdrawal from nature and reality, but a celebration of the artist's poetic devotion to her. It is true, we lack Monet's own words about his art, but in Geffroy, Mirbeau, and Clemenceau we have the testimony of close friends all of whom agree on the major issues I have raised here. Their writings must reflect Monet's ideas, since we know he was not timid about voicing them.

> To what Monet attempted to achieve [wrote Clemenceau], not one of his paintings fails to bear striking witness, sometimes liberally supported by its author's lively commentary. For no critique found him without a retort, and his rough tone and cutting words showed sufficiently that this man, benevolent and fond of laughing, had given too much of himself to his art to speak of it dispassionately.[34]

If I had to summarize Monet's views, I would rely on the meaning of the words cited by Clemenceau in his essay on the *Nymphéas*. The professional writer shows in Clemenceau's choice of words, and Monet's exact phrases must have been different, but I believe that this remarkable passage gives us the essence of Monet's naturalism and of his "decorative vision:"

> How I can still hear the gently authoritative tone of this friendly voice, in front of those demonstrations of nature, his Water Garden: "While you seek philosophically the world itself," he said with his pleasant smile, "I simply bend my efforts towards a maximum of appearances, in strict correlation with unknown realities. When one is on the level of concordant appearances, one cannot be very far from reality, or at least from what we can know of it. The only thing I have done is to look at what the universe showed me, in order to render witness to it by my brush. Is that not something? Your fault is to wish to reduce the world to your own measure, whereas, by increasing your knowledge of things, you would increase knowledge of yourselves."[35]

Chapter 6

Impressionism, Originality, and Laissez-Faire

With the advent of Symbolism in the late 1880s, and the growth of an anti-naturalist current in the paintings of younger artists (Seurat, van Gogh, Gauguin), Impressionist art came to be regarded as an unthinking form of naturalism. The Symbolist critics praised the new painters by claiming that their art was rich in intellectual, expressive, and decorative ideas, as opposed to Impressionism which, they believed, merely added a heightened color sense to the old Renaissance tradition of verisimilitude. Impressionist naturalism was dismissed by Félix Fénéon, Seurat's chief defender, in these derisive terms:

> The spectacle of the heavens, the water, greenery, varies from moment to moment, professed the first Impressionists. To imprint one of these fugitive appearances on the retina was their goal. Thus arose the necessity to paint a landscape in one seance and a tendency to make nature grimace in order to prove that the moment was unique and that one would never again see it.[1]

This view became commonplace in the twentieth century, and until the 1940s it was generally believed that in their mature work, Morisot, Degas, Monet, Renoir, Cassatt, and Manet were depicting their own society without analyzing it. They enjoyed theaters and promenades in the country and simply represented these innocent pleasures. Praise for them therefore fell not on their images of contemporary life, but on their innovations in color, brushwork, and other aspects of "pure painting," so congenial to the era of abstraction, given the premium it has placed on the formal components of painting.

Since the 1940s this view has been discredited, and scholars have expanded the range of issues eligible for analysis to include complicated interrelationships among painting, literature, and the history of Paris from 1848 to the 1880s.[2] We now know that Impressionism was not a simple-minded representation of color-light, and we are constantly reminded of the painters' innovations, for which the words "radical" and "revolutionary" are frequently used (especially by corporate sponsors of the recent spate of "blockbuster" Impressionist exhibitions). We have learned that Impressionism really was born of adversity and miscomprehension; its new brushwork, color, and spatial organization were subversive; its devotion to the immediate present was profoundly shocking; its subjects and

• From the *Radical History Review* 38 (1987): 7–15.

attitudes undermined the whole concept of what art was, what art schools should teach, and how art exhibitions should be organized.

All this is well worth pointing to, but were the Impressionists radicals? On the surface of it, no. Caillebotte, Degas, Manet, and Morisot were upper-class Parisians who can readily be assimilated with their peers, and who demonstrated no wish to make profound alterations of their society. Monet was the upstart son of a shopkeeper, eager to be accepted, and Renoir, the only Impressionist of artisan-class origins, was critical of the ruthlessness of urban-industrial society, but wanted to return to a premodern patrician order.[3] Pissarro was the only political radical among the painters, but he remains a special case, and he dealt with rural life, not with the urban and suburban society the others preferred.

What is needed in order to assess the label "radical" are inquiries along new lines. Further investigation of the artists' subjects, especially their preference for themes of leisure and entertainment, should be revealing.[4] Systematic study of the artists' clients and dealers, not yet undertaken, would certainly be rewarding. Many of their early patrons, for example, were not long-established members of high society, but wielders of new money: the financier Ernest May, the banker Albert Hecht, the retailer and speculator Ernest Hoschedé, the renowned baritone Jean-Baptiste Faure. The links between the new money and the new painting are doubtless there, but will remain speculative until someone does the work. In addition to these aspects of social history, we should look more deeply into the often discussed issues of the "caught moment," the hedonistic indulgence in natural light and out-of-doors living, the pronounced individualism of the painters, and their concern for originality. This chapter concentrates on the last two of these.[5]

The Impressionists' devotion to contemporary phenomena is now recognized as one of the key elements of their art. They looked to Paris and its suburbs for most of their subjects; even when they turned to the countryside, they represented it as though it were newly seen, free of the literary, historical, and moral overlays that had characterized the work of the preceding generation. They dealt in what are, after all, slight events in the history of humankind, mere ephemeral moments seized from the pleasure of leisure-time activities. Not only did they turn toward present-day subjects, they also emphasized features that pointed to the immediate and the momentary. There are many ways to represent a moored sailboat or a ballet rehearsal, but Monet and Degas used broken brushwork, indistinct contours, bright colors, and striking compositional geometry to induce in the viewer a sense of the spontaneous, the unresolved, that which is just now being seen. Impressionism, wrote César Graña:

> assumes a world in which *moments* can exist as total units of experience: where self-feeling, as well as the perception of others, has a new swiftness and, within that, a new, flickering poignancy; where the ephemeral and the unguarded can be memorable and must be followed and scanned by the painter with a flashing perceptivity of his own.[6]

Graña's words point to the combination of external observation and subjectivity that marked Impressionism. When the painters concentrated upon the illusion of what could be seen in the flash of a moment, they seemed to reduce experience to the self, unsupported by references to other moments, to other experiences. This was upsetting to many, for the viewer, required to concentrate on this one moment, was denied contact with other moments – with memory, in effect.

Denial of memory meant denial of history, a pervasive consequence of the Impressionists' orientation. "History" was not simply the discarded subjects of earlier painting, but the means by which they were rendered, particularly the structure of light and dark that gave conventional painting the satisfactory illusion of three dimensions. The exaltation of bright color and patchy brushwork was the Impressionists' way of presenting what one could see, without recourse to what one "knows" by virtue of traditional artistic training. This was only an *apparent* spontaneity, for Impressionism was just as artfully constructed as earlier painting. However, to many observers, then and later, the concentration on spontaneous vision and the absence of memory-trained techniques condemned the Impressionists to a superficial indulgence in pleasures. Max Friedlaender, gifted historian of Lowlands art, could not grant profundity to Impressionism because he believed that seeing was not just looking with the eyes, but with the judgments provided by memory and history:

> The man who knows most sees most; he sees more than is actually visible to him in a given instant and from a given standpoint. The Impressionists, however, were at pains to forget what they knew so as to notice only what fell within their field of vision. [. . .]
>
> The Impressionists, deliberately forgoing all criticism and judgment in respect of the phenomenal world, appealing neither to sentiment nor to sense of humor, absorbing the prismatic glitter of things with a positive neutrality, mark the visual art off from the art of poetry, from history, from satire, as also from the affecting, entertaining, instructive or informative type of narrative. The picture is no longer the exemplar of an idea, does not point beyond the visible, strikes us as something unique, individual, like a portrait.[7]

For this reason, Friedlaender denied the label "genre" to Impressionism. It lacked the moral ideas that he required for his definition. Similarly, Graña, while admiring the Impressionists, said that they cannot be called "naturalistic" because their art is one of "amiable lyricism" that mirrors but does not interpret contemporary life.[8]

The Impressionists' disavowal of memory and of history was one symptom of the gulf between present and past that opened ever wider with the spread of the urban-industrial revolution. History, mythology, and religion, for centuries the chief points of reference for painting, were discarded with surprising rapidity during the third quarter of the nineteenth century, first by the Barbizon artists in the second halves of their careers, then by the Impressionists (after youthful essays in traditional subjects). An education in Greek and Latin, in Homer and Virgil, and in the Bible, had little real function for the entrepreneurs of industrial capitalism: "If you're so smart, why ain't you rich?" These premodern subjects, which had been attached to monarchy, nobility, and theocracy, eventually ceased to underpin public education (private schools, out of class solidarity, retained the old curriculum for much longer). The Impressionists were ahead of most of their contemporaries when they denounced the Academy and its *retardataire* allegiance to those traditional sources.

To uproot the past was no easy step for the painters to take, and this is evident when we reflect on the upheavals it caused. Manet's mocking of history in his *Déjeuner sur l'herbe* and *Olympia* (both Musée d'Orsay, Paris), as well as other pictures of the 1860s, was linked to his defiance of the government's guardians of history – the directors of fine arts, the Academy, the juries of official exhibitions. The other Impressionists did battle with the government by organizing their own exhibitions, a step which effectively, by the end of the century, demoted the Academy's shows to minor status, and set the pattern for twentieth-century exhibitions, so often sponsored by independent artists' societies. A number of the Impressionists had only perfunctory periods of training in the Ecole des Beaux-Arts, and their example led to its rapid decline, if we are to judge by the pattern of artists who dominated early modernism. Few of them studied in sanctioned ways, and by ignoring government exhibitions, prizes, and fellowships, rendered them obsolete. The whole world of official painting came tumbling down, at least as far as alert young artists were concerned.

Because they turned toward contemporary subjects, the Impressionists had to disavow tradition and its institutions – hence their constant demands for freedom. Critics close to them made a virtual litany of this demand. Manet's friend Théodore Duret wrote of all "true artists" that they

> are vigorous persons, profoundly original, most often obeying in their methods of production a kind of instinct and inherent natural strength. Let all these individuals develop instead of trying to restrict them, let them freely express the outstanding aspects of their nature. Everything that will contribute towards assuring the individual his freedom of action will contribute to the development of the artist.[9]

The Impressionists and their supporters in the press demanded freedom from the restraints of official art policies. In this context, the term "freedom" has political meaning, for it paralleled the freedom from prior restraints that entrepreneurs were pleading for. Duret's words (including the phrase "methods of production"), could have served the cause of a Parisian businessman trying to market a product in the face of government restrictions that survived from an earlier era. Edmond Duranty, another friend of the Impressionists, after invoking the word "liberté" several times, used the famous economic phrase "laissez-faire, laissez-passer" to initiate a plea for freedom from "this bureaucracy of the mind, steeped in rules, that weighs on us in this country."[10]

Freedom, quite logically for the artists, was required both for the sake of producing their works (art historians recognize this) and for marketing them (most art historians avoid this). The *laissez-faire* market they fought for is the most obvious comparison with the commercial world. Having rebelled against the subjects of a prior age, they had excluded themselves from the patronage of government and church, and were forced to develop their own market. The role of private dealers greatly expanded in their era, and some of the painters, particularly Monet and Degas, were very clever in manipulating their markets. They played one dealer off another, learned various maneuvers to keep their prices up, and bypassed commercial galleries when they could reach clients directly. In December 1873 the Impressionists formed their own exhibition society, duly incorporated as a co-operative business, and began displaying their wares in rented quarters in the fashionable center of Paris.

Forced to seek their own outlets, the painters had to claim value for their product. This value was located in their originality, in the very way their works were produced. Their paintings were said to be the result of the creative individual working in freedom. Creativity, that is, was identified with the individual, not within the social, and originality was the precise locus of value. Originality in the business world was equated with invention, and it is revealing that both words are used repeatedly by the defenders of the Impressionists. Real artists, according to Duret, "are inventors, men who have an unusual character, an original way of feeling and, if they are painters, a touch, a sense of color, a way of drawing that are entirely personal." Their works are original because they do not imitate existing ones. They earn their way, furthermore, because they succeed "by painful labor, a tension of all their faculties, in giving form to their conceptions." And these forms are like other products whose originality guarantees their value: "new forms, original creations."[11]

By using the phrases "painful labor" and "original creations," Duret was crediting the Impressionists with two kinds of entrepreneurial virtue: hard, steady work and brilliant flashes of genius. These two values were often separated. Horatio Alger's boy heroes made it the hard way, with patience and dutiful attention to the boss's wishes. Victor Appleton's Tom Swift also made it by the end of each of his books, but it was invariably thanks to his remarkable inventive powers, such as building a giant searchlight in his garage. The Impressionists were more like Swift than like Alger's heroes, but Duret and other critics had to allay bourgeois fears by showing that genius was accompanied by hard work and skill.

The Impressionists' originality was based upon individuality and craftsmanship, and was therefore free of the monotonous effects of that unimaginative kind of work that emulates the perfectly finished product, that is, the industrial artifact. This product was equated with clever academic art, so that Duranty, in distinguishing the Impressionists from their imitators, again used the vocabulary of commerce. In France, he wrote, "the inventor disappears in favor of the one who takes out a patent on perfecting; virtuosity wins out over naïve awkwardness, and the vulgarizer absorbs the value of the man who has innovated."[12] The Impressionists' famous brushwork was cited constantly as proof of their "naïve awkwardness," of their honest and empirical response to nature, as distinct from the hated polish of conventional painting, where brushwork was suppressed, the smooth result constituting a sign of "skill." Mere polish in painting was equated with the despised values of the bourgeoisie, who confused skill with talent, and who valued mass production over the rare, imaginative, and hand-wrought piece.

What happened over the course of the nineteenth century was simply this: artists who remained within the sanctioned institutions of art did not have to cultivate very much originality (only enough to be noticed), because the system of prizes, government purchases, and church commissions gave them a living. The requirement was to conform enough to these institutions to guarantee continued subsidies and commissions – observing tradition was literally a way to make a living. How could artists outside this closed market earn their way? Like upstart businessmen, they had to develop a new product, and in the process they had to assert its newness, its originality. Their battles with tradition were a means of establishing this essential quality or originality that a few years later was translated into market value. "Radical" or "revolutionary" in relation to the dominant institutions, they were taken up at first by a handful of patrons, usually men of new fortunes, and therefore joined the advanced thrust of the rising bourgeoisie.[13] Their enemy was not the bourgeoisie as a whole, but its stodgiest representatives who were still mired in the past, whose protectionist attitudes thwarted progress. The painters, like other advanced entrepreneurs, had difficulty making their way at first, but this very difficulty was a sign of their originality, and a half-generation later (for most, when they reached their mid-forties) their originality was the very proof of their genius to a larger segment of the middle class, who then provided the income.

Thorstein Veblen, in *The Theory of the Leisure Class* (1899), offered an analysis of this phenomenon that should be applied to artistic originality:

> Hand labor is a more wasteful method of production; hence the goods turned out by this method are more serviceable for the purpose of pecuniary reputability; hence the marks of hand labor came to be honorific, and the goods which exhibit these marks take rank as of higher grade than the corresponding machine product. Commonly, if not invariably, the honorific marks of hand labor are certain imperfections and irregularities in the lines of the hand-wrought article. [. . .] The ground of the superiority of hand-wrought goods, therefore, is a certain margin of crudeness. This margin must never be so wide as to show bungling workmanship, since that would be evidence of

> low cost, nor so narrow as to suggest the ideal precision attained only by the machine, for that would be evidence of low cost.[14]

Veblen then went on to say that the "honorific" mark is not appreciated by the ordinary mortals who prefer the perfection of the machine-made, and therefore its appreciation is a way of distinguishing oneself from the common herd.

Originality and handcraft gave distinction and, eventually, great value to the Impressionists' paintings. They were not, therefore, radicals seeking the overthrow of their society, despite their flirtations with gypsies, urban itinerants, and other marginals. They were more like other aggressive members of the bourgeoisie, doing battle with outmoded institutions in order to push themselves and their culture in new directions. Nineteenth-century industrial society thrived on its critics, using them to lurch forward, to shed old ideas, painfully and awkwardly, in a process that bound together critic and target, each requiring the other.[15] The Impressionists were the vanguard of the bourgeoisie, not of any revolution. Of course it did not seem so at the time, not just because their work was new or "radical," but also because the world of entertainment and leisure that they favored was so opposed to the work ethic and the other moral underpinnings of the bourgeoisie.

From the vantage point of over a century later, it is easy to see this. Even so, historians have paid too little attention to the undercurrents flowing beneath the brilliant surfaces of Impressionist paintings. Their innovations have been largely seen in terms of style, and the social meanings of their forms and their subjects have remained too seldom explored. The history of Impressionism should be rewritten by integrating style and subject, individual and society. The whole history of modernism suffers still from formalism, including its latest manifestation, a trendy combination of semiotics and structuralism that gives a false veneer of newness, but that preserves the erroneous idea that art is somehow "pure," elevated above history into a realm of its own. Impressionism is a good place to start the necessary re-evaluation; it has replaced Renaissance painting as the art most widely admired and most sought after, because it built the foundations for the experience of modern life as it is comprehended and given structure in visual form.

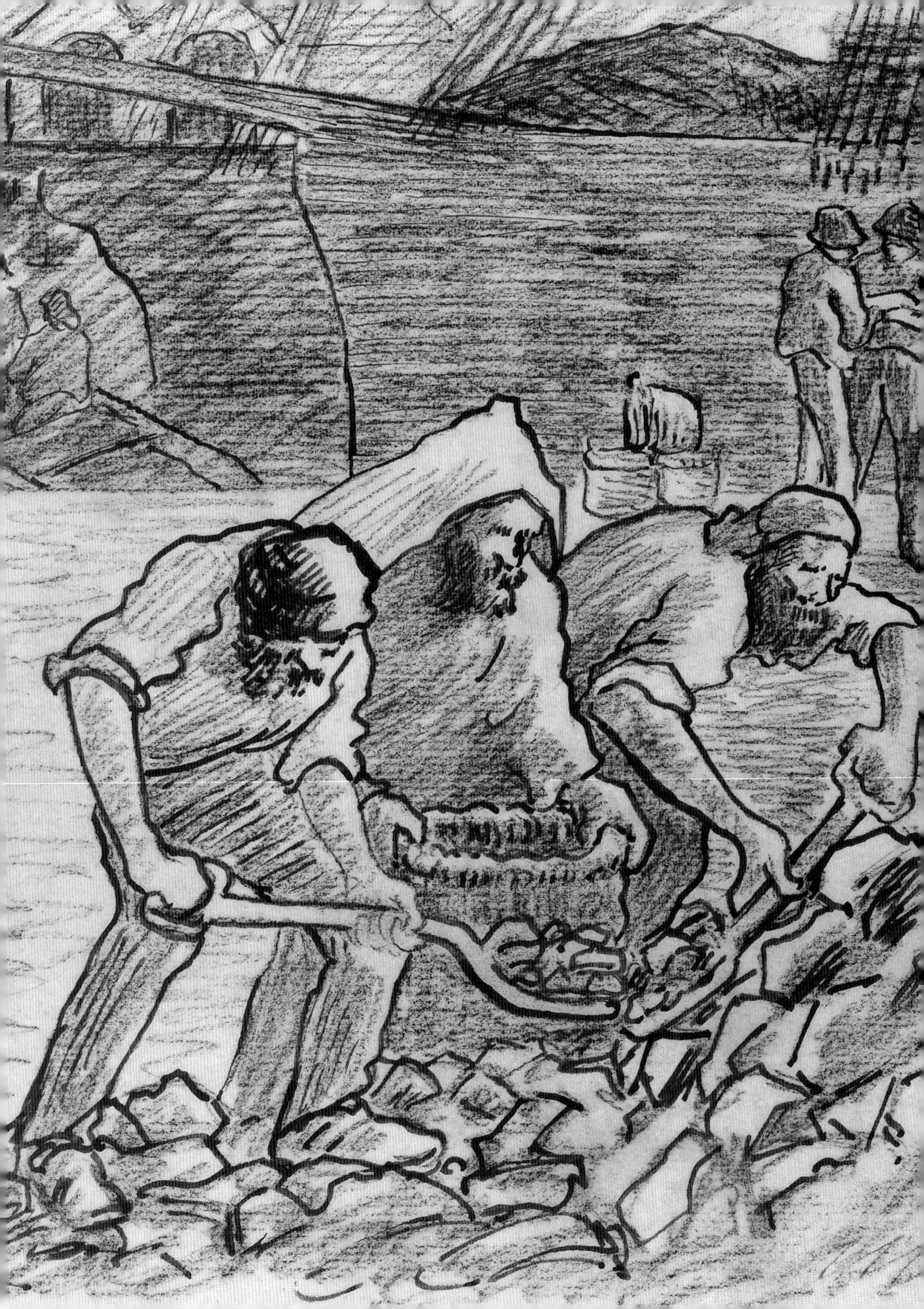

Chapter 7

Artists and Anarchism: Unpublished Letters of Pissarro, Signac, and Others

Justice en sociologie, harmonie en art: même chose.
– Paul Signac

The film biography of Vincent van Gogh, produced in 1956, was entirely characteristic of the middle of the twentieth century in treating his passionate social ideals as a symptom of a peculiar mental condition. This view ignores the social realities that help to form an artist's ideas, and explains away social convictions by reducing them to psychological aberrations. Yet van Gogh was by no means the only artist of the later nineteenth century who espoused humanitarian and radical political concepts. A surprisingly large number of artists who matured in France in the 1880s and 1890s were partisans of socialist-anarchist ideals, and it is rather an older artist, like Cézanne, living a hermit's life in the south, who is atypical of the period.

The unpublished correspondence of Jean Grave (1854–1939), France's leading Anarchist-Communist, is almost entirely with artists, and most especially with those painters at one time or another grouped together as Neo-Impressionists: Camille Pissarro, Paul Signac, Henri-Edmond Cross, Charles Angrand, Théo Van Rysselberghe, and Maximilien Luce. These letters provide the focus for an analysis of the Neo-Impressionists' attitudes toward society, all the more rewarding because, together with their friends among the Symbolist poets and critics, this group of artists endorsed one particular political creed.[1] Radical social views were not a new phenomenon in French art. The egalitarian convictions and social consciousness of Daumier, Courbet, and Millet had allied painting with progressive political thought earlier in the century. But the Impressionists, with the notable exception of Pissarro,[2] were indifferent to social questions in spite of their struggle for recognition in a hostile society. The tensions of the ebbing century, however, culminating in bloody strikes, terrorist bombings, and merciless police repressions, could not long be ignored. In this same period, workers' parties became a reality and socialist doctrines for the first time reached a wide public. In such an epoch it is small wonder that a great many painters and writers awoke

29 *(facing page)* detail of pl. 35.

• From *Burlington Magazine* 102 (November 1960): 473–82 (with Eugenia W. Herbert).

to social concerns and that the ever-widening gulf isolating the artistic avant-garde from the general public reinforced their sympathies with radical political movements.

So close were the ties between painting and literature in this era that it is not surprising to find a common pattern in both fields. Symbolism, the dominant movement in French and Belgian letters from about 1886 to 1900, manifested a politically radical side from its beginning, though it was not shared by all of its writers. "The social revolution will take place," wrote one of the important early Symbolist reviewers, "all coalitions will only serve to precipitate it."[3] At the height of the Symbolists' *mainmise* on French literature, one of its leading figures said of the bomb-throwing anarchist Ravachol, "a Saint has been born to us," and predicted that in the future property-less society Ravachol would be remembered gratefully as a victim of capitalism.[4] In spite of the esoteric nature of the writing, therefore, many Symbolists were very much concerned with radical social doctine: "They want to take part in the struggle, a thirst for action dominates the writers."[5] If for some of them sympathy with the far left went no further than an association with their own hatred of middle-class rule and a love of individualism, others endorsed the doctrines of Anarchist-Communism: Paul Adam, Gustave Kahn, Félix Fénéon, Emile Verhaeren, Bernard Lazare, Pierre Quillard, to mention only the most important.[6] It is no coincidence that the first four named were the friends and chief critical defenders of the Neo-Impressionists.

In the world of painting, sympathy with the far left was less widespread but nonetheless very important. It is true that most of the painters and sculptors associated with Gauguin and the Nabis were neo-Catholics and conservative, yet Théophile Steinlen, H.G. Ibels, Adolphe Willette, Félix Vallotton, and all of the Neo-Impressionists were directly associated with the anarchists.[7] Belgium's major sculptor of the period, Constantin Meunier, was steeped in socialist ideas.

The anarchism which awakened such sympathies needs, however, a word of explanation. It is more correctly called "anarchist-communism" and, far from being nebulous and negative, it was a well-articulated, positive doctrine.[8] It combined economic communism with individual anarchism. Collective ownership of the means of production was to be on a communal rather than a national scale, for man works ideally in small groups without the coercion of national laws and institutions (even socialist organization was considered coercive). Pierre Kropotkin (1842–1921), the intellectual leader of French anarchist-communism, rejected the romantic agrarian idea that the machine was evil, and placed the hopes of mankind on the efficiency of modern technology wedded to decentralized and largely autonomous productive units.[9] The active program of the anarchist-communists was to hasten the downfall of the present order, but because they did not believe in the efficacy of parliamentary action or in the creation of a syndicalist elite, they relied upon a combination of propaganda for their ideals and direct support of revolutionary activities. It was to the first of these that the artists were recruited (or, better, recruited themselves).

The dominant figure in the French anarchist-communist movement was Jean Grave. Not only did he emphasize the revolutionary potential of art more strongly than any of his fellow socialists, he also succeeded in enlisting artists in his cause to an extent far surpassing anything dreamed of by the leaders of other contemporary radical movements. Originally a shoemaker, he was one of those rare men who literally educated themselves. While still in his twenties he became Kropotkin's collaborator in Geneva. In 1885 he transferred the latter's weekly *Le Révolté* to Paris, and henceforth it was the most important organ of French anarchism through its successive phases as *La Révolte* (1887–94) and the *Temps nouveaux* (1895–1914).[10] From the beginning *La Révolte* kept up with avant-garde literature by means of a regular literary supplement. Grave's good sense led him to an appreciation of Symbolist writing although he was often impatient of its elitist tendencies. Through the supplement he hoped to bring before the worker a wealth of historical and literary material and, whether or not his efforts helped educate the workers, he maintained such a high level (publishing works by all the leading Symbolists) that among the subscribers to *La Révolte* were Mallarmé, Alphonse Daudet, Anatole France, J.K. Huysmans, Pierre Loti, Rémy de Gourmont, Lugné-Poe, and a host of others.[11]

Grave was somewhat slower to use the visual arts and went at it seriously only in 1896 with the conception of an album of lithographs which centers much of the correspondence with the Neo-Impressionists.[12] He no doubt took his initiative from his fellow anarchist Emile Pouget, who founded in 1889 the weekly *Père Peinard*, a journal of decidedly proletarian hue, written in slang.[13] Pouget's call for an alliance of art and the revolution was seconded by the contributions of Ibels, Willette, Luce, Valloton, Lucien Pissarro, and many less well-known artists, drawings that were quite frankly propagandistic in nature. *Père Peinard* usually had a large drawing on the front page, Ibels's *Chanson du gas* (pl. 30) being a typical example, and when Pouget was exiled to London in 1894 and 1895, he won the co-operation of Lucien Pissarro for his miniscule *Père Peinard* brochures (pl. 31). With Pouget's return to Paris in 1896, *La Sociale* supplanted *Père Peinard*, and continued to give an important place to art. Luce was commissioned to do a series of lithographs after the sculpture of Meunier, whose ennobling of the worker was obviously of great interest. Grave had deliberately given *La Révolte* and the *Temps nouveaux* a more intellectual flavor than the popular *Père Peinard*, and when in 1896 he decided to ask his painter friends for lithographs, he presented them with no editorial comment. This was the beginning of a collaboration that lasted until the outbreak of World War I.

By the mid-1890s then, Grave was already well acquainted with the Neo-Impressionists. It is unfortunately difficult to determine just when this acquaintance began in each case. His files were seized by the police in 1894 and few letters before that date survive. Apparently Maximilien Luce who, like Pissarro *père*, had a radical past of long standing, was the first to meet Grave. In the summer of 1888, in the full tide of the Neo-Impressionist movement (but when Pissarro was beginning to withdraw from the group), Luce asked Signac to write

30 *(right)* H.G. Ibels, *Chanson du gas*, 1893, cover of *Père Pleinard* (January 22, 1893).

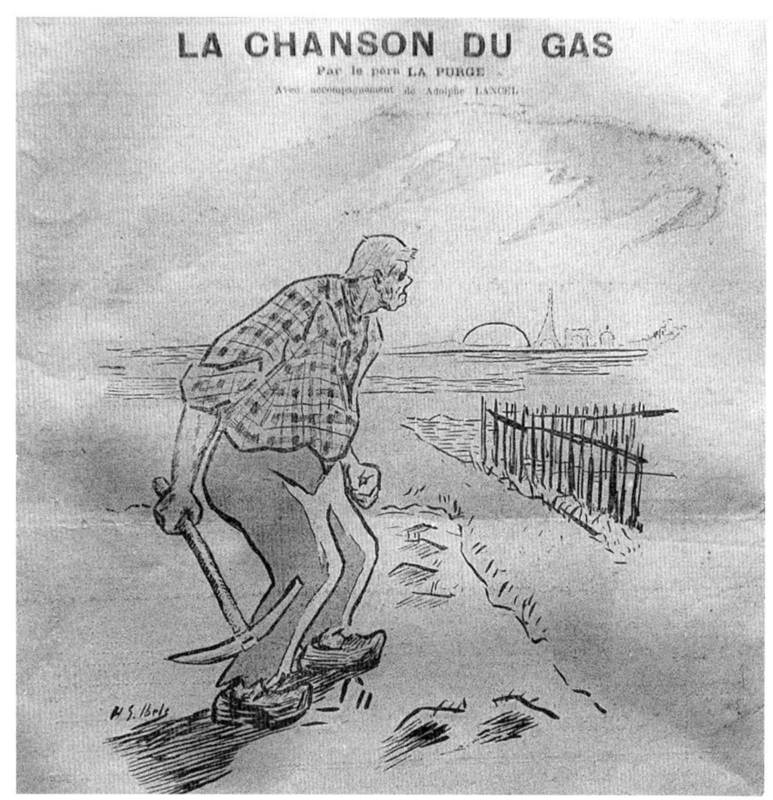

31 *(below)* Lucien Pissarro, *Il n'est pas mort* and *Tremble, plein de truffes!*, woodcuts for *Père Peinard*, September and November 1894.

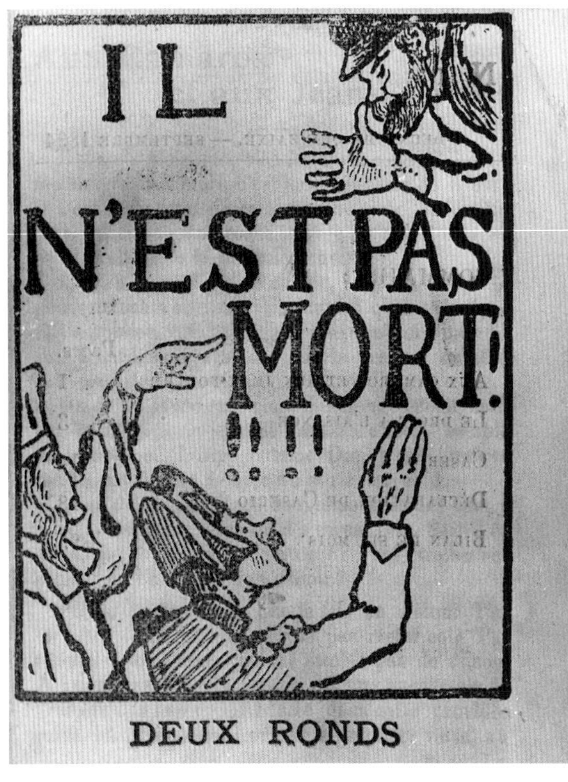

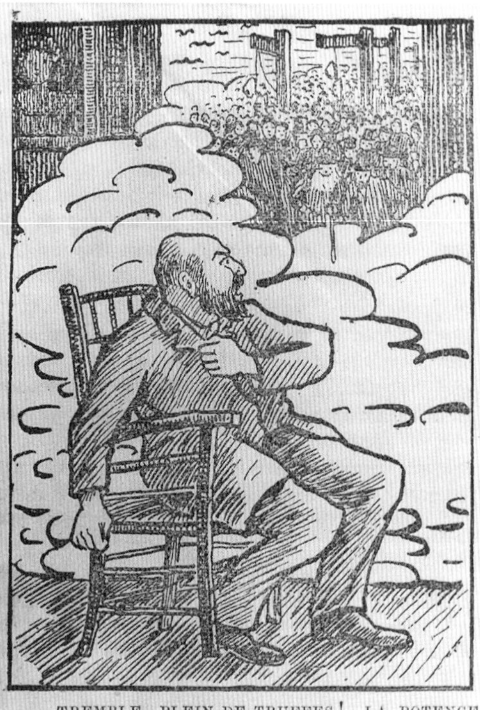

a letter for *La Révolte*, possibly at Grave's behest.[14] Signac's portrait of Luce drawn in 1890[15] shows him reading *La Révolte* – a means of characterizing Luce's well-known anarchist convictions – and by the following year Luce was contributing drawings to Pouget's *Père Peinard*.[16] Thereafter he was Grave's closest artistic collaborator, giving him innumerable lithographs and drawings, helping organize some lotteries for Grave's benefit and others for anarchist workers, and acting as intermediary between Grave, Pouget, and the artists.

Camille Pissarro knew Grave and Pouget at least by 1890, when they were all members of the short-lived *Club de l'art social*. Only Luce was more assiduous in helping Grave in his enterprises. Pissarro gave several drawings for the editor's publications, and both paintings and drawings for his lotteries. He got his friend Octave Mirbeau, the writer and critic, to defend Grave in the press and to write a preface for one of the anarchist's books. Perhaps the most remarkable testimony to the depths of his convictions is the number of times he sent money to Grave, an enormous sacrifice for one so much in need himself. In addition to frequent gifts of small sums, he twice paid the printing debts for the *Temps nouveaux*, each time amounting to more than 1000 francs.[17] He was no less helpful to Pouget, even sending him money when he was arrested in 1896.[18] At one time he contemplated writing an article for him,[19] and it was undoubtedly he who encouraged his son Lucien to offer Pouget and Grave a number of drawings.

Paul Signac, sympathetic to the anarchists since 1888 or earlier, was a good friend of Grave's before 1892, the date of their earliest surviving correspondence; he was on intimate terms with Pouget as well.[20] His library contained personally inscribed copies of Grave's books, testimony to the number of works Signac gave for his publications and lotteries. The warm tone of their correspondence indicates more than a casual friendship, which lasted into the 1920s.

Angrand and Cross seem to have met Grave only in the late 1890s, but they soon became good friends and occasionally exchanged visits. They provided Grave with a number of drawings, contributed to his lotteries, and showed in their letters an intimate knowledge of his and Kropotkin's writings. Van Rysselberghe hardly knew Grave, although he also gave him drawings (pl. 32), but he was an intimate of Elisée Reclus, the important Belgian geographer and anarchist-communist ally of Grave and Pouget.[21] He was also a friend of Pouget and harbored him in 1894 when the latter fled from France during a period of police persecution.[22]

Of the artists outside the Neo-Impressionist orbit who were close to Grave, Steinlen and Valloton were the most prominent. Their letters to Grave speak for themselves. Valloton probably met Grave first in the late 1890s, although his anarchist sympathies were obvious many years earlier, to judge from his prints (pl. 33). His last contact with Grave seems to have been about 1909, when he drew a cover for a *Temps nouveaux* brochure, after which he forsook his radical social ideals. Steinlen was almost as close to Grave as Luce, and aided him frequently right up to his death in 1923.

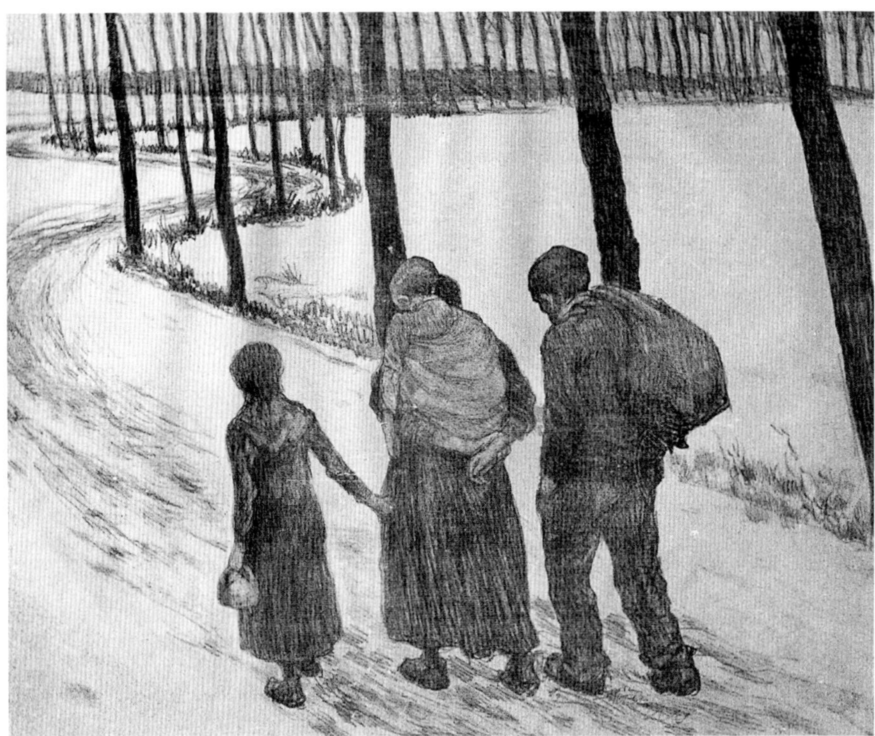

32 Théo Van Rysselberghe, *Les Errants*, 1897. Lithograph for *Temps nouveaux*, Album 7, 1897.

* * *

Once it has been established that the artists were friends and collaborators of the leading anarchist-communists, the logical question poses itself: what meaning did this alliance have for the artists, on the one hand, and for Grave and his colleagues, on the other? On the anarchist side the question is more readily answered. It is true that Grave, like Kropotkin, had a preference for art with a social message (although his tastes were more subtle than Pouget's), but he was nonetheless happy to accept the art of the Neo-Impressionists, for their honest portrayal of the life of the humble could serve the cause by exposing the injustices and inequalities of the existing social order. At the same time their artistic merits could educate the workers and prepare them for the richer existence promised by an anarchist future.

The problem is more complex in the case of the artists. If they had all indulged in overtly propagandistic art the answer would not be difficult to find, but such is not the case. On the contrary, they sat on the horns of a dilemma: their artistic judgment made them prefer subjects which were seldom obviously related to their political sympathies. This dilemma was compounded by another: they insisted upon the independence that art must maintain from nature and defended

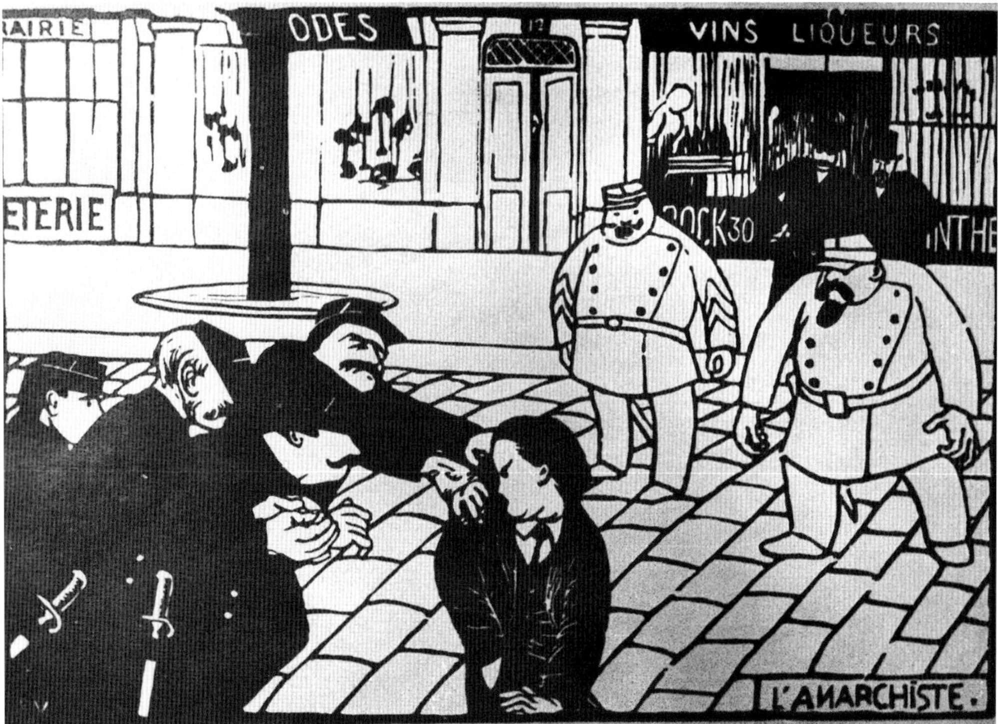

33 Félix Vallotton, *L'Anarchiste*, 1892. Woodcut. Formerly Collection Ginette Signac.

an art-for-art's sake position, yet they regretted the progressive weakening of their ties with nature. These interlocked problems can be stated succinctly in the form of a proportion: art-for-art's sake is to propaganda as art independent of nature is to the naturalistic tradition. To explain the equation, it will be necessary first to examine the works the artists gave to the anarchist press, then to see what light such an alnalysis can shed upon Neo-Impressionism as a whole.

Most of the drawings and lithographs given to Grave were simple views of humble people. For the *Temps nouveaux*, Camille Pissarro sent him two lithographs, *Les Porteuses de bois* in 1896 and *Les Sans-gîtes* (pl. 34) in 1898.[23] The first shows a group of female faggot gatherers, the second, a homeless couple and their child wandering along a country road. Pissarro drew a *Sower* (loosely based on Millet) for the cover of a lecture by Kropotkin that Grave published, and he also made a color lithograph of a plowman (pl. 19) for Grave's frontispiece to the literary supplement of June 1902 to the *Temps nouveaux*.[24] The lithographs by Van Rysselberghe and Cross in the series of the late 1890s represent homeless figures: those by Van Rysselberghe are like Pissarro's; one by Cross contrasts a vagabond seated in a somber foreground with peasants at work in a sunlit landscape. Although they are not directly propagandistic, these agrarian subjects were appropriate to anarchist-communism. If Kropotkin pleaded with the artists

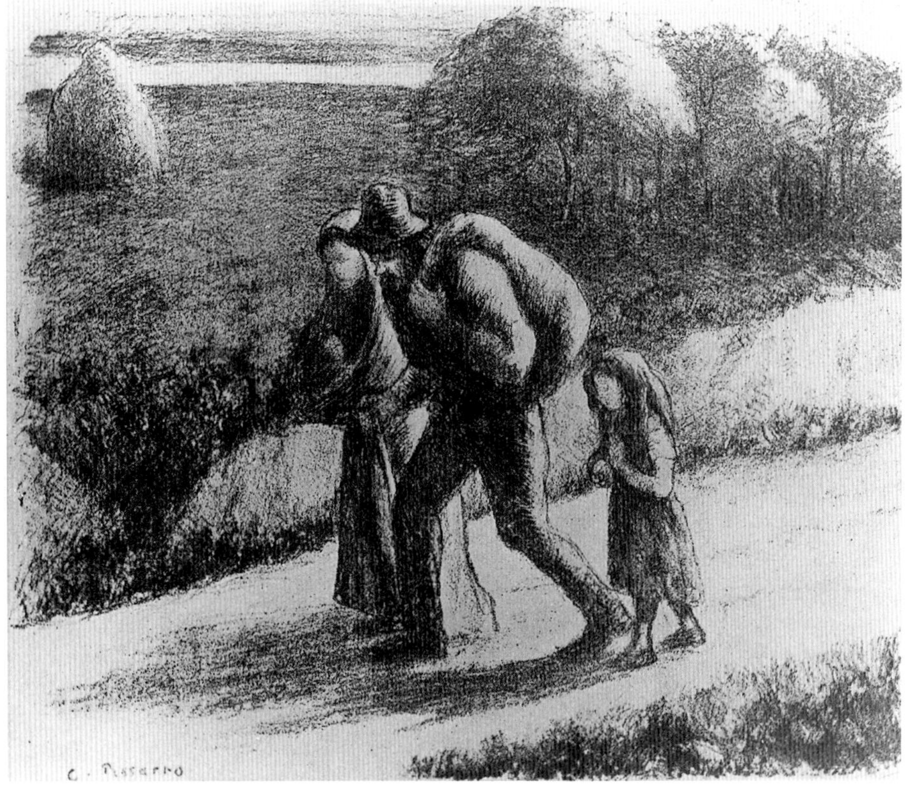

34 Camille Pissarro, *Les Sans-gîtes*, 1898. Lithograph for *Temps nouveaux*, Album 9, 1898.

to "Narrate for us in your vivid style or in your fervent pictures the titanic struggles of the masses against their aggressors; enflame young hearts with the beautiful breath of revolution," he also asked them to "show the people the ugliness of contemporary life" and the "ignominies of the present social order."[25] Simply by portraying workers and social outcasts, the painters were bringing truth before the public; truth about the existing order was by definition criticism of it.

Agrarian subjects were welcomed by the anarchists for another reason: in spite of Kropotkin's efforts to overhaul earlier anarchist theory in a scientific way, through the incorporation of industrial technology into the ideal society, he and his French followers could not shake a romantic love of the countryside. Their hatred of the manner in which the urban proletariat were oppressed led them to a hatred of industrial life and a glorification of the healthy life of the peasant, hence the apparent anachronism of rural images dedicated to "temps nouveaux." The peasant was, moreover, already a "decentralized unit" in society, whereas the urban worker had been forced into an economic and institutional pattern the anarchists wished to destroy. The very same orientation is seen in the letters of

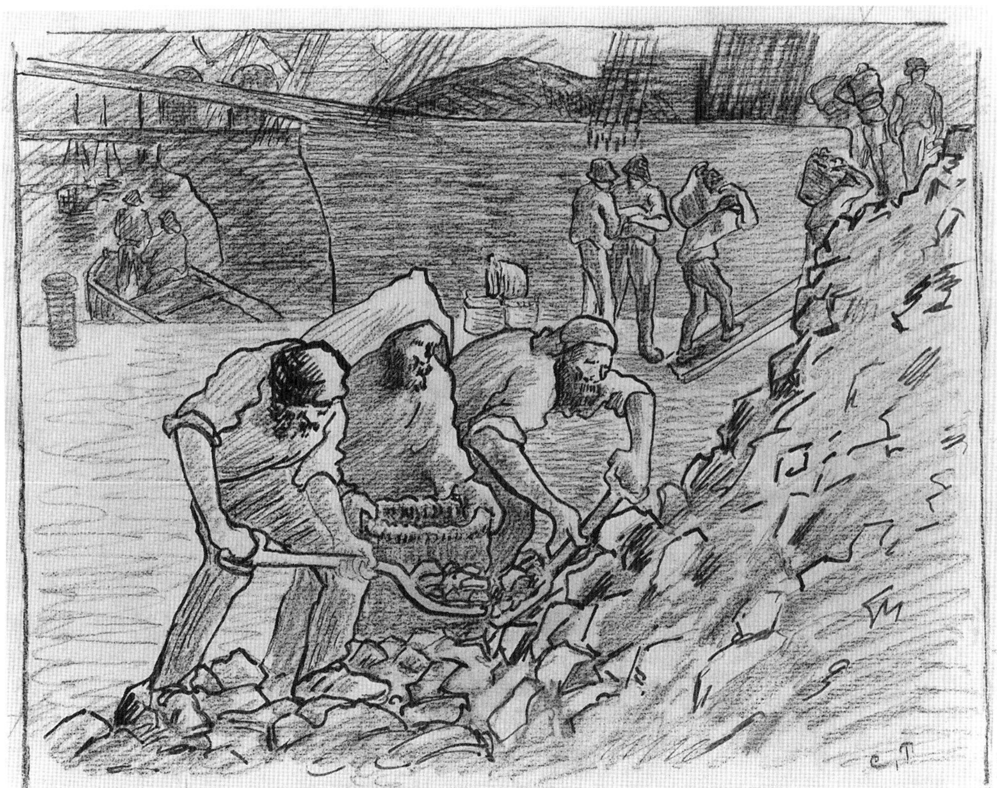

35 Camille Pissarro, *Stevedores*, 1893. Pen, ink, and charcoal on tracing paper, 9½ × 12¼ in. (24.1 × 31.1 cm.). Gift of Mr. and Mrs. Rodney L. White (Shelby Baier, Class of 1959). Mount Holyoke College Art Museum, South Hadley, Massachusetts.

Pissarro, Cross, and Signac. It is essentially romantic because it is born of nostalgia for the old and dislike of the new, inevitably triumphant, urban industrialization of life. Pissarro's assertion that "our ideas, impregnated with anarchist philosophy, spread through our work,"[26] refers to the dying naturalistic and anti-industrial tradition of the nineteenth century to which he clung (in both style and subject matter he remained close to Millet). The stevedores he drew (pl. 35) for a special issue of *La Plume* devoted to anarchism[27] could have been seen anytime during the nineteenth century, for they are a kind of worker who antedated the industrial revolution. Only once did he produce a series of truly radical drawings, the *Turpitudes sociales* of 1890.[28]

A good many artistic gifts to Grave and Pouget were nevertheless frankly propagandistic. Signac's *Démolisseurs* (1896) for the *Temps nouveaux* showed vigorous men that could only be interpreted as the workers demolishing the capitalist state. Years later he gave Grave a watercolor of an allegorical landscape representing the collapse of the present order (pl. 36).[29] The many drawings by Lucien Pissarro and Luce for Grave and Pouget are all quite inflammatory, as are those of their allies Steinlen, Valloton, and Ibels. Cross and Angrand occa-

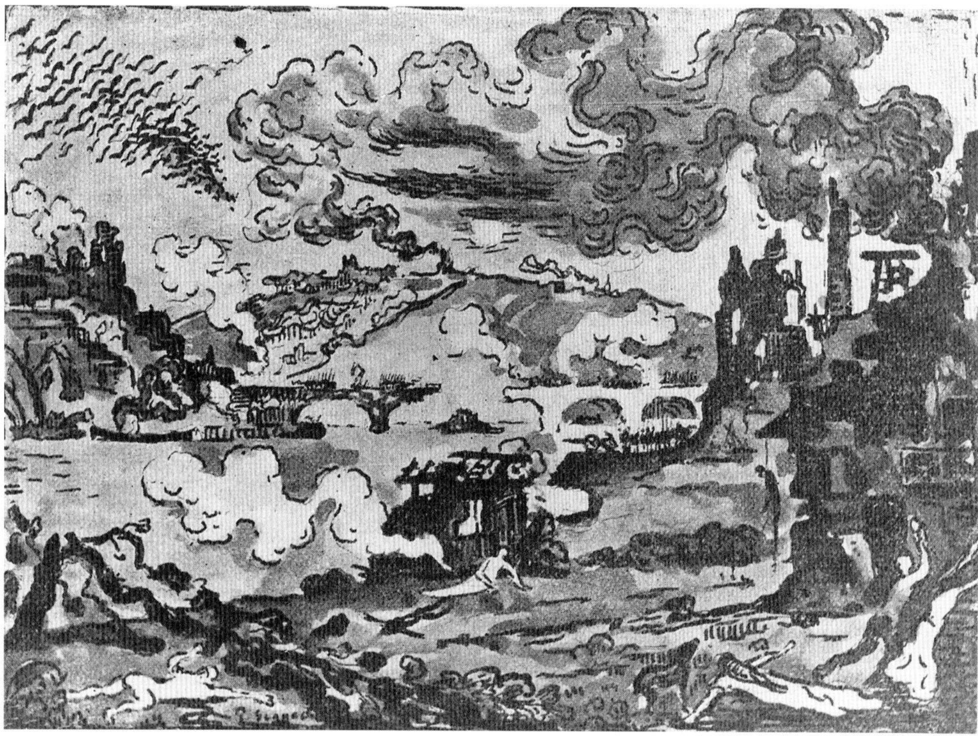

36 Paul Signac, *Collapse of the State*, cover of *Publications de "La Révolte" et "Temps Nouveaux"* 35 (July 25, 1925).

sionally overcame their timidity and produced militant subjects (pl. 37). Of the Neo-Impressionists, however, only Luce seemed really at home in this sphere, the others making a clear distinction between their occasional anarchist messages and their independent art. If they were willing to give Grave a propagandistic drawing now and then, they did not consider these bona fide works of art. Lucien Pissarro, in fact, went to some pains to make this clear.

> The distinction that you establish between "Art-for-art's sake" and art of social leanings does not exist. Every production that is really a work of art is social (whether the author wishes it or not), because the one who produces it makes his fellow creatures share the most vivid and clear emotions that he felt before nature's spectacles. [. . .] This work of pure beauty will have enlarged the esthetic conception of other individuals.[30]

Because capitalism has maintained workers and peasants in a state of ignorance, the artist must try to raise their level of artistic knowledge by painting as he sees best, not by diluting his work with easily understood, traditional elements which are reactionary in nature. Besides, Lucien wisely remarked, the individual autonomy sought by the anarchists must apply to artists, too, who should not be made subservient to an esthetic dictated by any collectivity.

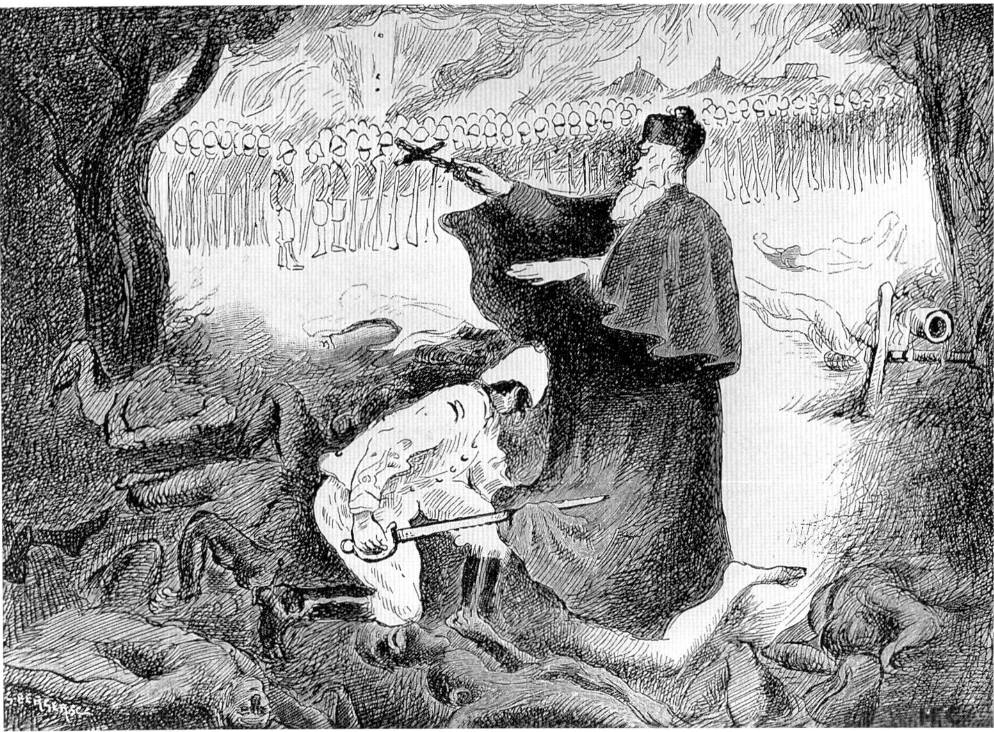

37 Henri-Edmond Cross, *Blessings*, 1903. Engraving by S. Berger after Cross's drawing, for Elisée Reclus, *Patriotisme-Colonisation* (Paris, 1903).

Signac on several occasions wrote an even more thorough defence of the artist's autonomy. By remaining true to their sensibilities, honest artists attack traditional artistic conventions beloved of the bourgeoisie, and thus give "a solid blow of the pickax to the old social edifice which, worm-eaten, is cracking and falling away."[31] The proof lies in the assumption of the bourgeoisie that radical artists are of necessity radical in their politics.

> Justice in sociology, harmony in art: the same thing. [. . .]
>
> The anarchist painter is not one who represents anarchist pictures but the one who, without concern for money, without desire for recompense, struggles with all his individuality against bourgeois and official conventions by making a personal contribution. [. . .]
>
> The subject is nothing, or at least is only one part of the work of art, no more important than the other elements: color, drawing, composition. [. . .]
>
> When the eye will be educated, people will see in paintings other things than the subject.
>
> When the society we dream of exists, when the worker, free of the exploiters who brutalize him, will have time to think and learn, he will appreciate all the diverse qualities of the work of art.[32]

He concludes that subject matter cannot be the determining factor in painting because it is a literary, not a painterly element. He reminds the anarchists that the official salons are full of paintings of workers and factories – sops to their middle-class consciences – yet no one pretends that these paintings are revolutionary.

If art could not be propaganda for the Pissarros, Signac, Cross, or Angrand, it does not mean that their subjects bear no relation to their political beliefs. Sympathetic portrayals of peasants and vagabonds had more than a casual relation to anarchist-communism, as we have seen, and are in strong contrast to the medievalizing annunciations or exotic peasantries of the conservative Nabis. There is another category of works given to the anarchist press which expresses their ideals: utopian visions of the future anarchist state. Signac specifically related his *Temps d'harmonie* (Mairie de Montreuil) to his anarchist faith, and Cross agreed with him that it was better to show people a vision of the anarchist state than present-day misery.[33] To a certain extent the Neo-Impressionists' scenes of bucolic happiness can be associated with their utopian dreams. In more than one letter Cross said that he was painting man as he would be in the future anarchist society. Views of peasants at work, gay fishermen on the shore, and idyllic landscapes were a kind of escape from the ugly present. The Neo-Impressionists' letters, especially Pissarro's, are full of references to the future when everyone will live in peace and tranquility like the peasants.

> I have just read Kropotkin's book. It must be admitted that if it's utopian, in any case it's a beautiful dream. And because we have often had examples of utopias become realities, nothing prevents us from believing that it will be possible one day, unless man sombers and returns to complete barbarity. [. . .] Kropotkin thinks that one has to live like peasants in order to understand them well; it seems to me that one has to be enthusiastic for one's subject to render it well, but is it necessary to be a peasant? Let's be artists first and we'll have the faculty of appreciating everything, even a landscape without being a peasant.[34]

By the end of the century, the seascapes and port scenes of Signac and the Provençal shore and dancing nymphs of Cross are also assimilated into their hopes for a utopian society. And yet they had a defensive attitude toward their subject matter and were referring to the utopian future in an attempt to explain to their political consciences what were primarily artistic decisions independent of anarchism. To understand this conflict, we should turn finally to a brief study of the position of Neo-Impressionism in the 1880s.

When Georges Seurat, the undisputed leader of the Neo-Impressionists, began his first independent painting and drawing in 1880, he turned to the peasant, whom he portrayed with obvious sympathy. His peasants are always at work, never resting, a tribute to their healthy, if burdened existence. The influence of Millet and Courbet upon these early works is a link with the socially conscious mood of the mid-century. Slowly becoming more aware of the urban industrial revolution, Seurat gradually shifted his attention to the city. A great many of his drawings from the years 1882 to 1886 are of the urban poor, the beggars, vagrants, and street vendors who will appear a decade later in the anarchist-communist press. He also drew industrial sites, and painted several views of the factories of Asnières and Courbevoie, the industrial suburb on the northwest fringe of Paris. In the background of *Bathing Place, Asnières* (National Gallery, London) of 1883–84 are the factories of Asnières, and the boys in the foreground are clearly sons of that working-class area.

At first glance, Seurat would seem to have abandoned his social consciousness in his later paintings of urban entertainments. But we have the word of his friends that the *Chahut* (Rijksmuseum Kröller-Müller, Otterlo) and similar subjects were satires upon the middle class.[35] Signac, writing about the Neo-Impressionists, said that

> by their picturesque studies of the worker towns of Saint-Ouen or of Montrouge, sordid and striking, by the reproduction of the broad and curiously colored appeal of a laborer next to a pile of sand, of a smith in the incandescence of his forge, or better yet by the synthetic representation of the pleasures of decadence: balls, chahuts, circuses, as did the painter Seurat who had so lively a feeling of the debasement of our transitional epoch, they bring their witness to the great social trial which is engaged between workers and Capital.[36]

Of course Seurat identified himself to a certain extent with the many people on the fringes of society whom he portrayed, entertainers as well as the urban humble. Only a few years later the young Picasso showed a similar interest in the destitute and in circus performers.

Seurat's early attraction to industrial scenes was shared by Signac, Luce, Angrand, Dubois-Pillet, and others.[37] It was in fact the painting of *la vie moderne*, the cry of progressive critics since Baudelaire, as well as the artistic merits of the Neo-Impressionists that won the admiration of the political radicals among the critics of the Symbolist period. Running through the praise of Paul Alexis, Georges Lecomte, Octave Mirbeau, Jean Ajalbert, Félix Fénéon, Gustave Kahn, Emile Verhaeren, and Jules Christophe is an open admiration of the new urban themes. All of those named except Alexis had close ties with the anarchist-communists (and Alexis was sympathetic to the cause). The Neo-Impressionists were also frequently defended by the left-wing press even when its writers did not know them personally.[38]

The activity of the Neo-Impressionists in the 1880s testifies to the sincerity of their social convictions. But they were equally sincere in the next decade when they had quite evidently forsaken subjects with an overt social message and had developed an art-for-art's sake position. How did they justify this apparent *volte-face*? Fearing he would be misunderstood, Signac defended his new attitude before his anarchist friends. The paintings of the Neo-Impressionists, he wrote:

> result from a purely esthetic emotion produced by the pictorial possibilities of things and beings and have the same social character, unconscious, that already marks contemporary literature, such as the novels of the Flauberts, the Goncourts, the Zolas and their followers, written with a purely literary intention, after lived experience, that have served the revolutionary cause more powerfully than all the novels in which political preoccupations take the lead over literary ones. [. . .]
>
> It would therefore be a mistake into which have fallen too often the best intentioned revolutionaries, like Prudhon, to demand systematically a precise socialist tendency in works of art, because this tendency will be found stronger and more eloquent among pure esthetes, painting what they see, as they feel it, and very often unconsciously giving a solid blow of the pickax to the old social edifice. [. . .][39]

As the decade of the 1890s progressed, the Neo-Impressionists became more and more aware of the logical conclusion that must be drawn from an art-for-art's sake position. Angrand, living the life of a recluse in the country near Rouen, was the major catalyst, prodding Signac and Cross with his profound questions. "He declares," wrote Signac in 1894, "that it's the searching around in nature which paralyzes us, that we know enough to draw a dog which won't look like a donkey, and that this suffices. The rest, arrangements of lines and colors, ought to be our sole preoccupation."[40] The conflict between a devotion to the abstract qualities of painting, and a lingering faithfulness to the naturalistic tradition, grew more acute. Cross spoke for the group when he wrote to Angrand in 1896:

> For a painting, you told me before, one problem suffices. In admitting that one might be well disengaged from the trap held out by nature with its astounding provocations, what can one paint? I find it an enormous difficulty to conciliate the choice of a subject with resolving a pictorial problem. [. . .]
>
> What method? Compose a harmony of tints at the studio table? Make sketches, then go out and search in the huge dictionary (Nature) for resemblances necessary to carry it out?
>
> As it is much more a question of the Neos creating harmonies of tints than harmonizing the tints of this landscape or that natural scene, the canvases that I am now painting remain distant from the goal.[41]

The Neo-Impressionists were never able to desert figurative subject matter, but because Signac and Cross had an imporant direct influence on Matisse, Braque, Puy, Valtat, K.X. Roussel, and other Fauve painters, their struggle with this crucial problem had important consequences.

And yet, paradoxically, it was precisely in the 1890s, when the artists had adopted this art-for-art's sake position, that their collaboration with the anarchist movement became most militant, as shown earlier. Thus a change in subject matter meant in no sense a desertion of the cause.[42] Certainly on Grave's side there was a farsighted concession to the artists. Much as he instinctively preferred somewhat propagandistic subject matter, he conceded that the artist could not yet hope to be fully understood by the masses. If, however, the artist did not ignore the people but instead took part in raising them to a higher cultural level, he could in the future expect an eager and grateful public, free of the corrupt taste of the bourgeoisie. Over and over again Grave insisted that in the future society the artist would be left in perfect freedom to express his concept of the beautiful, and declared his accord with Oscar Wilde that "art is the supreme manifestation of individualism."[43] It was this willingness to admit an esthetic consistent with his libertarian politics and to resist the snare of a more immediately tempting socialist realism that won Grave the lasting sympathy of so many artists.

With the passing of a century, we can today appreciate the unique position of the Neo-Impressionists and their friends, and its relevance to our own era.[44] They lived in a period that saw the formation of new social and labor movements, a period in which the "social question" was forcing older concerns into the background and imposing itself upon the attentions of all levels of society. Unlike the radical artists of the mid-nineteenth century, they did not believe in the idea of a progressive march of humanity toward a fraternal, harmonious society. They inclined instead to the conviction that social progress could not be expected without violence, without a concerted attack on all the institutions of the present and on its social hierarchy. The central issue was no longer monarchism or despotism versus republicanism, and therefore they did not, like Lamartine or Hugo earlier, think primarily in political terms. Their goal was a society resting on an egalitarian base, an ideal that would have frightened most of the radicals of the Romantic period whose motto had been "liberty and fraternity" rather than the dangerous "equality."

The general social ferment of the late century would not, in all likelihood, have sufficed to turn so many artists to the Anarchist-Communist movement if they had not considered themselves such signal victims of the social order. They saw little possibility of earning a respectable living from their art or of winning an appreciative public. Instead of limiting the blame for these circumstances to the nebulous villainy of bourgeois taste, they turned more concretely to the social organization of the present and indicted the capitalist system itself. Hence their hopes as artists as well as political individuals were centered on the construction of a new order in which art would meet with the justice that now eluded it. Their dreams of social justice converged with those of the Anarchist-Communists, the group of radicals which beyond all others emphasized human liberty as the goal of social reform.

Again in contrast to radical artists of earlier years, the Neo-Impressionists found it extremely difficulty to relate art to social ideals. To be sure, much of their work given to Grave had a clear social content, but these drawings and prints were usually of a journalistic sort and not a major part of their life's work. As political thinkers they were impassioned partisans in the social struggle; as artists they were afraid of sacrificing art to didacticism.

It is the conflict between art and political ideals that distinguishes the artists of the late nineteenth century from earlier artists of radical conviction, and makes them so important for the twentieth century. The difficulty in relating political beliefs to subject matter in art is an especially modern phenomenon. With the desertion of naturalism and easily recognized subjects, how can an artist communicate his political beliefs? Signac, Cross, Angrand, and the others are of significance because, on the threshold of abstract art, they wrestled with the dilemma and came up with the solution that has obtained ever since among most artists: an artist must remain faithful to his artistic sensibilities, for he will help destroy the old order through his *art*, not through its subject matter. The unwillingness of modern despotic governments to grant freedom to their artists is a proof of the significance of the Neo-Impressionists' problem. Freedom of choice in art is incompatible with preordained content.

The Neo-Impressionists also help us understand some of the attitudes of modern artists. Picasso, for example, was very much concerned with social themes in his early work (and looked to Steinlen's drawings of the 1890s that are closely related to the subject of this chapter), representing different kinds of people on the fringes of society. His self-identification with these beings is a particularly nineteenth-century attitude. Picasso did not become a truly twentieth-century artist until his development of Cubism, an art lacking overt political content. This change, foretold by the similar evolution of the Neo-Impressionists a generation earlier, marks the severance of art from conscious political expression and becomes typical of the modern period.

Perhaps their strongest ties with the twentieth century are found in the Neo-Impressionists' feeling of isolation, symbolized by their frequent portrayal of lonely wanderers. Their fondness for peasants and rural landscape looked forward to the anti-industrial orientation of many modern artists, whose subjects reflect the individual anarchism and escapism that is both the tragedy and the glory of modern art. The predominant rejection of industrial motifs, which extends to the public in their enthusiasm for van Gogh, Gauguin, Monet, and Cézanne, is tragic in so far as it reflects the position of men who feel themselves isolated from the reality of everyday life in an industrial-urban society, but it is also glorious because it represents a consistent and heroic fight against materialism, tawdriness, and facile acceptance of observable reality.

Chapter 8

Léger's *Le Grand Déjeuner*

Fernand Léger (1881–1955) was born in the Norman city of Argentan. After attending local schools, he became an architectural apprentice in nearby Caen, and then went to Paris in 1900. He continued to work as an architectural draftsman until 1903, when he began to study painting seriously at the Ecole des Arts Décoratifs and at the Académie Julian, as well as in private studios. Although much of his painting before 1910 was destroyed or lost, the broad stages of his artistic evolution are known. Like others of his generation, he passed successively through phases beholden to Impressionism, Neo-Impressionism, and Fauvism. In 1910 he emerged as one of the original Cubists, and among his friends were the painters Albert Gleizes, Jean Metzinger, and Robert Delaunay, the sculptors Constantin Brancusi, Jacques Lipchitz, and Alexander Archipenko, and the writers Guillaume Apollinaire, Pierre Reverdy, Maurice Raynal, and Blaise Cendrars.

Léger moved among the different exhibition societies and informal groups that constituted the Parisian avant-garde. The dealer D.H. Kahnweiler began showing his work in 1910, along with that of Picasso and Braque and in successive exhibitions his unique contributions to the development of Cubism appeared, including *Nudes in the Forest* (Kröller-Müller Museum, Otterlo) at the Salon des Indépendants in 1911, and *Woman in Blue* (Kunstmuseum, Basel) at the Salon d'Automne of 1912. Although he shared many ideas and some features of style with other Cubists, Léger went his own way. By 1914 he had developed a distinctive style based upon rendering three-dimensional units resembling segments of cones, cylinders, and other solids. Sometimes these seemed to represent no "subject" at all, at other times they were assembled in such a way as to form robot-like creatures, like those of his *Stairway* series.

Léger's career was suddenly uprooted by the outbreak of World War I. He served in the engineering corps during the worst of battles, the catastrophic months at Verdun. In 1916 he was gassed and was hospitalized with lung trouble until June 1918. He did a good many drawings while at the front, principally of fellow soldiers, usually shown at moments of leisure. He later wrote of his plunge into a new kind of realism, as opposed to the elitist abstraction of the prewar months. His great painting of the war years, *The Cardplayers* of 1917 (Kröller-

• *Léger's Le Grand Déjeuner* (exh. cat., Minneapolis Institute of Arts, and Detroit Institute of Arts, 1980): 9–37.

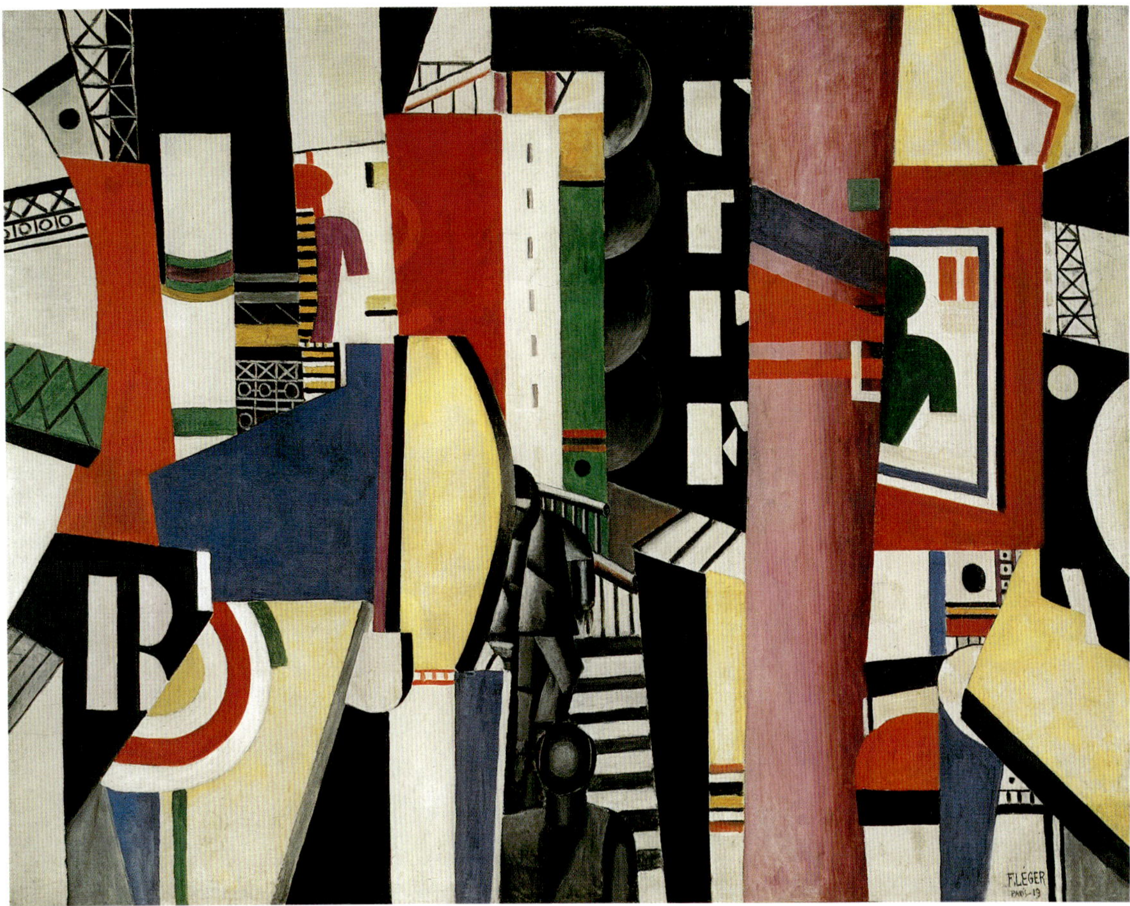

38 Fernand Léger, *The City*, 1919–20. 91 × 117½ in. (231.1 × 298.4 cm.). Philadelphia Museum of Art, A.E. Gallatin Collection.

Müller Museum, Otterlo), done in the hospital, shows three convalescent soldiers with cards, their mechano-morphic images emerging from a series of loosely jointed tubular, conical, and cubical shapes. In the hospital, Léger also produced a number of painted still-lifes, a great many drawings, and five illustrations for *J'ai tué* (1917–18), a piece of intensive prose in which his friend Cendrars, who had lost an arm in battle, recounts the trauma of hand-to-hand fighting. Here too Léger's visual language retains its geometric character and its avoidance of mere description, while conveying images of war machinery, soldiers, graveyards, guns, and (on the cover) the ghastly face of a dead German soldier.

In the waning months of war, Léger produced a number of paintings that already have the celebratory mood of victory, including *The Disks* of 1918 (Musée d'Art Moderne de la Ville de Paris). Here two soldiers, barely decipherable on the left edge, witness a new kind of urban geometry, dominated by huge colored disks that embody the dynamic forces of modern industrial life. The disks echo the brightly colored circles that Delaunay had featured in his paintings before the war. Léger must have felt a sympathy with Delaunay, since they were both intent upon making a viable language of Cubism, adapting it to subjects of modern life, and not just to studio still-lifes or café interiors. Indeed, in the years 1918 to 1920, Léger's subjects range very broadly over urban industrial life, in a mood of postwar euphoria. He painted several pictures of Bastille Day and of Armistice Day, and among his other major subjects are factory interiors, circus acrobats, still-lifes with machine-like parts (propellers, pistons, levers), tugboats, and city streets.

The City of 1919–20 (pl. 38) was regarded by Léger as the most important of his pictures from the period immediately following the war.[1] Although the work seems at first quite abstract, a close observation permits the viewer to interpret its images. We see a whole series of architectural planes, whose abrupt juxtapositions convey the dynamism of modern urban experience. Large letters and billboards point to the world of advertising which Léger admired so much, while girders to the left and right remind us of construction sites or supports for electric wires. In the center, below puffs of somewhat ominous factory smoke, two faceless men are descending outdoor stairs. They stand for the anonymity of urban encounters, the coexistence of strangers in an impersonal world which consists of a constant flux of different sensations. It is the "life of fragments," in the artist's own phrase, and a continuation of the excitement of the prewar years so admirably captured by Cubism. *The City* has something of the extraordinary, cut-up rhythms of Cendrars's *The End of the World Filmed by the Angel Notre Dame*, which Léger was illustrating at exactly the same time, in 1919: "Elevators rise and descend. Powerful projectors light up. Luminous signals. Optical colored telegraph. The departing train is seized, then brandished by the catapult of giant dynamos. An ultraviolet lightning bolt. A spiral unrolls. The train has left."[2]

The Evolution of *Le Grand Déjeuner*

It is against the fragmentation and ferment of *The City*, exhibited in 1920, that we must place *Le Grand Déjeuner* (pl. 39).[3] In his later letters (Appendices A and B), Léger emphasized the seeking of a new classicism which this picture represents: that is, a turning away from the excitable Cubism of *The City* towards a calmer, more obviously ordered style that looked back to the art of the classical tradition. It was an impulse felt by many Parisian artists from about 1920 onward, including Picasso, as well as Léger's eventual collaborators Amédée Ozenfant and Le Corbusier, founders of the Purist movement.

For both Léger and Picasso, the subject of the female nude was a logical means to explore a new classicism. It was a time-honored form in the French tradition, and both artists had painted nudes during the early Cubist period, before the

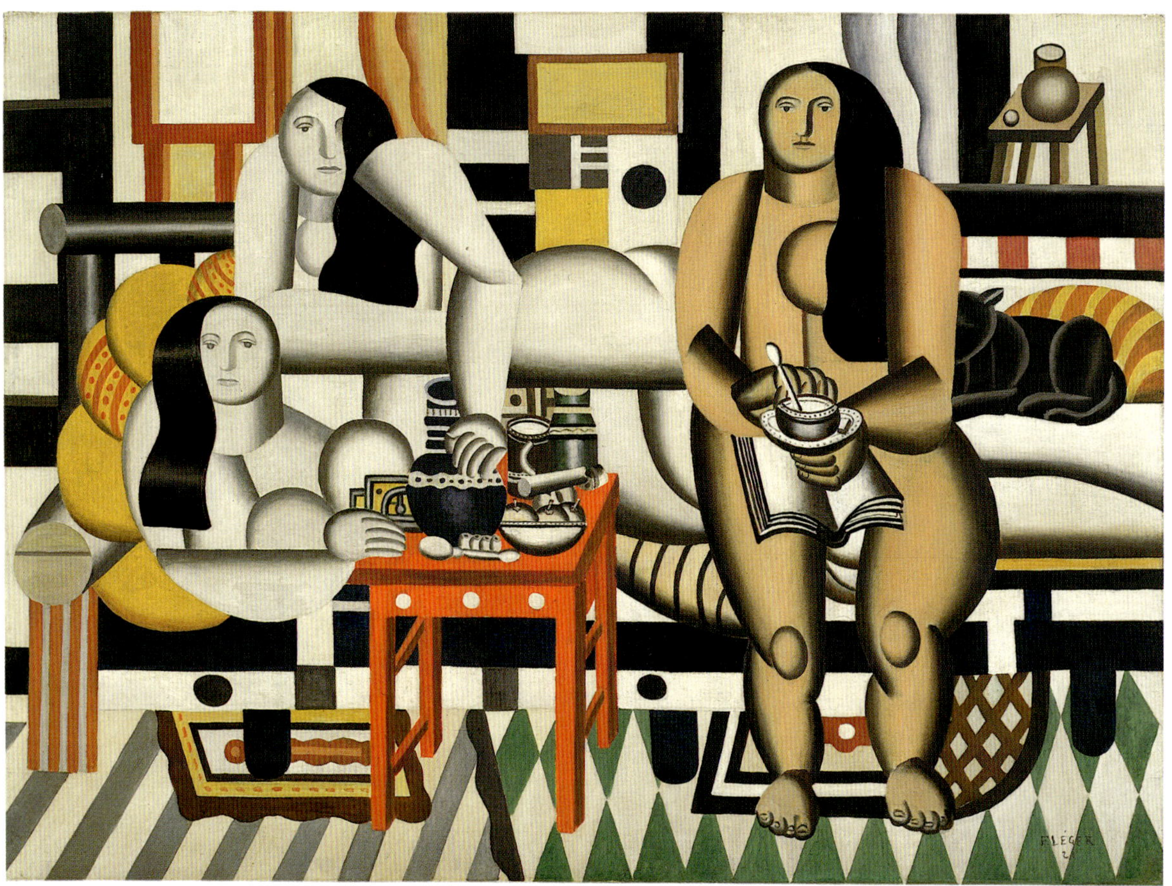

39 Fernand Léger, *Le Grand Déjeuner*, 1921–22. 72¼ × 99 in. (183.5 × 251.5 cm.). Museum of Modern Art, New York, Mrs. Simon Guggenheim Fund.

war. Beginning in 1920, Léger undertook a series of nudes which he continued for several years, and it is out of these paintings that *Le Grand Déjeuner* came. There is not a straight line of development leading from one of these paintings to another. Léger did not finish one picture before beginning a new one, but rather worked on a number of paintings simultaneously, moving back and forth among them, learning from each in a complicated way that no historian can reconstruct. Improvisation is at least as important a part of the artistic process as careful planning, and Léger's paintings, with their many repaints, give abundant evidence of constant changes of mind and therefore of a pragmatic learning process. Nonetheless, individual pictures can be analyzed for the lessons they offered Léger as he worked on his large composition, as long as one does not assume a straight chronological sequence.

In a letter to Alfred Barr (Appendix B) Léger said that *Le Grand Déjeuner* evolved at the same time as *Les Odalisques*, a painting he identified as in the Kahn collection, probably referring to the handsome composition formerly in the Burden collection (pl. 40). In this and several other paintings of nudes,[4] Léger

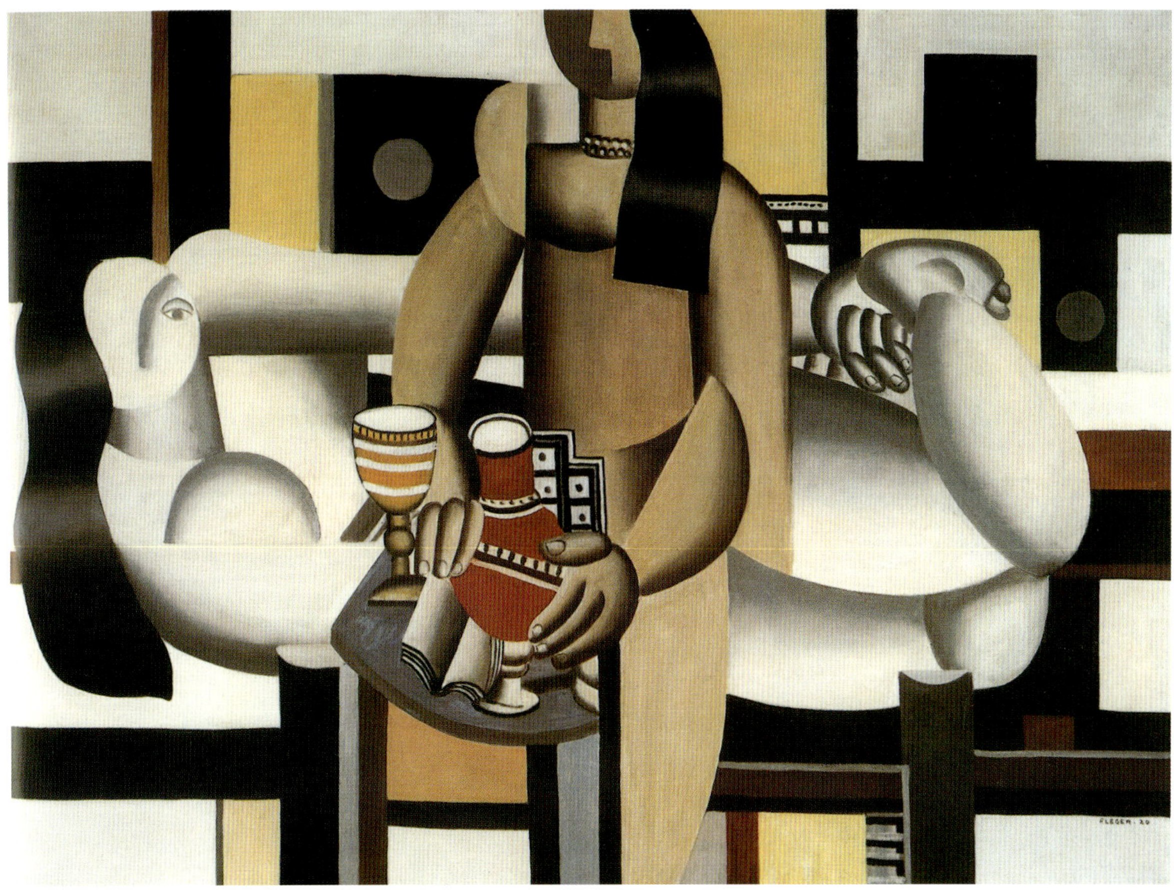

40 Fernand Léger, *Les Odalisques*, 1920. $27\frac{3}{8} \times 38$ in. (69.6×96.5 cm.). Formerly collection Mr. and Mrs. William A.M. Burden.

combined a horizontal figure, a vertical figure, and a still-life against a background of rectilinear elements, in essence much of the program for the large *Déjeuner*. The subject suited his search for a contrast to the dynamic modernism of *The City*. The word "odalisques" refers to the harem nudes of Ingres, Delacroix, and other painters of the Romantic era: "subjects or objects which have been treated during all the times by painters of other times" (Appendix B). The composition similarly reflects Léger's urge toward a new classicism; by taking up a theme sanctioned by tradition, he hoped to integrate art history, as well as past time, into the present. The classicism of the paintings of nudes is found in their well-resolved balance of horizontals and verticals, and also in their rounded, massive figures, so unlike the fragmented forms of most of his other paintings of 1917 to 1919.

In *Les Odalisques* the standing nude is of the terracotta color Léger eventually used for one figure in *Le Grand Déjeuner*, and it has the same effect: it brings the figure out towards us, clearly separating her from the other nude. In addition, the brightly colored still-life floats forward, an impression enhanced by the

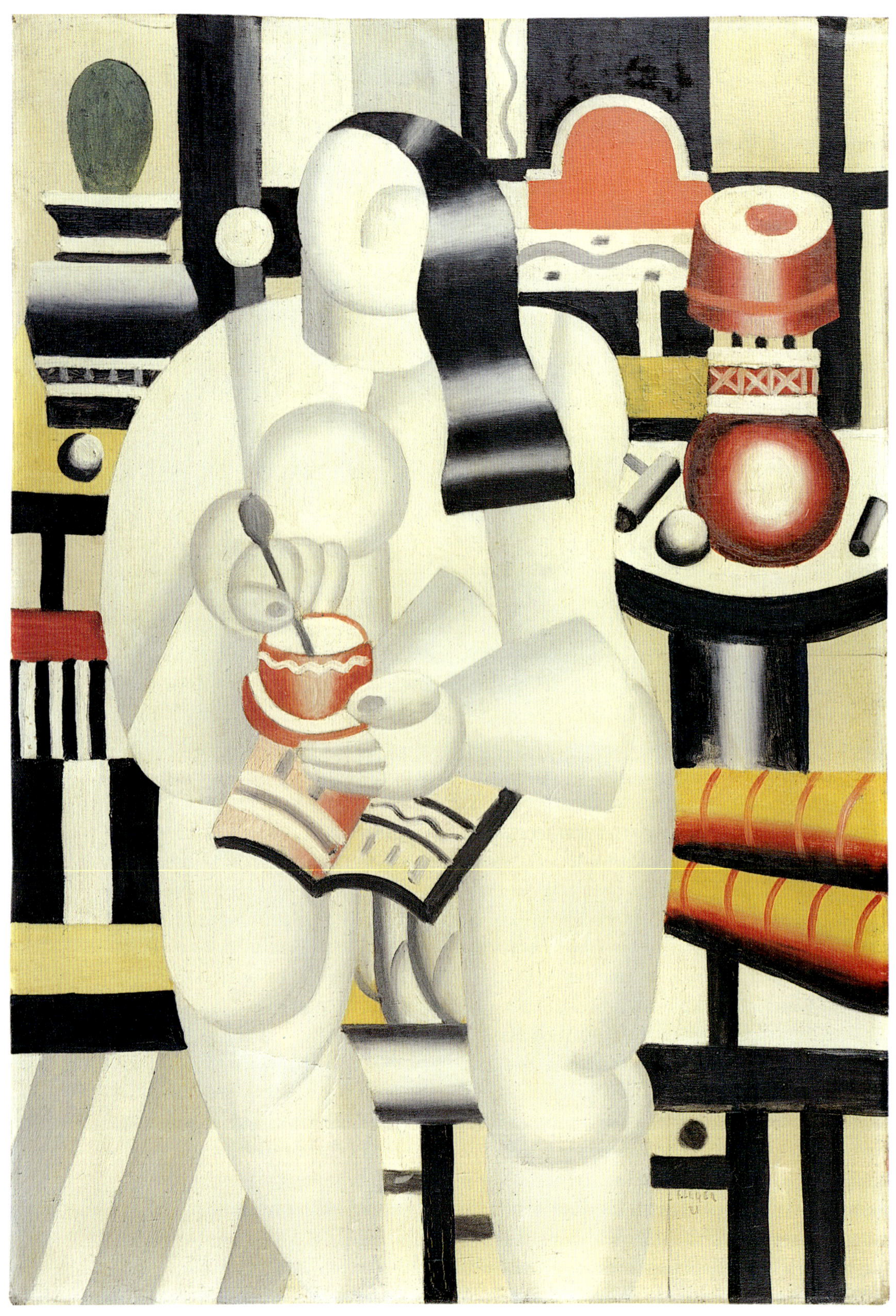

41 Fernand Léger, *Cup of Tea*, 1921. 36 × 26½ in. (91.5 × 67.3 cm.). Private collection.

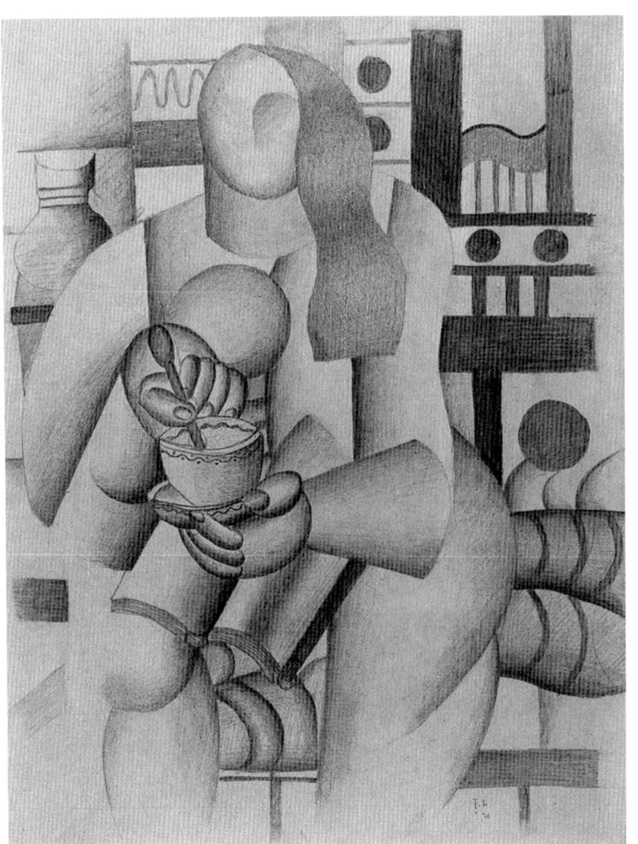

42 Fernand Léger, *Study for the Cup of Tea*, 1921. Pencil on paper, 18½ × 14 in. (47 × 35.5 cm.). Kröller-Müller Museum, Otterlo.

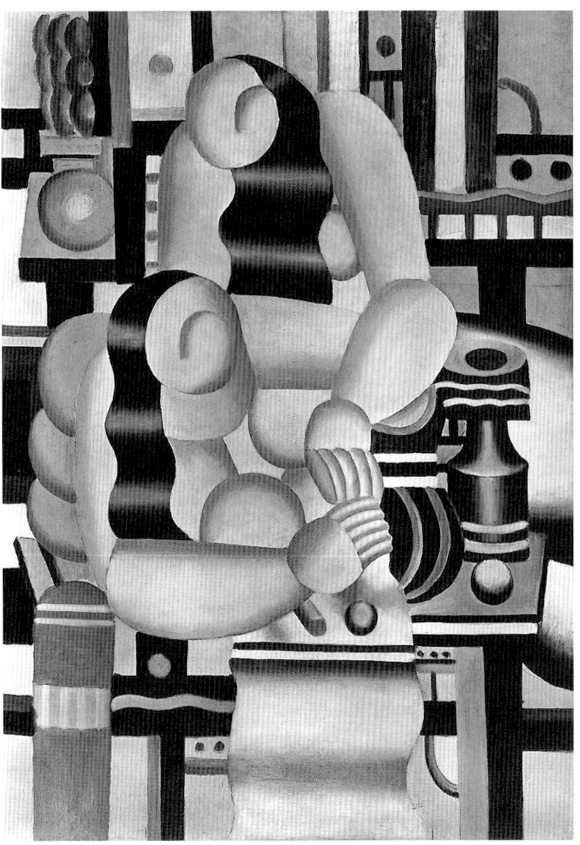

43 Fernand Léger, *Le Déjeuner*, 1921. 36¼ × 25½ in. (92 × 65 cm.). Musée National d'Art Moderne, Centre Georges Pompidou, Paris, AM 1984-585.

gesture of the standing nude, who grasps the large urn. This gesture has another purpose: it integrates the still-life with the nudes. The standing nude seems to be serving the other woman, and the book on the table adds an intellectual or, at least, a domestic note. It is here in *Les Odalisques* that Léger seems first to have thought of the meal and the book which he used subsequently in the *Le Grand Déjeuner* to convert a harem scene into an enigmatic breakfast of nude women.

The large *Déjeuner* is a mural-scale painting whose special problems were solved in a series of paintings and drawings. Léger's letters of 1942 and 1943 (Appendices A and B) name the several oils involved, although his use of the word "study" is ambiguous and often means "small version" or "variation upon," as much as "preparation for." The *Cup of Tea* (pl. 41) and *Le Déjeuner* (pl. 43) are paintings in their own right, although Léger called them "fragments," and they were probably conceived before the large composition was undertaken. The *Cup of Tea* is associated with a number of seated nudes, shown with a cup or book, sometimes with legs crossed or one leg doubled under. It has its own study (pl. 42), a drawing in the Kröller-Müller Museum, which also contributed to the three-figure composition: the woman's left forearm and the buttock-like

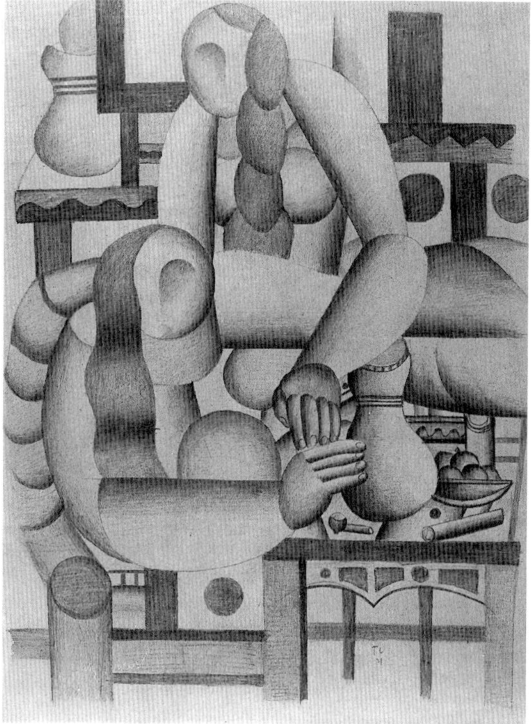

44 *(right)* Fernand Léger, *Study for Le Déjeuner*, 1921. Pencil on paper, 19¼ × 14⅜ in. (48.8 × 36.5 cm.). Kröller-Müller Museum, Otterlo.

45 *(facing page)* Fernand Léger, *Compositional Study for Le Grand Déjeuner*, 1921. Pencil on paper, 14½ × 20¼ in. (36.8 × 51.4 cm.). Kröller-Müller Museum, Otterlo.

thigh reappear in the large painting, but tipped over to the horizontal to become part of a reclining figure, one of the best examples of the shuffling of motifs which Léger performed so adroitly. The nude in the *Cup of Tea* lacks the double thigh, but has well-rounded volumes which are echoed in the vase and urn to either side. Her massiveness is subdued by the delicate grisaille rendering, which keeps her within the confines of the picture plane. In *Le Grand Déjeuner*, her warm-colored counterpart nearly jumps out from the surface.

Le Déjeuner (pl. 43), which anticipates the left side of the big canvas, also has its own drawing (pl. 44). The table in the drawing reappears, somewhat altered, in the main compositional drawing (pl. 45), as does the lateral extension of the nude's body. In *Le Déjeuner* the table and the buttocks differ from those in its preparatory drawing. The still-life on the table is simplified and partly covers the horizontal legs, preventing our eyes from sliding out of the picture. A tablecloth, in grisaille like the nudes, creates a strong vertical unity. The composition seems to derive ultimately from the two-figure group (pl. 40), but the vertical nude is placed in the background behind, instead of in front where she threatened to walk out of the picture. She is integrated with the reclining figure in another way: the two share an arm. The upper arm and the forearm of the reclining woman are the two forearms of her companion. To the left are the multiple orange pillows of *Le Grand Déjeuner*.

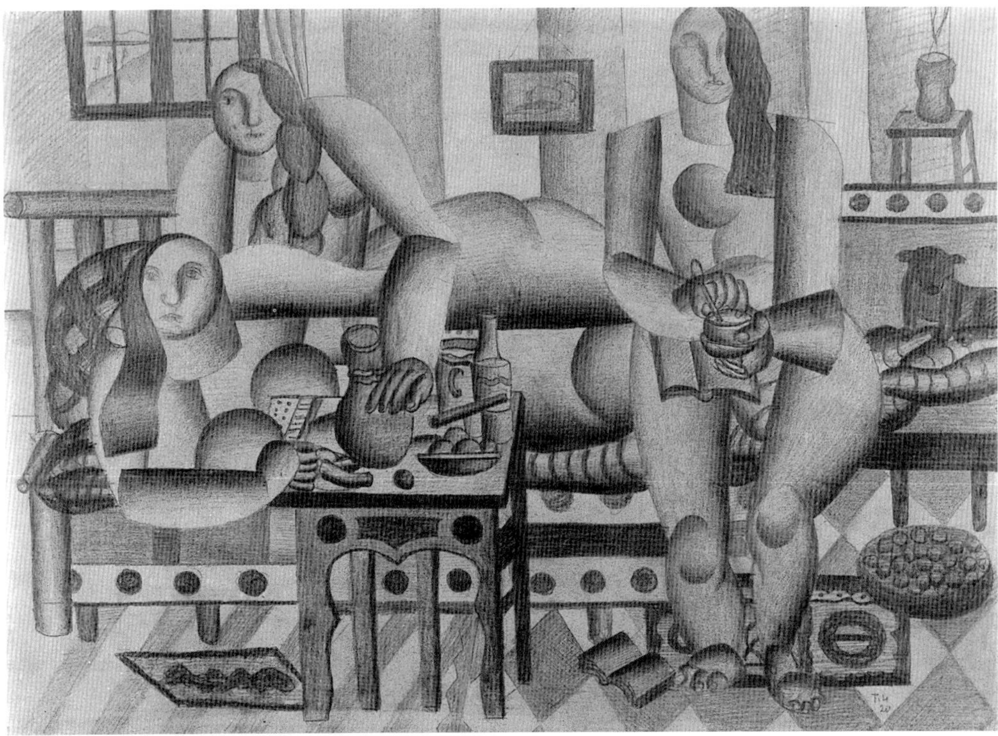

The compositional drawing (pl. 45) was probably done after the two oil "fragments" of the left and right sides, as a way of welding them into a single composition. It is closer in many details of pose and arrangement to the large painting than is either of the oils. The more three-dimensional rendering creates the environment of a single room, complete with window at the left rear, framed painting in the center, and view into another room at the upper right corner. There is a continuous floor plane, and a nearly continuous horizontal form, like a long sofa, which joins the three figures. The two women on the left still share one arm, but the upper nude's outstretched arm is now entirely hers, and has moved well to the right. It touches the urn, a change that gives to the still-life a more convincing spatial position, although in other regards it defies the conventions of illusionism. Some shared anatomy in the center joins the two women with the seated figure to the right. The upper portion gives a profile view of buttocks, derived from the drawing for the right figure (pl. 42); the lower portion comes from the thigh and kneecap in a painting of a reclining odalisque.[5] Together they are perceived as an extension of the reclining woman, although our mind tries to link them also with the other woman on the left.

The next stage in the development of the large painting is represented by the Minneapolis *Petit Déjeuner* (pl. 46).[6] Originally its seated figure was in grisaille, but Léger later reworked it in ocher. Otherwise the picture appears not to have

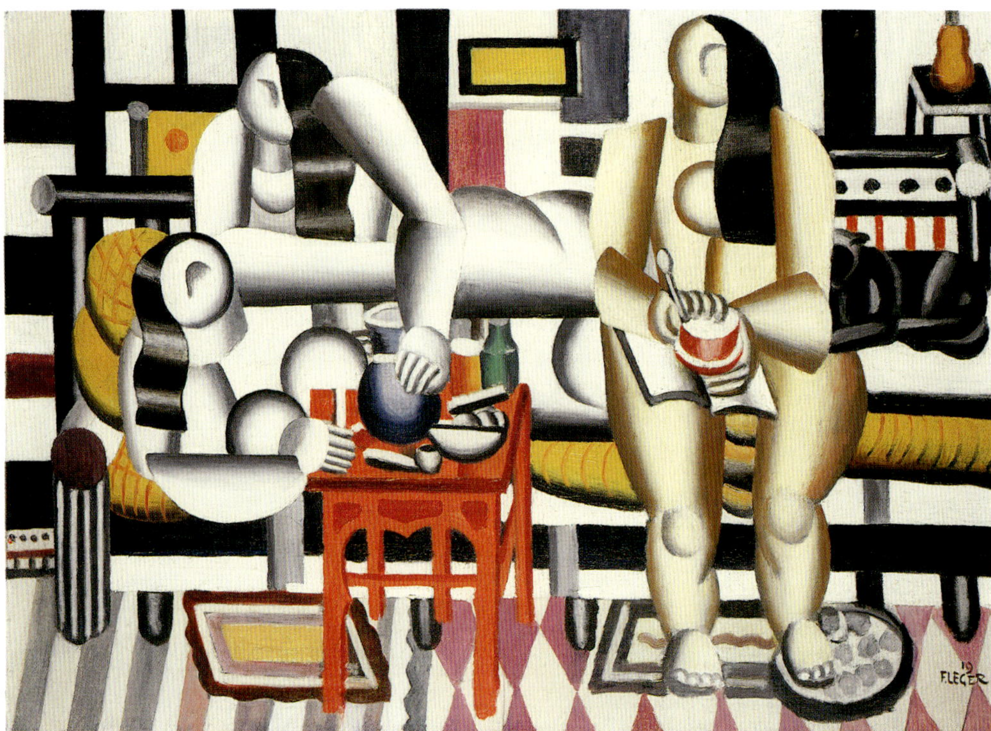

46 Fernand Léger, *Le Petit Déjeuner*, 1921. 27⅛ × 36¼ in. (69 × 92 cm.). Minneapolis Institute of Arts, Gift of Mr. and Mrs. Samuel H. Maslon.

been altered, except for the painting out of two small disks, one on the left edge and the other near the shoulder of the seated figure. That figure was moved closer to the other two than it was in the drawing, reducing the central expanse of thigh. Her form is closer to that in the drawing than that in the *Cup of Tea*, and a number of subtle alterations predict her pose in the final painting. To reduce the effect of a real person grasping a cup, Léger has removed her thumbs, and her hands, instead of holding the cup, now present it to the viewer. The book on her lap begins its rightward migration which will lead it from one leg, in the drawing, to a more central position in the large painting. Her left foot has been moved to the right and placed on the round cushion which is further away in the drawing. To her right, the several serpentine cushions have been replaced by one, further down, that continues the sofa motif from the center. The alert little dog of the compositional drawing is now more passive, and touches her body as proof of his symbolic role: fidelity (hence "Fido").

Many of the other changes from the drawing were calculated to render the scene less anecdotal. The window and the painting on the wall are reduced to skeletal rectangles, and the wide bands of the wall are repeated along the left edge, flattening the whole background. The prominent corner support of the sofa

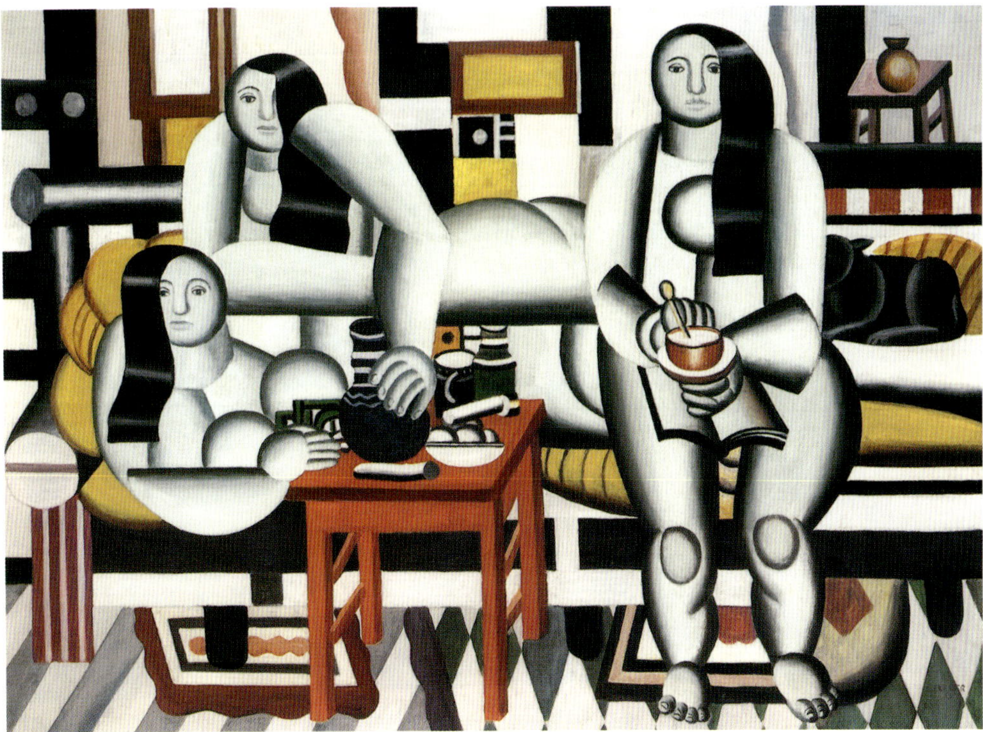

47 Fernand Léger, *Le Petit Déjeuner*, 1921–22. 40⅛ × 53⅛ in. (102 × 135 cm.). Private collection.

is redrawn to give it greater autonomy as a pictorial form, and the bottom cushion is accordingly pushed to the right. To echo the rectilinearity of the top and side, the horizontal underpinnings of the sofa are greatly simplified and the floor plane is unified by eliminating the book and consolidating the rugs and floor tiles. The two rear legs of the bright red table, which in the drawing are ostentatiously pushed forward, are now placed further back, although they still appear misplaced by conventional standards.

The other *Petit Déjeuner* (pl. 47), larger than the Minneapolis picture, is nearer to the final composition. Furthermore, its three grisaille figures give us an idea of how the final painting would have looked before its seated figure was repainted. Some features of this canvas disclose that it, too, was repainted, and that underneath the present surface are features of the Minneapolis composition. The red table, although now more conventionally rendered, once had three disks on its front edge, a momentary echo of the complicated pattern of the earlier table. The top of the head of the seated woman was originally more like that of the Minneapolis version, but nearly an inch of it was painted out to make the contour more rounded. Similarly, the repaints on the reclining nude's hair show that it once had a narrower fall.[7]

Other compositional alterations that appear in the larger *Petit Déjeuner* are more significant for the final painting, and a few of them restore at least some of the three-dimensionality of the principal drawing (pl. 45). The window at the upper left acquires a double-thick edge, suggesting an open casement thrown back to the wall; to its right and to the right of the seated woman, a curtain appears, a deliberate reverberation of the women's hair which will be reinforced in the large oil. In the upper right corner the table reacquires the more conventional aspect it had in the compositional drawing, and in so doing creates a deeper space. This more tangible space is evident elsewhere; below the table, the dog now has its own striped cushion, which seems to stretch the divan all the way to the right edge – the more so since the grisaille rectangle that is under the dog in the Minneapolis picture is now more like an oversized human leg.

Further down on the right side, the orange cushion or bedding has disappeared, on its way to becoming the second outsized leg of the final painting, and still lower, the floor bends back more, thanks to the new shape of the rounded cushion and the removal of the horizontal white band at that point. Along the floor on the far side, the small rug does not float forward on the surface quite so much, because it is pinned down by the leg of the divan. Conventional perspective is nonetheless defied by the angled placement of the scalloped strip (originally the border of the large striped rug which covers the left half of the floor), and by the squaring-off of the once tubular corner leg of the sofa. The two cushions behind the reclining nude have become four, and on the table the several vessels have more definite shapes and decorated surfaces. The enigmatic red rectangles on the table's left edge have assumed their ultimate character: pieces of toast in a wire holder. The balloon-breast behind the toaster is now firmly anchored, thanks to the appearance of a segment of adjacent torso missing from the Minneapolis painting.

The most pronounced change is the introduction of facial features. In the Minneapolis variant and in the two "fragments" each of the women has a bird-like nose and brow that recall the severe curves of Brancusi's abstract sculpted heads. By giving them eyes, nose, and mouth (no ears, but then Léger seldom puts handles on his pots), Léger adds to the space of the picture in two ways. In one sense, the features articulate the volume of the heads. In another, two of the figures establish contact with our own eyes and thereby create an interplay between the painted space and our own.

The Completion of *Le Grand Déjeuner*

In the fall of 1921, viewers at the Paris Salon d'Automne had the first opportunity of matching gazes with the women of the large canvas itself.[8] Léonce Rosenberg, with whom Léger had a regular contract, lent the painting, and it was credited to his collection when it was reproduced in *Esprit Nouveau* in

December (pl. 48). That photograph is the only evidence we have of the early state of the painting, which was reworked in 1922 after Léger had taken it back from Rosenberg (exchanging it for the "more pleasant picture" *Mother and Child*, now in the Kunstmuseum, Basel; see Appendices A and B). It was doubtless very austere in appearance, with its figures all in grisaille, an effect we can guess at by imagining the second *Petit Déjeuner* (pl. 47) at the scale of the large canvas. We cannot be sure of all the alterations that Léger made, but many of them can be discovered by studying the visible repaints, as well as by comparing the painting with the *Esprit Nouveau* photograph. The two horizontal zones to the right, below the dog, are both in grisaille now, although the lower one seems to have been painted first in yellow, as in the Minneapolis version. The importance of this change is considerable, for now these two zones have become the extended legs of the reclining nude, carrying her body all the way to the right edge in a conscious search for unity.

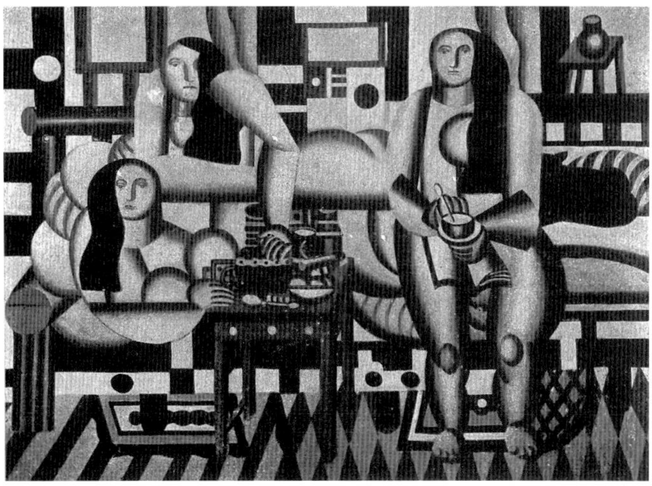

48 Fernand Léger, reproduction of *Le Grand Déjeuner* in *Esprit nouveau*, December 1921.

Elsewhere several decorative motifs were eliminated after the Salon d'Automne exhibition. To the left of the seated woman's leg, one disk was removed from the white horizontal strip, and above that strip, two white portions were covered over in dark blue to form a more continuous dark base for the divan. In the upper left corner a prominent disk was painted out. Nearly all the minor changes tended towards the reduction of decorative elements (one exception is found on two yellow- and red-striped pillows behind the reclining nude, which were given their rows of dots only in the reworking).

The most important changes that Léger made after the painting's return from the Salon d'Automne concern the seated woman to the right. The lower part of her hair was curved to the right, exposing more of her torso. Both forearms were altered, at the left by enlarging the wrist, on the right by exchanging a curved bottom edge for the straight one. Léger made the saucer wider and added the sugar cube, and he also expanded the volume of the open book. All these differences, small as they may seem, give the figure more three-dimensional mass. Of course the fundamental change, the striking idea, was to repaint her in terracotta color. The warm tone brings the figure to the foreground, and simultaneously creates a deeper space on her side of the composition.

Two of Léger's letters to Alfred Barr (Appendices A and B) give an explanation for the alteration of the seated woman. By separating her from the other two, he intended to emphasize a more spatial reading, which he associated with easel painting, as distinct from wall or mural painting. An easel painting can be moved from place to place and consequently its specific environment cannot be determined by the artist. Léger was therefore eager that the painting leap out from the wall, as it were, in order to control any space in which it might be hung. Earlier he had written that "in a flat, I'm satisfied if my picture controls the room, if it dominates everything and everyone."[9] A mural painting, on the other hand, although it may be "romantic" in its expression, according to Léger, has a known, fixed position.[10] It adheres to the wall on which it is placed and does not seek to invade the viewer's space.

The contrasting natures of easel and wall painting which, Léger wrote to Barr, were for him a lifelong preoccupation, are displayed in *Le Grand Déjeuner*, despite the dominance of "the easel side." It is this conflict between the illusion of three dimensions and the actual flat surface that is at the heart of the picture's visual excitement. Toward the bottom of the canvas, for example, the viewer is struck by the powerful illusions of the red table, which slants effectively back into imaginary depth, and of the foreshortened feet of the seated woman which seem to thrust out in front of the surface. And yet, lacking the shadows of traditional art, these same forms float curiously atop the flat patterns of the floor. Seen as a whole, the composition somehow encompasses both the illusion of volume and mass, seen principally in the women, and the flat patterns of architectural surface. These "flat" patterns themselves are restless, however, and the viewer finds some of them forming holes through the composition while others jump forward. Similarly, the bulk of the two grisaille nudes fades into flatness at certain points, an effect aided by the repetition of similar off-white tones in other parts of the canvas. At times, because of the many zones of white, the two nudes seem to loom out of the background, part of it and yet detaching themselves from it.

Le Grand Déjeuner, like most other works by Léger, thrives on such internal contrasts. Instead of settling into a peaceful harmony, the painting finds a balance of opposing elements which sufficiently neutralize one another to hang together, all the while threatening to come apart. When we stare at the canvas we participate actively in this struggle, and we come to realize that for Léger this is not merely a play of formal elements but the very essence of his art. "I apply the law of plastic contrasts," he wrote in 1923. "I group contrary values together: flat surfaces opposed to modeled surfaces; volumetric figures opposed to the flat façades of houses; molded volumes of plumes of smoke opposed to active surfaces of architecture; pure, flat tones opposed to gray, modulated tones or the reverse."[11]

In most of his writings, from 1914 onward, Léger insisted on contrast as his principle of organization. In paintings of the prewar years, for example, puffs of smoke and curves of women's bodies were set against the straight-edged masses of architecture. These were contrasts of growing, organic shapes against inert ones, and embodied fundamental oppositions of life; the human against the environment, the lifelike against the inert, the colored against the colorless. For Léger, this was a social and not just a formal conception. To recognize that life was a dialectical interaction between opposed forces, he believed, was to be a man of the vanguard. Already in 1914 he castigated the bourgeoisie for its fear of contrast: "Contrast has always frightened peaceful and satisfied people; they eliminate it from their lives as much as possible, and as they are disagreeably startled by the dissonances of some billboard or other, so their lives are organized to avoid all such uncouth contact."[12]

In Léger's letters to Barr of 1942 and 1943, he associated the contrasts of classic and romantic, and of easel and mural, with *Le Grand Déjeuner*, and when he wrote of having reworked the painting in 1922, he said, "I decided to strengthen the contrasts." The painting includes his whole lexicon of contrasts: straight vs. curved, soft vs. hard, flat vs. rounded, vertical vs. horizontal, color vs. black and white, human vs. architectural, organic vs. inert. These contrasts are not so ruthlessly maintained as to forbid interrelationships, however. Flat disk, circular, and oval ends of tubular furniture, and oval mouths of containers have their counterparts in the women's breasts, eyes, heads, and kneecaps; undulating curtains and rug patterns repeat the rhythms of failing hair; spoon, egg cups, vases, and fruit have the swelling volumes of the nudes, and they establish analogies of containment and growth; pillows offer close approximations to female form.

Because contrast, in Léger's view, is the vital principle of modern life, it extends deeply into his esthetic. A painting gives witness to two powerful opposites, the subjective (the artist's mind) and the objective (the "real world"), each needing the other, and together duplicating the conflicts that are the essence of modern life. "Art is subjective, that is understood," he wrote in 1923, "but a controlled subjectivity based on 'objective' raw material. That is my absolute opinion. Plastic work is 'the ambiguous state' of these two values, the real and the imagined. The difficulty is to find a balance between these two poles; to cut the difficulty in two and take only one or the other, to make either pure abstractions or imitations of nature, is really too easy and avoids the problem as a whole."[13]

The artist's job is to create something entirely new, but by incorporating references to the world outside his mind he escapes the trap of purely personal effusion. His art is a social art because of its dialog with reality. This is why Léger consistently denied abstraction, and why, after the war, he congratulated himself on rediscovering the subject matter of modern life, thanks to his wartime experience with fellow soldiers, the ordinary people of France. "And then, the return to the subject, trying still to set plastic contrasts against each other. I rarely abandon the subject, even now. I keep the subject as much as my desire to create something new will allow. If I do leave it behind, it is only to obtain greater intensity."[14]

Léger's New Humanism

The "subject" of *Le Grand Déjeuner* was explained in Léger's letter of 1943 (Appendix B) in very plain terms: "some women's bodies, one table, a dog, every time's subject without any expression of evocation." It is phrases like the last that have convinced too many people that Léger's subjects are unimportant. Critics and historians have too thoroughly absorbed the aggressive doctrine of early modern art, which proclaimed the triumph of formal values over "subject." Léger's letters make it clear that he was searching for "monumental figures," for a new classicism in opposition to the dynamism of *The City*. He wanted a "controlled subjectivity" that would permit objective references to dominate "romantic" expressiveness. In this he looked back to artists who were labeled both "classical" and "primitive," and whose work is characterized by a singular detachment that struck their contemporaries as a lack of expression: Ingres, Seurat, and Cézanne.

In *Le Grand Déjeuner*, themes of dynamic modernism were supplanted by one that had been "treated during all the times." It was a renewal of contact with historical themes, treated with an objectivity of expression guaranteeing that it would surmount personal feeling and contemporary preoccupations. Léger set about making a pictorial résumé of great art themes of the past. Odalisques and harem scenes have already been discussed; his three nudes, although they do not look like specific paintings of the past, also recall such works as Seurat's *Models* (Barnes Foundation, Merion), three nudes of remarkably dispassionate character, or Puvis de Chavannes's several paintings of three pensive semi-nudes. The choice of three figures was no accident. Like Seurat and Puvis, Léger wished to renew the old traditions represented by three nudes: the Three Graces, the three rivals for the judgment of Paris, or the three major visual arts (painting, sculpture, architecture). Léger's friend Delaunay had symbolized the city of Paris by three nudes in an ambitious painting of 1910–12 (Musée National d'Art Moderne, Centre Pompidou, Paris), and Léger's first great painting, *Nudes in the Forest* (Kröller-Müller Museum, Otterlo), also used three figures in an enterprising, if still undeciphered, homage to man's power to build. *Le Grand Déjeuner* stands in a long Western tradition of art in which ideas are vested in images of the human body.

Léger was not alone in this new humanism, for there was a broad current of classicism that marked art in Paris from 1920 onward. Leading art journals (including *Esprit Nouveau* and others with which Léger collaborated) discussed and reproduced antique sculpture as well as works in the classical tradition, among them paintings by Poussin, David, Ingres, Corot, and Seurat. Picasso's contribution to the new classicism was especially important, and some of his paintings of nudes and half-draped figures of 1920 and 1921 deliberately evoke classical antiquity. His *Three Women at the Spring* of 1921 (pl. 49) is one of the best known of these and it has often been compared with Léger's *Déjeuner* (they are often placed in the same room at the Museum of Modern Art, New York). They share a massiveness of scale and – in conventional terms – inexpressive, dispassionate facial features. Some observers have gone so far as to claim that Léger's painting was derived from Picasso's, but this ignores the fact that the *Déjeuner* evolved logically from Léger's own earlier work. Léger was doubtless stimulated by Picasso's example, but their common roots in the classicizing tradition is the best explanation for the characteristics shared by these two paintings.

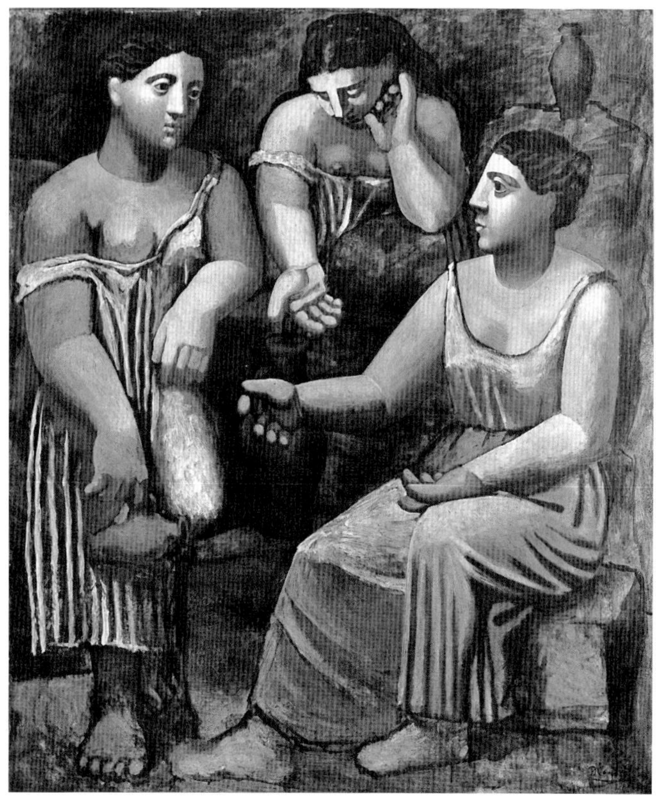

49 Pablo Picasso, *Three Women at the Spring*, 1921. $80\frac{1}{4} \times 68\frac{1}{2}$ in. (203.9 × 174 cm.). Museum of Modern Art, New York, Gift of Mr. and Mrs. Allan D. Emil.

Le Grand Déjeuner is no stodgy derivation from past art, of course, and we would miss its unique flavor if we failed to see its humor. Léger frequently decried the "beautiful subjects" of traditional art, and insisted that painting must be modern. He would have found Picasso's *Three Women at the Spring* too full of nostalgia for the past, in his terminology, too "romantic." To him, his *Déjeuner* was more modern because, although it incorporated aspects of past art, it did so by mocking it. He wanted to outrival great art of the past by remaking it in his own guise. This is an old habit of French artists. Manet had remade the reclining Venus in his famous *Olympia*, and in their different ways, Degas, Renoir, Seurat, Gauguin, Cézanne, Maillol, and Matisse had reclaimed for themselves the theme of the female nude, usually presented, as in Léger's work, in moments of leisure. Degas, for example, rescued the nude from the pastiches of unimaginative contemporaries and placed her in a domestic setting, with startling results.

Léger's willful mocking of tradition (which for him included the artists just named) was confessed in his letter to Barr: "Traditionally *Le Grand Déjeuner* can be connected to the Romance period, I think (Appendix A)." His wish to counteract the dynamism of *The City* by embracing subjects of the past had its humor: he took a "beautiful subject" from the romantic era and used his own art to make it classical. This is a perverse display of ego, to take a romantic subject and discipline it by its supposed opposite, all the while denying to it the usual attributes of erotic appeal. "It is the classical line, [in] my opinion, [to] put the subject or the object inside, behind the pictorial expression. The romantic is just the contrary, I believe; the subject or object come before, in expressive feeling" (Appendix B).

Léger would have been amused by our contemporary phrase "sex object," for he has made his women into objects by refusing to give them any conventional sexual appeal. He has further prevented men from seeing them simply as sexual partners, despite their origins in the odalisques, by surrounding them with domestic references. They are having breakfast, and the seated figure has been reading. The dog is the traditional symbol of fidelity, the opposite of the sensual cat which Manet had preferred. More than anything else, however, overt sensuality is forbidden by the fact that the three figures are not real women, in the fiction of the picture, but works of art. Léger's evocation of past art constitutes a kind of visual quotation. His three nudes are art works within a work of art. Two of them are colored like marble statues and the third like a terracotta sculpture.

The marvelous, admittedly intellectualized humor of this composition lies in its very improbability: the introduction of classical sculptures into a modern domestic setting. Léger had something of the deadpan humor of Seurat who, in his *Models* (Barnes Foundation, Merion), placed three nudes in his studio and flatly called them "models." Like Seurat, his most important forebear in early modern art, Léger was probably aware of an antique prototype in the legend of Xeuxis at Croton, who chose several models in order to combine their best qualities into one ideal figure. Or perhaps he thought of Paris, confronting two goddesses and Helen in order to choose one as the paramount beauty. Since we, the viewers, are put in the position of the artist, whose figures are staring out at us, we become Xeuxis or Paris, confronted by a notable triad of historic nudes.

Women and Men of Leisure

Léger's art-nudes are easily distinguished from other inhabitants of his interiors. *Women in an Interior* (pl. 50) is the most beautiful of several pictures that include clothed figures (here strongly colored in orange and wine-red) with the nudes. We accept the child and the clothed woman as "real" persons who have entered the domain of the nudes. The reclining nude has been given her own set of arms, and embraces the child, although her hand can also be viewed as belonging to the clothed woman. The seated nude has her forearm and book confounded with the standing woman, and the nude to the rear, her coloring altered, further confuses the spatial and noumenal reading by reaching out over the reclining nude.

Such combinations of art-nudes and clothed figures do not occur often in Léger's oeuvre; far more common are interiors where no such ambiguities arise, that is, scenes in which the figures, although far from illusionistic, are "real"

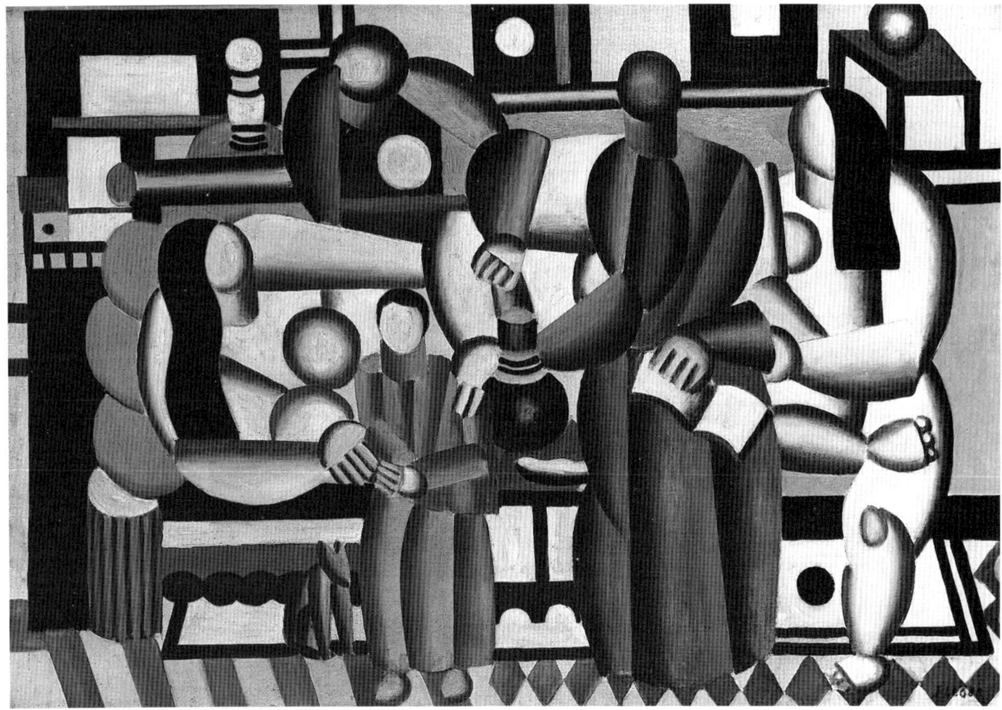

50 Fernand Léger, *Women in an Interior*, 1921. 25⅜ × 36¼ in. (64.5 × 92 cm.). Musée National d'Art Moderne, Centre Georges Pompidou, Paris.

within the limits of their special worlds. The two figures in *Women in an Interior* have upper bodies rather like those of the figures in *Le Grand Déjeuner* but, because they are provided with skirts, they are readily accepted as a clothed mother and daughter standing by a "real" window and flanked by two tables. There is a whole set of compositions related to the *Mother and Child* (Kunstmuseum, Basel) which Léger gave Rosenberg in exchange for *Le Grand Déjeuner*. These place the figures partly inside a living room and partly outside on a balcony through open French windows. Most of these show a clothed mother, reclining with a book in her hand, and a clothed child, but at least one, *Three Persons before a Garden* (formerly Mr. and Mrs. Ralph F. Colin), shows a father standing behind his wife and child.

The clothed figures in these and other paintings, in specific family relationships, make the nudes of *Le Grand Déjeuner* all the more clearly understand-able as very different creatures, as painted art works. This range of domestic interiors hints at other relationships which extend the meaning of the *Déjeuner*: all of them show figures at leisure. To understand why this is so, we should, in turn, look briefly at Léger's other subjects and how they evolved after World War I.

In the last years of the war, and in the immediate postwar years, Léger was absorbed in the dynamism of urban-industrial life. A good many paintings show silhouettes of men in factory interiors and in city streets. This is the realm of modern man, who leads a Promethean life, and the urban environment itself is characterized by frenetic activity, as in *The City* (pl. 38). In one extended series beginning in 1917, Léger represented tugboats bringing produce to the city, often with one or two male figures standing nearby as witnesses to this vital activity. Working, building, and provisioning the city are the realm of the male for Léger, as distinct from that of the female. (To a certain extent these men continue the activity of the military engineer whom Léger had drawn during the war.) The mood of exultation celebrated in *The City*, the joyful plunge into the fragmented life of modern man, reigned over Léger's subjects into 1921. Then the great change began which is chiefly celebrated in *Le Grand Déjeuner*, and in this new mood, the allied themes of women and leisure gradually take over.

Léger's new humanism was a response to his growing feeling that the frenetic pace of modern life needed the discipline of calmness and order, a feeling he shared with Ozenfant and Le Corbusier, and other artists in Paris. In an essay of 1924 he likened himself both to doctor and to priest, bringing relief from the cacophony of factory and city, and helping create through art a "society without frenzy, calm, ordered, knowing how to live naturally within the Beautiful without exclamation or romanticism."[15] With his nudes of 1920, he began to use women as symbols of release from labor, or even as symbols of the reward for labor. *Le Grand Déjeuner*, announced as a counterweight to *The City*, is the central masterpiece of this period in which women are identified with leisure, and both of these are associated with art history, since art of the past is also a release from the present.

Leisure is not, for Léger, a frivolous escape from modern life. It is earned by modern man. Léger was an optimist who believed that modern technology would release man from drudgery. This is why, even in the factory pictures of 1917 to 1920, he seldom showed men actually working: they usually stand or sit, nearly inactive, because man has produced machinery which does the work for him. Léger's wartime drawings, including the illustrations for Cendrars's *J'ai tué*, likewise show men standing near or sitting on machinery, but not engaged in battle.

In this connection, one of the largest classifications of Léger's subjects should be mentioned. The "animated landscapes," begun in 1921, encompass several dozen paintings. Typical of them is the fine *Animated Landscape* (pl. 57). It shares with *Le Grand Déjeuner* the turn towards a "society without frenzy, calm, ordered," and is more directly a re-formation of *The City*. It is best explained by the fact that *The City*, a year or so after Léger had finished it, came to stand for "romantic" excitement, insufficiently disciplined and (perhaps unconsciously) too close to the excitement of the war years. As those years receded, a yearning for peace and order grew stronger, and the result in *Animated Landscape* is a new utopian vision of the modern city. It is as though the many wartime drawings of soldiers at rest, standing near farmhouses or their field kitchens, had grown into a vision of peacetime leisure, earned by war and earned by the labor of modern factories. The men of *Animated Landscape* stand outside a city where billboard forms deliberately clash with nature to assert man's triumph over her.

Léger's optimism was shared by many in the early 1920s, especially by social reformers, both capitalists and socialists, whose hopes for the future were vested in rapid industrialization, and who stressed the virtues of earned leisure. The same optimism had stood behind the leisure subjects of Impressionism, Post-Impressionism, and early modern art. In constant references to his origins in Impressionism, Léger pointed to the "Nordic" character of modern life. "Nordic" was defined as a dynamic plunge into modern life, in contrast to "southern" character, marked by slowness and resistance to modernization. Leisure-time subjects of the Impressionist period generally express this optimism, and many of Monet's paintings show pleasure boats alongside railroad bridges, the peaceful cohabitation of industry and relaxation. Seurat's *Bathing Place, Asniéres* (National Gallery, London) is a worthy ancestor of Léger's *Animated Landscape*, by virtue of showing boys and men enjoying leisure against the backdrop of factories and bridges.

Le Grand Déjeuner and *Animated Landscape*, therefore, take their place logically in the explication of Léger's ideal society. Man stands next to his city, his factory, and his tugboats. His domain is the street or the wharf. Woman is never shown there, for her realm is the interior. She is the nude, woman as sexual partner, woman as inspirational muse and as work of art. In other guises she is standing next to her child, or reclining with a book, enjoying her cultured leisure. She stands by the luncheon table as maker of meals, and she decorates the interior with the flowers she is often shown holding. In one series of pictures, both of her functions are shown: one figure is a nude, reclining, while one or two clothed women stand nearby, often holding flowers. In this domestic world, boys are only occasionally shown, men hardly ever. The male is present only as the presumed viewer (and therefore as Léger the painter) to whom this ideal world is being presented. For all his social idealism Léger, like most males of the period, accepted and even glorified the separate provinces of male and female, both worlds serving the male.

"Geometric Necessities"

Different though their two realms are, *Le Grand Déjeuner* and *Animated Landscape* are linked by an underlying social conception which posits that a rational, ideal society consists of both industry and leisure. The two paintings are linked also by the conspicuous geometry of their forms. Léger's geometry is so fundamental to his conception of art and of society that, like his theory of contrasts, it permeates all aspects of his painting. "A picture organized, orchestrated, like a musical score, has geometric necessities exactly the same as those of every objective human creation (commercial or industrial achievement)."[16]

Léger believed that geometry was the expression of rationality and order, as opposed to private emotions, of decisiveness, as opposed to middle-class softness, of impersonal clarity, as opposed to subjective vagueness.[17] Geometry was not simply discovered in nature and imitated by the artist. It was not, as it had been in Renaissance Christian thought, the hidden harmony of nature, one which was revealed by the artist-genius, authorized by God to disclose his secrets. It was instead a social and artistic pattern that man creates, the very proof of his triumph over nature, and nature was equated with imitative representation in art. Far from being alone in this conviction, Léger shared it with Le Corbusier and Ozenfant, with artists of the De Stijl group, with members of the Bauhaus, and with Russian Constructivists. The revolutionary Russian critic Filippov declared in 1921:

> The psychology of art established two kinds of artistic imagination – the *reproductive* and the *constructive*. The first of these proceeds from ready-made forms already existing in nature and life reflects them in the representation or distorting mirror of visual art. The second, audaciously and actively, contrasts Man's creation with Nature's creation by expressing the instinct of life, its beauty and its energy and, instead of imitating and reflecting its ready-made forms, creates completely new forms as signs and symbols of Man, the conqueror of Nature.[18]

Geometry was the visible sign of the reason and order which artists would help bring to the new society. It spoke for qualities of utility and economy, as opposed to the vagaries and the inconsistencies of nature. Flat industrial textures, smooth and unmodeled, replaced the "romantic" textures of traditional brushwork in painting, and strong local colors, reduced to primaries and secondaries, displaced the atmospheric nuances of imitative color.

Geometry was both modern and social in its character for Léger because it was the desired expression of order that linked painter, architect, and engineer. Collaboration among artists, rather than subjective individualism, was a product of the mood of reconstruction that came out of the war.[19] Léger lived up to his goals by collaborating with film-makers, architects, writers, musicians, and choreographers,[20] and he looked especially towards architecture as the leading art, given its direct social function. For many painters of the 1920s, this aspiration toward architecture supplanted the prewar concern for music, which now seemed to smack of subjective individualism. "I would, then, bring about a new architectural order: the architecture of the mechanical. Architecture, both traditional and modern, also originates from geometric forces."[21]

Geometry and architecture were often equated in Léger's art, as indeed they are in the forms of *Le Grand Déjeuner* and *Animated Landscape*, and both were associated with the mechanical. This association is not based simply on the appearance of machinery, but concerns the creativity of man who imposes order on nature thanks to the forces of organized thought, which are conceived of as geometrical. Geometry is non-imitative and even anti-natural because it stands for the instruments which modern man uses to change nature. Modern technology has altered the environment, and therefore art cannot any longer support a falsehood, the immutability of nature, which it does when it merely imitates her forms.

Even before World War I, Léger had declared his faith in the new machine world, symbolized by the disruptive geometry of the billboard. After the war, he insisted over and over again that a painter is bound to his environment and that "the contemporary environment is clearly the manufactured and the 'mechanical' object; this is slowly subjugating the breasts and curves of woman, fruit, the soft landscape."[22] He nevertheless warned against the error of the Futurists and other "romantics" who glorified the dynamic movement of machinery. His very French sense of *pondération*, of imposing restraints on the emotions, led him instead towards the new classicism of *Le Grand Déjeuner* and *Animated Landscape*, in which man rises above his subjectivity, for "every pictorial work must possess this momentary and eternal value that enables it to endure beyond the epoch of its creation."[23] The geometry of Léger's painting, embracing the ethic of the new machine world, speaks for the "momentary," but in its ties with the disciplined forms of classical art, it also speaks for the "eternal."

It seems paradoxical that the assertive geometry of Léger's painting can stand both for modern technology and for the continuity of classical art, yet if we assess the nudes in *Le Grand Déjeuner*, for example, in these terms, the mechanism whereby he brings these opposing natures together becomes clear. His nudes have already been likened to classical sculpture, and to the controlled forms we associate with Poussin, David, Ingres, Seurat, or Maillol. On the other hand – and here he finds his distance from the penetrating nostalgia of Picasso's *Three Women at the Spring* (pl. 49) – his women have an unnatural smoothness, a sense of finish that likens them to machines, or to robots, hybrid forms of man and machine which are often vessels for our fantasies. In order to give his robot-nudes a potential for movement, Léger exaggerates the separateness of lower and upper arms, hinging them as one might a mannequin's limbs. To the extent that Léger's figures can be considered objects (or are they illusions of objects?), he has succeeded in his goal of combining art with life, man with his tools. "I have never enjoyed copying a machine," he wrote in 1925. "I invent images from machines as others have made landscapes from their imagination. For me, the mechanical element is not a fixed position, an attitude, but a means of succeeding in conveying a feeling of strength and power."[24]

Few people will deny strength and power to Léger's painting, but many will find one particular quality puzzling, if not offensive: the anonymity and the impersonality of his figures. Léger's denial of "romantic" and individual qualities, however, required this detachment. People and non-human forms must be both anonymous and impersonal (also objective: like objects), because this guarantees that they spring from the mass of society, and constitute its forces. Impersonality and anonymity certify their lack of individualism and give emphasis to production of something that is socially useful. Forms must appear to be reproducible, to come from mass production, to serve the common good. Lack of "personality" is equated with subordination of the individual to society. Like contemporary Russian Constructivists, Léger equated "good taste" and traditional painting with individualism, which lacked social utility. Although he made his works by hand, he gave them the appearance of impersonality in order to suppress the self, and to proclaim those features which, because they are "rational" and geometric, seem to be interchangeable and therefore suitable to mass production. In other words, the social value of his art is found in its very impersonality.

Logically this view means that Léger, like the Russian Constructivists, preferred the anonymous worker to the egocentric artist. It was the artisan who was at the center of the new society, Léger wrote. This is why he insisted more than once on his rediscovery at Verdun of ordinary Frenchmen, *le peuple*, for they were closer to the new reality than artists mired in the past. This is also why he envied the worker. In several variations upon *The Typographer* of 1919 (including those in the Kröller-Müller Museum, Otterlo, and the Philadelphia Museum of Art),[25] he shows the bust of a mechano-morphic man who is facing an easel on which there is a composition with a few large letters. The drawing (private collection) for this series makes it clear that the typographer is really the artist, for there is a canvas stretcher and a framed picture to the rear, as well as a still-life. Because Léger had been designing illustrations and the typography for Cendrars's *La Fin du monde* in 1919, his identification with the printer-artisan was not farfetched.

Better known than this composition is *The Mechanic* (pl. 51), a figure often recognized as Léger's *alter ego*.[26] This robust man stands before a display of geometry which we accept as machinery or as a factory environment, although no piece of it is recognizable – proof enough of Léger's inventiveness and of the commonality of our assumptions. In French, "mécanicien" has several meanings; here the nautical tattoo makes it likely that Léger's virile man is an engine-room machinist, perhaps associated with the many steam tugs whose exteriors Léger interpreted in the series already mentioned. (A better English title would be *The Engineer*.) His arms are marked by bulging muscles, in contrast to the smooth arms of the women in *Le Grand Déjeuner*. In effect he is the triumphant male for whom these nudes exist. He does not need to be shown working, for his dominance is more fully expressed in his assured composure – leisure once more being the appropriate counterpart of labor.

The Primitive and the Classical

Léger's machinist evokes more than the modern world of technology. Like the nudes of *Le Grand Déjeuner*, he also reminds us of past art, particularly of

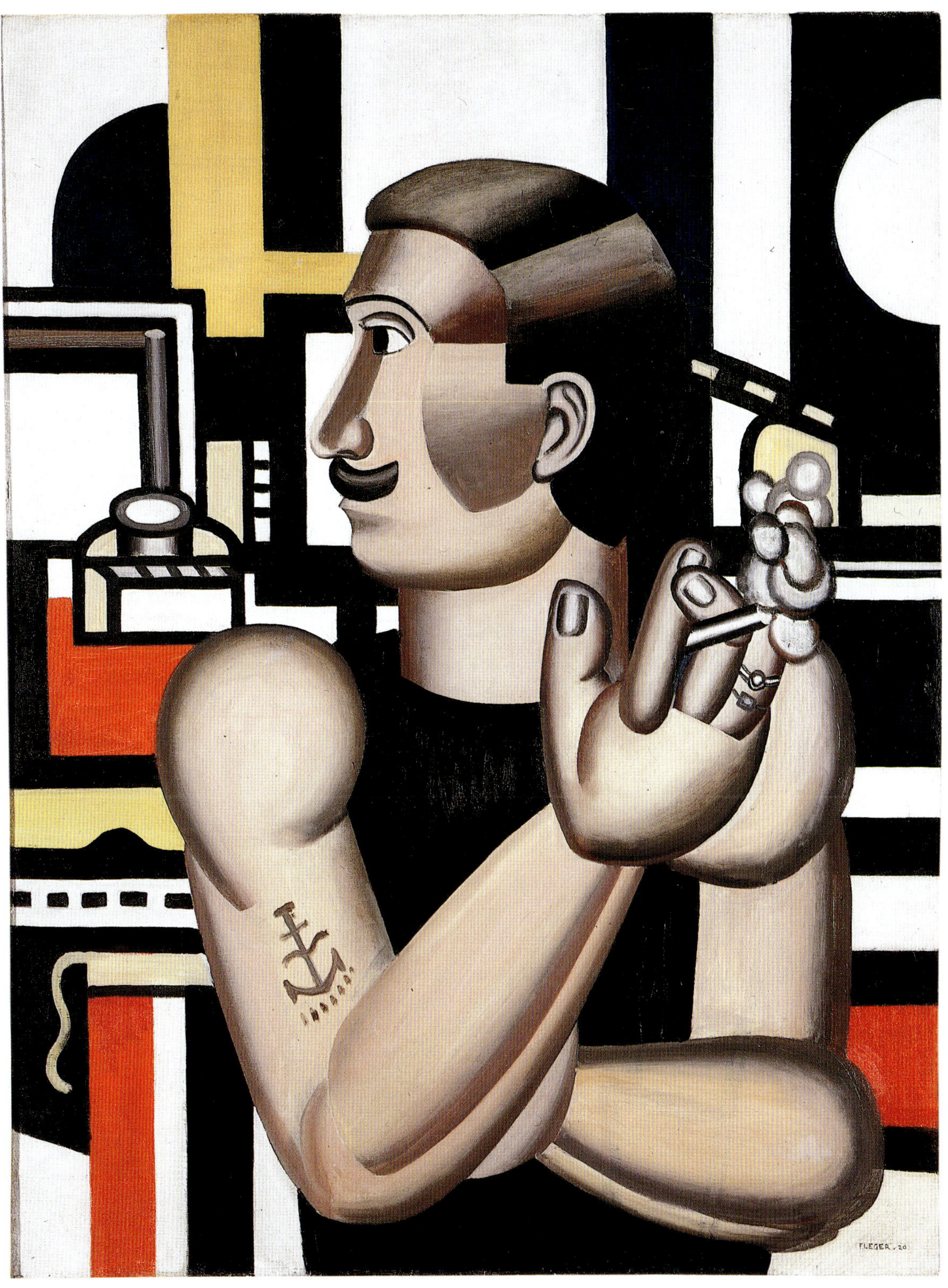

51 Fernand Léger, *The Mechanic*, 1920. 45½ × 34¾ in. (115.5 × 88.5 cm.). National Gallery of Canada, Ottawa, purchased 1966.

art usually called "primitive." Christopher Green has compared his work to Assyrian sculpture,[27] and one thinks also of the Douanier Rousseau whom Léger is known to have admired, particularly of Rousseau's portrait of *Pierre Loti* (Kunsthaus, Zürich). That the image of worker would be associated with primitive art, and the recent "primitive" Rousseau, is only natural. Léger's admiration of *le peuple* extended to those artists who, he believed, were free of the taint of imitation, who were truly creative. In his letter of 1922[28] and in many of his essays he asserted that the so-called primitive artists are superior to Renaissance painters because they placed no false ideas, derived from others, between themselves and their works of art.

This idea, well articulated in the nineteenth century by Ruskin, was widespread in early modern art and was an essential part of the defense of "conceptual" as opposed to "visual" or imitative art. It can be found in the major statements on Cubism by Léger's associates Gleizes and Metzinger, Kahnweiler, Rosenberg, Raynal, Reverdy, and others. "Primitive" art was thought to arise from collective, social impulses, as distinct from the subjectivity of the individual artist, and to express "conceptual" ideas. These ideas supplanted imitation and represented a new synthesis that merged the eternal values of past art with the needs of the present. Because this synthesis was said to be based on "constructive" principles rather than on the sensuality of traditional art, it was discoverable also in well-designed artifacts and machines, the products of engineers and workers who, free of elitism, unwittingly built objects that could rival art. This is why *The Mechanic* and *Le Grand Déjeuner* have their geometric units: Léger's proof that he had sounded the depths of his own era, and also the depths of the great traditions of art.

There is good reason to emphasize *art* rather than the machine when talking of Léger. Yes, his paintings seem mechanical when compared with works characterized by highly expressive brushwork; they seem all the more polished and impersonal when reduced to the scale of a catalog reproduction. Seen closely, however, the canvases show evidence of handicraft and changes of mind which we would not expect to find in a machine. Stucco-like brushwork shows traces of the moving hand, and lines are not always drawn with the aid of a straightedge. They reveal instead the slight undulations natural to gestures based on rotating wrist and pivoting elbow. For all the talk of metal machinery, the impersonality that Léger sought was that of the good piece of ceramic or the well-crafted wooden tool that can still reveal the hand of its creator. Creativity and the joy of his craft were too strong in Léger to be suppressed in an actual machine-like perfection. That is instead one of the poles he approaches, but to attain it would be too great a self-abnegation, too thorough a capitulation to "objective raw material," and there would be no room for that other essential quality, subjectivity. "The work of art is the ambiguity between these two elements," and subjectivity is one of these elements, although it is a "controlled subjectivity." This helps explain why Léger retained recognizable subject matter and a personal facture, unlike the Russian Constructivists who approached more closely the goal of machine-like impersonality in order to suppress individuality.[29]

Léger's painted parts are not really mechanically rendered, nor are they interchangeable. He is more like the engineer than the machinist, more like the inventor who devises the preliminary model than the worker who supervises its production. Although Léger longs for a reconciliation of artist and artisan, he is aware of their distance. Is the artisan everything, he asks?

> No. I think there are some men above him, very few, who are capable of elevating him through their plastic concept to a height that towers over the primary level of Beauty. Those men must be capable of viewing the work of the artisan and of nature as raw material, to be ordered, absorbed and fused in their brains, with a perfect balance between the two values: the conscious and the unconscious, the objective and the subjective.[30]

Léger's esthetic structure would collapse if it failed to join art and life. "I am a firm believer in a slow and continual inroad brought about by the manufactured object which holds the secret of any Renaissance we may have. A man living for a long time in the environment of these stern geometric forms will unconsciously find himself won over by them."[31] But the machine environment – transformed rather than imitated – is only part of Léger's foundation. His letter of 1942 (Appendix A) is very revealing, for when Barr asked him whether or not *Le Grand Déjeuner* exhibited the influence of the machine, he said no, and spoke instead of art. He pointed out first that his early painting *Nudes in a Landscape* (i.e., *Nudes in the Forest*) already had blocky volumes, by which he meant that his art had evolved consistently, not requiring a sudden interjection of machine influences to explain its monumental geometry. He then referred to the stream of art before the Renaissance. Other writings let us know that by this he wished to join the forms of the *Déjeuner* to the "utmost simplification" of primitive art, and therefore that Barr must not think his figures were inspired by machines.

Léger's "primitivism," like Picasso's, was not based upon a very exclusive canon. He referred admiringly to whole cultures – Egypt, Greece, Rome, pre-Renaissance Europe – but he also confessed his love of several of the most sophisticated artists in the Western tradition: David and Ingres, whom he mentions most often, and also the Le Nain brothers, Poussin, Corot, and Cézanne. These artists are often called "classical" because they form part of a long tradition traceable to antiquity in which a clear perception of order is paramount, as opposed to the emotional expressiveness of "romantic" artists. In his letters to Barr, Léger used the word "classical," but in his numerous essays, he used "primitive" nearly as often. Although this is confusing, it is not inconsistent. The concepts are closely allied in his thought because they share an emphasis upon constructive geometry and the willful imposition of clear pattern, instead of imitative representation. Furthermore, in their own day, David,

Ingres, Corot, Cézanne, and Seurat were each recognized by contemporary critics as being primitive, on the one hand, and classical, on the other. It has been a commonplace of modern writers to apply both terms to Léger himself, as well as to Picasso.[32]

Léger succeeds in reconciling more than the primitive and the classical. He is an astounding artist, who by his "law of plastic contrasts" manages to bring together a whole host of opposed qualities: the human and the machine, the living and the inert, the round and the flat, the real and the imagined, the primitive and the technological, the classic and the romantic. And the miracle is that he does not weaken or soften these disparate elements, but lets them jostle one another in an unusual pictorial competition. He is the "director of objects" who arranges his forms, emblematic of the conflicts and contradictions of modern life, so that they create a world of dynamic balance.

The nude women in *Le Grand Déjeuner* are a calming and reassuring presence, but they startle us. They are like art objects from the past, suddenly deposited in a modern environment of noisy and angular geometry. Léger always likened his own era to a state of war. "If I stand facing life, with all its possibilities, I like what is generally called the state of war, which is nothing more than life at an accelerated rhythm. The state of peace is life at a slack rhythm."[33] Like Phidias at the time of the Peloponnesian Wars or David on the eve of the French Revolution, Léger responded to the tensions of his society by a severely controlled art, an art whose greatness lies in stretching taut, almost to breaking point, forms and ideas that are suspended between the poles of calmness and frenzy, objectivity and subjectivity, harshness and softness. "I profoundly admire my epoch," Léger wrote in 1925. "It is hard and sharp, but with its immense senses it sees clearly and always wants to see more clearly, whatever may happen. It is the end of obscurity, of chiaroscuro, and the beginning of the state of enlightenment. Too bad for those with weak eyes."[34]

Chapter 9

Léger, the Renaissance, and "Primitivism"

In August 1925, facing his first one-man exhibition in the United States, Fernand Léger must surely have wished to put his best foot forward. He wrote out longhand for Katherine Dreier (who had invited him to exhibit with the Société Anonyme in New York) a suite of seventeen aphorisms. Among them are these three:

> The colossal error is to believe that the Italian Renaissance is a beautiful period of art. It's exactly the opposite.
>
> The Italian Renaissance is total decadence, where everything is imitated, sensualized, sentimentalized.
>
> The Italian Renaissance is bad because it's hazy, vague, soft, sentimental, sensual, descriptive, imitative.[1]

What are we to make of these polemical assertions in view of the fact that Léger has always been placed by historians in the center of the "Call to Order" of the early 1920s, when he, Picasso, and other Parisian artists displayed renewed contact with the arts of classical antiquity, the Renaissance, and of individuals like Poussin, David, Ingres, and Seurat?[2] The answer is found in Léger's conception of the "primitive," which he opposed to the Renaissance in most of his abundant lectures and essays. We learn who these primitives were in another of the aphorisms he sent Dreier: "These are the Chaldeans, the Egyptians, the primitives, the Romanesque, the Gothic, etc." In writings of the 1930s he added "popular arts," Chinese, Indochinese, and Aztec arts to this list. Except for Giotto, whom he mentioned several times, he rarely named individual primitive artists, limiting himself to an occasional passing reference to Clouet, Fouquet, Memling, and Piero della Francesca. He had mixed praise for a few later artists who have some of the virtues of the primitives: Poussin, the Le Nain brothers, David, Ingres, Corot, Cézanne, and the Douanier Rousseau.

To explore Léger's opposition of Renaissance and primitive is one of the best ways of appreciating the particular resonance of his art. Eventually it will let us see that in his mind there was no incompatibility between the Call to Order and his hatred of the Renaissance. By always specifying the Italian Renaissance (he

• From *Hommage à Michel Laclotte* (Paris, 1994): 642–47.

mentions pejoratively Raphael, Leonardo, and Michelangelo), and by declaring it inferior to the Romanesque and Gothic eras, Léger allows us to trace his views to the prewar years. Thanks to the work of Mark Antliff,[3] we now know that by 1913 the increasing polarization of left and right had led a number of Léger's friends in Cubist circles to sympathize with "Celtic nationalism," a nativist movement that was opposed to the Italianate, Catholic, and monarchist classicism of rightists like Charles Maurras. Léger's lifelong preference for the Gothic and his vehement attacks on the Renaissance were developed as a consequence of this prewar opposition of left and right which, in vanguard art circles, englobed the long-standing conflict between modernists and the Ecole des Beaux-Arts.

In this conception, articulated cogently by Léger's friend Albert Gleizes,[4] the height of Christian art had been reached with the Romanesque and early Gothic in France. It was a product not of isolated heroes, but of *le peuple*, particularly of artisans later called "primitive" who embodied the virtues of the French collectivity in their architecture and the paintings and sculptures that decorated them. Gleizes and others of like persuasion believed that the modern French worker was the heir of this tradition, and that collective, syndicalist activity was the way to the future, not bourgeois individualism (which actually supported the statist collectivism of rightists like Maurras). The enemy was the right which wanted to perpetuate the Latinate conceptions that still dominated official art circles. From this vantage point, the influence of the Italian Renaissance had been a contamination. It had introduced a concern for appearance, that is, for a Graeco-Latin humanism that the French had transformed creatively in the Middle Ages, but that was now returning as a foreign import.

By 1915 the fervor of wartime mobilization altered the terms of this antagonistic relationship, although it did not bring left and right closer together. As we have learned from the work of Kenneth Silver,[5] the Latinate classicism championed by the right, with its associations of reason, order, and construction, became identified with wartime France, as distinct from "Gothic" and barbaric Germany. The left had to accept this patriotic view so, denied its former opponent, Celtic nationalism and its Bergsonian underpinnings faded away. From 1917 onward into the era of the Call to Order there developed a pronounced Italianate neoclassicism in the art of many Paris-based artists, including Picasso, Braque, Severini, Gris, de la Fresnaye, and Metzinger.

Léger, we know, joined this classicizing current. He changed from the dynamic Cubism of pictures like *Disks* and *The City* (pl. 38) to such pictures as the much calmer *Le Grand Déjeuner* and *Animated Landscape* (pls. 39 and 57). The dynamism of those early postwar pictures was appropriately linked to the frenzy and intensity of life in the streets, but now, after 1920, Léger wanted to help bring about a "society without frenzy, calm, ordered, knowing how to live naturally within the Beautiful without exclamation or romanticism."[6] Given this shift, it was perfectly logical of him to assimilate antique statuary and architecture with emblems of modernity, and to acknowledge admiration of several of the great classicizing artists, including Poussin, David, and Ingres. Why then – to return to our central question – did he renounce the Italian Renaissance, traditionally considered the great restorer of classicism?

The answer is that he divorced the idea of classicism from the Renaissance and attached its values instead to the "primitive."[7] This amounted to a rephrasing of his basic predilections of the prewar years. He could still denounce the Italian Renaissance, but now he adopted many of the values traditionally associated with it and placed them alongside the primitive. Other participants in the Call to Order made the same adaptation. In the pages of avant-garde art magazines from 1920 onward were featured early Greek sculpture, Fouquet, Clouet, the Le Nain brothers, Poussin, Ingres, Corot, and Seurat (who displaced Cézanne as the leading precursor), all of them artists who, it was said, avoided copying appearances and instead stressed the "conceptual" over the "imitative."[8]

This list of sanctioned artists should remind us that there had long been a tradition of redefining the classical in terms of the primitive. Maurice Quaï and the Barbus rebelled against David because he was not sufficiently like the early Greeks; Ingres's voluptuous and serpentine nudes were at first seen as a primitive break with Davidian correctness; the German Nazarenes, the British Pre-Raphaelites, and a number of Ingres's mid-century pupils preferred early Renaissance art to that of Raphael, Leonardo, and Michelangelo; Puvis de Chavannes won widespread acceptance with his archaizing Hellenism; Seurat was dubbed "a modernizing Puvis", and several supportive critics referred his art to Egypt and the Italian primitives; Cézanne was a modern primitive. Léger was conscious of continuing this current.

> For example, if one wants to survey French painting from the fourteenth century to the present, two currents, two schools, are distinguishable: one classic, starting with the primitives and including Poussin, David, Ingres, Corot, Rousseau. [. . .] The other, more romantic current, which begins in the eighteenth century and includes Delacroix, the impressionists, the surrealists.[9]

For modernist artists and writers, "primitive" was not pejorative, and instead bore the meaning of first, or original. This could mean the first artists or first works of what would become a classical style, hence the defenders of Cubism, struggling to legitimate the new art in the prewar years, and anxious to separate themselves from the traditionalists of the right, had insisted that the classicism of each era was rooted in the initial novelty of its own energies, and was not to be defined by comparisons with earlier epochs.[10] It is this conception which allowed Léger and other modernists to devote themselves to contemporary subjects and a new style without feeling that they had divorced themselves from the past. They believed they were recapitulating the primitive phase of earlier classicisms. Léger preferred "the early Greeks" (*les Grecs d'origine*)[11] to Hellenistic and Roman artists, and he declared that the Impressionists were primitives. "The impressionists are the great originators of the present movement; they are its primitives."[12]

Although Léger shared these ideas with fellow modernists, he carved out a distinctive place, first and foremost in his painting, but also in his activities as a prolific lecturer and essayist. To disguise his actual classical heritage, he insisted upon the immediately modern. Who else but Léger would make references in his paintings to steam tugs, café bars, billboards, accordions, shop windows, soda siphons, and "éléments mécaniques," but also to classicizing nudes and still-lifes of fruit and flowers? And, whereas Gleizes increasingly turned toward Christian ideals and had withdrawn from leftist politics by the mid-1920s, Léger insisted upon an utterly secular content, and became more and more engaged, eventually becoming recognized as one of the leading artists of the Popular Front.

Renaissance Errors

To comprehend Léger fully, we must now turn to the personal inflection he gave to ideas widespread during the Call to Order, ideas that had their origin in prewar Cubism and which he would carry on with only modest qualifications until his death in 1955. This analysis begins with his contrast of the Italian Renaissance with the "primitive." The first of the errors of the Italian Renaissance, for Léger, is the imitation of nature. "It is the error of *imitation*, of the servile copy of the subject, as opposed to the so-called primitive epoch that is great and immortal precisely because it invented its forms and methods."[13] Imitation is wrong because it is a substitute for invention. "A poor, twisted Christ of the twelfth century is infinitely more moving and more beautiful through the sensibility it contains than the leg of a statue by Michelangelo."[14] Moreover, natural objects are beautiful in themselves and cannot be improved upon by imitation. Instead, artists should seek non-imitative equivalents that embody the subjective in dialog with the objective, and that are entirely new "objects." There is a risk, for this dialog involves references to the objective world that can border upon imitation. "Subtlety lies in making distinctions, for being inventive can come very close to being imitative. Certain primitives, and pictures by Ingres, by David, for example, are very close to being imitative."[15]

The second error is the *beau sujet*, that is, a hierarchy of traditionally sanctioned subjects, rather than a recognition that all subjects and all objects can be grist to the artist's mill. Further, the "beautiful subject" smacked of sentiment and sensuality, instead of the desired objectivity. The continuing worship of the Renaissance, of imitation, and of the beautiful subject is laid at the door of "that malady that is the Ecole des Beaux-Arts."[16] Its tired formulae have the sanction of officialdom, and so "the French, who have a weighty artistic tradition behind them, often make such errors."[17] Léger's disgust with the Beaux-Arts perpetuates the struggle of modernist artists with academic juries and teachings, the struggle that had come to a head with Impressionism. From the 1860s onward, modernism's virtues of freedom, intense color, lack of "finish," and the like, were literally defined by opposition to the teachings of the Ecole.

The third grievous error of the Italian Renaissance was the championing of individualism, which supplanted the collectivism that had marked primitive epochs. Because individuals arrogate powers to themselves, they deprive themselves of the healthy resources of society, that is, they are not in a creative dialog with their epoch. Paradoxically, however, while Léger regretted that individualism had undermined the collective art he wished to see established, he was also in the odd position of defending individual creativity against the corporate authority of the Ecole.

The fourth sin of the Renaissance was its championing of easel painting over the mural. Léger admitted that wall decoration continued in the Renaissance, but lamented that it was gradually vitiated by "the beautiful subject" and by bourgeois individualism which was satisfied only by the selfish ownership of mobile objects. An ardent democrat, Léger regretted that so much art had become the privilege of the wealthy few, and had drained away energies from the public arts. Nonetheless, although be lamented the hegemony of easel painting, Léger recognized that the virtues of modernism were vested in creative individuals.

> The isolated man, insofar as he is an individual creator, will control the direction of the arts and the plastic occurrences for a long time to come. The easel painting is his proper means of expression.[18]

> When the creative artist is filled with doubt, there is nothing to justify his seeking to attach himself to some standard of judgment set up in the past. He must run his own risks. His loneliness is great. Such is the drama lived through by all men upon whom has been laid the destiny of inventing, creating, constructing.[19]

Primitive Virtues

What is there among the "primitive" arts that spoke so powerfully to modern artists? For his part, Léger characterized primitive epochs by the simple mechanism of opposition to the Renaissance. Just as the word "leisure" is comprehensible only because "work" is posited, or "early" has meaning only if we think of "late," so primitive art was the antiphonal response to his conception of the Renaissance. Primitive arts did not imitate, they invented; they did not set up a hierarchy of subjects and quality, but accepted a whole variety; they spoke for the collective, not the individual; they favored art of public scale, not easel paintings.

Rather than observe the imitative modeling of the Renaissance tradition, primitives used unmodeled surfaces and "pure color." Although each primitive era has its own standards, they share a non-imitative style, based upon color unadulterated by Renaissance modeling, and upon "the vertical arrangement of the isolated object to obtain a decorative or plastic value."[20] Of course this is a defense of modernist abstraction, but Léger distinguished himself from his colleagues by his insistence upon the "object" and its epistemological reality. (It is probably for this reason that he neither made collages nor created the effects of transparency that Moholy-Nagy and Lissitzky favored.) "The feeling for the object," he wrote, "is already in primitive pictures – in the works of the high periods of Egyptian, Assyrian, Greek, Romanesque, and Gothic art. The moderns are going to develop it, isolate it, and extract every possible result from it."[21] The object was always there in art, but it was covered over by the subject, and must be freed from its imprisonment in Renaissance modeling and perspective. This extends to the human figure which should shed its sentimental and expressive trappings and become an object.

> In contemporary modern painting, the object must become the *leading character* and dethrone the subject. Then, in turn, if the person, the face, and the human body become objects, the modern artist will be offered considerable freedom. [. . .] At this moment, to the mind of the modern artist, a cloud, a machine, a tree are elements as interesting as people or faces.[22]

If primitivism teaches the primacy of the object, it also shows that there is no hierarchy of quality, subject, or object, and therefore no one kind of realism to act as exemplar. Realism results from looking closely at one's surroundings, and each primitive era found its own kind, suitable to its conditions. The highest reality for Léger is in the art object itself, not in the natural world, but he did not endorse pure abstraction because he believed that the artist's subjectivity is inevitably in colloquy with the objective world. New art is a new realism based upon this colloquy, and modern objects inevitably enter into its formulation: the Eiffel Tower, a foot under a table, a cloud, a woman's fingernail, a tree trunk, a poster. Everything has an equal object-value, and it is up to the artist to choose wisely among them to create a beautiful painting.

To the individualism of the Renaissance, Léger opposed the collective nature of primitive eras. Moderns are not yet ready to develop a new collective art because they are still trapped in the solitude of the individual. "I know that *collective forces* are on the march, and that the individual as king must be swallowed up, must fall into line, that individual egotism has often taken advantage of this situation."[23] Léger's salutation to "collective forces" took on a special urgency in the 1930s, when his lifelong radicalism flowered under the Popular Front, but already before World War I he had insisted on the primacy of the collective. His leftism, that is, was not an opportunism born of the 1930s, but a consistent set of beliefs that underpins his aesthetic. "I am convinced that we are approaching a conception of art as comprehensive as those of the greatest epochs of the past: the same tendency to large scale, the same collective effort."[24]

In that essay of 1913, and consistently later, he cited the Gothic as the era that could best provide lessons for the hoped-for evolution toward a collective art. "Our cathedrals [. . .] are the result of intelligent and sensitive collaboration. They are the achievement of many people. We must redraw the contract."[25] This was a conception that had been most famously stated in the middle of the nineteenth century by Ruskin, and sustained by the international Arts and Crafts movement, but it was also well rooted in French art. In their different ways, Millet, Monet, Pissarro, Renoir, and the Nabis associated the Gothic with natural energies and with the virtues of the anonymous artisan. The French Gothic was opposed to the Italian Renaissance (can we imagine Monet painting a classical façade?) which they believed responsible for introducing individualism and scholarly knowledge that undermined the more collaborative, popular, and primitive art of the Middle Ages. It is this belief that merged with Celtic nationalism in the prewar years.

Art for the Public

The fact that Léger perpetuated an already established ideal of the Gothic does not deny the vitality it acquired in his esthetic. He believed that in an era of illiteracy, the cathedral, with its comprehensive narrative and symbolic ornamentation, was a truly popular art that transmitted a whole culture's thought. However, Gothic architecture's ornamental and representational surfaces were no longer needed once Gutenberg's movable type provided another medium for cultural texts.[26] Now, in the modern era, color photography, cinema, and popular art forms "have effectively replaced and henceforth rendered superfluous the development of visual, sentimental, representational, and popular subject matter in pictorial art."[27] Once again painters should collaborate with architects in the decoration of public spaces (it is painters who are specialists in color, therefore best equipped to contribute to "polychromed architecture"), but without the now unnecessary subjects and imitations of the Renaissance tradition. Instead they should go back to the underlying principles of Gothic art, using "conceptual realism," the true coupling of the beautiful and the collective. Addressing contemporary architects, Léger said:

> Your mission is to replace the sentimental and outmoded church with an equivalent work, beautiful in itself and capable of detaching humanity from the grip of religions. You have at your disposal this need for verticality which obsesses the world, this need of elevation by the vertical. You have the round form – the ball – which satisifies the mind. These two abstractions are there: render them human and stirring, but do not reduce architecture to an esthetic and linear problem. [. . .] The modern monumental building must be the equivalent of the byzantine and the romanesque – equally rich and both "dans la durée" and in its own time.[28]

With such reasoning, Léger became one of the chief spokesmen among French painters for the revival of mural art, the central subject of many of his lectures and essays. In essence collaborative, mural art could overcome the dilemma of the isolated individual. Fortunately modern architecture has stripped walls of their imitative Beaux-Arts encrustation, and hence there is room for a revival of the mural.[29] Unfortunately, however, Léger had to place this "mural Renaissance" in the future because, he said, modern architects resisted the need for collaboration with painters. They were elitists who ignored the needs of the people for beautiful and instructive ornamentation, who excluded them by their radically unornamented walls. Obviously this reflected Léger's frustrations at being restricted to easel painting but he became more optimistic after 1933 when he began to win commissions for art of public scale,[30] benefiting from the social consciousness that had become widespread in that decade (public murals, though of different content, characterized art of the 1930s in Russia, Italy, the United States, and Mexico). "Put your plans back in your pockets," he told architects, "go out into the streets, listen to them breathe, you must make contact, steep yourselves in raw materials, walk in the same mud and dust."[31]

From the outset of his career, Léger had insisted upon the ordinary artifacts of modern life, including the sights and sounds of the street, as the source of artistic energy. The anonymity and impersonality of Léger's images, those immediately identifiable qualities of his painting, had to be objective and detached because this guaranteed that they sprang from the mass of society, indeed that they constituted its forces. Lack of "personality" and expressiveness he equated with subordination of the individual to society. Although Léger's works are full of *pentimenti* and seldom machine-like, he gave them the appearance of impersonality in order to proclaim those features which, because they are rational and geometric (not "vague, soft, sentimental, sensual"), seem to be interchangeable and therefore suitable to mass production. For that reason, the artisan is superior to the typical modern artist.

Regrettably, the artisan has been schooled to think that "art" is for the rich bourgeoisie in the museums (which close their doors in late afternoon, just when workers leave their factories). This definition of a false art will remain in place until society evolves in the direction of a "new collective social art," an art which will be modern but which will also look toward the "primitive and popular artists of before the Renaissance."[32] Logically, then, Léger assimilated the "primitive" of past and present with the anonymous modern artisan (he admired the Douanier Rousseau). Like medieval men, artisans will eventually realize that the ordinary objects they fabricate (although now with the aid of modern machinery) have the pure colors and functional shapes that constitute art. In other words, Léger gave a particular leftist inflection to what was, after all, a common idea among the avant-garde, the belief in a kind of folkloric honesty among peasants and workers, as among early "primitive" peoples.

Of course artisans need someone to point the way, and so Léger carved out a place for himself and other vanguard artists in this construction of a new collectivity. A few artists (he would not have used the word "elite") were to guide the artist to the highest levels of beauty.[33] Only the best modern artists can rival the effects of cinema, radio, and the photo-montages of posters and billboards. Their large, clean forms and colors, divested of the unsuitable remnants of Renaissance imitation, will eventually win over the worker because they are based instead upon the shapes of modern life. Furthermore, the upper classes have abdicated responsibility by remaining mired in the past, so it is *le peuple* who are "poetry's last great refuge."[34] Have they not invented argot, that most modern and living language, that imaginative transposition of reality?

It is here that Léger distinguished himself from most other artists of the avant-garde: he constructed a world parallel to argot. Not for him the minotaurs of Picasso, the magic forests of Max Ernst, or the austere geometries of Mondrian. They and he are equally modern but it is he who invented a pictorial language of bicycles, door keys, pipes, balusters, giant letters, and abstract form-objects, a visual argot whose popular forms gave new life to the nudes, plants, clouds, and landscapes of tradition. Modern and traditional, primitive and classical, impersonal and unique, his art is that rarest of artifacts, an offering to all of society. It is a language that can provoke discomfort with the status quo, that can use the vulgate to create astonishing poetry, that uses a new realism to give life to what is, after all, a conservative doctrine: the desire for harmony. In Léger's ideal world we would find both a provincial housewife and an urban worker.

> Go into the shop of a little dressmaker in the provinces. Have the patience to watch all through a fitting that a local businesswoman is having. To get the effect she wants, she will be more meticulous, more exacting than the most elegant Parisian. This stout, fifty-year-old lady, she too wants to achieve a harmony that is appropriate for her age, her environment, and her means. [. . .]
>
> The world of work, the only interesting one, exists in an intolerable environment. Let's go into the factories, the banks, the hospitals. [. . .] Let's bring in color; it's as necessary as water and fire. Let's apportion it wisely, so that it may be a more pleasant value, a psychological value; its moral influence can be considerable. A beautiful and calm environment.
>
> Life through color.
> The polychromed hospital.
> The colorist-doctor.[35]

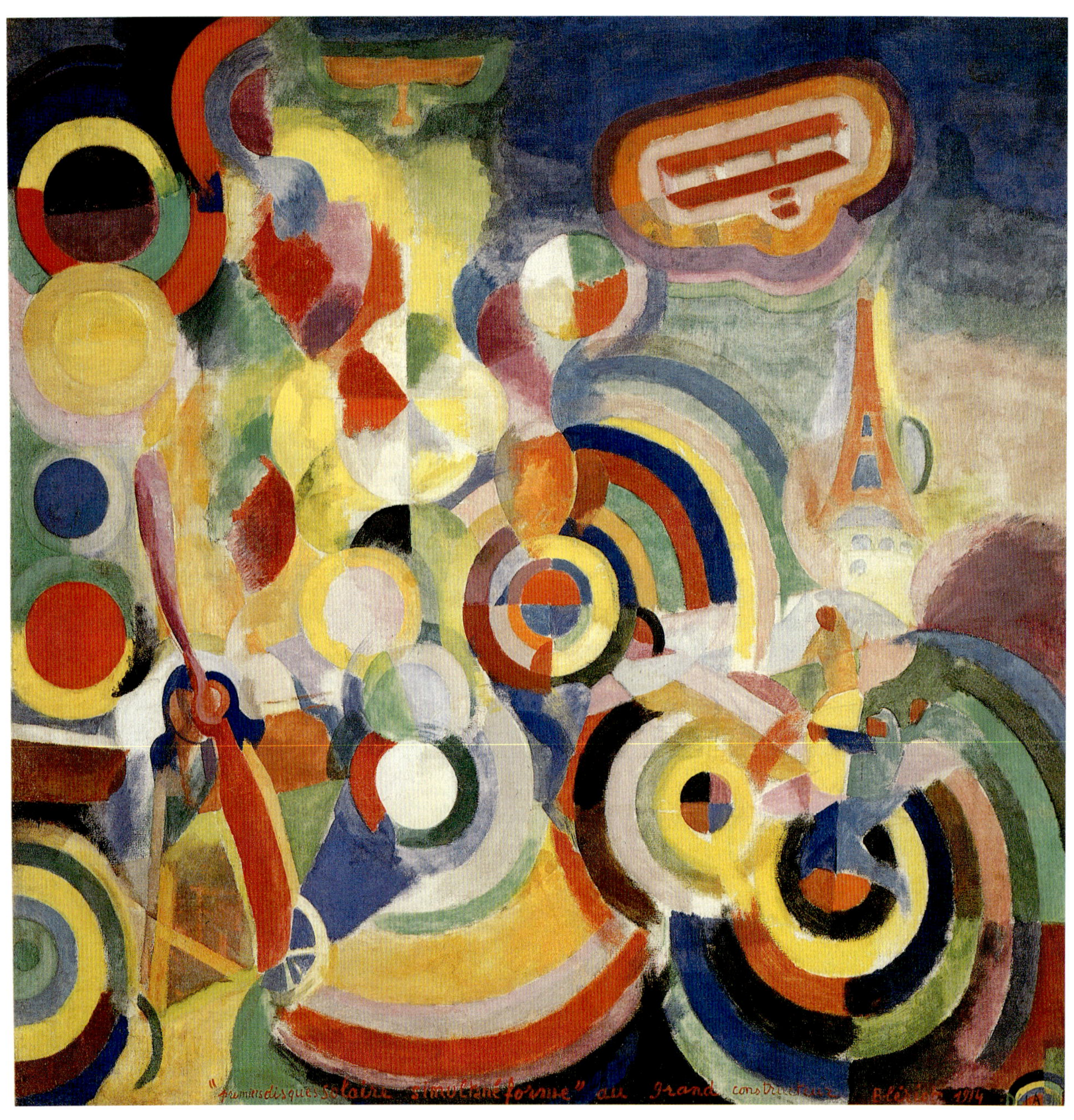

52 Robert Delaunay, *Homage to Blériot*, 1914. $98\frac{5}{8} \times 99$ in. (250.5×251.5 cm.). Oeffentliche Kunstsammlung Basel, Kunstmuseum.

Chapter 10

The Arrival of the Machine: Modernist Art in Europe, 1910–1925

I approach the subject of art and technology rather like one of the blind men in the old story about the discovery of the elephant. The whole beast is too large to encompass at once, yet if I put my hand on the trunk I would not be describing the leg, if on the leg, then I would not be describing the head. As a historian more comfortable with concrete cases than broad generalizations, I here investigate one portion of this elephantine subject, trusting that this is an adequate sample of its complexity. I limit myself to the years bracketing World War I, when modernist painting and sculpture first paid wide attention to modern machinery, science, and industry.

I write "modernist" and not "modern" for of course when we look outside the modernist canon to the whole range of visual culture – illustrations in the press, prints, photographs, film – we find lots of images of modern industrial and scientific forms. These would constitute a rich body of material for a study of art and technology but I have set them aside as a future project and write here about some of the art that has become central to our cultural constructions by virtue of its dominance in public exhibitions, museums, the press, and in the literature of art history. I am aware that it is not really the past we are talking about when we study the history of modernist art but our present culture, its desires, its fears, its expectations. Another limitation: I do not deal with the material side of art (the changing sources of its pigments, for example), although a study of this realm would show the imbrication of the visual arts in industrial techniques and products.

Before 1910

Why was it that avant-garde art kept the machine at arm's length until about 1910? In the two preceding decades most figures and settings of modernist art were far removed from industrial forms of the modern city. Various kinds of "primitivism" became virtually synonymous with modernism, ranging from

• From *Social Research* 64, 3 [special issue on "Technology and the Rest of Culture"] (fall 1997): 1273–1305.

techniques in painting, sculpture, and printmaking to images of peasants and non-European peoples.[1] Some artists, most notably Gauguin, sought out "primitive" places far from the modern city. Advanced taste at the turn of the century celebrated Cézanne's Provençal landscapes, van Gogh's and Pissarro's peasants, Rodin's and Renoir's nudes, Gauguin's Tahitians, Signac's Mediterranean ports, and Monet's waterlilies. For, as the industrial revolution had taken an ever firmer hold on culture in the nineteenth century, modernist art had become increasingly associated with urban and suburban leisure and premodern or primitive "nature." Monet's famous paintings of the Gare St. Lazare in 1877 do not argue with this observation, because he never again painted any machines or, indeed, any industrial setting. His next fifty years (born 1841, he died in 1926) were devoted to non-Parisian scenes, climaxing in hundreds of pictures of his water gardens which, by the end of the twentieth century, had become the most sought-after objects for blockbuster exhibitions.[2]

The extraordinary popularity of Monet's waterlilies in our high-tech era can remind us that "art" and "nature" are not fixed realities but constantly changing mental constructions. Often intertwined in the nineteenth century, they embodied release from the tensions of the workplace. They were compensatory domains, hence the dramatic rise of landscape and paintings of rural life as the industrial revolution took hold. In technique and style, a parallel to this is found in modernists' love of handcraft in opposition to the uniformity of academic art which they likened to machine production. Instead of machine-age regularity, it was instinct and spontaneity, considered natural, that characterized early followers of the modernist Arts and Crafts movement and their championing of individualism. Their sign was the irregularity of handwork which Thorstein Veblen identified as the "honorific mark" that conferred value.[3]

As the most obvious materialization of modern industry, the machine did not become important in advanced painting until the half-decade before World War I. I will shortly demonstrate that this was so by pointing to leading examples, but first I want to puzzle over the reasons for this sudden adoption after long delay, one of the fundamental mysteries of modernist painting and sculpture. Of course it is involved in the across-the-board innovations of Cubism, Italian Futurism, Russian Cubo-Futurism, and British Vorticism, but merely to say so is not to explain why machine imagery suddenly loomed so large. Until about 1910 the machine was the enemy of all that modernist artists held dear: handcraft, creativity, individuality, and the marks of original expression. It bore the taint of mass-produced polish, an uncreative "perfection" that reduced the worker to a mere robot; it was also tainted by association with the money-grubbing bourgeoisie rather than with the free-spirited and marginalized artist.

If the machine were to be accepted by the vanguard, indeed to be taken as a leading sign of modernity, then it could no longer be considered the enemy. What permitted this *volte-face*? One factor was that by the end of the century the heirs of the international Arts and Crafts movement had accepted some industrial methods of production. The principle of the primacy of handcraft could appear to be maintained while in fact it was being rapidly undermined. For example, the art press increasingly used mass-production methods and photographic "process prints" to reproduce the effects of handcrafted images. When industry could be treated as the servant of creativity, there was no longer such a gap between handwork and the machine. Symptomatic of this change was the dedication of the Deutscher Werkbund in 1907 (Peter Behrens, Hermann Muthesius, Henry van de Velde, and others) to "the ennoblement of handiwork through the union of art, industry and handcraft."[4]

Another possible factor in accepting the machine as part of modernity rather than its opponent was the rapid increase of machinery in daily life. Bicycles and automobiles were commonly seen in the first years of the century, so were domestic sewing-machines and electric lighting. Cheaper means of photographic reproduction allowed advertisers in the daily and periodic press to increase pictures of domestic appliances and machines, while the cinema became the newest form of mechanized entertainment. In offices, there were now typewriters, pneumatic tubes, and dictating machines. In the outdoor environment one saw subways, elevated trains, trams, and seaport cranes. All these were quite new or a vast extension of preceding inventions, and so the machine became a normal, if not a fully domesticated feature of daily urban life. By contrast, the industrial engines, locomotives, and steam tractors of the nineteenth century were more external, more like monstrous invaders which could not be domesticated.

Of course the familiarity of the machine in daily life did not mean that it appeared in the work of all modernists, nor that it was an indispensable aspect of modernism. Picasso's and Braque's paintings and collages (glued-together newsprint and other fragments) evoke café and studio still-lifes or nudes: "fine arts" subjects rather than machinery. Modernity is found in their new language of fragmentation as well as in the evocations of contemporary intellectual life. The hegemony of their art is so great that Cubism generally is identified with them, and historians therefore pay little attention to the "Epic Cubists"[5] who identified modernity with the segmented imagery of such structures as locomotives, iron girders, and airplanes.

Typical of prewar Epic Cubism is Albert Gleizes's *Landscape* (pl. 53), centered upon a city of excitable units of geometric architecture and scattered iron girders. Nearly abstract but recognizable pictographic forms identify railroad signals and a locomotive charging towards a river bridge while above the angular city, factory chimneys and smoke mark the nearby suburbs.[6] Jacques Villon made three paintings of factory machinery interpreted in the dynamics of pictorial structure,[7] and his brother Raymond Duchamp-Villon sculpted a *Horse* (pl. 56) that combined machine parts with the organic rhythms of that animal. (The third brother, Marcel Duchamp, also investigated the look and meaning of machinery, as we shall see when we turn to Dada art.)

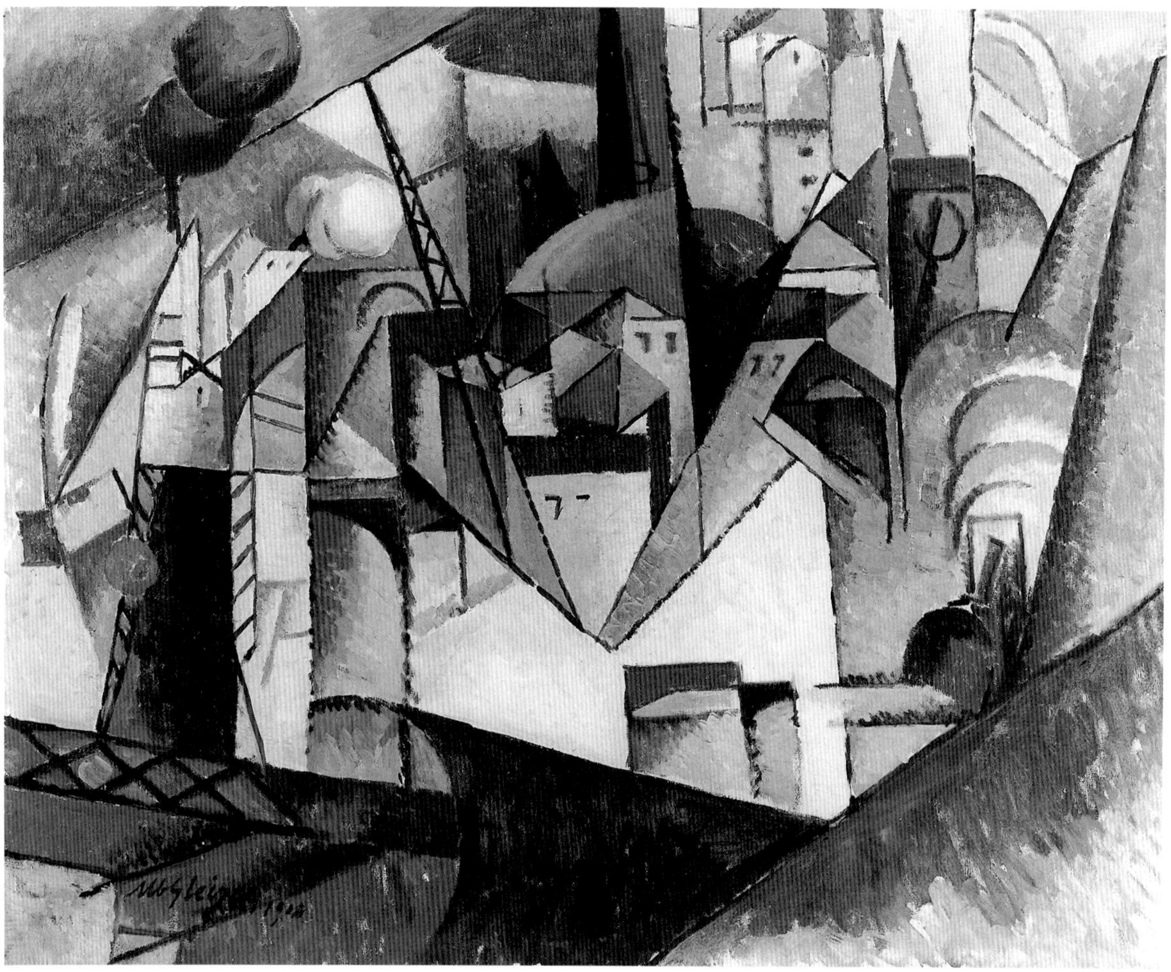

53 Albert Gleizes, *Landscape*, 1914. 28⅞ × 36½ in. (73.3 × 92.3 cm.). Yale University Art Gallery, New Haven, Collection Société Anonyme.

Another Epic Cubist, Robert Delaunay, dealt with the modern city and modern engineering. In a number of paintings from 1910 onward he featured the Eiffel Tower of 1889 as the leading symbol of the new Paris. It appears in the upper right corner of his *Homage to Blériot* of 1914 (pl. 52), a modern history painting and a masterpiece of Epic Cubism that summons up the famous aerial crossing of the English Channel in 1909. Above are two airplanes while in the lower left, intertwined with other forms, is the large propellor and undercarriage of another airplane. Dominating the whole canvas are swirling disks whose partitioned colors call up the moon (cool colors) and the gaseous fireball of the sun (hot colors), forms of celestial dynamism linked with the machines that let humans overcome gravity. Delaunay hoped to engage the viewer in his conception of simultaneity, in which perception, stimulated by the optics of painted color, would bring awareness of transcendent ideas of expansion and movement. Both form and subject would reveal the pervasive universal flux in which modern machinery takes its place.[8]

"Simultaneity" was defined differently by the Italian Futurists although they also linked it with the modern city and machinery. For them it is not as rarified a term as Delaunay's but instead a concept of immediacy, in which implied movement involves the spectator in an active engagement with the politics of modernity. The Futurists proclaimed modern technology as the instrument that would wrench their country violently into the modern world. Carlo Carrà's *What the Street Car Told Me* (1910–11, on loan to the Städtische Galerie, Frankfurt) uses vivid diagonals and tumbling geometry to suggest the interpenetration of a careening bus with nighttime lights, reflections, and passers-by. It is fully as abstract as the work of Gleizes or Delaunay but has a visceral immediacy foreign to their more aloof calculations.

It was not pictures of machines but pictorial dynamism that expressed the new industrial age. Even less representational than Carrà's canvas is Giacomo Balla's *Speeding Automobile* (Museum of Modern Art, New York). Here, and in several variations on this theme, Balla embodied machine movement in a nearly abstract geometric vivacity partly inspired by motion photography. Balla's work seems to give visual form to some of the famous sentences from F.T. Marinetti's "Futurist Manifesto" of 1909:

> We affirm that the world's magnificence has been enriched by a new beauty: the beauty of speed. A racing car whose hood is adorned with great pipes, like serpents of explosive breath – a roaring car that seems to ride on grapeshot is more beautiful than the *Victory of Samothrace.*
>
> We will glorify war – the world's only hygiene – militarism, patriotism, the destructive gesture of freedom-bringers, beautiful ideas worth dying for, and scorn for women.[9]

The latter phrase, of course, is one of the most flagrant proofs of the links between male sexism and violence, well hidden in Cubism but overt in Futurism.[10] In 1911 and 1912 the Futurists were ardent supporters of Italy's war with Turkey and the use of aerial bombardment in Libya. Then, after the onset of World War I in August 1914, they did everything to help push Italy into the conflict on the allied side, publishing pro-war pamphlets, organizing meetings, and the like. When Italy joined the allies in May 1915, the Futurist leader Marinetti mustered most of the group into a military motocycle corps that he organized. Subsequently he and several other Futurists joined Mussolini's new Fascist order and in the 1920s became propagandists for rapid industrialization. Was it not Mussolini who called Marinetti "the Saint John the Baptist of the Fascist movement?"

Elsewhere, before the war, the machine was associated with radical modernism. In England in 1913, Jacob Epstein sculpted his original *Rock Drill* (later dismembered) by incorporating pieces of a real drill atop a metal tripod. Later he cast in bronze the uppermost portion, a geometrized torso surmounted by a head in the shape of a welder's helmet.[11] In British Vorticism, Wyndham Lewis and his colleagues on the eve of war proclaimed in masculinist terms echoing Futurism that modernity meant violent upheaval. Lewis's prewar *Plan of War* of 1914 (lost, known from a photograph) is abstract, but full of slashing geometry loosely related to diagrams of battle maneuvers. His elaborated drawing *Combat no. 2* (Victoria & Albert Museum, London) of the same year, also a prewar work, shows mechano-morphic men fighting, their forms having the dynamic geometry of his abstract constructions. With the onset of war, he and other Vorticists specialized in pictures that indulge in the mechanisms of wartime violence, for example, Christopher Nevinson's *A Bursting Shell* of 1915 (Tate, London) or Edward Wadsworth's *War Engine* of the same year (now lost). The latter, although abstract, includes elements that were clearly patterned on pistons of an internal combustion engine.

Among the Cubo-Futurists in Russia, Natalia Goncharova had frequently included wheels, gears, and other parts of machinery in her work by 1913, such as *Weaver* (National Museum of Wales, Cardiff) and *Airplane over Train* (Art Museum, Kazan). Olga Rozanova similarly employed elements of machinery, as in her *Metronome* of 1913–14 (State Tretyakov Gallery, Moscow). The association of machinery with modernism did not require the latest kind of industrial form. Goncharova's mechanized loom and Rosanova's metronome had been around for a century, and Kasimir Malevich's *Knife Grinder* (1912, Yale University Art Gallery, New Haven) uses a very old machine to symbolize his modernist "principle of glittering" (written on the back of the canvas). Russian artists also made numerous mechano-morphic forms, including Malevich's costumes for *Victory over the Sun* (1913), and *Médrano* (1915, Guggenheim Museum, New York) by the Paris-based Alexander Archipenko. Their forms, by the way, have an engaging sense of humor in contrast to the rather horrifying mechano-morphic inventions of the British Vorticists and the Italian Futurists.

War and Revolution

With the outbreak of World War I, the machine took on a new and terrifying presence, so much so that the war itself was embodied in the airplane, aerial balloons, the submarine, and motorized vehicles of all sorts, as well as in the ubiquitous cannons, machine guns, barbed wire, and gas masks. The design of airplanes and airborne armaments evolved with great rapidity, as did that of both military and civilian motor vehicles. Military needs also greatly increased the use and awareness of radio transmissions and the telephone. Before the war

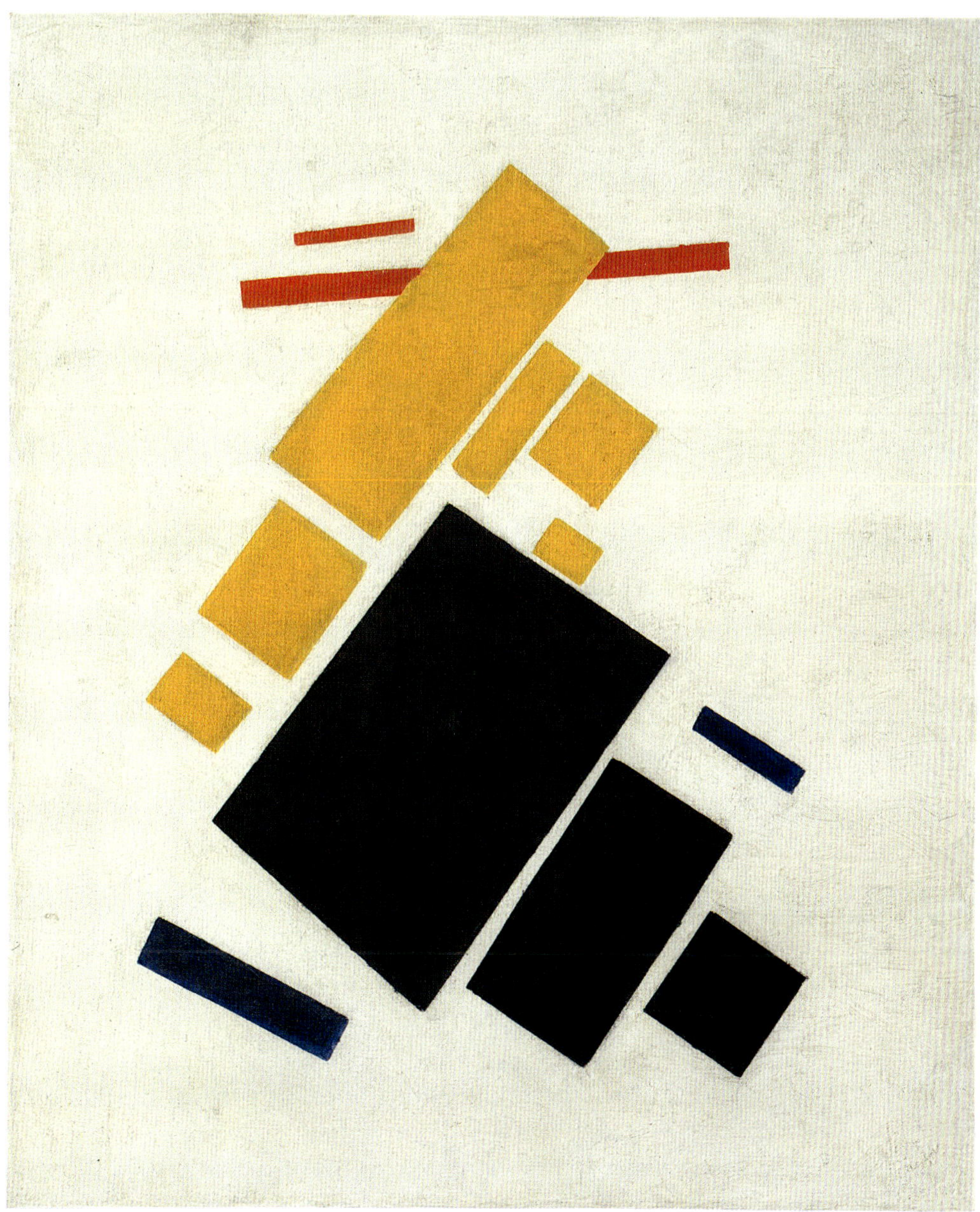

54 Kasimir Malevich, *Suprematist Composition: Airplane Flying*, 1914. 22⅞ × 19 in. (58.1 × 48.3 cm.). Museum of Modern Art, New York.

ended, illustrated journals were full of praise for the new designs, rightly associated with the needful economies of wartime industry. In this perspective, old-fashioned handcraft seemed anachronistic in both artistic and social terms. It was now far easier to equate modernity with industrial forms than before the war.

In Russia the war meant a violent break with the tsarist past. Some artists claimed a stake in the future by getting rid of all representations of the real world, after passing through several years of Cubo-Futurism during which they had retained representational clues. Naturalistic representation was associated with the tsarist past, whereas the new language of abstract art, established by 1915, could speak for the future. Malevich's *Suprematist Composition, Airplane Flying* (pl. 54), exhibited in December 1915, is a case in point. In Delaunay's painting (pl. 52) the images of airplanes are still needed but in Malevich's, the dark rectangles at the bottom of the frame suggest the weight of earthbound forms, the yellow ones float above these, and our eye is led upward to the faraway red stripe. When writing about his art Malevich referred to airplanes and to extra-terrestial satellites: "We are the highest point in the race of contemporary life, the kingdom of machines and motors and their work on earth and in space."[12] He likened modern technology's defeat of earth-born gravity to his self-invented Suprematist forms which he declared to be a new visual language utterly free of references to the natural world. Similarly, Vladimir Tatlin's sculptures shown in the same exhibition of 1915 were entirely abstract, and one *Corner Relief* (subsequently lost) was suspended on wires to free it metaphorically from contact with the earth.

The Russian Revolution of 1917, born of wartime events, led to the adoption by some party leaders of the radical language of abstraction.[13] Aware of the value of cultivating the artistic avant-garde, they reached out to wielders of a new visual language. In 1918, for the first anniversary of the October Revolution, Nathan Altman designed the speakers' rostrum in St. Petersburg by surrounding the old column of Alexander with gigantic geometric forms, a new abstract language for a new society. Two years later Tatlin unveiled his towering *Monument to the Third International* (known through photographs and drawings) in the lobby of the meeting place of world communism. It was a model for a central government structure to be built in glass and steel, those products of modern industry that take over the role of stone, brick, and wood. Inside the external spiral, which symbolized the ever-evolving social forms of revolution, there were to be three rooms that would revolve on electric motors. A huge cube, which would rotate once a year, housed the legislature. Above it a pyramid, housing the executive, would rotate once a month, while at the top a cylinder, enclosing the agitation and information center, would revolve once a day. The revolution was to be served not by traditional Euclidean forms but by visionary geometry that would transform the world thanks to modern engineering. A second version of the "Tower," as it is called, was the centerpiece of the USSR's exhibition in the World's Fair of 1925 in Paris: an official sanction of its symbolic language.

For Soviet revolutionary artists (we now group them together as "Constructivists" although in the polemics of the time this term was a more limited one), the word "art" smacked of products isolated from the masses by faulty bourgeois conceptions. "Art" designated objects for private pleasure, so radical artists

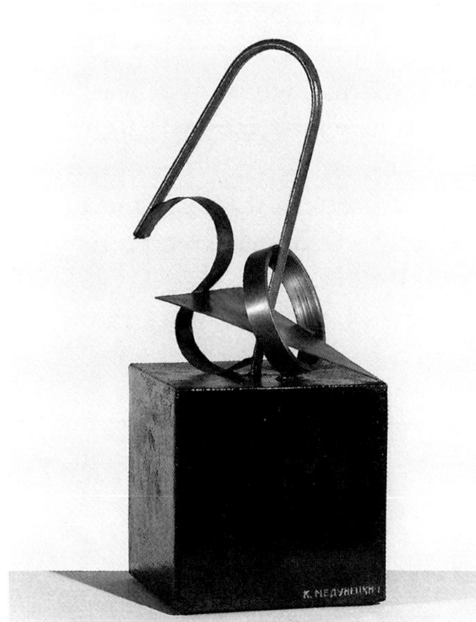

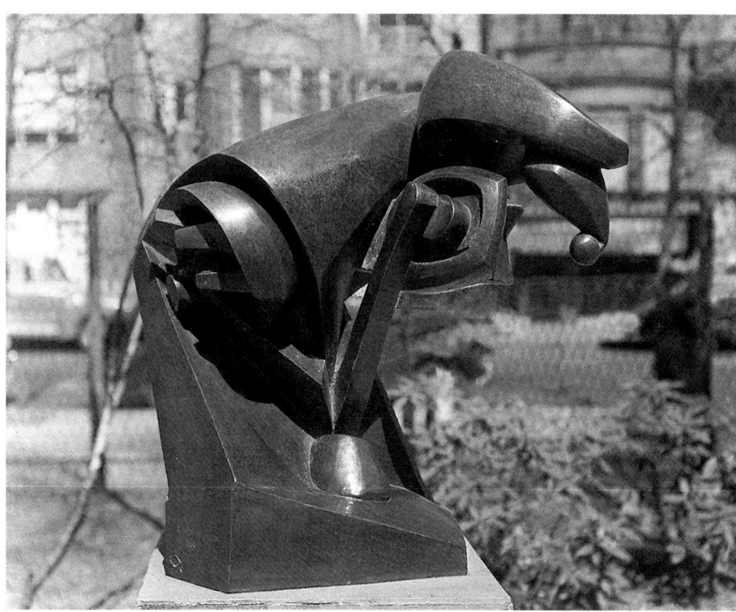

55 *(left)* Konstantin Medunetsky, *Spatial Construction*, 1919. Tin, brass, steel, and painted iron, 18⅛ in. (46 cm.) high. Yale University Art Gallery, New Haven, Collection Société Anonyme.

56 *(right)* Raymond Duchamp-Villon, *Horse*, 1914. Bronze (cast *c.* 1930–31). 40 × 39½ × 22⅜ in. (101.6 × 100.1 × 56.7 cm.). Museum of Modern Art, New York, Van Gogh Purchase Fund.

instead talked about "laboratory experiments." Artists were now frequently called "artist-engineers," and their work was to be closely related to factory production. The critic Boris Arvatov wrote that the progressive artist "is not merely a performer but a constructor-inventor; he can give engineering a higher creative form."[14] Engineering, that is, cannot stand by itself but needs this new specialist of form, a "constructor-inventor." Thanks to his mastery of visual form, the constructor supplies that which the ordinary technician lacks.

Konstantin Medunetsky's *Spatial Composition* (pl. 55), exhibited with the Society of Young Artists in 1921, shows the artist-engineer at work. His deceptively simple shapes, in four different metals, form a subtle set of relationships. From one corner of the cubical base of painted metal, a brass triangle slants upward. It passes through a steel ring to reach an S-shaped strip of tin. To the upper end of the tin strip is attached an iron parabola, suitably painted red to inhibit rust. This parabola curves up and then down, piercing the brass triangle and reaching the other end of the S-strip. It forms a spatial plane that controls all the forms, each of which touches the base at only a tiny point.

Because Medunetsky borrowed his materials directly from industry, leaving them without any marks of his own touch, his sculpture seems worlds apart from Raymond Duchamp-Villon's *Horse* of 1914 (pl. 56), the major sculpture of Epic Cubism which in its day seemed so radical. The difference between them – only seven years separate them – is one measure of the extraordinary gap that the war had opened out in modern culture. Duchamp-Villon not only intended to use bronze, the traditional sculptor's material (his plaster was cast after his wartime death), he also merged images of machine and horse. On both sides of his sculpture rise simulacra of crankshafts, and in the back is a ring of plugs that resemble the chuck of a lathe. For Medunetsky, after war and revolution, this would have been an old-fashioned object that joined machine and organism into a "romantic" piece of art. It provided no lessons to engineers on the logically organized yet inspirational uses of their materials.

Many Russian Constructivists treated their function as an equivalent to that of Communist Party leaders. They would direct workers and peasants away from handcrafts towards the acceptance of machine production. Both artists and party cadres sought socially efficient forms, new forms that could embody modern industrial materials and techniques rather than hated individualism and naturalism, associated with the defunct regime of the tsars. Artists and party leaders alike had the same view of World War I: it destroyed the old – in art as in society – to make way for the new.

Art in Russia was not as isolated as its rhetoric sometimes suggested. In 1919 Walter Gropius had become the director of the Bauhaus, reorienting Weimar's earlier design school in a moment of postwar socialist euphoria. By 1923 that euphoria had waned, and the school was transforming its utopian mandate to one that would wed design to enlightened capitalist commerce and industry. The Bauhaus emphasized not "art" but the examination of the possibilities inherent in industrial materials, sometimes echoing the Russian "laboratory experiments." It is true that Wassily Kandinsky and Paul Klee had studios at the Bauhaus and continued their individual fine arts work, but their teaching was subordinated to the school's investigation of new principles of design in all media. Bauhaus exhibitions were devoted to products and materials of industrial and commercial utility, and by the mid-1920s some designs entered production, ranging from Marcel Breuer's "Wassily" chair to Marianne Brandt's Kandem bedlamp.[15]

The French "Rappel à l'Ordre"

In postwar France there was no equivalent to the Bauhaus or the Constructivists' schooling. New energies came from diverse vanguard artists but victorious France underwent no upheaval comparable to those in Germany and Russia; its government stressed continuity, not radical change. For the overt endorsement of modern technology, we should turn to Fernand Léger and to his allies Le Corbusier and Amédée Ozenfant; the latter two founded Purism in 1918. Purism's importance was enhanced by the influential review *Esprit Nouveau*, which Ozenfant and Le Corbusier launched in 1920. Lasting until 1925, it was

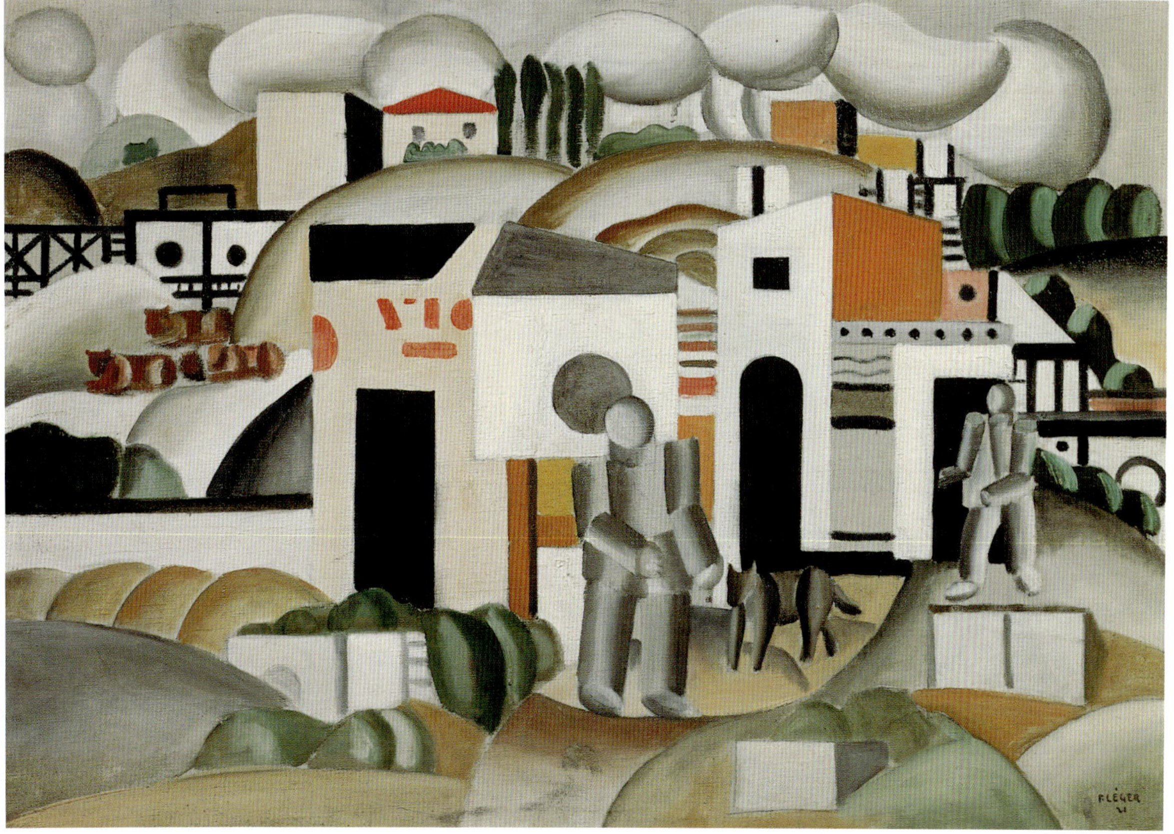

57 Fernand Léger, *Man with a Dog (Animated Landscape)*, 1921. 25⅝ × 36¼ in. (65 × 92 cm.). Private collection, London.

one of the major outlets for the "Rappel à l'Ordre" ("Call to Order") that characterized the postwar years in the Parisian avant-garde. ("Rappel" carries the meaning of recall, or return, hence "Retour à l'Ordre" ["Return to Order"] was an alternative phrase.)

Kenneth Silver has shown the close connection of wartime and postwar rhetoric in France to that of the Call to Order, a vanguard embrace of modern industry with esthetic clarity that had long been attached to the classicizing underpinnings of French culture, as contrasted to supposed Germanic emotionalism and individualistic expressiveness. Le Corbusier, for example, like Malevich, used the airplane to attach wartime inventiveness to modernity. The airplane, he wrote in *Vers une architecture* (1923), "mobilized invention, intelligence, and daring: imagination and cold reason. It is the same spirit that built the Parthenon." He also explicitly linked Roman engineering with the ethos of French reconstruction, proposing that the word "Roman" meant "unity of operation, a clear aim in view, classification of the various parts."[16]

Like the Bauhaus artists and Constructivists, the Purists and Léger derived a lot of their energies from the war but, lacking the outlets provided by a radicalized society, they poured their reactions into the broad stream of postwar reconstruction. They occupied the familiar role of avant-garde artists whose work in a stable society is provocative, perhaps leading to reform, but is not revolutionary. Léger's friend and sometime collaborator Le Corbusier, as Mary McLeod has demonstrated, was an enthusiast for Taylorism, the American concept of rationalized serial production that he deemed essential for France's vast program of reconstruction.[17] Taylorism was also put forward in Soviet Russia but there it could be folded into party-managed industry, whereas Le Corbusier could imagine it only in the context of progressive capitalism.

At the center of the Call to Order, Léger deserves special attention.[18] His art of the early 1920s insisted upon a close relationship of art and industry. His *Animated Landscape* of 1921 (pl. 57) is a utopian vision for the modern world, one of a large number bearing the same title that speak for an optimistic reading of postwar reconstruction. He embraced continuity by retaining representational imagery, discarded by Russian Constructivists who were so anxious to cut all ties with the past. Triumphing over nature is a billboard city (Léger loved billboards and disliked "do-gooders" who opposed them),[19] for the countryside is dedicated to supplying its wants. Cows ruminate peacefully in the distance near buildings which suggest industrialized agriculture, organized to feed the city. City and country share the landscape because their premodern separation has been bridged by the logic of industrial order. It is the same industrial organization, the fruit of human rationality, that lets men stand passively by the city, freed from the sweat of manual labor by the power of mind over raw nature. Earned leisure is the triumph of modernity, signaled here by the domestic coupling of man and dog, a masculine counterpart to Léger's frequent treatment of equally impersonal women enjoying household leisure.

Like Constructivist and Bauhaus geometry, Léger's forms do not embody the appearance but instead the logic of machine production. His numerous essays frequently make the point that to imitate machines would be to indulge in mere descriptive naturalism. He is therefore rather close to the Russian Constructivists despite his representational imagery. He was not then a member of any party, as far as we know, but he was on the political left (if only, in Soviet terms, a bourgeois liberal). He put ordinary artisans at the center of his social credo. In his essay of 1924, "The Machine Aesthetic," he wrote as follows:

> The artisan regains his place, which he should always have kept, for he is the true creator. It's he who daily, modestly, unconsciously creates and invents the pretty trinkets and beautiful machines that enable us to live. His unconsciousness saves him. The vast majority of professional artists are detestable for their individual pride and their self-consciousness; they make everything wither.[20]

Like the Constructivists, therefore, Léger aligned himself with democratic forces, opposing elite artists by taking on the role of a vanguard leader who works on behalf of disfranchised artisans and workers.[21]

The Machine Esthetic

Léger, the Russian Constructivists, Bauhaus artists (and more distantly, the American "Precisionists" Charles Demuth and Charles Sheeler) were allied by the "machine esthetic," a concept already in vogue by the time Léger used it in 1924. For them art should be the expression of industrial culture. Its forms and techniques were said to be analogous to machine production because both art and machinery process raw materials for new forms and uses. Machines do not automatically have economical structures or suitably modern appearance, so industry needs specialists in form who can instruct both engineers and public in the logic and beauty of rational means. Geometric form is the basis both of the new visual language and of industrial culture, because of the long-standing associations that define it in Western culture: measurement, order, rationality, construction, and impersonality. It is a concept that is shared by society, and therefore cannot be claimed as unique to any individual. Thanks to geometry, the *impersonality* of artistic forms guarantees a visual language suitable to mass production and social engineering, hence both the unmarked industrial surfaces of Medunetsky's *Spatial Construction* and the impersonality of Léger's images are programmatic assertions.

For adherents of the machine esthetic, nature and naturalistic art were equated with prewar society. In the postwar era, humans can triumph over nature thanks to the new technologies; they must not continue merely to follow nature but instead must transform her. And it is "her" in this very masculine set of beliefs. "The contemporary environment is clearly the manufactured and 'mechanical' object; this is slowly subjugating the breasts and curves of woman, fruit, the soft landscape – inspiration of painters since art began."[22] Postwar reconstruction made idealists into "constructors" and "artist-engineers," not mere artists.

The least common denominators of the international machine esthetic can be summarized under six headings. Geometry is their common expression, which is why geometric abstraction had such powerful resonance in the postwar era.

Construction vs. destruction. The postwar world requires the destruction of prewar hierarchies. The war had a cleansing effect because it destroyed monarchy and naturalism in the arts; reconstruction is based upon violent upheaval; progressive politics and progressive art are allies.

Rationality. A social term of broad currency, "rationality" enfolds the esthetic associations of reason, order, utility, and economy. It speaks for the conscious and manmade in opposition to the subjective and private (associated with the prewar era), and for the secular because geometric harmony is no longer conceived as a revelation of the divine. Men create, they do not "discover" or "reveal."

Triumph over nature and naturalism. Nature is equated with the traditional, the accidental, the irregular (divine purpose is no longer believed in), and the imitative, as distinct from secular modernism in which geometry represents industrial triumph over the "natural" forms of prewar social organization (monarchies were defeated).

Anonymity, impersonality, anti-individualism. The social and artistic enemy is individualism and emotive expressionism, which are anti-social. The anonymous worker and *le peuple* are to be celebrated. Because modern humans use machines as tools in social co-operation, personal brushwork in art and handmade irregularities in industry must be discarded. The anonymous in art and the impersonal in machinery, symbolized by geometric form, are the signs of the subordination of the individual to social good.

Aspiration towards architecture. The machine esthetic in painting and sculpture claimed architecture as the favored sister art, in contrast to the prewar vanguard's preference for music, now considered too personal. Postwar reconstruction obviously favored the most socially useful of the arts, not just in its accomplished structures, but also in its production by teams of designers and workers. Architecture is the quintessential social collaboration. Léger titled one of his pictures *Architecture* (1923, private collection) and El Lissitzky's pictures and graphics, no matter how abstract, are full of three-dimensional simulacra of architectural forms.

Reproducibility, economy of means. Mass production must triumph over isolated handcrafts and individualism to bring the largest benefits to the most people. Geometric forms in industry and in art embody the logic of reproducibility and its social benefits. Although Léger and the Constructivists crafted their work by hand, they gave it the appearance of impersonality to proclaim the suppression of the self. The social value of their art lies in its apparent suitability to mass production. Logically, as the prescient Meyer Schapiro realized in 1937, the esthetic terminology of abstraction was borrowed from economics and industry. After World War I, he wrote:

> the older categories of art were translated into the language of modern technology; the essential was identified with the efficient, the unit with the standardized element, texture with new materials, representation with photography, drawing with the ruled or mechanically traced line, color with the flat coat of paint and design with the model or the instructing plan.[23]

The Dada Opposition

This chapter so far has discussed artists whose work embraced positive attitudes toward humankind's ability to use new industrial techniques to alter both art and society. Other modernists, however, adopted opposed viewpoints, and we must now consider them. Leading the way before 1918 was Marcel Duchamp, that heir of nineteenth-century dandyism whose mocking attitude toward rationality and toward art itself has come to be regarded as a fundamental manifestation of modernism.[24] Seeking alternatives to conventional painting after 1912, he created objects that could only be understood in terms of the conceptions they led to when their appearance was linked with Duchamp's words for them. Word and concept, that is, were inextricably fused with the visual to escape what Duchamp regarded as the limitation of "retinal art."

One of his best-known objects is *Fountain*, a porcelain urinal turned on its back but unaltered except for his signature as "r. mutt." In 1917 it was rejected by a vanguard exhibition society in New York (and was subsequently lost), presumably because of its potential for scandal but also because it did not seem to be "art" at all. Duchamp's radical act (appreciated much more in the 1960s than in 1917) was to declare that art was pure concept, that an ordinary manufactured object could be transformed by that declaration, and that "originality" did not require artistic handwork. Two years earlier Duchamp had begun working on his large *Bride Stripped Bare by her Bachelors, Even* (Philadelphia Museum of Art), a work on glass "uncompleted" in 1923, and then repaired in 1936 to incorporate prominent cracks in its glass. Readable only if one is privy to some of the many explanatory notes Duchamp published, the "large glass" is a structure of frustrated mechanical sex, a complicated and immensely rich mechanomorphic world that became an object of pilgrimage in the 1960s. Duchamp's work was at the center of what came to be known as "New York Dada," notable for its frequent assaults upon conventional ideas about the machine world and about art. Morton Schamberg exhibited metal pipes in a miter box as *God* (1918, Philadelphia Museum of Art), and Duchamp's French sidekick Francis Picabia made paintings and drawings using the imagery and style of diagrams of machines. Some were "portraits" of notable figures (Alfred Stieglitz was rendered as a diagrammatic camera), others were instances of mechanical sex rendered in gears and pistons, including *Amorous Parade* (1917, private collection, Chicago).

Although Duchamp's prewar work had adumbrated the Dada spirit, it was only during World War I that Dada became established as a broad if loosely co-ordinated activity. The name itself was provided in 1916 by the group led by Hugo Ball at the Café Voltaire in Zürich (Hans Arp, Sophie Tauber, Tristan Tzara), and adopted the next year by Duchamp, Picabia, and their American colleagues.[25] The New York and Zürich groups retreated from the war but instead of joining anti-war groups they adopted attitudes of sardonic withdrawal, acting out the belief that in face of war's monstrosities, the only sanity was unreason. In the aftermath of the war other Dadaists treated the machine as the agent of destructive violence, and insisted that rationality was inherently oppressive. Various manifestations of international Dada rapidly spread from New York and Zürich to major centers of European culture. It became a notorious phenomenon of postwar culture until about 1924, when Surrealism took over and transformed Dada's waning energies. Dada was not an organized movement but its disparate practitioners had similar caustic, often bitter reactions to the consequences of mechanization, particularly in light of the war.

It was in postwar Germany that Dada gained the largest number of adherents, doubtless because there the mood of defeat and upheaval gave greater outlet to anti-war and anti-rational beliefs than was true in victorious France and communist Russia. Already in 1918 a group of Dadaists in Berlin had linked Dada with the war. Listen to the echoes of war and postwar trauma in the language of their manifesto:

> Life appears as a simultaneous muddle of noises, colors and spiritual rhythms, which is taken unmodified, with all the sensational screams and fevers of its reckless everyday psyche and with all its brutal reality. [. . .] Dada is the international expression of our times, the great rebellion of artistic movements, the artistic reflex of all these offensives, peace congresses, riots.[26]

In the first major Dada exhibition in Berlin, in 1920, a pig in military uniform dangled from the ceiling, near a large painting by Otto Dix of *War Cripples* (formerly Stadtmuseum, Dresden), a savage indictment of war which made a mockery of any hopes for postwar recovery. Elsewhere in that exhibition was a huge collage by Hannah Höch, *Cut with the Kitchen Knife Dada through the last Weimar beer belly cultural epoch of Germany* (Nationalgalerie, Berlin).[27] Höch's cut-outs from the mass press echo "these offensives, peace congresses, riots," and the overall rhythms of her polemical collage express "screams and fevers." In the upper left there is the head of Einstein from which spring machine forms and the word "Dada." In the upper right is the deposed Kaiser Wilhelm surrounded by Weimar political and military leaders; his mustache consists of two wrestlers. Machine forms abound throughout the collage, countered by many images of women, shown as the antithesis of masculine machinery and military culture. (It is a female who "cuts with the kitchen knife.") As Maud Lavin has shown, negative and positive connotations swarm throughout the collage: images of both human and machine movement, excitement, and riotous liberation, not just "anti-machine" connotations.

Photo-collage was a subversive handmade form particularly prominent among German Dadaists, notably Höch, John Heartfield, and Raoul Haussman. In contrast to Picasso, who avoided photographic reproductions in his prewar collages, and who personalized his borrowings with his own drawing, the German Dadaists rarely added any drawing of their own to their montages, instead using clippings from the machine-based mass media to promote resistance and activism. In doing so, they attacked the old concept of "originality" and the wholeness of earlier art, and therefore assaulted the supposedly rational means of representation itself, not just the rationality of industry and mechanized war. (It is worthwhile remembering that Léger held the opposite point of view, and therefore never used photographic reproduction nor, indeed, collage.)

Max Ernst

Max Ernst, less overtly political than the Berlin Dadaists, introduced a technique closely related to photo-collage and equally subversive. From 1919 through 1921 he made a number of Dada works by taking sheets from a compendious publication of 1914 whose engravings represent all sorts of objects, charts, and images used in school instruction.[28] He suppressed some of their objects and altered others by coloring the sheets with gouache, paint, and drawing, occasionally pasting on fragments borrowed from this and other publications. For *Hydrometric Demonstration of Killing by Temperature* (1920, private collection), Ernst converted a page of laboratory equipment into a compartment of machine-like objects that protrude into a blue sky. This bizarre composition looks like a premonition of Hitler's crematoria but in 1920 it would have conjured up a menacing factory. *Two Ambiguous Figures* (1919, private collection) transforms another sheet into mechano-morphic creatures sporting goggles reminiscent of gas masks.

Showing greater distance from the war, *Sheep* of 1921 (pl. 58) converts a group of geometric objects used in primary education to a strange vision. Set in a desert landscape where a reindeer sled disappears in the distance, these objects

58 Max Ernst, *Sheep*, 1921. Gouache and collage over catalog page, 4⅝ × 6¼ in. (11.2 × 16 cm.). Musée National d'Art Moderne, Centre Georges Pompidou, Paris.

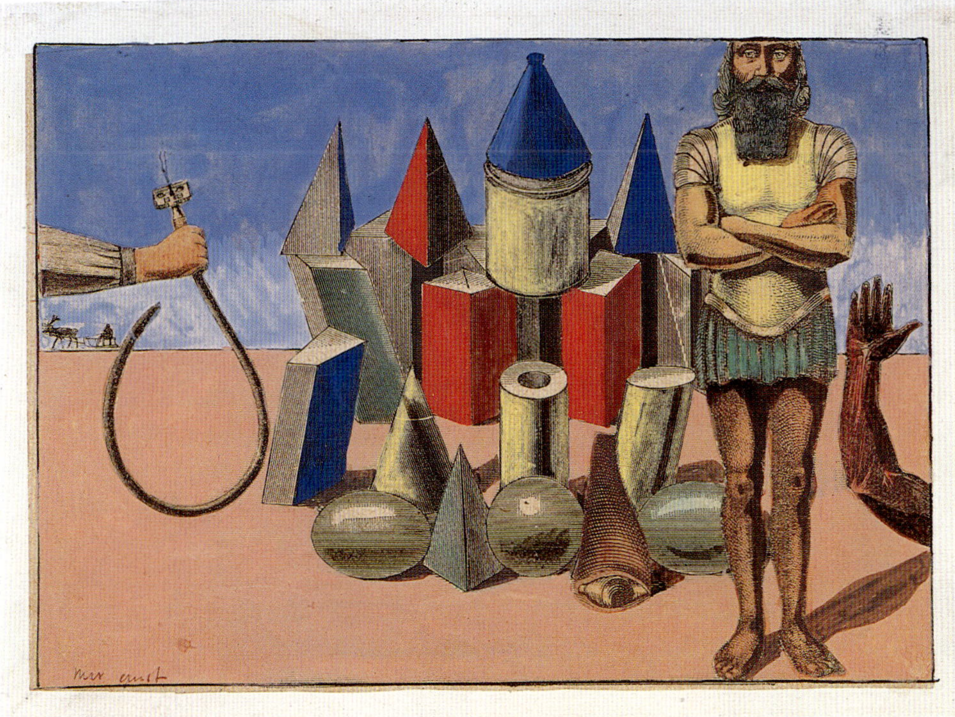

originally dedicated to rational investigation (object lessons!) have become otherworldly forms watched over by an ancient warrior. Of the two flanking arms, one mysteriously brandishes a tube and petcock, while the other is flayed, its horror partly mitigated by recognition that it was borrowed from a medical chart. Three years before Surrealism was founded, we are already in a world of unreason, all the more upsetting because the very instruments of rational discourse are used to deny the logic of construction and understanding.

In paintings unaided by collage, and therefore more like the procedures of traditional art, Ernst pursued the same attack upon reason and, by extension, upon the mechanical world. The central image of *Elephant Celebes* of 1921 (pl. 59) was inspired by a photograph of a double-legged structure of dried clay made by the Konkomba people of western Sudan to store their grain.[29] Ernst's elephantine form would defy the descriptive powers of the group of blind men. The Africanness of its "primitive" shape is mixed with its opposite, mechanistic forms. At the top, geometric shapes recall both the "metaphysical art" of Giorgio de Chirico of the prior decade and the turrets of armored vehicles of World War I.[30] The monstrous "trunk" looks like industrial tubing but terminates in an organic image of a bull's head and napkin, perhaps threatening the woman in the lower right, or already feasting on her absent head. Paradoxically, the eyes of the bull can be read as a headless woman's breasts, and the horns as her arms. Either reading sets up a dialog with the decapitated nude, whose mutilated form also resonates strangely with the phallic tower behind. The age-old theme of "the world upside down" appears in the two fish who swim in the sky, but the downward-spiraling smoke to the right makes us think of that modern wartime disaster, a stricken airplane or observation balloon, all the more so because the landscape resembles an airfield.

No such monster and no headless nudes could ever disturb the balanced and optimistic worlds that Léger created. He and Max Ernst are a study in unparallel lives, for although both lived in the muck and mire of World War I trenches, witnesses to untold slaughter of their comrades, they established opposed viewpoints in their art. The earth of Léger's *Animated Landscape* (pl. 57) is not an airfield for a clanking monster, but a productive countryside that will feed his billboard city. His robotic figures are not mutilated, but constructed of impersonal geometry that stands for the positive capacities of human reason to replace hard labor with rational instruments. He will orchestrate material forces towards a new social harmony in which Ernst's irrational inventions could have no place.

For Léger, in victorious France, and for the Russian Constructivists, in the midst of building a new political order, the dehumanization of war was a spur towards ideals of social reconstruction, as it was for Gropius and the Bauhaus. By contrast, for Ernst and many other artists in Germany, the dehumanization of wartime violence and civilian suffering was tragic proof that humans will use coercive social order, impersonality, and the machine to destroy life. The

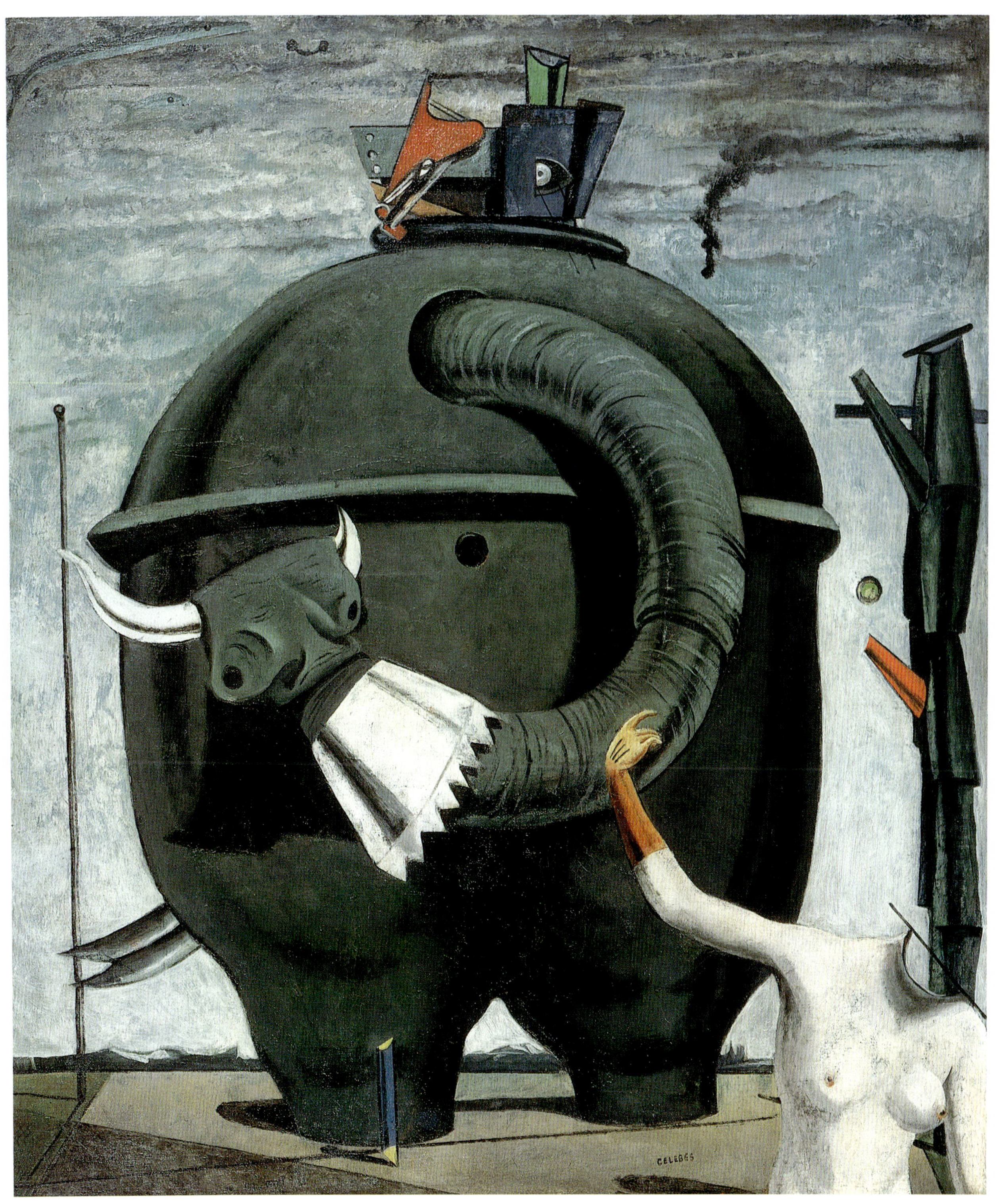

59 Max Ernst, *Elephant Celebes*, 1921. 49¼ × 42½ in. (125 × 108 cm.). Tate Modern, London.

wondrous potential of modern technology therefore had to be countered with its dangers. The Dadaists could accuse Léger, the Russian Constructivists, and the Bauhaus of serving both capitalism and communism by making the machine into an instrument of social order. The radical nature of Dada art is to have exposed the social consequence of the machine world: social order can be imposed to become social control. This is an essentially political stance because it recognized that the machine was not the classless instrument of a better world but a symbol of the control of some humans by others. The machine and other emblems of reason caricatured by the Dadaists spoke for the *lack* of control by the victims of social order.

The Machine Then and Now

This chapter has marked out the gap between those who greeted the arrival of the modern machine as the harbinger of a new utopia, and those who looked upon it with despair. From Leo Marx and Langdon Winner we have long been aware that this opposition has characterized modern culture since the onset of the industrial revolution. All I have hoped to do is to document that critical moment revolving around World War I when modernists elevated the machine to the dominant structures and subjects of painting and sculpture.

It is true that there were some cross-currents between the Dadaists and the technological optimists of the machine esthetic. Both sides believed that old ideas had been destroyed by the war and that traditional naturalism could not suit the new era that humankind was entering in the postwar years. Dada artists were not unrelievedly against all ramifications of the machine. Hannah Höch and Raoul Haussman emphasized its uses for destruction and social control but they were also struck by the potential of modern machines to release the human imagination. Some Dada artists came close to Constructivist geometry, particularly Kurt Schwitters, whose collages and reliefs after 1921 often take on a regularity bespeaking rational organization. On the other hand, the attacks that Dada made on the old order were so engaging that a number of artists associated with the machine esthetic flirted with it. Before he went to the Bauhaus, László Moholy-Nagy composed a number of frankly Dada works, and Alexander Rodchenko's photo-montages for Mayakovsky's poem *Pro Eto* (1923) have a decided Dada exuberance. However, although these cross-currents reflect mutual awareness among the avant-garde, they do not deny the broad oppositions that I have sketched out.

Although prior generations had their machine optimists and detractors, it was only in the turbulent second decade of the twentieth century that modernists felt obliged to deal head-on with the arrival of the machine, particularly in the aftermath of World War I. In fact, the visit this chapter has made to art of that decade seems to take us back to a kind of naïve or archaic world. Since then,

Surrealism, science fiction, frequent wars, apocalyptic atomic power, and microcomputing have all intervened to prevent us from seeing into technology with such doubtful clarity.

For us today, technology's intersections with artistic culture are so varied and intertwined that those old polarities no longer seem a sufficent description of modern beliefs. The astonishing rise of science fiction has been possible because of the widespread belief that modern technology, symbolized by machines, gives humans the capacity to build whole new worlds but also to destroy, the two capacities in dangerous alliance, no longer readily separable. In fact, science fiction, although its origins predate the twentieth century, became a major element in advanced industrial culture only after World War I; its rise to prominence roughly coincided with the development of Surrealism.

In our present culture, many of us actually share the ideas embodied in both Ernst and Léger. We place great hopes in the latest advances of technology. We travel about in wondrous machines but we find in current films, television, and computer games an unending display of high-tech machinery dedicated to violent ends. In science fiction we are nearly always under the threat of imminent violence, and can find images that more or less look like both Léger and Ernst. The separation of illusion from reality, of human organisms from machines, is no longer evident, as we can see when we walk by the game arcades in our shopping malls or read about sophisticated work on cognitive computing machines.

Appendices

Three typed letters to Alfred H. Barr, Jr., from Fernand Léger: *Three Women* (*Le Grand Déjeuner*) Collection File, Department of Painting and Sculpture, Museum of Modern Art, New York. Léger typed these letters in somewhat imperfect English, which has been retained below (with only minor alterations in punctuation and spacing). The third (Appendix C) is published for the first time in the present volume. I am again grateful to my colleagues at the Museum of Modern Art for their authorizations.

Appendix A

80 West 40th Street
New York City

November 13th [1942]

Dear Mr. Barr:
Here is the answer to your questions:

1) Was this painting conceived as a mural decoration?

It is for me, an easel painting – because of the subject and of the intentions of perspective that it contains.

The mural art, at my opinion, must avoid to destroy a wall or, if you prefer, to come out of the wall. By the will of the volumes and by their strength, "the three women" attack the wall and are a painting more than a decoration.

2) I know of one complete preliminary study in the collection of Meric Callery.[1] Did you make any other composition studies? If so, do you know where they are?

There are, prior to Mrs Callery's preliminary study three other composition studies, first in date (dimensions 30 Figure). The two first ones,[2] very unfinished are, I believe, at the Chateau de Chambord where Huisman (at the beginning of the present war) had sent for me 60 of my pictures (I hope that they are still there!). The third composition study[3] had been painted at the request of Léonce Rosemberg (for one of his customers who wished one exemplary of this size).

Of most, there are two more pieces (canvasses of 30 Figure). The study for the section on the right side is at Paul Rosemberg's under the title "La tasse de chocolat."[4] The study for the section on the left side is at Kahnweiller's.[5]

3) Did you begin *Le Grand Déjeuner* before Picasso began his *Three Musicians*? Do you feel that there is any connection at all between these two pictures for each is, in its way, the painter's masterpiece of the same year and period?

If I consider the dates of the pictures. *Three Musicians* are from 1923,[6] *Le Grand Déjeuner* from 1921. About a connection between them, I should think more with *La Ville* from 1919. Because of the technic of the flat colours and strong colours. It is, I believe, the picture *La Ville* which has given the taste of stronger colours in Cubism.

4) Did you tell me that you changed the color of one of the three figures in the large composition?

When the definitive picture *Le Grand Déjeuner* was finished, it was bought by Léonce Rosemberg. But when the picture has been taken to his gallery, Léonce Rosemberg was afraid of the severity of the painting. At his request I took it back and gave him instead of it: "La mère et l'enfant" (collection Laroche)[7] a more pleasant picture and less important one, at my opinion. It is during this time that I decided to strenghten the contrasts and emphasized more and more the strenght of the painting by painting the personage at the center[8] in ochre. The side easel painting was then reinforced.

5) Do you consider the *Grand Déjeuner* a Cubist painting?

Your question is embarrassing for the reason that I am unaware of what is called Cubism. If Cubism means Picasso, Braque, grey period, montmartroise period, "Le Grand Déjeuner" has absolutely nothing to do with it. "Cubism" was too related to abstract painting.

On the other hand, if Cubist means: will of the volumes, then, I am more Cubist than all the others, specially in *Le Grand Déjeuner*.

6) Do you agree that the forms of the machine influence the style of *Le Grand Déjeuner*?

No, because the will of the full volumes is already in the "Nus dans le paysage" (1909–1911) collection Kroeller Moller, Hollande. The utmost simplification of the volumes is in all the ancient works before the Renaissance. Traditionally *Le Grand Déjeuner* can be connected to the Romance period, I think. But for emphasized the strenght and intensity, I have dislocated the volumes. One arm comes before the torso, one leg comes before the thigh.

In 1911 I was called: Tubist by Vauxcelles. Therefore all that precedes the mecanical period.

7) Looking back on the picture from 20 years after, what is your opinion of it?

If I look back to my work, three major pictures are dominating all of it. *La*

Ville, *Le Grand Déjeuner*, et *La Composition aux perroquets*.[9] Between these three phases, an important number of paintings are more or less binded to these three major works.

When I have seen exhibited by you *Les 3 femmes* have appeared to me much calmer, fixed than before. Perhaps the colors have already lost of their action.

It is a painting more classical, I think, than *La Ville*, a little romantic by the sentiment of evocation of a modern city. *Les 3 femmes* evokes nothing it is that: classicism.

Your brown background is perfectly well choosen for a canvas on which one the light colors dominate. Perhaps that the presentation, new to me, emphasized the classical direction of the work.

I think that I have answered nearly to the questionary. I am to your disposition for more development if you wish it.

Very cordially Yours
[signed: F Léger]

[P.S.:]

I shall be very pleased to see one picture of my last manner in your muséum and I am wishing that you will "find the money"!!!

My present wish would be too, to find one wall to realise the "Men in the space"[10] in the technic of the picture, which one, I believe, interest you. Can you help me to find this wall? It is not for me a purpose of money. I have never been very preoccupied with this question.

I would like now to realise a big mural painting which would be the culminating of my two years work in the U. S. A.

One University's wall, one college, the White House, Sing Sing!! Why not? Think of it. You are, I believe, admiraby in place for that. I shall be very grateful to you.

One amusing story around *Le Grand Déjeuner* (ceci "entre nous"):

Paul Rosemberg has just bought this picture around 1922 or 23,[11] somthing like that. I believe – this between us – that the painting made him afraid.

Alphonse Kahn at this time was very actif around my work. He had a great authority rue de La Boëtie and was leading an active campaign to have Paul Rosemberg buying *Le Grand Déjeuner*. Paul had come some times to look at the picture without saying a single word. One day, he took his decision and the picture was bought.

Alphonse Kahn felt very happy. He called me to the phone and asked me if I had seen Paul Rosemberg since he had bought my picture. I told him: No. Then he said textually: – "Don't disturb him, he is a little bit sick, I believe il a du mal a digérer *le Grand Déjeuner*, son estomac n'est pas habitué à ces sortes de choses. Wait a little!"

Appendix B

Fernand Léger
80 West 40th Street
New York City

November 20th, [1943]

Dear Mr. Barr:
This is the answer to your new interrogations.

1) When did I make the first study? – At the end of 1920, I think. It follows (or was made in the same time) the Odalisques (Coll. Alphonse Kahn)[12] which are already the "idea of the Grand déjeuner." Perhaps would it be possible to discover the exact dates in Les Cahiers d'Art or in Teriade's book.[13]

2) I have thought in terms of monumental figures after La Ville and in reaction against this last painting.

All my life, I have been in conflict between the mural idea and the easel painting idea. When I have realized La Ville (mural) I felt the imperious need for an easel painting: "Le grand déjeuner," like a contrary strength. So more or less consciously, after one realization of some elements taken out of modern life, to try on subjects or objects which have been treated during all the times by painters of other times. One background of classicism dominate in myself, I believe, some romantic pranks sometimes as: La Ville 1919, Les Disques 1920, Les plongeurs (modelled) 1941–42[14] but some women's bodies, one table, a dog, every time's subject without any expression of evocation. It is the classical line, at my opinion. To put the subject or the object inside, behind the pictorial expression. The romantic is just the contrary, I believe; the subject or object come before, in expressive feeling. I have lived this uneasiness all my life and Le Grand déjeuner is one ot [sic] my classical fighting won.

3) The picture should have been completed after its return from Léonce Rosemberg's. I believe that one of the sketches[15] admits of the retouch in ochre. Probably Spring 1922.

Very sincerely yours
[signed "F Léger"]

Appendix C

Fernand Léger
80 West 40th Street
New York City

October 28th, 1943

Dear Barr,

I have seen "Le grand déjeuner" in place. It is very well and the frame too, is perfect! It is not, of course, the opinion of Paul Rosemberg who is missing his "pretty gilded frame."

Compliments for all of it.

Very sincerely
Yours
[signed "F Léger"]

[P.S.:]

I am just thinking that if any day you are wishing to replace "Les Musiciens (1921)" de Picasso with another important picture of same dimensions I should be very pleased to entrust you one of mine which would have never been exhibited before.

A curious story about "Le grand déjeuner"

During the exhibition of my works at the "Museum of Chicago" (after this one at the Modern Art Museum) I was asked there by a gentleman who was wishing to speak to me. I went there, and found a rather stern fellow, clergy man looking, very reserved, French speaking.[16]

He took out of a document case a photograph of "La Grande jatte" by Seurat and another one of "Le grand déjeuner" striped by some blue and red lines (both of photographs.

This appeared rather mysterious to me. "Excuse me to bother you, he told me, but I wanted to show you my researches. The classical French art is commanded by some conscious or inconscious geometrical laws. In the present case, I am obliged to see the analogies of the horizontal and vertical dominant lines in this two paintings.

What do you think about it? For me, did he add, it is a racial law and you *cannot* runaway out of it. On the contrary of it, romanticism . . . etc. etc."

I kept listening to him with much attention and looked at him. He was a pure American fellow, tall, dry, dogmatic but passionnate with his problem.

It is unnecessary to tell you that I had never suspected this fact and it is this particular American, for me an unknown man, who had come to reveal me this discovery.

He went out, rather satisfied with my ignorance but he did not leave any address.

[Signed "F. L."]

Notes

Preface

1 "*Theoretical.* And where did you find that written down, or tell me what school you attended where you could have heard what you tell me? *Practical.* I never had other book than the heavens and the earth, known to all, and it is given to all to know and read this beautiful book." Millet's notes from Bernard Palissy, *Oeuvres complètes* (Paris, 1844), in the Moreau-Nélaton papers concerning Millet, Cabinet des Estampes, Bibliothèque Nationale, Paris.

2 Richard Powers, *Three Farmers on their Way to a Dance* (New York, 1985, reprinted 1987): pp. 98–99.

1 Industry in the Changing Landscape

1 This does not mean that abstract art itself depends upon a false teleology, but that patterns of historical thought, addressed to all periods of art, unwittingly absorbed twentieth-century attitudes and set subject matter aside in favor of the formal components of art.

2 See Greg M. Thomas, *Art and Ecology in Nineteenth-Century France* (Princeton, 2000).

3 Daubigny's illustrations are the subject of the dissertation by Madeleine Fidell, *The Graphic Art of Charles François Daubigny* (New York, 1974); see also her "A Sketchbook by Daubigny: Traveling by Rail during the Reign of Louis-Philippe," *Master Drawings* 38, 1 (2000): 3–28. Michel Melot has provided a new catalog of Daubigny's prints, *L'Oeuvre gravé de Boudin, Corot, Daubigny, Dupré, Jongkind, Millet, Théodore Rousseau* (Paris, 1978). The standard biography of the artist remains that of Etienne Moreau-Nélaton, *Daubigny raconté par lui-même* (Paris, 1925); new information and excellent reproductions are found in the monograph by Madeleine Fidell-Beaufort and Janine Bailly-Herzberg, *Daubigny* (Paris, 1975).

4 "[N]ous procurent-elles abondamment de ces illusions de repos, de liberté, de solitude, qui sont presque du bonheur." In *L'Artiste*, cited in Moreau-Nélaton, *Daubigny*, p. 69.

5 For Lachambeaudie, see Carel Lodewijk de Liefde, *Le Saint-Simonisme dans la poésie française entre 1825 et 1865* (Haarlem, 1927). The best-known edition of the *Fables* was published by Bry in Paris in 1855. My translations of excerpts from Lachambeaudie in this chapter are quite literal, without any attempt to provide equivalents of his poetic language.

6 Lachambeaudie was exiled in 1851, but the 1855 edition of his *Fables* was given a prize citation by the Académie Française.

7 "Mon vieux, décidément, j'ai du malheur. Tout ce que je voulais faire est rasé: arbres coupés, plus d'eau dans la rivière, maisons abattues! Aussi, en désespoir de cause, je me sauve et vais voir si le Père Eternel n'a pas dérangé les montagnes du Dauphiné. J'espère

que non." Cited in Moreau-Nélaton, *Daubigny*, p. 63.

8 "Ce pauvre Barbès est donc sorti de prison? As-tu lu ce qu'il a dit sur la guerre? Ils sont ici plus ou moins ratapoils, et les mots guerre et victoire ne sont pas épargnés. Quand on observe le grand calme de la nature, les querelles vaines des cabinets européens, comme dit Pierre Dupont, vous apparaissent bien davantage, et on se demande à quoi ça sert de tuer des gens qui ne sont pas las d'être vivants." Cited in Moreau-Nélaton, *Daubigny*, p. 65.

9 Raymond Williams, *The Country and the City* (New York and London, 1973), is the most brilliant treatment of this theme.

10 My own interest in Argenteuil as an especially revealing case history began in 1964, and thereafter that subject entered into my lectures. The present chapter is closely based on the sixth of ten Slade Lectures delivered at Oxford University in the winter of 1978. My work, however, had been based on available secondary sources and guidebooks for Argenteuil. Paul Tucker, in his *Monet at Argenteuil* (New Haven and London, 1984), has gone far beyond my preliminary study and has used archival and contemporary sources to document a very persuasive interpretation both of Monet's paintings and of changing Argenteuil. For Monet in the context of his generation, see John Rewald, *History of Impressionism* (New York, 1946, rev. ed., 1973), my *Impressionism: Art, Leisure, and Parisian Society* (New Haven and London, 1988), and Paul Tucker's *Claude Monet: Life and Art* (New Haven and London, 1995). The basic monograph is Daniel Wildenstein, *Claude Monet: Biographie et catalogue raisonné*, 5 vols. (Lausanne and Paris, 1974–85).

11 Such compositions have been traced to Japanese prints and to Whistler's paintings, but this is one of the countless instances of art historians limiting themselves to known traditions and looking only for the purely visual. A prototype for Monet's compositional structure can be found in earlier illustrations of rail and highway bridges. The artists of these illustrations frequently chopped off the two ends of a bridge to heighten the sense of its leaping across the page. See, for example, Eugène Chapus, *De Paris au Havre* (Paris, 1855), a railroad guide in which more than one bridge is shown in that fashion, with one or more boats on the water underneath. (Daubigny did some of the illustrations for this book, but those of the bridges are not signed.)

12 Tucker, *Monet at Argenteuil*, supplies abundant proof of this; much evidence can be found in successive editions of guidebooks to Paris and its environs, in which boating at Asnières and Argenteuil looms ever larger as the century progresses.

13 See Emile de Labédollière, *Histoire des environs du nouveau Paris* (Paris, 1861); in addition to its text about boating, this book is graced by amusing illustrations by Gustave Doré.

14 Old guidebooks and maps make this clear but again, Tucker, *Monet at Argenteuil*, has provided detailed and new information.

15 *View of Argenteuil, Winter* (1874), Nelson Gallery-Atkins Museum, Kansas City.

16 Wrongly dated 1872 by Wildenstein, *Claude Monet*, vol. 1, no. 227; the date of 1874 is confirmed by comparison with dated pictures, and by the fact that it is this painting on Monet's easel in the picture by Manet of 1874, *Claude Monet in his Studio Boat*, Neue Pinakothek, Munich.

17 Rodolphe Walter, "Les Maisons de Claude Monet à Argenteuil," *Gazette des beaux-arts* 6, 68 (December 1966): 333–42, recapitulated and extended (with many letters of the period) in Wildenstein, *Claude Monet*, vol. I, pp. 58ff.

18 Adolphe Joanne, *De Paris à Saint Germain, à Poissy et à Argenteuil* (Paris, 1856): 5–6.

19 Elisée Reclus, "Du sentiment de la nature dans les sociétés modernes," *Revue des deux mondes* 63 (May 15, 1866): 352–81.

20 See map in Walter, "Maisons de Claude Monet," p. 333.
21 See Juliet Wilson-Bareau, *Manet, Monet, and the Gare Saint-Lazare* (National Gallery of Art, Washington, and Musée d'Orsay, Paris, 1998).
22 Concluding lines of Lachambeaudie's "Les Deux rivages," *Fables*.

2 City vs. Country

This chapter had its origin in a lecture delivered at Reed College, Portland, Oregon, on April 23, 1968, as part of a series on "The City in Nineteenth Century America, England and France." I am grateful to my colleagues associated with that series, particularly to Charles Rhyne and John Rothney, and for help in obtaining photographs, also to Jacques Foucart, Linda Nochlin and Vagn Poulsen. The most valuable works for this study were: Meyer Schapiro, "Courbet and Popular Imagery: An Essay in Realism and Naiveté," *Journal of the Warburg and Courtauld Institutes* 4 (1940–41): 164–91; Stanley Meltzoff, "The Revival of the Le Nains," *Art Bulletin* 24 (September 1942): 259–86; Linda Nochlin, "Gustave Courbet's Meeting: A Portrait of the Artist as a Wandering Jew," *Art Bulletin* 49 (September 1967): 209–22; and Timothy J. Clark, "A Bourgeois Dance of Death: Max Buchon on Courbet," *Burlington Magazine* 111 (April–May 1969): 208–12, 286–90. For publications after 1970, see my *Jean-François Millet* (exh. cat., Réunion des Musées Nationaux, Paris, and Arts Council of Great Britain, London, 1975–76); T.J. Clark, *Image of the People* and *The Absolute Bourgeois* (both 1973, reissued Berkeley, 1999), and Nina Lübbren, *Rural Artists' Colonies in Europe, 1870–1910* (Manchester, 2001).

1 See my *Impressionism: Art, Leisure, and Parisian Society* (New Haven and London, 1988).
2 Delacroix, May 16, 1853, in André Joubin, ed., *Journal de Eugène Delacroix*, 3 vols. (Paris, 1950), vol. 2, pp. 51–53.
3 Among the best books of the period, offering demographic charts and intelligent analyses, are: Eugene Bonnemère, *Histoire des paysans depuis la fin du moyen age jusqu'à nos jours 1200–1850*, 2 vols. (Paris, 1856); Jules Brame, *De l'Emigration des campagnes* (Paris, 1859); Léonce de Lavergne, *Economie rurale de la France depuis 1799* (Paris, 1860); and S.C. Valny, *Etudes sur la dépopulation des campagnes* (Auch, 1862).
4 Brame, *De l'Emigration*, pp. 93–94; the facts summarized in this discussion are found in the books listed in n. 3, but Brame's is perhaps the most convenient to use.
5 Bonnemère, *Histoire des paysans*, vol. 2, p. 399.
6 T. Thoré, *Salon de 1847* (Paris, 1847): 142. "Nous avons vu des tableaux de Millet qui rappellent à la fois Decamps et Diaz, un peu les Espagnols, et beaucoup les Lenain, ces grands et naïfs artistes du dix-septième siècle auxquels la postérité n'a pas encore accordé leur place légitime parmi les meilleurs peintres de l'école française." This is one of the rare references to the brothers not included in Meltzoff, "The Revival of the Le Nains."
7 See Emile Bouvier, *La Bataille réaliste 1844–1857* (Paris, 1913).
8 Pierre Dupont, *Chants et chansons*, 4 vols. (Paris, 1851–54), vol. 1, p. 6.; the publisher's prospectus claimed that Dupont's songs would inspire peasant and worker, and Baudelaire's introduction attached them to the mood of 1848. Dupont's preface, an overt attack upon Louis Napoleon, ends with a veritable peroration, echoing the Saint-Simonists, in favor of entering the new "industrial movement" of society with the republican collaboration of "work, science and love, the reign of truth."
9 Castagnary, *Philosophie du Salon de 1857*, in *Salons 1857–1870*, 2 vols. (Paris, 1892), vol. 1, p. 7. "La peinture religieuse et la peinture historique ou héroique se sont graduellement affaiblies, à mesure que s'affablissaient comme organismes sociaux, la théocratie et la monarchie auxquelles elles se réfèrent; leur élimination, à peu près complète aujourd'hui, amène la domination

absolue du genre, du paysage, du portrait, qui relèvent de l'individualisme: dans l'art comme dans la société, l'homme devient de plus en plus homme."

10 The essential biography for Millet remains Etienne Moreau-Nélaton's *Millet raconté par lui-même*, 3 vols. (Paris, 1921).

11 The version exhibited is probably the one now in the Yamanashi Prefectural Museum, Kofu, Japan; the contemporary version is in the Museum of Fine Arts, Boston. Alexandra Murphy believes that the Boston version was the one exhibited in 1851. See her *Jean-François Millet* (exh. cat., Museum of Fine Arts, Boston, 1984), no. 18.

12 T. Delord in *Charivari* (January 7, 1851).

13 F. Sabatier-Ungher, "Salon de 1851," *La Démocratie Pacifique*. This and the preceding citation form part of an anthology of contemporary criticism of Millet that was gathered together for Quincy Adams Shaw, and which is now with the Shaw papers in the Museum of Fine Arts, Boston. "Va, sème, pauvre laboureur, jette à pleines mains le froment à la terre! La terre est friande, elle produira, mais l'année prochaine, comme celle-ci, tu seras pauvre et tu travailleras à la sueur de ton front, car les hommes ont si bien fait que le travail est une malédiction, le travail qui sera le seul véritable plaisir des êtres intelligents dans la société régénérée. Le geste a une enérgie toute michelangesque et son ton une puissance étrange [. . .]; c'est une construction florentine. [. . .] C'est le Démos moderne."

14 In *La Presse*, cited by Moreau-Nélaton, *Millet*, vol. 2, p. 42.

15 Marius Chaumelin, *Salon Marseillais de 1859* (Marseille, 1860): 57.

16 Olivier Merson, *Exposition de 1861, la peinture en France* (Paris, 1861): 221.

17 Alexandre Dumas, *L'Art et les artistes contemporaines au Salon de 1859* (Paris, 1859): 118.

18 Letter of February 1, 1851, cited in Moreau-Nélaton, *Millet*, vol. 1, p. 91. "Vous êtes assis sous les arbres, éprouvant tout le bien-être, la tranquillité dont on puisse jouir; vous voyez déboucher d'un petit sentier une pauvre figure chargée d'un fagot. La façon inattendue et toujours frappante dont cette figure vous apparaît vous reporte involontairement vers la triste condition humaine, la fatigue. Cela donne toujours une impression analogue à celle que La Fontaine exprime dans sa fable du bûcheron!"

19 Castagnary, *Salons*, vol. 1, p. 24. "Cette toile, qui rappelle d'effroyables misères, n'est point, comme quelques-uns des tableaux de Courbet, une harangue politique ou une thèse sociale: c'est une oeuvre d'art très belle et très simple, franche de toute déclamation. Le motif est poignant à la vérité; mais, traité comme il l'est, dans le plus haut style, avec largeur, sobriété et franchise, il s'élève au-dessus des passions de parti, et reproduit, loin du mensonge et de l'exagération, une des ces pages de la nature vraies et grandes, comme en trouvaient Homère et Virgile." For an illuminating discussion of the different conceptions of gleaners' roles in rural society, see Liana Vardi, "Construing the Harvest: Gleaners, Farmers, and Officials in Early Modern France," *American Historical Review* 98, 5 (December 1993): 1424–47.

20 Bonnemère, *Histoire des paysans*, vol. 2, pp. 418–19.

21 From an undated autobiography that Millet wrote later, cited in Alfred Sensier, *La Vie et l'oeuvre de J.-F. Millet* (Paris, 1881): 44. "Et Paris, noir, boueux, enfumé, où j'arrivai un soir, fut pour moi la plus pénible, comme la plus décourageante des sensations. Ce fut un samedi de janvier que j'arrivai le soir à Paris, par la neige; la lueur des réverbères presque éteints par le brouillard, la quantité immense de chevaux et de voitures qui se heurtaient ou s'entrecroisaient, les rues étroites, l'odeur et l'air de Paris, me portèrent à la tête et au coeur, au point de me suffoquer. Je fus pris par une crise de sanglots que je ne pouvais arrêter."

22 Letter to Sensier of January 25, 1851, cited in Moreau-Nélaton, *Millet*, vol. 1,

p. 89. "Si vous voyiez comme la forêt est belle! J'y cours quelquefois à la fin du jour, après ma journée, et j'en reviens, à chaque fois, écrasé. C'est d'un calme, d'une grandeur épouvantables: au point que je me surprends ayant véritablement peur."

23 Castagnary, *Salons*, vol. 1, p. 17. "C'est une vérité vieille, que les églogues et les idylles ont presque toujours été le contre-coup d'agitations sociales. Froissés par le tumulte du monde, les poètes, les rêveurs se réfugient dans la paix des champs, dans la contemplation de la nature calme et sereine."

24 Castagnary, *Salons*, vol. 1, p. 59. "La *Pose du télégraphe électrique dans les rochers du cap Gris-Nez* (Pas-de-Calais), est un paysage ferme et vigoureux, qui ne mérite qu'un reproche, mais capital. Pourquoi ce télégraphe électrique? Que signifie-t-il, je ne dis pas dans cette toile, mais dans toute toile? Qu'y a-t-il de commun entre ce fil d'archal, ce produit industriel, utile, et le paysage, recherche et expression du beau dans la nature? Evidemment c'est un non-sens."

25 Bonnemère, *Histoire des paysans*, vol. 2, p. 371.

26 E.H. Gombrich, *Art and Illusion* (Oxford and New York, 1960).

27 One of the best repertoires of peasant imagery from Egypt to the early twentieth century is Paul Brandt's splendid *Schaffende Arbeit und bildende Kunst*, 2 vols. (Leipzig, 1927).

28 See my *Nature's Workshop: Renoir's Writings on the Decorative Arts* (New Haven and London, 2000).

29 Benedict Nicolson, "The Anarchism of Camille Pissarro," *The Arts* 2 (1947): 43–51; see also chapter 7 below (from an article first published in 1960). For more recent publications, see Martha Ward, *Pissarro, Neo-Impressionism, and the Spaces of the Avant-Garde* (Chicago, 1996); John Hutton, *Neo-Impressionism and the Search for Solid Ground: Art, Science and Anarchism in Fin-de-Siècle France* (Baton Rouge and London, 1994), and T.J. Clark, *Farewell to an Idea* (New Haven and London, 1999).

30 See Debora Silverman, *Van Gogh and Gauguin: The Search for Sacred Art* (New York, 2000).

31 Griselda Pollock, "Van Gogh and the Poor Slaves," *Art History* 11, 3 (September 1988): 406–32.

32 Sensier, *Millet*, pp. 101–02. "l'art n'est pas une partie de plaisir. C'est un combat, en engrenage qui broie. . . . Je ne suis pas un philosophe, je ne veux pas supprimer la douleur, ni trouver une formule qui me rende stoïque et indifférent. La douleur est, peut-être, ce qui fait le plus fortement exprimer les artistes." How apt the machine metaphor is for van Gogh as well as for Millet!

33 For references to writings by Fred Orton and Griselda Pollock, and Denise Delouche, see chapter 3.

3 Peasants and "Primitivism"

1 The exhibition included, in roughly chronological order, Jean-Jacques de Boissieu, Olivier Perrin, François-Hippolyte Lalaisse, Adolphe Hervier, Charles Jacque, Adrien Lavieille, Millet, Alphonse Legros, Jules Laurens, Jules Bastien-Lepage, Camille and Lucien Pissarro, Auguste Lepère, Gauguin, Emile Bernard, Armand Seguin, Théophile Steinlen, Henri Delavallée, Tony Beltrand, and Henri Rivière.

2 See Eugen Weber, *Peasants into Frenchmen* (Stanford, 1976), and Annie Moulin, *Peasant and Society in France since 1798*, trans. M.C. and M.F. Cleary (Cambridge, 1991). I relate internal migration and peasant imagery in chapter 2 above.

3 For Courbet, see Timothy J. Clark, *The Absolute Bourgeois: Artists and Politics in France, 1848–1851*, and his *Image of the People: Gustave Courbet and the 1848 Revolution* (London, 1973); for Millet, see my *Jean-François Millet* (exh. cat., Réunion des Musées Nationaux, Paris, and Arts Council of Great Britain, London, 1975–76).

4 Marilyn Brown, *Gypsies and Bohemians: The Myth of the Artist*

in *Nineteenth-Century France* (Ann Arbor, 1985), and Jerrold Siegel, *Bohemian Paris* (New York, 1986). See also Nina Lübbren, *Rural Artists' Colonies in Europe, 1870–1910* (Manchester, 2001).

5 Colin Rhodes, *Primitivism and Modern Art* (London and New York, 1994).

6 It was Thorstein Veblen in 1899 who showed that primitive handwork acquired cultural and monetary value in capitalism. "Hand labor is a more wasteful method of production; hence the goods turned out by this method are more serviceable for the purposes of pecuniary reputability; hence the marks of hand labor come to be honorific, and the goods which exhibit these marks take rank as of higher grade than the corresponding machine product." *The Theory of the Leisure Class* (New York, ed. 1953): 114.

7 Meyer Schapiro analyzed the role of popular arts and primitivism in Courbet's circle, giving major place to Champfleury (Jules Husson-Fleury, 1821–99), in "Courbet and Popular Imagery: An Essay in Realism and Naïveté," *Journal of the Warburg and Courtauld Institutes* 4 (1940–41): 164–91. For the establishment of folklore studies in the 1870s and 1880s, see Weber, *Peasants into Frenchmen*, pp. 471–72 and *passim*.

8 Champfleury, *Histoire de l'imagerie populaire* (Paris, 1869). The phrases cited below come from the revised edition of 1886.

9 Charles Saunier and G.M. Texier-Bernier, *Auguste Lepère: Peintre et graveur* (Paris, 1931): 161–62.

10 Richard Shiff, "The Technique of Originality," *Cézanne and the End of Impressionism* (Chicago, 1984): 55–152.

11 See Michel Melot, "La Notion d'originalité et son importance dans la définition des objets d'art," in *Sociologie de l'art*, ed. Raymonde Moulin (Paris, 1986): 191–202. See also chapter 6 below.

12 Denise Delouche, *Peintres de la Bretagne* (Mayenne, 1977), and her *Les Peintres et le paysan breton* (Baillé, 1988). The former is a detailed study of the imagery of Brittany from 1800 to 1860; the latter is a broader study encompassing the whole century.

13 Caroline Ford, *Creating the Nation in Provincial France: Religion and Political Identity in Brittany* (Princeton, 1993): 29–30 and *passim*.

14 *Guenn*, which went through thirty-eight editions, was based partly upon Pont-Aven and partly upon nearby Concarneau (Delouche, *Peintres et le paysan*, p. 157). The author's full name is Blanche Willis Howard von Teuffel (1847–98).

15 Fred Orton and Griselda Pollock, "Les Données bretonnantes: La prairie de représentation," *Art History* 3 (September 1980): 314–44. Delouche, *Peintres et le paysan*, *passim*, points out that the ceremonial coifs that Gauguin and Bernard called "medieval" were really developed over the course of the eighteenth and nineteenth centuries.

16 Ford, *Creating the Nation*, pp. 94–96.

17 Weber, *Peasants into Frenchmen*, ch. 28 and *passim*; Annie Moulin, *Peasant and Society in France since 1798*, trans. M.C. and M.F. Clearly (Cambridge, 1991): ch. 3 and *passim*.

18 For the classic study of the growing acquaintance with non-European arts in the later nineteenth century, see Robert Goldwater, *Primitivism in Modern Art* (New York, rev. ed., 1966), ch. 1. Need it be said that there are deep-seated relationships among colonialism, the bare-skinned hedonism of Gauguin or Matisse, and modern tourism? See also Gill Perry, "Primitivism and the 'Modern,'" in *Primitivism, Cubism, Abstraction*, ed. Charles Harrison et al. (New Haven and London, 1993): 3–43.

19 Patricia Leighten, "The White Peril and *L'Art nègre*: Picasso, Primitivism, and Anticolonialism," *Art Bulletin* 72, 4 (December 1990): 609–30.

20 Letter of July 20, 1863, in Etienne Moreau-Nélaton, *Millet raconté par lui-même*, 3 vols. (Paris, 1921), vol. 2, p. 145.

21 Philippe Burty, "Les Eaux-fortes de M. J.-F. Millet," *Gazette des beaux-arts* 1, 11 (September 1861): 262.
22 Weber, *Peasants into Frenchmen*, p. 457.

4 Courbet's *Mère Grégoire* and Béranger

This is a revised version of the paper I read at the Courbet symposium of 1979, first published in *Malerei und Theorie: Das Courbet-Colloquium 1979*, ed. Klaus Gallwitz and Klaus Herding (Frankfurt am Main, Städtische Galerie im Städelschen Kunstinstitut, 1980): 75–89. In preparing the 1980 essay I was substantially aided by Susan Wise, then Assistant Curator at the Art Institute of Chicago, who shared with me all the information, photographs, and other documents in her possession. I also benefited from an exchange of correspondence with Hélène Toussaint of the Louvre, Paris, following the symposium. We did not agree on many matters, but my interpretation was partly shaped by her conjectures.

1 For Courbet's *Mère Grégoire*, the essential reading is as follows: Susan Wise, "La Mère Grégoire," in *European Portraits 1600–1900 in The Art Institute of Chicago* (exh. cat., Chicago, 1978): 74–77; Robert Fernier, *La Vie et l'oeuvre de Gustave Courbet*, 2 vols. (Paris and Lausanne, 1977–78), vol. 2, no. 167; Hélène Toussaint, "La Mère Grégoire," in *Gustave Courbet* (exh. cat., Grand Palais, Paris, 1977), no. 45; Toussaint, "Le Réalisme de Courbet au service de la satire politique et de la propagande gouvernementale," *Bulletin de la Société de l'Histoire de l'Art Français* (December 1, 1979): 233–44. For Béranger's poem, see *Oeuvres complètes de P.-J. de Béranger* (Paris, 1836). The poem is undated but is assumed to have been composed about 1820.
2 John Keefe, formerly Curator of Decorative Arts at the Art Institute of Chicago, identified this object as, in all likelihood, a Spanish screen from Córdoba, popular in the nineteenth century (information communicated by Susan Wise). I am very grateful to Mr. Keefe and Ms. Wise for identifying the screen. Presumably, it was an old photograph that led Fernier, *Vie et l'oeuvre*, to identify it as a mirror. Toussaint, in "Réalisme de Courbet," continued to believe it is a mirror, and used its symbolism to aid her interpretation.
3 Grandville's illustration appeared also in the Brussels edition of *Oeuvres complètes* (1844). Born Jean Ignace Isidore Gérard (1803–47), the artist preferred "J.J. Grandville."
4 For Béranger, the best source is the monumental study by Jean Touchard, *La Gloire de Béranger*, 2 vols. (Paris, 1968). See also Pierre Brochon, *La Chanson française*, vol. 1: *Béranger et son temps* (Paris, 1956).
5 Brochon, *Chanson française*, pp. 12ff., and Toussaint, "Réalisme de Courbet," p. 235.
6 Brochon, *Chanson française*, p. 21. See also Emile Bouvier, *La Bataille réaliste* (Paris, 1913).
7 Pierre Dupont, *Chants et chansons*, 3 vols. (Paris, 1851–53), vol. 1, p. 6.
8 Touchard, *Gloire de Béranger*, vol. 1, pp. 391–98, 412–35.
9 Jean-François Millet is among those painters who based a work on a song by Béranger: "Les Etoiles filantes" of *c.* 1848–50 (National Museum of Wales, Cardiff).
10 See Touchard, *Gloire de Béranger*, vol. 2, pp. 357ff. and *passim*.
11 Arthur Arnould, *Béranger, ses amis, ses ennemis et ses critiques* (Paris, 1864): 68ff.
12 Touchard, *Gloire de Béranger*, vol. 2, p. 315.
13 Arnould, *Béranger*, pp. 160ff.
14 Susanna Barrows, "After the Commune: Alcoholism, Temperance and Literature in the Early Third Republic," in John Merriman, ed., *Consciousness and Class Experience in Nineteenth-Century Europe* (New York, 1979): 205–18.
15 Compare, for example, the tone of the first and the third volumes of Dupont's *Chants et chansons*.
16 Siegfried Kracauer, *Orpheus in Paris: Offenbach and the Paris of his Time* (London, 1938).

17 The rather special vulgarity of Béranger's poem is probably the reason for its omission in all English anthologies of his work. The fact that Courbet's is *Mère* and Béranger's *Madame* Grégoire is of no significance. The two words are virtually interchangeable in this context and, in fact, are so interchanged by Castagnary, in his letter to Courbet of 1873 (see p. 75 below), and in Randon's text for his caricature of 1867 (pl. 27).

18 Barrows, "After the Commune," p. 207.

19 Subsequent to my initial presentation of this observation in Frankfurt, Mlle. Toussaint became convinced that the flower was indeed a symbol of the Republic. However, by a complicated route, and convinced that the painting dates from 1849, she reached the conclusion that Courbet's intention was to satirize the Republic, not the Empire. See Toussaint, "Réalisme de Courbet," pp. 236–41. I am unable to accept her early date for the painting, nor can I follow her ingenious but finally unconvincing argument.

20 Georges Riat, *Gustave Courbet peintre* (Paris, 1906).

21 Alexandre Schanne, *Souvenirs de Schaunard* (Paris, 1886).

22 Charles Léger, *Courbet* (Paris, 1929): 41. "The painter reimburses in part what he owes Mme Andler for his keep, assuring that she will lose nothing by waiting, besides, he will do her portrait, for which two studies exist, under the name of *Mère Grégoire*." Wise, "Mère Grégoire," made the wrong deduction from this text, for the phrase "he will do her portrait" is articulated by Léger on his own behalf; he was not using indirect discourse to attribute the words to Courbet.

23 Gerstle Mack, *Gustave Courbet* (New York, 1951): 154, pointed out that Schanne confused Courbet's trips to Montpellier in 1857 and to Le Havre in 1859 by combining features of both excursions.

24 Riat, *Courbet*, p. 366.

25 Schanne, *Souvenirs*, p. 296.

26 Toussaint, "Réalisme de Courbet," p. 239, convincingly identified the model as Henriette Bonion, who is represented in several of Courbet's paintings. The small portrait of her in the Musée Fabre, Montpellier, can now be identified with her and closely resembles the woman in the Art Institute's painting.

27 I am very grateful to Susan Wise for transmitting to me the results of the restoration carried out in 1977 by Alfred Jakstas, then conservator at the Art Institute. Richard R. Brettell, former Curator of European Painting at the Art Institute, pointed out to me that the pattern of cusping on the inserted piece indicates that it had been nailed on its own stretcher for as much as two years before it was incorporated into the larger canvas.

28 Riat, *Courbet*, p. 366.

29 "C'est moi qui aie collé la tête de la Mère Grégoire sur cette grande toile, toujours par économie." Letter dated March 26, 1874, in the Cabinet des Estampes, Bibliothèque Nationale, Paris, cited by Toussaint, "Réalisme de Courbet," p. 244. Wise, "Mère Grégoire," at the time unaware of this letter (as I was then), correctly raised doubts about the supposed mutilation of the picture by another hand.

30 Théophile Silvestre, *Histoire des artistes vivants* (Paris, 1856): 273.

31 Ibid., p. 278.

32 Fernier, *Vie et l'oeuvre*, no. 168 (48 × 39.5 cm) is clearly a study for the Chicago head. Another painting (ibid., no. 169), in the Petit Palais, Paris, is also said to be both Mme. Andler and Mére Grégoire, but bears no resemblance to the Chicago or the Morlaix pictures. See also n. 27 above.

33 Zacharie Astruc, "Les 14 Stations du Salon," *Quart d'Heure* (July 20, 1859), cited in Riat, *Courbet*, p. 173.

34 It was not the first or the last musical work inspired by "Madame Grégoire." In May 1830, Rochefort, Dupeuty, and de Livry had put on a vaudeville piece, *Madame Grégoire ou le cabaret de la pomme de pin*. Exactly fifty years later, at the Menus Plaisirs in Paris, a musical play called *Madame Grégoire* was presented by Burani, Ordonneau, and

Okolowicz. Touchard, *Gloire de Béranger*, vol. 2, pp. 638ff., showed that throughout Courbet's years in Paris, there was on average more than one public presentation each year drawn from Béranger's songs.

35 *Moniteur des arts* 151 (February 23, 1861), kindly communicated by Mlle. Toussaint.

36 "Madame Grégoire" remained in the popular consciousness until the end of the century, when she was displaced by other favorites. In 1879, for example, a frequent visitor to Paris evoked Béranger to recall the old times he feared were lost: "You fancied that the bonny buxom hostess sitting behind the counter was 'Madame Grégoire;' that it was the 'Petit Homme Gris' who had just ordered another pint and that it was the 'Gros Roger Bontemps' who was playing at tonneaux [a game played with barrels] in the garden with Lisette;" see George Augustus Sala, *Paris Herself Again in 1878–9*, 2 vols. (London, 1879), vol. 2, p. 6.

37 For the views of these and other contemporaries, see Touchard, *Gloire de Béranger*, vol. 2, pp. 394ff. Touchard paid very little attention to Proudhon, for reasons that are not clear.

38 Arnould, *Béranger*, pp. 257–96. Arnould reprinted extensive passages from the suppressed *De la Justice dans la Revolution et dans l'Eglise*, on the grounds that those passages had not raised the censors' ire. Proudhon scholars seem to have overlooked this publication.

39 T. Thoré, *Salon de 1845, précédé d'une lettre à Béranger* (Paris, 1845): xxii–xxiii.

5 Monet's Cathedrals

1 Steven Levine, *Monet and his Critics* (New York, 1976). Levine's purpose was to deal with all aspects of the criticism of Monet, and there was little occasion for him to dwell on the decorative to the extent that I do in this chapter. However, he alertly signals the issue on numerous occasions, and repeatedly offers wise observations (see "décor" and "décoratif" in his index). See also Levine's "Décor/Decorative/Decoration in Claude Monet's Art," *Arts* 51 (February 1977): 136–39. For Monet's *Cathedrals* and for issues related to this chapter, see Paul H. Tucker, *Monet in the '90s* (exh. cat., Boston Museum of Fine Arts, 1989), and his *Claude Monet: Life and Art* (New Haven and London, 1995), and also Tucker et al., *Monet in the 20th Century* (exh. cat., Boston Museum of Fine Arts, 1998).

2 Key phrases in the original French are noted here; the original publication of this essay includes the full texts in French of all quotations.

3 Ernest Chesneau, introduction to Edouard Guichard, *Dessins de décoration des principaux maîtres* (Paris, 1881): 14.

4 Camille Mauclair, "Critique de la peinture," *Nouvelle Revue* 96 (September 15, 1895): 314–33, as cited in Levine, *Monet and his Critics*, pp. 208–09.

5 Georges Lecomte, "L'Art contemporain," *Revue indépendante* 23, 66 (1892): 1–29 (4–5). Richard Shiff (personal communication) points out that this is a longer version of articles published serially in the Brussels review *Art moderne* (February 14, 21, and 28, 1892).

6 Lecomte, "Art contemporain," p. 10. "à rendre en leur intensité fugace les rapides effets naturels [. . .] par un rendu plus synthétique et plus réfléchi."

7 Ibid., pp. 12–13. "Elles sont belles de la seule beauté plastique, par la science des arrangements, les accords de lignes et de tons."

8 Octave Mirbeau, *Exposition Claude Monet – Auguste Rodin* (exh. cat., Georges Petit, Paris, 1889): 13, cited in Levine, *Monet and his Critics*, p. 106.

9 Octave Mirbeau, "Claude Monet," *Art dans les deux mondes* (March 7, 1891): 183–85, cited in Levine, *Monet and his Critics*, p. 118. "l'illumination des états de conscience de la planète, et les formes supra-sensibles de nos pensées."

10 Gustave Geffroy, *Claude Monet: Sa vie, son oeuvre*, 2 vols. (Paris, 1924), vol. 1, p. 89, presumably written in 1898.

"ce double découpage ornementale des branches profilées sur le ciel et réflétées par l'eau, cette ruelle de feuillage où glisse la délicieuse fantasmagorie du ciel et des nuées. [. . .] Paysages familiers et rêvés, formes sombres, fantômes lointains, évocations mystérieuses, miroirs limpides."

11 Lecomte, "Art contemporain," p. 14.

12 Ibid., p. 15. "Ce ne sont plus des simplifications de formes, mais bien des ablations de formes."

13 Ibid., p. 23.

14 Ibid., p. 29. "par réaction contre les religiosités renaissantes [. . .] dans la justice des nouveaux groupements sociaux."

15 George Heard Hamilton, *Claude Monet's Paintings of Rouen Cathedral*, (London, 1960), evoked contemporary religious attitudes in regard to the *Cathedrals*, and he pointed out that Monet so framed his pictures as to eliminate the cross on the central pinnacle. However, although he reminded the reader that Monet was a non-believer, Hamilton was content to raise the issue in this provocative fashion, without further comment. See also Ségolène Le Men, *La Cathédrale illustrée de Hugo à Monet* (Paris, 1998).

16 Camille Mauclair, "La Réforme de l'art décoratif en France," *Nouvelle Revue* 98 (February 15, 1896): 724–46, cited in Levine, *Monet and his Critics*, pp. 210–11. "c'est un art descriptif et déformateur, c'est un groupement de spectacles dont le propre est d'être *vu*."

17 Camille Mauclair, "Choses d'art," *Mercure de France* n. se. 14 (June 1895): 357–59, cited in Grace Seiberling, *Monet's Series* (New York, 1980): 173.

18 Kenneth Clark, *Landscape into Art* (London, 1949; ed. New York, 1976): 177.

19 Mentioned briefly by Hamilton, *Monet's Paintings of Rouen Cathedral*, p. 25, but otherwise ignored by modern historians of Monet.

20 Léon Bazalgette, *L'Esprit nouveau* (Paris, 1898): 376. "Cette caresse du jour au mélancolique visage du sanctuaire d'antan, cette alliance des pierres vénérables et du soleil toujours vivant."

21 Ibid., p. 384. "mais qu'ils étaient éternellement unis, consubstantiels et solidaires." In substituting nature for godhood, Bazalgette offered a perfect example of John Ruskin's "pathetic fallacy."

22 Ibid., pp. 385–86.

23 Ibid., pp. 389–90. "La vie déborde de ses toiles, dépouillée de tout symbole, de tout artifice, de tout mensonge."

24 Georges Clemenceau, "Révolution de Cathédrales," *La Justice* (1895), rev. ed. in Clemenceau, *Claude Monet: Les Nymphéas* (Paris, 1928). "baignée des vagues lumineuses qui se heurtent et se pulvérisent en éclaboussures d'étincelles."

25 Levine, *Monet and his Critics*, p. 183, points out that in reprinting the 1895 article in his book of 1928, Clemenceau cut out this strong sentence: "Je m'aperçois alors que pendant que mon faible curé se met à la torture pour s'ébahir de miracles que ne sont pas, je vois, moi, au soin d'un perpétuel prodige que m'affole et m'enivre de réalités miraculeuses."

26 Clemenceau, "Révolution de Cathédrales," p. 88. "Et ces cathédrales grises, qui sont de pourpre ou d'azur violentées d'or, et ces cathédrales blanches, aux portiques de feu, ruisselantes de flammes vertes, rouges ou bleues, et ces cathédrales d'iris, qui semblent vues au travers d'un prisme tournant, et ces cathédrales bleues, qui sont roses, vous donneraient tout à coup la durable vision, non plus de vingt, mais de cent, de mille, d'un milliard d'états de la cathédrale de toujours dans le cycle sans fin des soleils. Ce serait la vie même, telle que la sensation nous en peut être donnée, dans sa réalité la plus vivante."

27 Ibid., "vingt révélations merveilleuses," "miracles," "divine brume."

28 A. F., "Les Petits salons, Claude Monet," *Gil Blas* (June 12, 1895), cited in Seiberling, *Monet's Series*, p. 247. "Silence! le monument de fumée, où la lumière sculpte des allégories, semble environné de voiles légères; mais le soleil séduit et attire à les clochetons, semblables à des

jet d'eau figés, et c'est alors comme une assomption de la cathédrale."

29 Most studies of Ruskin's influence in France emphasize Proust, Bergson, and the turn of the century, but J. Autret's *Ruskin and the French before Marcel Proust* (Geneva, 1965) showed that significant attention was paid to him from 1860 onward, coincident with the rise of Impressionism. In the 1890s, Robert de la Sizeranne became the leading French Ruskinian. His *Ruskin et la religion de beauté* (Paris, 1897) enjoyed four editions in three years, preceding Proust's first articles on the English writer in 1900, the year of Ruskin's death.

30 See my *Nature's Workshop: Renoir's Writings on the Decorative Arts* (New Haven and London, 2000), which includes discussions of Ruskin and Morris in France.

31 The proposal, never acted upon, was published posthumously by Lionello Venturi, *Les Archives de l'Impressionnisme*, 2 vols. (Paris, 1939), vol. 1, pp. 127–29.

32 Janine Bailly-Herzberg, ed., *Correspondance de Camille Pissarro*, 5 vols. (Paris, 1980–91), vol. 4, letters no. 1138 (May 26, 1895) and 1140 (June 1, 1895).

33 Clemenceau, *Claude Monet*, p. 123.

34 Ibid., pp. 122–23. "Car aucune critique ne le trouvait sans riposte, et le ton bourru et le mot à l'emporte-pièce montraient assez que cet homme, bienveillant et rieur, avait trop donné de lui-même à son art pour en pouvoir parler avec détachement."

35 Ibid., pp. 101–02. "'Tandis que vous cherchez philosophiquement le monde en soi, [. . .] j'exerce simplement mon effort sur un maximum d'apparences, en étroites corrélations avec les réalités inconnues. Quand on est dans le plan des apparences concordantes, on ne peut pas être bien loin de la réalité."

6 Impressionism, Originality, and Laissez-Faire

1 Félix Fénéon, "Le Néo-Impressionnisme," *Art moderne* 7 (May 1, 1887): 139.

2 The key work in the revision of Impressionism is T.J. Clark's *The Painting of Modern Life: Paris in the Art of Manet and his Followers* (New York, 1985), a brilliant, original, and often tendentious interpretation (incorporating, amended, two influential earlier articles). My regret is that he pays insufficient attention to Degas, and little at all to Monet and Renoir. See also my *Impressionism: Art, Leisure, and Parisian Society* (New Haven and London, 1988).

3 See my *Nature's Workshop: Renoir's Writings on the Decorative Arts* (New Haven and London, 2000).

4 Among the rare studies of the art market in late nineteenth-century art are Nicholas Green, "Dealing in Temperaments: Economic Transformation of the Artistic Field in France during the Second Half of the Nineteenth Century," *Art History* 10 (March 1987): 59–75, and Robert Jensen, *Marketing Modernism in Fin-de-siècle Europe* (Princeton, 1994).

5 Only after the original publication of this essay did I find Michel Melot's article "La Notion d'originalité et son importance dans la définition des objets d'art," in *Sociologie de l'art*, ed. Raymonde Moulin (Paris, 1986): 191–202. Melot's incisive article concentrates on the relation of the quantitative rarity of an object to "originality," demonstrating that its value as property lies behind metaphysical, esthetic, and other considerations of the term.

6 César Graña, "Impressionism as an Urban Art Form," in *Fact and Symbol* (New York, 1971): 83–84. Welcome though this view was in 1971, it has been superseded by Clark's *Painting of Modern Life*. Clark embeds the idea of "flickering poignancy" in the social history of Haussmannian Paris, particularly well in his first chapter.

7 Max Friedlaender, *Landscape, Portrait, Still-life* (New York, 1963): 224–26.

8 Graña, "Impressionism," p. 74 and *passim*.

9 Théodore Duret, "Les Peintres français en 1867," cited in George H. Hamilton,

Manet and his Critics (1954, ed. New York, 1969): 110.

10 Edmond Duranty, *La Nouvelle Peinture*, 1876, ed. Marcel Guérin (Paris, 1946): 50–51.

11 Théodore Duret, "Edouard Manet," in his *Critique d'avant-garde* (Paris, 1885), pp. 121–22. Richard Shiff, *Cézanne and the End of Impressionism* (Chicago, 1984) offers by far the most incisive analysis of the new marks and forms of Impressionism, and he deals extensively with the issues of originality in artistic processes. He limits his discussion to esthetics, however, and does not incorporate social history.

12 Duranty, *Nouvelle Peinture*, p. 54.

13 See Albert Boime, "Entrepreneurial Patronage in Nineteenth-Century France," in *Enterprise and Entrepreneurs in Nineteenth- and Twentieth-Century France*, ed. E.C. Carter, R. Forster, and J.N. Moody (Baltimore, 1976): 137–207.

14 Thorstein Veblen, *The Theory of the Leisure Class* (1899, ed. New York, 1934): 159–60.

15 In addition to Marx, this process has been studied by Georg Simmel, especially in his essay "Conflict," in *Georg Simmel on Individuality and Social Forms*, ed. Donald N. Levine (Chicago, 1971): 70–95. See also Siegfried Kracauer, *Orpheus in Paris: Offenbach and the Paris of his Time* (New York, 1938), Jerrold Siegel, *Bohemian Paris* (New York, 1986), and Green, "Dealing in Temperaments."

7 Artists and Anarchism

Letters to Jean Grave mentioned in this article were published in the *Burlington Magazine* 102 (December 1960): 517–22. We owe to Ginette Signac, Colette Chambelland, Jean Maitron, John Rewald, and Pierre Angrand our sincerest thanks for their help in our researches. The late Mme. Signac put at our disposal her father's archives (hereafter referred to as the Signac Archives), and her collection of drawings and prints of the artists discussed in this chapter. Monsieur Maitron, director of the Institut Français d'Histoire Sociale, was the first to realize the importance of Grave's correspondence and generously allowed us to study it. Mlle. Chambelland, librarian of the Institut Français d'Histoire Sociale, went to great trouble to procure us copies of some of the documents. The late Mr. Rewald gave us access to his personal library and lent us some photographs, and the late Monsieur Angrand made available his uncle's correspondence, at the same time providing us with collateral information about the letters.

1 A brief analysis of the political views of the artists of the Symbolist period is given by John Rewald in his *Post-Impressionism from van Gogh to Gauguin* (New York, 1956): 147–84. Cogent analyses of the Neo-Impressionists and anarchism are found in Eugenia W. Herbert, *Artists and Social Reform in France and Belgium, 1885–1898* (New Haven, 1961), John Hutton, *Neo-Impressionism and the Search for Solid Ground: Art, Science and Anarchism in Fin-de-siècle France* (Baton Rouge, 1994), Martha Ward, *Pissarro, Neo-Impressionism, and the Spaces of the Avant-Garde* (Chicago, 1995), and Robyn S. Roslak, "The Politics of Aesthetic Harmony: Neo-Impressionism, Science, and Anarchism," *Art Bulletin* 73 (September 1991): 381–90.

2 For the pioneering account, see Benedict Nicolson, "The Anarchism of Camille Pissarro," *The Arts* 2 (1946): 43–51. Nicolson's thorough discussion of Pissarro's anarchist views is the source of the statements about Pissarro in this chapter, unless otherwise indicated.

3 Anonymous, "Courrier social," *La Vogue* 1 (April 11, 1886): 27.

4 Paul Adam, "Eloge de Ravachol," *Entretiens politiques et littéraires* 5 (July 1892): 29. The name of this important Symbolist review is especially significant.

5 Bernard Lazare, "Les Livres. La Conquête du pain," *Entretiens politiques et littéraires* 4 (April 1892): 183.

6 Jean Grave's autobiographical history, *Le Mouvement libertaire* (Paris, 1930),

mentions many of the Symbolists and reproduces letters from several.

7 And by 1905, Kees van Dongen and Franz Kupka also (Grave, *Mouvement libertaire*, pp. 219–20). K.X. Roussel gave Grave a drawing, presumably at about the same time, reproduced years later in *Publications de "La Révolte" et "Temps nouveaux"* 30 (November 15, 1924).

8 The best sources for late nineteenth-century anarchism are Grave, *Mouvement libertaire*, and Jean Maitron, *Le Mouvement anarchiste en France*, 2 vols. (Paris, 1975).

9 For a thorough bibliography of writings by and about Kropotkin, see the bibliography in Maitron, *Mouvement anarchiste*.

10 Grave, *Mouvement libertaire*: pp. 59, 70, claimed that *La Révolte* and *Temps nouveaux* had a weekly circulation of 8000 during most of this period.

11 From the subscription list seized by the police in 1894: Archives Nationales, Paris, Dossier $F^7$12506.

12 Published in the continuation of the original article in the *Burlington Magazine* 102 (December 1960). For *Temps nouveaux* and its visual art, see Aline Dardel, *"Les Temps nouveaux" 1895–1914: Un Hebdomadaire anarchiste et la propagande par l'image* (exh. cat., Musée d'Orsay, Paris, 1987). Her documented account superseded that of the present article by filling out the record of the prints that Grave published.

13 Fewer artists subscribed to *Père Peinard* than to *La Révolte*, but among them were Pissarro, H.G. Ibels, Octave Mirbeau, Georges Lecomte, and Jean Ajalbert: Archives Nationales, Paris, Dossier $F^7$12506. The last three were staunch defenders of the Neo-Impressionists.

14 Undated letter (summer 1888) from Signac to Luce (Signac Archives). No letter by Signac was published in *La Révolte* until 1891.

15 Reproduced in Rewald, *Post-Impressionism*, p. 141.

16 Adolphe Tabarant, *Maximilien Luce* (Paris, 1928): 37, estimated the number of Luce's contributions to *Père Peinard* at 100.

17 Grave, *Mouvement libertaire*, p. 295.

18 Pissarro to Lucien, March 17, 1896, in *Correspondance de Camille Pissarro*, ed. Janine Bailly-Herzberg, 5 vols. (Paris, 1980–91), vol. 4, letter no. 1217.

19 Pissarro to Lucien, May 5, 1891, in ibid., vol. 3, letter no. 658. "Luce asked me if you and I might like to draft some anarchist ideas on the role and asso-ciation that artists could have in an anarchist society; to indicate in a few words the direction artists' work would take under absolute liberty without the terrible shackles of messieurs the capitalists-collectors-speculators and dealers; the development that artistic ideas would undergo, the love of beauty and the purity of our sensations, etc. No need for it to be well developed, G. Lecomte would take charge of the writing; it would only be [a sketch of] ideas."

20 Letters from Grave and Pouget (Signac Archives).

21 It was through Van Rysselberghe that the Neo-Impressionists were chosen in 1894 to decorate a huge terrestial globe that Reclus planned to build for the World's Fair of 1900: Signac to Cross, December 17, 1894 (Signac Archives). Unfortunately this project was never realized.

22 Van Rysselberghe to Signac, undated [1894] (Signac Archives). The interlocking friendships among anarchists, painters, and writers are made clear by the fact that Verhaeren, a close friend of the Neo-Impressionists since 1886, was also a friend of Reclus.

23 Loys Delteil, *Le Peintre-graveur illustré* 17 (Paris, 1923), nos. 153, 154. *Les Sans-gîtes*, which means *The Homeless*, is there entitled *Les Trimardeurs* (*Tramps*), a middle-class rather than working-class name. See John Hutton, "'Les Prolos Vagabondent:' Neo-Impressionism and the Anarchist Image of the Trimardeur," *Art Bulletin* 72 (June 1990): 296–309.

24 Delteil, *Peintre-graveur*, no. 194. In the original article in 1960, we confused the 1898 *Sower* with the 1902 *Plow*, and wrongly identified an album cover

by Auguste Roubille as the work of Signac; we thank Aline Dardel, *Temps nouveaux*, for the corrections.

25 Grave, *Paroles d'un révolté* (Paris, 1885): 66–67.

26 Pissarro to Lucien, April 13, 1891, in Pissarro, *Correspondance*, vol. 3, letter no. 653.

27 May 1, 1893. This issue, highly favorable to anarchist-communism, included articles by Kropotkin, Grave, and Reclus, and drawings by Camille and Lucien Pissarro, Luce, and Ibels.

28 André Fermigier, *Turpitudes sociales / Camille Pissarro* (Geneva, 1972).

29 Reproduced in *Publications de "La Révolte" et "Temps nouveaux"* 35 (July 25, 1925).

30 Letter to the editor, *Temps nouveaux* 1, 32 (December 7–13, 1895): 1.

31 "Impressionnistes et révolutionnaires," *La Révolte* 4, 40 (June 13–19, 1891): 4. Signed "un camarade impressionniste," the article was without question written by Signac.

32 Unpublished and undated manuscript in the Signac Archives, probably from about 1902. It was a lecture clearly aimed at workers and their anarchist leaders.

33 Signac–Cross correspondence (Signac Archives).

34 Pissarro to Mirbeau, April 21, 1892, in Pissarro, *Correspondence*, vol. 3, letter no. 774.

35 For example, Gustave Kahn, writing of *Chahut*: "if you search at all costs a symbol [. . .], you will find one in the hieratic structure of this canvas and its subject, a contemporary ignominy." "Seurat," *Art moderne* 11 (1891): 109.

36 Signac, "Impressionnistes et révolutionnaires."

37 From 1886 to 1888 such subject matter became so closely attached to the Neo-Impressionists that their strong influence in Belgium was marked by the sudden appearance there of similar industrial scenes.

38 For example, Robert Bernier, "Le Socialisme et l'art," *Revue socialiste* 13, 77 (May 1891): 599–604, and A. Hamon, *La France sociale et politique* (Paris, 1892), *passim*.

39 Signac, "Impressionnistes et révolutionnaires."

40 From the diary entry for November 27, 1894 (Signac Archives), this extract is included in John Rewald, "Extraits de journal inédit de Paul Signac," *Gazette des beaux-arts* 6, 36 (July–September 1949): 108.

41 Cross to Angrand, November 19, 1899, from the archives of the late Pierre Angrand.

42 That the Neo-Impressionists did not dilute their radical convictions in the 1890s is attested to not only by their contributions to Grave, but also by their steadiness in face of the hysterical government persecution of anarchism which reached its peak in 1893 and 1894. Luce found himself in prison with Fénéon, charged with conspiracy in an anarchist plot (they were both acquitted), and Pissarro and Kahn fled to Belgium to avoid a similar fate. See Pissarro's letters to his son from June through September, 1894. In one of them he wrote "Our friends are successively leaving France. Mirbeau, Paul Adam, Bernard Lazare, Steinlen, Hamon were due to be arrested; they fled in time" (July 30, 1894, in Pissarro, *Correspondence*, vol. 3, letter no. 1023). Luce documented this moment of crisis in his album *Mazas*, including scenes of his and Fénéon's incarceration.

Another indication of the Neo-Impressionists' devotion to the progressive cause is found in their adherence to the Ruskin–Morris doctrine which would bring art to the working class. In the late 1880s Signac had worked with the scientist friend of the Symbolists and Neo-Impressionists, Charles Henry, and provided him with charts and a poster for a talk Henry gave to the furniture workers of the Saint-Antoine district in 1890 (lecture of March 27, 1890, published the following year as *Harmonies de formes et couleurs*). Growing out of his work with Henry was his desire to provide artisans with instruments that would improve the quality of their work (Signac to van Gogh, April 1889, in *The Complete Letters of Vincent van Gogh*, 3 vols., Greenwich, Conn.,

1958, vol. 3, no. 584a). Several other Neo-Impressionists were imbued with Ruskin–Morris ideals, especially Lucien Pissarro who joined the Hammersmith group in London. Grave was very sympathetic to this activity and was, in fact, among the first in France to print excerpts from the writings of Morris and his group.

43 Grave, *La Révolte* 4, 13 (July 10–17, 1891): 2.

44 This article was written in 1960, when there was far more interest in social change than now, in 2002.

8 Léger's *Le Grand Déjeuner*

References to the exhibition for which this essay served as the introduction have been eliminated here, and so have several paragraphs devoted to specific pictures in that exhibition. For further reading, in addition to the works cited below, see the exhibition catalogues *Fernand Léger*, ed. Hélène Lassalle (Musée d'Art Moderne, Villeneuve d'Ascq, 1990); *Fernand Léger 1911–1924: The Rhythm of Modern Life*, ed. Dorothy Kosinski (Kunstmuseum Wolfsburg and Kunstmuseum Basel, 1994); *Fernand Léger*, ed. Christian Derouet (Musée National d'Art Moderne, Centre Pompidou, Paris, 1997); *Fernand Léger* ed. Carolyn Lanchner (Museum of Modern Art, New York, 1998); and *L'Esprit nouveau: Purism in Paris*, ed. Carol S. Eliel *1918–1925* (Los Angeles County Museum of Art, 2001). See also Christopher Green, *Cubism and its Enemies: Modern Movements and Reaction in French Art, 1916–1928* (New Haven and London, 1987); Matthew Affron, *Fernand Léger and the Spectacle of Objects* (PhD dissertation, Yale University, New Haven, 1994); and Mark Antliff and Patricia Leighten, *Cubism and Culture* (New York, 2001).

1 See Appendix A. I reproduce here and in Appendix B two letters Léger wrote to Alfred H. Barr in 1942 and 1943, in which he answered questions that Barr had wisely put to him. For the current volume I have added a third letter to Barr, previously unpublished, an amusing one because of the suggestion of replacing Picasso's *Three Musicians* with one of his own, and because of the encounter with Daniel Catton Rich (unnamed but well described).

2 Blaise Cendrars, *La Fin du monde filmée par l'Ange Notre-Dame* (Paris, 1919), n. p. "Des ascenseurs montent et descendent. De puissants projecteurs s'allument. Signaux lumineux. Telégraphie optique colorée. Le train en partance est saisi, puis brandi par la fronde des dynamos géants. Un éclair ultra-violet. Une spirale se déroule. Le train est parti."

3 Léger usually called the painting *Le Grand Déjeuner*, but sometimes *Trois femmes*. *Three Women*, in English, gradually supplemented the original title. "Déjeuner" by itself means "luncheon;" "grand" refers to the size of the painting. "Petit déjeuner" is the phrase for "breakfast," and the toast and eggs of the big picture show that breakfast is indeed the meal referred to. Léger would have enjoyed the idea of wrestling with the title *Le Grand petit déjeuner*. The smaller versions (pls. 46 and 47) are appropriately called in French *Le Petit Déjeuner*.

4 Several paintings of seated and reclining nudes were included in the 1980 exhibition and discussed in the original essay. *Les Odalisques* is the only one of these to be retained here.

5 *Femme couchée*, 1921, no. 4 in the 1980 exhibition, lent by the Perls Gallery.

6 That is, the next stage among known works. The Minneapolis variant is one of the two "unfinished" studies (the other has not yet come to light) mentioned in the letter of 1942 (Appendix A). The replica commissioned by Léonce Rosenberg, probably in 1922, was in the Zoubaloff collection, and then it was with the Beyeler Gallery in the 1970s. The Minneapolis painting was done in 1921, despite its date of 1919. Léger often signed and dated works long after they were done, when he was about to dispose of them, and many are misdated. This may be the result of faulty memory but, because almost all such dates are earlier than they should be, Léger may have intended to claim priority of invention.

7 Other *pentimenti* include painting over the pattern of lozenges on the foot cushion (lower right), and the suppression of the prominent disk in the pinkish-white rectangle near the shoulder of the seated woman. The fact that both patterns are found in the final canvas means that they were probably still visible in plate 47 while it served as a model. In this hypothesis, plate 47 was retouched only after the large canvas was finished.

8 This exhibition was not previously recorded; omitted also from the history of the picture was its exhibition in New York in November 1925, when it was included in Léger's first one-artist show in America, organized by Katherine Dreier for the Société Anonyme. See also chapter 9 below.

9 Letter to Léonce Rosenberg published as "Correspondance," *Bulletin de L'Effort moderne* 4 (April 1924), editorially dated there 1922. Translated by Charlotte Green for *Léger and Purist Paris*, ed. John Golding and Christopher Green (exh. cat., Tate Gallery, London, 1970–71): 85–86 (85).

10 One token of Léger's originality is his reversal of the usual association of "romantic" with easel painting and "classical" with mural art.

11 Léger, "Notes on the Mechanical Element," 1923, in *Functions of Painting*, ed. Edward F. Fry, trans. Alexandra Anderson (New York, 1973): 29.

12 Léger, "Contemporary Achievements in Painting," 1914, in *Functions of Painting*, p. 13.

13 Léger, "Notes on Contemporary Plastic Life," 1923, in *Functions of Painting*, p. 26.

14 Letter to Daniel Henry Kahnweiler, December 11, 1919, incorporated in his "A Tall Redheaded Norman," in *Homage to Fernand Léger*, special issue of *XXe Siècle*, ed. G. di San Lazarro (New York, 1971): 3–8 (4).

15 Léger, "The Spectacle: Light, Color, Moving Image," 1924, in *Functions of Painting*, pp. 35–47.

16 Léger, "Notes on the Mechanical Element," in *Functions of Painting*, p. 28.

17 Many writers have posited the influence of Mondrian and De Stijl on Léger, but the relationship is better described as one of shared ideas. Léger's rectilinear and flat geometry was a constant feature of his painting from 1918 onward.

18 Alexei Filippov, "Production Art," in *The Tradition of Constructivism*, ed. Stephan Bann, trans. John Bowlt (New York, 1974): 22.

19 This phenomenon has been analyzed by Kenneth Silver in "Purism: Straightening up after the Great War," *Artforum* 15 (March 1977): 56–63, and in *Esprit de Corps: The Art of the Parisian Avant-Garde and the First World War, 1914–1925* (Princeton, 1989).

20 Including the architect Mallet-Stevens, the writers Cendrars, Goll, and Malraux, and the film-maker l'Herbier. When Léger designed sets for Rolf de Maré's Ballets Suédois, he collaborated closely with the composer Darius Milhaud and the dancer-choreographer Jean Borlin. See my "'Architecture' in Léger's Essays, 1913–1933," in *Architecture and Cubism* ed. Eve Blau and Nancy J. Troy (Cambridge, Mass., 1997 [conference papers, Canadian Center for Architecture, 1993]): 77–88.

21 Léger, "The Machine Aesthetic: The Manufactured Object, the Artisan, and the Artist," 1924, in *Functions of Painting*, p. 53. It is worth remembering that Léger began professional life as an architectural apprentice.

22 Letter to Léonce Rosenberg, in *Léger and Purist Paris*, p. 86.

23 Léger, "Contemporary Achievements," in *Functions of Painting*, p. 11.

24 Léger, "The Machine Aesthetic: Geometric Order and Truth," 1925, in *Functions of Painting*, p. 62.

25 Need I add that this active figure is a man, in contrast to the passive women of *Le Grand Déjeuner*?

26 Although dated 1920, it was more likely done later, probably in 1922.

27 Christopher Green, *Léger and the Avant-Garde* (New Haven and London, 1976): 199–201.

28 Letter to Léonce Rosenberg, in *Léger and Purist Paris*, pp. 85–86. See chapter 9 below.

29 Léger's later adherence to the Communist Party (1945) should not be allowed to push too far to the left his attitudes of the 1920s. He was then a "left liberal," much concerned with the individual's role in society and with artistic subjectivity. Although he castigated the bourgeoisie, his perception of society in a perpetual state of competition and conflict, one in which the strong win out, is actually that of entrepreneurial capitalism.

30 Léger, "The Machine Aesthetic: The Manufactured Object," in *Functions of Painting*, p. 60.

31 Letter to Léonce Rosenberg, in *Léger and Purist Paris*, p. 86.

32 For penetrating discussions of primitivism and classicism in Cézanne, see Richard Shiff, *Cézanne and the End of Impressionism* (Chicago, 1984), chs. 12 and 13, and "Cézanne and Poussin: How the Modern Claims the Classic," in *Cézanne and Poussin: A Symposium*, ed. Richard Kendall (Sheffield, 1993): 51–68.

33 Léger, "The Machine Aesthetic: Geometric Order and Truth," in *Functions of Painting*, p. 64.

34 Ibid., p. 65.

9 Léger, the Renaissance, and "Primitivism"

1 "L'erreur colossale est de croire que la Renaissance Italienne est une belle époque d'art. C'est exactement le contraire. / La Renaissance Italienne est une décadence totale, où tout est imité, sensualisé, sentimentalisé. / La Renaissance Italienne est mauvaise parce qu'elle est floue, vague, molle, sentimentale, sensuelle, descriptive, imitative." Léger's manuscript communications are among the Dreier papers in the Beinecke Library, Yale University, New Haven. The aphorisms and a short preface that the artist had requested of Carl Einstein were translated for the catalog of the exhibition held in November 1925, at the Anderson Galleries, and are retranslated here.

2 For the "Rappel à l'Ordre" (sometimes the "Retour à l'Ordre"), see Kenneth Silver, *Esprit de Corps: The Art of the Parisian Avant-Garde and the First World War, 1914–1925* (Princeton, 1989); Christopher Green, *Cubism and its Enemies: Modern Movements and Reaction in French Art, 1916–1928* (New Haven and London, 1987); and Université de Saint-Etienne, *Le Retour à l'ordre dans les arts plastiques et l'architecture, 1919–1925* (Saint-Etienne,1975). See also chapter 10 below.

3 Mark Antliff, *Inventing Bergson: Cultural Politics and the Parisian Avant-Garde* (Princeton, 1993), esp. pp. 106–34. My discussion here does not do justice to the depth and subtlety of Antliff's book, especially since I have extracted ideas from a text devoted primarily to the role of Henri Bergson's ideas among vanguard artists and writers.

4 Antliff, *Inventing Bergson*, ch. 2 and *passim*, and the work of the late Gleizes scholar Daniel Robbins: "From Symbolism to Cubism: The Abbaye de Créteil," *Art Journal* 23 (winter 1963–64): 111–16; *Albert Gleizes 1881–1953: A Retrospective Exhibition* (exh. cat., Guggenheim Museum, New York, 1964); and *The Formation and Maturity of Albert Gleizes* (PhD dissertation, New York University, 1975).

5 Silver, *Esprit de Corps*. Taken together, the persuasive analyses of Antliff and Silver provide the context for interpreting Léger's ideas, and I am much indebted to them both.

6 Léger, "The Spectacle: Light, Color, Moving Image," 1924, in *Functions of Painting*, ed. Edward F. Fry, trans. Alexandra Anderson (New York, 1973): 47.

7 Léger's juxtaposition of the classical and the primitive was carefully detailed by Christopher Green, but in purely stylistic terms (*Léger and the Avant-Garde*, New Haven and London, 1976). See chapter 8, n. 32 above.

8 These preferences of the "Rappel à l'Ordre" were pointed out in Green, *Cubism and its Enemies*, and put in the context of broader intellectual currents

in Silver, *Esprit de Corps*. It should be noted that the term "conceptual" was one of the phrases most *à la mode* in prewar Cubism.

9 Léger, "Color in the World," 1938, in *Functions of Painting*, pp. 126–27.

10 Antliff, *Inventing Bergson*, p. 116, shows this idea to be a particularly Bergsonian one, and refers tellingly to an essay by H.-M. Barzun, "D'un art poétique moderne" (November 1912), in which this idea is developed.

11 Léger, "Color in the World," in *Functions of Painting*, p. 128.

12 Léger, "The Origins of Painting and its Representational Value," 1913, in *Functions of Painting*, p. 4.

13 Léger, "The Machine Aesthetic: The Manufactured Object, the Artisan, and the Artist," 1924, in *Functions of Painting*, p. 57.

14 Léger, "The Wall, the Architect, the Painter," 1933, in *Functions of Painting*, p. 93.

15 Léger, "Notes on Contemporary Plastic Life," 1923, in *Functions of Painting*, p. 27.

16 Léger, "The Machine Aesthetic: The Manufactured Object," in *Functions of Painting*, pp. 57–58.

17 Léger, "The New Realism," 1935, in *Functions of Painting*, p. 113.

18 Léger, "Color in the World," in *Functions of Painting*, p. 126.

19 Léger, "The New Realism Goes On," 1937, in *Functions of Painting*, p. 114.

20 Léger, "The Street: Objects, Spectacles," 1928, in *Functions of Painting*, p. 79.

21 Léger, "The New Realism," 1935, in *Functions of Painting*, p. 109. In that volume "romane" (romanesque) was mistranslated as "Roman," a grievous error given Léger's dislike of the Roman.

22 Léger, "The Human Body Considered as an Object," 1945, in *Functions of Painting*, pp. 132–33.

23 Léger, "Color in the World," in *Functions of Painting*, p. 129.

24 Léger, "Origins of Painting," in *Functions of Painting*, p. 8.

25 Léger, "The Wall, the Architect, the Painter," in *Functions of Painting*, p. 99.

26 Léger, "Origins of Painting," in *Functions of Painting*, p. 9.

27 Ibid.

28 "Votre mission est de remplacer l'église sentimentale et déclassée, par l'oeuvre d'équivalence, belle en soi et capable de dégager l'humanité de l'emprise des religions. Vous avez à votre disposition ce besoin de verticalité qui obsède le monde, ce besoin d'élévation par la verticale. Vous avez la forme ronde – la boule – qui satisfait l'esprit. Ces deux abstractions sont là: rendez-les humaines et émouvantes, mais ne reduisez pas l'architecture à un problème esthétique et linéaire. [...] Le monument moderne doit être à l'équivalence du byzantin et du roman – aussi riche et aussi 'Dans la durée' et dans le temps." Léger gave this address at a conference held in Athens on August 9, 1933; see "Discours aux architectes," *Annales techniques* 2, 44–46 (October–November 1933): 1159–62. It was Matthew Affron, then completing his doctorate (*Fernand Léger and the Spectacle of Objects*, Yale University, New Haven, 1994), who kindly supplied me with this text, and it is Mark Antliff, *Inventing Bergson*, who showed the Bergsonian context of Léger's phrase "dans la durée" [in enduring time] even though Léger's Bergsonism had become much adulterated by 1933.

29 Léger, "The Wall, the Architect, the Painter," in *Functions of Painting*, p. 94.

30 1935: decoration of the gymnasium of the French pavilion at the Exposition Internationale in Brussels. 1937: murals for the Vélodrome d'Hiver and the Palais de la Découverte in Paris. 1939: sets for J.-R. Bloch's *Naissance d'une cité* at the Vélodrome d'Hiver. After World War II Léger's activity as artist of public surfaces greatly increased, with numerous commissions for both secular and religious spaces.

31 "Mettez vos plans dans vos poches, descendez dans la rue, écoutez-les respirer, vous devez prendre contact, vous tremper dans la matière première, marcher dans la même boue et la même poussière." Léger, "Discours aux architectes," p. 1161. From the days of Celtic nationalism before the war, Léger retained the belief that the continuity of the French race was

found in *le peuple*, not in its ruling classes.

32 Léger, "The New Realism Goes On," in *Functions of Painting*, p. 115.

33 Léger, "The Machine Aesthetic: The Manufactured Object," in *Functions of Painting*, p. 60.

34 Léger, "The New Realism Goes On," in *Functions of Painting*, p. 118.

35 Léger, "The Spectacle," in *Functions of Painting*, pp. 45–46.

10 The Arrival of the Machine

For this chapter I am generally indebted to Lewis Mumford, *Technics and Civilization* (New York, 1934); Meyer Schapiro, "Nature of Abstract Art," *Marxist Quarterly* 1 (January–March 1937): 77–98; Pierre Francastel, *Art et technique aux XIXe et XXe siècles* (Paris, 1956); Leo Marx, *The Machine in the Garden* (New York, 1964); Langdon Winner, *Autonomous Technology. Technics-out-of-Control as a Theme in Political Thought* (Cambridge, Mass., 1977), and Linda Henderson, *The Fourth Dimension and Non-Euclidean Geometry in Modern Art* (Princeton, 1983). For the era just before and after World War I, I have learned especially from Jeffrey Herf, *Reactionary Modernism: Technology, Culture, and Politics in Weimar and the Third Reich* (Cambridge and New York, 1984); Kenneth Silver, *Esprit de Corps: The Art of the Parisian Avant-Garde and the First World War, 1914–1925* (Princeton, 1989); and Richard Cork, *Vorticism and Abstract Art in the First Machine Age*, 2 vols. (Berkeley, 1976).

1 See chapter 3 above.

2 See Paul Tucker et al., *Monet in the 20th Century* (exh. cat., Boston Museum of Fine Arts, London, Royal Academy, 1998–99). Irony of ironies: a branch railway bisected Monet's property; he built a tunnel under it to reach his water garden.

3 Thorstein Veblen, *The Theory of the Leisure Class* (1899, ed. New York, 1934): 159–60 and *passim*. I have pointed out the appropriateness of Veblen in this regard in chapter 6.

4 Eva Forgács, *The Bauhaus Idea and Bauhaus Politics*, trans. John Bátki (Budapest, 1995): 6.

5 It is Daniel Robbins who defined "Epic Cubism" as the work of Gleizes, Delaunay, Le Fauconnier, and others whose concern for programmatic themes distinguishes them from Braque and Picasso. He coined the term in his *Albert Gleizes 1881–1953: A Retrospective Exhibition* (exh. cat., Guggenheim Museum, New York, 1964), and pursued the concept subsequently in publications on Jacques Villon, Jean Metzinger, and Henri Le Fauconnier.

6 See the entry on Gleizes by Robbins in *The Société Anonyme and the Dreier Bequest at Yale University*, ed. Robert L. Herbert, Eleanor S. Apter, and Elise K. Kenney (New Haven and London, 1984): 301–03.

7 Jacques Villon, *Le Petit Atelier de mécanique*, 1913 (Phillips Collection, Washington), *L'Atelier de mécanique*, 1914 (private collection), *L'Atelier de mécanique*, 1914 (Gallery of Fine Arts, Columbus, Ohio).

8 For Delaunay's writings defining "simultaneity" and other issues, see *Robert Delaunay: Du Cubisme à l'art abstrait, documents inédits*, ed. Pierre Francastel (Paris, 1957). For the Bergsonian import of these ideas, see Mark Antliff, *Inventing Bergson* (Princeton, 1993): 40–41, 50, 53–54, 108, and 132. We should note that Delaunay's target-like forms also recall the multi-colored disks figured in books on color theory (one of Delaunay's preoccupations). When the disks are spun at high speed by simple machines, the colors merged, hence permitting a quantification of the constituent hues.

9 Filippo Marinetti, "First Futurist Manifesto," 1909, in *Futurist Manifestos*, ed. Umbro Apollonio (New York, 1973): 21–22.

10 The phrase linking a car with the Greek sculpture is usually cited without including the phrase "that seems to ride on grapeshot," thereby softening Marinetti's war-like imagery. William Valerio's *Boccioni's Fist: Italian Futurism and the Construction of*

Fascist Modernism (unpublished dissertation, Yale University, New Haven, 1996) is a brilliant analysis of the relationship of violence and proto-Fascist politics with the aggressive masculinity and partly repressed homoeroticism of the Futurists.

11 Because Epstein stripped the sculpture of its metal drill when he made the later bronze in 1916, Cork interprets it as the supplanting of prewar optimism by a sense of impotence and forlornness in face of the war's disasters (*Vorticism*, vol. I, pp. 134–35).

12 Kasimir Malevich, "Architecture as a Slap in the Face to Ferro-Concrete" (April 1918), in his *Essays in Art 1915–1933*, ed. Troels Andersen, trans. Senia Glowacki-Prus (New York, 1971): 63.

13 For Russian and Soviet art, see Sheila Fitzpatrick, *The Commissariat of Enlightenment: Soviet Organisation of Education and the Arts under Lunacharsky, October 1917–1921* (Cambridge and New York, 1971); Camilla Gray, *The Russian Experiment in Art 1863–1922*, ed. Marian Burleigh-Motley (London, 1986); Christina Lodder, *Russian Constructivism* (New Haven and London, 1983); *Art into Life: Russian Constructivism 1914–32* (exh. cat., Henry Art Gallery, Seattle, 1990), *The Great Utopia: The Russian and Soviet Avant-Garde, 1915–1932* (exh. cat., Guggenheim Museum, New York, 1992).

14 Boris Arvatov, *Art and Class* (1923), excerpt in *The Tradition of Constructivism*, ed. Stephen Bann (New York, 1974): 47.

15 For the Bauhaus, see Hans Wingler, *The Bauhaus* (Cambridge, Mass., 1969); Claudine Humblet, *Le Bauhaus* (Lausanne, 1980), and Forgács, *Bauhaus Idea*.

16 Both citations from Kenneth Silver, "Purism: Straightening Up After the Great War," *Artforum* 15, 7 (March 1977): 56–63.

17 Mary McLeod, "'Architecture or Revolution:' Taylorism, Technocracy, and Social Change," *Art Journal* 43 (summer 1983): 132–47.

18 For Léger, see Fernand Léger, *Functions of Painting*, ed. Edward F. Fry, trans. Alexandra Anderson (New York, 1973); Silver, *Esprit de Corps*; Christopher Green, *Léger and the Avant-Garde* (New Haven and London, 1976). See also the exhibition catalogs *Fernand Léger*, ed. Hélène Lassalle (Musée d'art moderne, Villeneuve d'Ascq, 1990); *Fernand Léger 1911–1924: The Rhythm of Modern Life*, ed. Dorothy Kosinski (Kunstmuseum Wolfsburg and Kunstmuseum Basel, 1994); *Fernand Léger*, ed. Christian Derouet (Musée National d'Art Moderne, Centre Pompidou, Paris, 1997); and *Fernand Léger*, ed. Carolyn Lanchner (Museum of Modern Art, New York, 1998).

19 Léger, "Contemporary Achievements in Painting," 1914, in *Functions of Painting*, p. 12.

20 Léger, "The Machine Aesthetic: The Manufactured Object," 1924, in *Functions of Painting*, p. 59.

21 By the standards of Marxism, Léger's definitions of artisan and worker are naïve. It is true that unlike Picasso and most other contempory vanguardists he often painted men identified as factory workers, but in his writings he included among artisans the modest shopkeepers who designed their own window displays, and he repeatedly endorsed capitalist competition as the essential structure of society.

22 Léger, writing in 1919, cited by Christopher Green and John Golding, *Léger and Purist Paris* (exh. cat., Tate Gallery, London, 1970): 85–86.

23 Schapiro, "Nature of Abstract Art," *Marxist Quarterly*, p. 97.

24 For Duchamp, see William Camfield, *Marcel Duchamp Fountain* (Menil Collection, Houston, 1987); Pontus Hultén, Jennifer Gough-Cooper, and Jacques Caumont, *Marcel Duchamp: Work and Life* (exh. cat., Palazzo Grassi, Venice, 1993); Francis Naumann, *New York Dada, 1915–23* (New York, 1994), and Linda Henderson, *Duchamp in Context* (Princeton, 1998).

25 For Dada, see Hans Richter, *Dada: Art and Anti-Art* (London, 1965);

William Rubin, *Dada and Surrealist Art* (London, 1969); Dawn Ades, *Dada and Surrealism Revisited* (exh. cat., Arts Council of Great Britain, 1978); Helena Lewis, *Dada Turns Red: The Politics of Surrealism* (Edinburgh, 1988); Marc Dachy, *The Dada Movement, 1915–1923* (New York, 1990); and Naumann, *New York Dada*.

26 Cited in Richter, *Dada*, p. 106.

27 For Höch, see Maud Lavin, *Cut with the Kitchen Knife: The Weimar Photomontages of Hannach Höch* (New Haven and London, 1993).

28 This was the sales catalog *Kölner Lehrmittel-Anstalt* published by the Hugo Inderau firm, an exhibitor in the industrial exhibition of 1914 in Cologne. Ernst's use of the catalog (he made twenty-five overpaintings from it) is documented by Dirk Teuber in *Max Ernst in Köln: Die rheinische Kunstszene bis 1922*, ed. Wulf Herzogenrath (exh. cat., Kölnischer Kunstverein, 1980): 206–74. For Ernst, see also Roland Penrose, *Max Ernst's Celebes: The 52nd Charlton Lecture* (University of Newcastle upon Tyne, 1972); Werner Spies, *Max Ernst Collages: The Invention of the Surrealist Universe* (New York, 1991); and William Camfield, *Max Ernst: Dada and the Dawn of Surrealism* (Munich and New York, 1993).

29 Penrose, *Max Ernst's Celebes*, pp. 14–15.

30 I am indebted to Richard Cork (*Vorticism*, vol. 2, pp. 258–60) in my observations of *Elephant Celebes*, although I think he pushes analogies with the war rather too far.

Appendices

1 That is, plate 47.

2 Not identified.

3 Private collection, Chicago.

4 Plate 41.

5 Plate 43.

6 Correctly 1921 (Léger's revealing error).

7 Now Kunstmuseum, Basel.

8 He meant the figure to the right.

9 Musée National d'Art Moderne, Centre Pompidou, Paris.

10 Perhaps one of several versions of *Divers* (Museum of Modern Art, New York, and elsewhere).

11 After 1925 (Léger's error).

12 Probably plate 40.

13 "Fernand Léger," special issue of *Cahiers d'art*, 1933; E. Tériade, *Fernand Léger* (Editions Cahiers d'art, 1928).

14 *Disks* (Musée d'Art Moderne de la Ville de Paris); *Divers* (perhaps the version in the Museum of Modern Art, New York, or that in the Art Institute of Chicago).

15 Apparently the Minneapolis *Petit Déjeuner*.

16 This is an easily recognized description of Daniel Catton Rich, subsequently Director of the Art Institute of Chicago, and author of *Seurat and the Evolution of "La Grande Jatte"* (Chicago, 1935), in which linear diagrams were reproduced.

Principal Writings by Robert L. Herbert

* In the present book
** Portions in the present book

"Seurat's Drawings," in *Seurat: Paintings and Drawings*, ed. Daniel Catton Rich (exh. cat., Chicago, Art Institute, and New York, Museum of Modern Art, 1958).

"Seurat in Chicago and New York," *Burlington Magazine* 100 (May 1958): 146–55.

** "Artists and Anarchism," with Eugenia W. Herbert, *Burlington Magazine* 102 (November 1960): 473–82; (December 1960): 517–22.

"Millet Revisited," *Burlington Magazine* 104 (July 1962): 294–305; (September 1962): 377–86.

Barbizon Revisited (exh. cat., Museum of Fine Arts, Boston; Toledo Museum of Art; Cleveland Museum of Art; California Palace of the Legion of Honor, 1962–63).

Seurat's Drawings (New York, 1963).

The Art Criticism of John Ruskin, ed. and intro. (New York, 1964).

Modern Artists on Art, ed. and intro. (Englewood Cliffs, NJ, 1964; enlarged edition, Mineola, NY, 2000).

Neo-Impressionists and Nabis in the Collection of Arthur G. Altschul, ed. and intro. (exh. cat., Yale University Art Gallery, New Haven, 1965).

"Millet Reconsidered," *Museum Studies* (Art Institute of Chicago) 1 (1966): 29–65.

Neo-Impressionism (exh. cat., Guggenheim Museum, New York, 1968).

* "City vs. Country: The Rural Image in French Painting from Millet to Gauguin," *Artforum* 8, 6 (February 1970): 44–55.

"Seurat's Theories," in *Les Néo-Impressionnistes* (Paris and Lausanne, 1970), trans. *The Neo-Impressionists*, ed. Jean Sutter (London and Greenwich, Conn., 1970): 23–42.

"Neo-Classicism and the French Revolution," in *The Age of Neo-Classicism* (exh. cat., Arts Council of Great Britain, 1972): lxxii–lxxv.

David, Voltaire, 'Brutus' and the French Revolution (London and New York, 1972).

"Les Faux Millet," *Revue de l'art* 21 (1973): 56–65.

"Baron Gros's Napoleon and Voltaire's Henri IV," in *The Artist and the Writer in France: Essays in Honour of Jean Seznec*, ed. Francis Haskell et al. (Oxford, 1974): 52–72.

"A Color Bibliography," *Yale University Library Gazette* 49 (July 1974): 13–59; 52 (January 1978): 127–65.

Jean-François Millet (exh. cat., Réunion des Musées Nationaux, Paris, and Arts Council of Great Britain, London, 1975–76).

Millet's "Gleaners" (exh. cat., Minneapolis Institute of Arts, 1978).

"Method and Meaning in Monet," *Art in America* 67 (September 1979): 90–108.

* "Courbet's *Mère Grégoire* and Béranger," in *Malerei und Theorie: Das Courbet-Colloquium 1979*, ed. Klaus Gallwitz and Klaus Herding (Städtische Galerie im Städelschen Kunstinstitut, Frankfurt am Main, 1980): 75–89; revised version in

Museum Studies (Art Institute of Chicago) 13, (1987): 24–35.

** *Léger's Le Grand Déjeuner* (exh. cat., Minneapolis Institute of Arts, and Detroit Institute of Arts, 1980).

"Parade de cirque de Seurat et l'esthétique scientifique de Charles Henry," *Revue de l'art* 50 (1980): 9–23.

* "Industry in the Changing Landscape from Daubigny to Monet," in *French Cities in the Nineteenth Century*, ed. John M. Merriman (New York, 1981): 139–64.

The Société Anonyme and the Dreier Bequest at Yale University: A Catalogue Raisonné, ed. with Eleanor S. Apter and Elise K. Kenney (New Haven and London, 1984).

* "The Decorative and the Natural in Monet's *Cathedrals*," in *Aspects of Monet*, ed. John Rewald and Frances Weitzenhoffer (New York, 1984): 160–79.

"Monet's Turf," *New York Review of Books* (October 11, 1984): 43–45.

* "Impressionism, Originality, and Laissez-Faire," *Radical History Review* 38 (1987): 7–15.

Impressionism: Art, Leisure, and Parisian Society (New Haven and London, 1988).

Seurat (exh. cat., Réunion des Musées Nationaux, Paris, and Metropolitan Museum, New York, 1991).

"Art and 'Accuracy'," *New York Review of Books* (August 12, 1993): 35–36.

* "Léger, the Renaissance, and 'Primitivism':" *Hommage à Michel Laclotte* (Paris, 1994).

Monet on the Normandy Coast: Tourism and Painting, 1867–1886 (New Haven and London, 1994).

"Courbet's Lost Laundresses," *Art in America* 88 (February 1995): 80–85, 107.

"Impressionists on Stage," *New York Review of Books* (November 2, 1995): 44–47.

** *Peasants and "Primitivism," French Prints from Millet to Gauguin* (exh. cat., Mount Holyoke College Art Museum; Museum of Art, Rhode Island School of Design; University of Chicago, Smart Museum of Art, 1995–96).

"Degas & Women," *New York Review of Books* (April 18, 1996): 46–48.

" 'Architecture' in Léger's Essays, 1913–1933," *Architecture and Cubism*, ed. Eve Blau and Nancy J. Troy (Cambridge, Mass., 1997 [conference papers, Canadian Center for Architecture, 1993]): 77–88.

* "The Arrival of the Machine: Modernist Art in Europe, 1910–25," *Social Research* 64, 3 [special issue on "Technology and the Rest of Culture"] (fall 1997): 1273–1305.

"Renoir the Radical," *New York Review of Books* (November 20, 1997): 8–10.

"Monet our Contemporary," *New York Review of Books* (November 19, 1998): 18–22.

"Goodbye to All That," *New York Review of Books* (November 4, 1999): 28–31.

Nature's Workshop: Renoir's Writings on the Decorative Arts (New Haven and London, 2000).

"*La Becquée* de Millet entre 1848 et 1860," *Revue du Louvre et des Musées de France* 50, 3 (July 2000): 60–69.

"Signac et les paysages de l'art social," *48/14* [Musée d'Orsay, Paris] 12 (February 2001): 74–83.

Seurat: Drawings and Paintings (New Haven and London, 2001).

"Spirits on Canvas," *New York Review of Books* (June 21, 2001): 42–47.

"Introduction" to Jean Renoir, *Renoir My Father* (New York, 2001; Renoir's memoir, Paris, 1962).

Photograph Credits

In most cases, photographs have been supplied by the owners or custodians of the works. Other sources and additional credits are as follows:

Oeffentliche Kunstsammlung Basel, Martin Bühler: 52
Courtesy Museum of Fine Arts, Boston: 15, 28
© National Gallery of Canada: 51
© 2000. The Art Institute of Chicago. All Rights Reserved: 24
© 1983 The Detroit Institute of Arts: 10
© Ole Haupt: 16
© 2001 The Museum of Modern Art, New York: 49, 56
© 2002 The Museum of Modern Art, New York: 39, 54
© Photo CNAC/MNAM Dist. RMN: 43, 58
© Photo RMN – H. Lewandowski: 2, 3, 11
Yale University Photographic Services: 20
Photo John Webb: 59
Photo by Graydon Wood, 1992: 38

Copyright Bylines

© ADAGP, Paris and DACS, London 2002: *frontispiece*, 1, 7, 8, 9, 10, 11, 28, 36, 38, 39, 40, 41, 42, 43, 44, 45, 46, 47, 48, 49, 50, 51, 53, 57, 58, 59
© L & M Services B.V. Amsterdam 20020203: 52

Index

Page numbers in *italics* indicate illustrations